THE FUTURE OF FUTURITY

THE LEWIS HENRY MORGAN LECTURES

Kathryn Mariner and Llerena Guiu Searle, Co-directors

THE   FUTURE

OF   FUTURITY

Affective Capitalism and Potentiality
in a Global City

PURNIMA MANKEKAR

&   **AKHIL GUPTA**

DUKE UNIVERSITY PRESS
Durham and London
2025

© 2025 DUKE UNIVERSITY PRESS

Project Editor: Ihsan Taylor
Designed by A. Mattson Gallagher
Typeset in Minion Pro and Futura Std
by Westchester Publishing Services

Library of Congress Cataloging-in-Publication Data
Names: Mankekar, Purnima, [date] author. | Gupta, Akhil, [date] author.
Title: The future of futurity : affective capitalism and potentiality in a global city /
    Purnima Mankekar and Akhil Gupta.
Other titles: Lewis Henry Morgan lectures.
Description: Durham : Duke University Press, 2025. | Series: The Lewis Henry Morgan
    lectures | Includes bibliographical references and index.
Identifiers: LCCN 2024035208 (print)
LCCN 2024035209 (ebook)
ISBN 9781478031536 (paperback)
ISBN 9781478028321 (hardcover)
ISBN 9781478060604 (ebook)
Subjects: LCSH: Contracting out—India—Bangalore. | Labor mobility—India—Bangalore. |
    Industrial management—India. | Capitalism—Social aspects—India—Bangalore.
Classification: LCC HD2368.I4 M36 2025 (print) | LCC HD2368.I4 (ebook) |
    DDC 658.7/23095487—dc23/eng/20241217
LC record available at https://lccn.loc.gov/2024035208
LC ebook record available at https://lccn.loc.gov/2024035209

To Lata, with love

Contents

Foreword

Purnima Mankekar and Akhil Gupta delivered the Lewis Henry Morgan Lectures in October 2017. Their public lecture, "Future Tense: Capital, Labor, and Technology in a Service Industry," was followed by a workshop in which invited scholars and members of the Department of Anthropology provided feedback on the manuscript for this book. Formal discussants included Anne Allison (Duke University), Carla Freeman (Emory University), Kiran Mirchandani (University of Toronto), Andrew Willford (Cornell University), and Llerena Searle (University of Rochester). Mankekar and Gupta's lecture continued a tradition that began with Meyer Fortes in 1963. Since then, the Lewis Henry Morgan Lectures have pushed the discipline in new directions and generated an archive of ethnographic and theoretical innovation. The lectures were conceived by Bernard Cohn in 1961 and have been organized and edited over the years by Alfred Harris, Anthony Carter, Thomas Gibson, Robert Foster, and Daniel Reichman. This is the first book in the series for which we have the pleasure of writing a forward.

In this book, Mankekar and Gupta examine business process outsourcing (BPO), an industry that provides services at a distance through technological mediation. Though employing only a small percentage of Indians, the BPO industry has an outsized impact, garnering widespread popular and scholarly attention since the first call center was established in India in 1999. Mankekar and Gupta's ethnography emphasizes the contradictions that emerge as agents and clients build rapport over geographic, temporal, and cultural differences. BPO workers do not just recite scripts or memorize culturally appropriate greetings; they connect intimately with customers, comforting, supporting, cajoling, and advising them while fixing their computers or booking their holiday travel. Yet agents' relations with their clients are structured by their position as service workers: even as agents learn intimate details of clients' lives, they must refrain from judgment; even as they endure racist rants, they must not talk back "unprofessionally," lest they face material consequences.

In placing young Indian workers—many from oppressed caste and lower-class backgrounds—in positions of servitude to consumers in Australia, the United States, and the United Kingdom, the industry recapitulates and reconfigures colonial histories and racial ideologies that have cheapened labor in postcolonial nations. This labor arbitrage, fueled by transnational racial capitalism, today reverberates with echoes of nineteenth-century ideas about social development, including those of Lewis Henry Morgan. In *Ancient Society* (1877), Morgan sets out a vision of human progress that links technological capacity to intellectual and social development. As he grappled with the promise and upheavals of American capitalism, Morgan looked to the past to understand the development of property-based states from kinship-based societies, in the process creating a civilizational ladder that positioned certain groups as "behind" or "ahead" of others. Even if repudiated by contemporary anthropologists, these social-evolutionary ideas live on—not only in Marx and Engels's writings but in modernization theory and in widespread conceptions of development.

While capitalism may be organized more globally than before, as Mankekar and Gupta argue in the introduction, with capitalists in the Global South accumulating capital in ways that disrupt North/South, First World–Third World dichotomies, development discourses continue to shape people's social imaginaries. A linear notion of progress, anchored in the geographic unit of the nation-state, motivates an understanding of India lagging behind other nations in a race for economic growth and technological advancement. *The Future of Futurity* both grapples with this legacy and troubles it by attending to the experiences of those within the BPO industry.

In this context, India's BPO industry powerfully suggests that "catching up" is now possible. Mankekar and Gupta argue that the same uneven development that makes India a place to recruit service workers provides a scaffolding for Indian workers to aspire to new ways of life. The industry's high salaries (relative to other industries in India) allow for agents to strive for class mobility, understood in India in relational and familial terms. Agents provide health insurance to their parents and pay for siblings' education while building middle-class lives for themselves and contributing to the upward mobility of the nation as a whole. Such striving is so ethnographically palpable that Mankekar and Gupta describe it as an "affective formation" of futurity.

However, in the lived experiences of BPO agents, futurity is tinged with uncertainty and anxiety, such that time is disjointed rather than unilineal. Rapidly changing technology and corporate needs make BPO work unstable in ways that shape agents' striving. As Bangalore sleeps, agents work to serve clients in different time zones, respond in real time to unpredictable interactions, and make do with a work schedule that wreaks havoc with bodily rhythms and clashes with religious and familial duties. These "disjunctive temporalities" configure agents' bodies—even as those bodies frustrate and exceed corporate discipline. *The Future of Futurity* masterfully traces relationships between global structures and agents' affective experiences, without reducing one to the other.

Llerena Guiu Searle
Kathryn Mariner

Department of Anthropology
University of Rochester
November 2023

Acknowledgments

We began this project in 2009 and concluded it in 2016. In conducting our longitudinal ethnographic research, we have depended on the generosity of many people who have given us their time, insights, and knowledge. Many of these people have also showered on us their hospitality and affection, without which such a long-term and intensive project would have been unsustainable. We are grateful to the owners, CEOs, CTOs, and managers at the three companies who gave us permission to work in their organizations: they remain unnamed but our gratitude to them is immeasurable. This set of introductions offered us opportunities to enter the "shop floor" and sit in on training sessions of BPO agents, which, in turn, generated many of the insights presented in this book. It is also from this initial access to agents, supervisors, and other employees that we managed to draw the sub-set of employees who spent time with us in successive years and who gave generously of their time and energy to share their experiences, yearnings, aspirations, and anxieties. Our indebtedness is greatest to the people who continued to meet us year after year and offered us the gift of entering their lives and their stories. In this book, we have amalgamated the narratives and worldviews of several of our interlocutors into composite figures in order to protect their identities. While individual identities are shielded and individual biographies necessarily obscured, we have intended to portray the multidimensionality of the lives of our interlocutors, their relationships with each other and their families, and their hopes and fears for the future.

Our friends in Silicon Valley and in Bengaluru were immensely helpful to our project, and we thank them for making this project possible. Among them, Arun Kumar and Poornima Kumar, Vasudev Bhandarkar, Saritha Rai, and Mr. and Mrs. J. K. Chandna were particularly generous in sharing with us their professional and personal networks. Without their help, we would have been unable to get access to the firms where we eventually conducted our fieldwork.

This long-term project has also drawn sustenance from the feedback and support of colleagues in forums where we presented our research. One of our first full-length presentations from this fieldwork was at a workshop "Rethinking Global Capitalism through Intimate Industries," organized by Rhacel Parreñas, Rachel Silvey, and Hung Cam Thai at Pomona College on March 7, 2013. At that time, we were still in the midst of intensive fieldwork, and the comments and feedback we received from other participants and, subsequently, from anonymous reviewers at the journal *positions* were extraordinarily helpful in how we proceeded with our research. We remain in debt to Rhacel, Rachel, and Hung Thai for providing us with the opportunity to present observations and analysis that, at the time, felt to us preliminary. Purnima Mankekar would like to thank audiences at her keynote at the conference Global South Asia, in July 2017, organized by Ramaswami Harindranath at the University of New South Wales, Australia.

We presented the entire manuscript at a workshop that accompanied the Henry Lewis Morgan Lecture at the University of Rochester in 2018. We want to thank the then chair, Dan Reichman, and Bob Foster for inviting us, and an amazing set of interlocutors for giving us detailed and insightful feedback: Andrew Willford, Anne Allison, Kiran Mirchandani, Carla Freeman, and Llerena Searle. Other faculty at Rochester also were generous with their insights, including John Osburg and Tom Gibson. Early versions of chapter 1 and chapter 4 benefited from comments received during two panels at the 116th Annual Meeting of the American Anthropological Association in 2018: "Gender Politics: Engaging the Legacy of Sherry Ortner" and "Revisioning American Capitalism through a Cosmopolitan Lens: Engaging the Legacy of Sherry Ortner." We are particularly grateful for comments by discussants John Jackson and Anna Tsing and feedback from members of the audience. We thank Joe Masco and Deb Thomas for inviting us to submit a version of chapter 1, "Mobility, Emplacement, Translation," in their terrific edited volume, *Sovereignty Unhinged*, and for the outstanding feedback we received from them and from anonymous reviewers that enabled us to strengthen our argument in the chapter and, beyond that, in this book. A preliminary version of chapter 4 was presented by Purnima Mankekar at the Gender Studies Colloquium at the University of Melbourne in July 2018. We are very grateful to Tamara Kohn for inviting Purnima Mankekar to present at this colloquium and to faculty and students who provided excellent feedback.

Versions of the chapters in this book have been presented at the following venues: the Anthropology Department at Deakin University, the Stanford Center for South Asia, the Culture, Power, Social Change (CPSC) interest group at UCLA, the University of Melbourne Anthropology Seminar Series, the EGROW webinar series, and the LSE Anthropology Seminar Series. We are grateful to the audiences at all these venues for their thoughtful questions and queries that pushed our thinking further.

We have been fortunate indeed in our academic careers to have as our primary editor Ken Wissoker, whom we met first as an acquisitions editor at Duke University Press, and who later became editor-in-chief and editorial director. His keen eye for what makes an interesting theoretical intervention and his vast knowledge of overlapping fields has been a continued source of inspiration. Most of all, we thank him for his support in all our professional endeavors and personal adventures. We are grateful to Ryan Kendall and Ihsan Taylor for their diligence, patience, and hard work in putting together this manuscript in its final stages.

We cannot thank Cari Costanzo enough for her magnificent editorial suggestions and her insightful feedback on our manuscript. Our colleagues, staff, and students in the departments of Anthropology, Asian American Studies, Gender Studies, and Film, Television, and Digital Media at UCLA, and at the School of Culture and Communication and the Department of Anthropology (School of Social and Political Sciences) at the University of Melbourne have always been a source of support and intellectual companionship. We are deeply indebted to all our students and research assistants who have helped with the library research and with going over the manuscript with such care (listed in alphabetical order): Izem Aral, Bradley Cardozo, Hannah Carlan, Aditi Halbe, Nafis Hasan, Remy Kageyama, Jananie Kalyanaraman, Sucharita Kanjilal, Derek Lu, Tanya Matthan, Sumita Mitra, Leah Nugent, Prahas Rudraraju, Tulika Varma, Donghyoun We, and Alesi Woodward-Hart.

We are grateful for the loving support of our friends across the three continents where we have made our home during the writing of this book. Our work would not have been possible without a wonderful set of friends and interlocutors in Bengaluru: Saritha Rai, Namas Bhojani, Carol Upadhyay and A. R. Vasavi at NIAS, Devesh Nayal and the entire Nayal family, Nausheen and Ibraiz Siddique, and Sajai Singh and Sapana Taneja. In Los Angeles, Melbourne, and the San Francisco Bay Area, we have been supported and nourished (in every way) by Hannah Appel, Vasudev and Vrinda Bhandarkar, Aomar Boum and Norma Mendoza-Denton, Jessica Cattelino and Noah Zatz, Keith Camacho, Jane Collier and the late George Collier, Cari Costanzo, Andy Dawson, Erin Debenport, Rachel Fensham, Inderpal Grewal and Alfred Jessel, Lieba Faier, Laurie Hart, Chris Healy, Grace Hong, Dolly Kikon, Tammy Kohn, Arun and Poornima Kumar, Anna Laursen, Rachel Lee, Nadeem Malik, Kathleen McHugh, Aamir Mufti and Saloni Mathur, Sherry Ortner and Tim Taylor, Ravi and Ruchi Oswal, Haripriya Rangan, Sherene Razack and Larry Brookwell, Mukta and Harsh Sharangpani, Shu-mei Shih and Adam Schorr, Urmi Thakur, Karen Umemoto, Ethiraj Venkatapathy and Julia Jaroch, Sylvia Yanagisako and the late John Sullivan, David Yoo, and Audrey Yue.

We thank our families for their love and support: Aruna and Harsh Bhargava, Akash Bhargava and Elizabeth de Leon, Gauri and Amit Gangoli, Lucy Mankekar, Tara and K. P. Mohanan, and Rahul Aggarwal have always been there for us. Purnima is grateful to her sister Aruna for the daily "kavaj" of protection. Our mother Meena Gupta has been a source of love, support, and good humor. Veena Dubal (our beloved "Veenie Didi"!), you are the daughter of our hearts, our firstborn: we are so blessed that your love suffuses our lives. Purnima would like to thank her spiritual sister, Danielle Hart, for the walks, long chats, meals, shared confidences, and unstinting love and support: you have helped me weather many storms and celebrate an equal number of triumphs, and not a day goes by when I am not grateful for your presence in our lives.

Kamla Mankekar did not live to see this book come to fruition, but her fierce sense of ethics, insistence that a world of ideas and ideals is always worth fighting for, and feminist politics shape every word in the pages that follow. George Collier, much-loved mentor and loyal friend, we miss you: you are not with us, but you continue to be a beacon of integrity and dignity and shape us in more ways than we could ever express.

To Deeya Shivani, the light of our lives: your sparkling intelligence and wit, your resilience, courage, and integrity, and your infectious joie de vivre are nothing short of inspirational. You bring joy (and sleepless nights!), laughs and pranks, culinary experiments, and adventures to our world.

Witnessing your journey and your numerous triumphs has been the most precious gift we could ever have received.

We dedicate this book with love to Lata Mani, without whom Bangalore would never have become home. We thank her for always showing us a path forward no matter what our challenges, for her emotional and spiritual guidance, for all the love and support she has bestowed upon our family over the past several years, and, most of all, for the grace that she brings to all the spaces that she inhabits.

INTRODUCTION

Disjunctive Temporalities, Discrepant Futures

Preethi joined Serenity, the small business process outsourcing (BPO) firm where we began our fieldwork in Bengaluru in 2009, immediately after she received her pre-university course (PUC) diploma.[1] Her mother had died while she was in high school and she had helped her father raise her three younger siblings. Preethi was energetic, driven, highly articulate, and independent in her thinking. Her father had disapproved of her joining a BPO; he had preferred that she seek a job in the multinational bank where he was a security guard. But she interviewed at Serenity and was recruited as an agent. Like all BPO agents, she worked long hours, usually at a time when her family was asleep. Depending on her shift, she would frequently get home just as her siblings were getting ready for school. Her father had forgiven her for working in a BPO because her salary helped pay for the tuition of her siblings. She hoped that they would go to college, something she wasn't able to do because her family couldn't afford it; she had also saved enough money to make repairs to their crumbling, two-room apartment. Still, her father remained deeply ambivalent about her job; he had difficulty accepting that she had to work at night. Preethi, meanwhile, was proud of her accomplishments, and especially that she could support her entire family. She could now hope for a more secure financial future for herself and her family, but she was also nervous about how long she could work at this relentless pace.

Preethi's imagination of her future was expansive: she looked at the possibilities that lay ahead with enthusiasm and confidence. She had already been promoted to the position of team leader and felt sure that she would one day become a manager in Serenity's HR division. Her feelings about the future were also laced with anxiety and apprehension. She worried about many things: being laid off, burning out, getting emotionally exhausted facing the constant disapproval of her father and community, and being able to marry someone who would support her in case her in-laws disapproved of her work in a BPO. She was, at once, excited and tense about what the future held for her.

The Future of Futurity will introduce you to people like Preethi, people that you are likely to have encountered but never met. If you live in the Global North, they are the people who call you when you sit down to dinner to offer a deal on a vacation, or the ones to whom you might vent while trying to resolve problems with a new computer. They are the intimate strangers who read your lab reports overnight so that the results are in your physician's inbox first thing in the morning. Or they could be the person calling you about your credit card debt. We are referring to the army of young men and women who are employed by a large industry responsible for the outsourcing of service work on a transnational scale. We draw on diachronic research with these workers in the outsourcing industry, commonly referred to as "agents," who live in Bengaluru, a metropolis in the southern Indian state of Karnataka, and perform affective labor for customers in countries like the United States, the United Kingdom, and Australia.

But what is it like to be an agent in the sprawling BPO industry?[2] What does it *feel* like to perform affective labor for customers one has never seen and is unlikely to ever meet, including troubleshooting for them, attending to their needs, answering their questions, and putting up with their frustration? How does working in the BPO industry open up different pathways for navigating a globalized world and for imagining one's future in such a world? And what do these imaginings of the future suggest about the relationships between futurity, capital, and technology that shape the contemporary moment?

BUSINESS PROCESS OUTSOURCING AND MUTATIONS OF CAPITALISM

So what are BPOs and what do they signify for the young men and women who work in these companies? *Business process outsourcing* refers to the provision of a range of long-distance services by Indian companies to corporations in countries like the United States, the United Kingdom, Australia, and other parts of the world. BPOs are part of the Information Technology Enabled Services (ITES) sector where the performance and monitoring of labor is facilitated by information and communication technology. The ITES industry is founded on the communication of information and affect. Initially, data entry and data transcription projects (or "processes" as they are termed in the industry) were outsourced to India. Very quickly, ITES expanded to include customer service. The economies of big cities and some small towns took a new turn, and so did the financial prospects of hundreds of thousands of young men and women. The first call center was established in India by General Electric in 1999 (Solomon and Kranhold 2005); by 2015, BPOs employed almost 700,000 people and constituted a USD 26 billion industry (Reuters 2008).[3]

Accurate statistics about India's BPO industry are difficult to obtain because its data is lumped with the IT industry. The BPO sector's annual revenues in the 2020–2021 financial year were estimated at USD 38 billion, recording an annual growth of almost 8 percent (Nasscom 2018, 2020; Press Trust of India 2020; *Economic Times* 2021). In 2019–2020, the total global market of BPOs was estimated at USD 221–226 billion (Grand View Research 2022; Phadnis 2020; Snowdon and Fersht 2016). In this industry, the largest firm had less than 6 percent market share (Everest Group 2019). We worked with three companies that we selected on the basis of their size: the largest company had 0.2 percent of the global market share but employed almost twenty-six thousand people worldwide; the second company had only 0.1 percent of the global market share with almost six thousand employees worldwide; and the third company was much smaller, with about a thousand employees at its peak. The last company struggled to stay afloat, went through a succession of CEOs, and we heard persistent rumors that its owner had put it up for sale. When we last checked, we learned that it had been shuttered, although it had not yet been sold.

Contrary to the image that "monopoly capital" dominates the industrial landscape, the BPO industry resembles ideal-typical models of competitive markets. Throughout our fieldwork we found a wide scattering of companies with a significant number of employees, each with a small share of the total market: unlike some older branches of manufacturing, three or four large companies did not control 50–80 percent of the industry. Secondly, no matter where companies were headquartered (United States, United Kingdom, France, and India are the leading countries), their operations were usually dispersed across multiple sites. Almost all companies in the industry employed large numbers of people in India and the Philippines, but they also had smaller units in Central America (Costa Rica, Guatemala, Honduras, El Salvador), North America, central and eastern Europe (Romania, Hungary, Czech Republic, Poland), the United Kingdom and Ireland, South America (Colombia, Brazil, Argentina), North Africa (Morocco), western Europe (Germany, France), and Australia. Therefore, large and small companies competed with each other in all of these different sites simultaneously.

Apart from being competitive and dispersed geographically, the BPO industry is global in two additional ways. First, and most obviously, the industry connects people globally through the circulation of information and affect. As subsequent chapters will demonstrate, BPOs manifest a distinct form of transnational racial capitalism that shapes the attribution of value and worth to the labor and lives of workers in Global South locations like Bengaluru, mediates processes of translation and mistranslation that shape their affective labor, and regulates their mobility, immobility, and emplacement. The offshoring of service work has, to some extent, reconfigured the pathways laid down by histories of colonization and imperialism, not least because former English-speaking colonies with cheaper labor (for example, India and the Philippines) have become the primary centers of BPO work (Bajaj 2011). The BPO industry is global in another sense. It started out using the difference between labor costs in the United States and in India and other parts of the Global South (labor arbitrage) to offshore back-office work and lower-end customer contact work (call centers). If one were reading Émile Durkheim in a global context, the rise of call centers and BPOs was about the global division of labor, in which more routinized, Taylorized, office work was being done in a lower-cost location. But if one were to add to Durkheim a postcolonial lens, it would follow that the people doing the more routinized, low-cost labor were located in former colonies: their familiarity with the language, history, and mores of the former colonizers made them appear especially well-suited to the type of affective labor required for these jobs.[4]

BPOs have enabled affective labor to be performed at a distance due to technologies of communication. The first technology to be introduced was high-speed telephone lines, followed by the World Wide Web and satellite communication technology. In recent years, the movement of consumers to new technology platforms such as mobile phones and tablets has made apps, chatting, and artificial intelligence (AI) more important. Offshoring was a logical outcome of the outsourcing that US firms had long practiced domestically. For example, since the price of real estate in San Francisco was so high, companies moved all their accounting, human resources, quality control, and warehouses to cheaper, remote locations in the East Bay. However, when call centers were first exported to locations such as India, the big advantage for US companies to shift overseas lay not only in the much lower cost of labor (we discuss the *production* of lower cost or cheap labor shortly); more significantly, it lay in the fact that they could recruit people with a far higher skill set than the workers who worked in call centers in the United States (Mirchandani 2005, 108, 113). The first generation of call center workers in India were almost all graduates of elite schools and colleges. But when other types of companies such as banks, consulting firms, and others moved their operations to India, these higher-skilled workers were no longer attracted to call center employment and moved to more lucrative jobs. By 2008, the socioeconomic composition of call centers and BPO agents in Bengaluru had changed with college graduates comprising a tiny minority.

Our primary objective in this book is to diagram the fraught relationship between the lifeworlds generated by affective capitalism and futurity as an ontological formation. At a historical moment when a global pandemic compelled us to confront the fault lines of inequality and precarity, when a surge in authoritarianism has rendered fragile our assumptions about the state, civil society and liberal notions of freedom and choice, and when the planet itself is under threat, can we even imagine a future? What is the future of futurity in contexts of rapacious capitalism(s), the impunity of state surveillance and violence against marginalized communities, and the "great derangement" of the devastation of the planet (Ghosh 2016)? What is the relationship between BPO agents' aspirations and anxieties regarding their individual future and the generation of futurity as an affective-temporal regime? How might rethinking capitalism, in all its mutations and contradictions, enable us to rethink the future of futurity? And what might the future of futurity have to do with relationality and potentiality?

MUTATIONS OF CAPITAL

What kinds of distinctions do we invoke in our theorization of global capitalism, racial capitalism, semiocapital, and affective capitalism that threads through this book? In using these terms we reference an *assemblage* that has different, interwoven, and discontinuous components and, here, we sketch them briefly in anticipation of our arguments in the chapters to come. Bengaluru's BPOs offer an exemplary lens to engage these processes in how they push back against totalizing, homogeneous, and universalist conceptions of "capital," which, in turn, is assumed to have a logic that is as inexorable as it is homogeneous. *Our goal, however, is decidedly not to represent Bengaluru's BPOs as a "local" or "particular" form of capitalism.* On the contrary, we aim to parochialize dominant assumptions about capitalism by asking: How do BPO agents' struggles, lifeworlds, and forms of becoming compel us to rethink how we theorize capitalisms in all their multiplicity and contradiction?

Global capitalism refers to the uneven and contradictory expansion of capitalism geographically (Lenin [1917] 1939). Marx postulated that geographic expansion is an inherent tendency of capitalist development for three important reasons that reduce costs and increase competitiveness: capitalists look for cheaper sources of raw material, produce where the wage bill is lower, and sell where markets for their products exist to prevent the crisis of realization. Marx himself situated revolutions in transportation and communications infrastructure as the critical axis through which geographic expansion occurs, a phenomenon that he labels "the annihilation of space by time."[5] BPOs are an important example of these spatially expanding tendencies in capitalism because it was the introduction of new communication technologies that enabled this form of labor to be conducted at a distance, allowing companies to take advantage of lower labor costs by opening up back-office operations and call centers halfway across the globe.

The Future of Futurity is about how the disjunctive temporalities undergirding India's New Economy exemplified by BPOs offer an opportunity to theorize the future of futurities.[6] The changing nature of global capitalism provides us with one important axis to (re)theorize futures and futurities. Old geographies of capitalist firms from the Global North spreading in a colonial or imperial manner in the Global South are less persuasive now as compared with a few decades ago (Rofel and Yanagisako 2019). In many traditional manufacturing sectors, the expansion of firms from the Global South to the Global North is just as conspicuous as the movement in the other direction. Indian firms have grown into some of the largest companies worldwide in traditional manufacturing and are opening up or acquiring businesses in the Global North rapidly. For example, Tata Motors, one of India's largest conglomerates, has manufacturing units in Argentina, South Africa, Great Britain, and Thailand, and research and development centers in South Korea, Great Britain, and Spain. They produce Jaguar and Land Rover branded vehicles in Britain and commercial vehicles in South Korea under the Tata Daewoo label.

How might rethinking the relationship between the spatiality and temporality of capitalist expansion enable us to examine the future of futurity? A radically rethought version of the classical Marxist theory of combined and uneven development may help us better understand the contemporary global capitalist system (Trotsky [1938] 1973, [1918] 2008; Van der Linden 2007). The theory of combined and uneven development was produced to account for the failure of capitalist development to close the gap between rich and poor areas of the world, between the First World and the Third World, between Global North and Global South.[7] This is a geography—a shorthand—that we have become accustomed to in thinking about difference and divergence in the global capitalist economy. However, this territorially based view of rich and poor areas may have outlived its utility: we may now need a new geography of the production of wealth, poverty, and the middle class in which territorial space matters less than social space and temporality.[8] The multiple futures of global capitalism do not index territorial entities like the United States, China, and India, entities in whose terms all our economic and political discourse is organized. New geographies of accumulation are creating and exacerbating pockets of steep inequality *within* societies rather than simply across them. Billionaires are multiplying most rapidly in what has been termed the Global South, while a sixth of the US population sinks below the poverty line (Credit Suisse 2015). These new geographies of inequality are the result of patterns of capitalist accumulation that create within countries a small island of wealth, a somewhat larger peninsula of middle-class prosperity (growing in India, China, and Brazil but shrinking in the United States, Japan, and Europe), and a sea of poverty in all places. Few analytic frameworks have attempted to explain the *simultaneous* rise of the superrich, the growth of the middle classes, and the creation of a class of desperately poor people. Yet, without such a framework, we can understand neither the position of those who work in BPOs nor the wider context in which BPOs have flourished nor where they might be headed in the future. In a situation marked by the emergence of discrepant futures, what can we say about futurity, about that which is immanent?

Our discussion of semiocapitalism draws on Franco "Bifo" Berardi and Michael Hardt to diagram the reconfiguration of capitalism with the manipulation of symbols and code; this, it has been argued, is part of the reorganization of capitalism that has become ascendant with the rise of computers, software, information technology, and AI.[9] In *The Future of Futurity*, we make several assertions that fly in the face of dominant assumptions of semiocapital. Against conceptions of semiocapital as disembodied, we insist on foregrounding both the embodied labor implicated in affective capitalism as well as the inextricable entanglement of bodies, technologies, and organic and inorganic matter that are foundational to it. In arguing that the labor of semiocapital is affective, we problematize assumed boundaries between cognitive, emotional, and corporeal labor engaged by bodies that are *formed* at the intersection of caste, class, race, and gender. Against the proposition that semiocapital is sustained by the uninterrupted flow of information across the world, we draw attention to the generation and circulation of affect that are far from seamless but are, in fact, beset with blockages and misunderstandings, missed understandings, and translations that fail. Additionally, far from assuming that semiocapital "transcends" location and place, we insist that the affective capitalism of Bengaluru's BPOs is powerfully refracted by the city as an actant. Rather than simply providing a "context" or "site" for the establishment of BPOs, the city's material infrastructures (including those that remain incomplete, in suspension, or in ruins), the resilience of more-than-human life forms, the recharging of religious and linguistic conflict, and the spatialities of the cruelties of caste and gendered violence are profoundly imbricated in the generation of affective capitalism (Sreenath 2020).

Our understanding of *racial capitalism* is indebted to the work of Cedric Robinson (2019, [1983] 2020), who has argued that capitalism builds on, exploits, and *deploys* existing axes of inequality rather than simply replacing it with class; class inequality is always already intersectional with other forms of inequality; and that the long history of racism is baked into capitalism from its beginning rather than an unfortunate byproduct or illegitimate remnant from the past. In the case of BPOs, colonial logics of race are not simply reenacted or reproduced but are actively reconstituted. They are transformed—they change form—but they do not disappear. Our understanding of racial capitalism is deeply indebted to Asian American studies scholars who have long argued that labor and the attribution of value, and their implications for migration and immigration as much as for indenture and other forms of servitude, are always-already refracted by race (for instance, Lowe 2015; Glenn 1985, 1992, 2012; Hune 1989; Ong 1999). We draw on but also extend theorizations of intimate labor, care work, and affective labor performed by Asian bodies in a transnational circuit of service and servitude (Choy 2003; Gottfried and Chun 2018; Kang 2010; Parreñas 2001; Parreñas, Thai, and Silvey 2016; P. Sharma 2020) to highlight how the BPO industry is sustained by and reconfigures racial capitalism outside Atlanticist and Americanist frameworks of race.[10] These perspectives profoundly shape our theorization of the affective labor of BPO agents in Bengaluru who, while they do not physically migrate, engage in forms of virtual migration contingent on the extraction of surplus from racialized bodies emplaced by transnational discourses of race, racialism, and value. In particular, our theorization of Bengaluru's BPOs is in dialogue with scholarship on BPOs and call centers in the Philippines, a country with a markedly different colonial history than India but which nevertheless offers valuable points of comparison and contrast with the forms of racial capitalism congealing in Indian BPOs (Errighi, Bodwell and Khatiwada 2016). Engaging these histories of empire and coloniality hence enables us to track contemporary *mutations* of racial capitalism in contexts marked by affective capitalism.

In our theorization of *affective capitalism* we radically problematize assumptions about the "expansion" of capitalism into new domains of social life, and its colonization of consciousness. Affective capitalism is not "outside" other domains of sociality but is, fundamentally, coproduced with it; thus, for instance, the rhythms of affective labor are thoroughly entangled with the temporalities of the body, of ritual, and of family relations. At the same time, BPOs depend on a form of value extraction predicated on the modulation of affect: affective labor is meant to produce affective states and dispositions. Of course, affective labor is not unique to BPOs because it is the mainstay of several other service industries as well. However, the conjunction of affective work done across geographic and social distance represents a distinctive mode of surplus production that is typical of BPO work.

INTERJECTION

It is past midnight, and we are already exhausted—the long drive from our home to this BPO has been full of nail-biting moments. There are times when we have felt that our taxi will slam into another vehicle, a streetlamp, a building, the cart of a street vendor: our nerves are in shreds. We are being brought to the BPO by a van that transports agents to work. The speed of the van as it rushes through the city underscores the urgency of getting agents to work on time, for unpunctuality can lead to the failure of a process—an unmitigated disaster for the entire team. We are unaccustomed to the speed and marvel at how BPO agents cope with it. We will learn subsequently that speed, collision, and gridlock—literally and figuratively—are a fundamental part of their lifeworlds.

This is our first time on what we learn later is called the "shop floor," where agents do their work. We arrive disheveled and disoriented. It is pitch-dark outside, the blackness of the night a constant reminder of the slumbering city around us. But here, on the shop floor, the adrenaline—and tension—is palpable, much like a newsroom just before a deadline. The walls of the large room in which the agents are sitting are bare except for a poster that jubilantly announces the excitement and adventure of cruise travel (we have been informed that the agents are working on a process or project contracted to them by a leading European cruise agency). These young men and women, most of whom look like they are in their early twenties, are sitting in small cubicles that crowd the room: the cubicles are placed cheek by jowl and are also bare, strangely bereft of any personal effects, photographs, or any other decoration. The agents are sitting in various postures that make visible the tension that runs through their bodies as they concentrate on the calls they're making, the packages they're supposed to sell, the deals they're obligated to clinch. The air is filled with electricity. Some agents sit crouched in their seats, almost as if they wish to disappear into them—it appears to us that they have failed to make a sale and their bodies display the fatigue, disappointment, and anxiety that seems to course through them. Every now and then the tension in the air is punctuated by claps, as when an agent is successful in selling a travel package to a client thousands of miles away from where they sit in their cramped cubicle. Once in a while, an agent rushes up from their seat, waving their arms joyously in a spontaneous, unrehearsed dance of triumph. A young woman, at most a year or two older than some of the agents, is the team supervisor and she makes her rounds, patting the shoulder of an anxious agent stooping over his monitor, his palm on his forehead, in despair because he has lost his client. A few more failed sales and he can lose his job. A young man sitting next to him turns to look at him sympathetically and clicks his tongue in support, knowing that he could be in his shoes the next night or even later that same night.

AFFECTIVE AND POLITICAL ECONOMIES

The BPO industry demonstrates how conjunctions between global capitalism, racial capitalism, and semiocapitalism produce affective capitalism as distinct assemblages. BPOs hence offer extraordinary insights about the mutual imbrication of capitalism(s), futurity, and the building of lifeworlds. This does not mean that there exists some seamless integration of these aspects of capitalism—there is friction between them to be sure, and they articulate differently depending on the industry, its location, and its history, to name but a few of the factors that *generate* capitalism rather than are simply "impacted" by it. Although the BPO industry has neither the prestige nor glamor of software and higher-end industries such as business consulting and R&D industries, or the working-class credentials of mining, steelwork, or automobile production, it is exceedingly productive as a site to think about the multiple articulations of global capitalism, racial capitalism, semiocapitalism, and affective capitalism that characterize capitalism in the present.

Following the work of the Gens collective, we take it as a given that capitalism and other domains of sociality are coconstituted (Bear et al. 2015), with implications for how we can understand futurities. Capital*ism*—rather than *capital* as an abstract entity, which is assumed to have a "logic," agency, or will of "its" own—is never singular; nor is it distinct from sociality, emotion, and affect. Capitalism can be irrational, unpredictable, and, above all, supple— all the time *needing* to reinvent itself in relation to other temporalities and other socialities. Far from colonizing realms of social life from the "outside," it is intimately imbricated with sociality. BPOs underscore how the heterogeneous temporalities of affective capitalism generate distinctive futurities in various alignments and misalignments with the temporalities of the body and family, mobility and immobility, and translation and mis(sed) translation. The disjunctive temporalities of affective labor compel us to reconceptualize the *interweaving* of work and life in the futurities generated by affective capitalism.

The worlds and lives of BPO agents demonstrate the "braiding" of political and affective economies (J. Menon 2021). Policies of the Indian state, the demands of multinational capitalism, and the affective assemblage represented by the scrambling of past, present, and future in the chronotopes of Bengaluru have converged to produce formations of futurity that, while particular to this place, also provide a fecund site for theorizing futurity at this sociohistorical juncture. Bengaluru is not unique in how it enacts and represents the tense adjacency of different temporalities (T. Srinivas 2018; see also S. Srinivas 2016). The city represents itself as the hub of technological progress, but this reach toward a (post)modern future coexists with the invocation of a supposedly glorious past of Brahminical and Hindu supremacy in which "lower" castes are kept in their place; this is a golden age from which Muslims and other religious minorities have to be expunged (Assadi 2002; Gatade 2014). Neoliberal economic policies may well have spawned some of these fantasies of past glory which must then be "reclaimed" in order to build an exclusionary vision of national(ist) futures.

BPOS AND REGIMES OF LABOR

As contemporary instantiations of affective capitalism, BPOs are predicated on the circulation of signs, information, and affect.[11] However, the establishment of BPOs in Bengaluru is part of a long history of IT companies in the city; their distinctiveness, therefore, does not lie in their being harbingers of capitalism centered on the production and manipulation of symbols.

Besides, the creation and manipulation of affect have always been a part of capitalist economies (Hardt 1999, 96; Bear et. al 2015; Yanagisako 2002): affective production, communication, and exchange are generally dependent on human contact, whether this contact is actual or virtual. Furthermore, kin work, caring work, and other forms of invisible labor have existed both within capitalist labor processes and in pericapitalist spaces (Hardt 1999, 96; Tsing 2015). In other words, agents' engagement in care work is not unique to BPOs.

What, then, is distinctive about the labor of BPO agents and why do we characterize it as affective? After all, every labor process has some measure of affect built into it—the pleasure experienced by an assembly-line worker in a finished automobile, the pride of a craftsperson in a beautifully produced garment, or even the frustration experienced by someone whose job is monotonous and boring. The labor of BPO agents produced commodities that were largely intangible—for instance, satisfaction, a feeling of being cared for, and brand loyalty. The products of labor were modes of feeling and, above all, a sense of connectedness with the company.

Affective labor hence lies at the core of BPO work for three reasons: Affect was the *product* of the labor of BPO agents. It was generated through the *confluence* of cognition, emotion, corporeality, and technology—agents' labor was predicated on affectively charged modes of connectivity and exchange with customers and each other. And the creation and circulation of affect in BPOs through these interactions and the labor process was *generative*: it produced agents as specific kinds of subjects. The affective labor at the core of the work performed by BPO agents entailed their entire being. BPOs hence differ from other offshore outsourcing industries in at least three critical dimensions: affective labor is central to the work process; affect is the chief output of this labor; and the laborer's connection to the customer is live and interactive, creating conjoined and disjunctive temporalities across disjointed locales. As part of the larger transnational service industry, BPOs foreground how the production and extraction of affective labor from the Global South have become important mechanisms for capitalist reproduction (Parreñas 2001, 2005; Vora 2015).

Affective intensities charged the atmosphere of BPOs in powerful ways. The demands on agents were intense and stringent. Each quarter, they were given a report card with a grade (A, B, C, D) based on their performance of affective labor. Agents consistently receiving the lowest grade for several quarters running were fired. Conversely, those receiving the highest grade were rewarded with promotions and bonuses. Bonuses were linked with performance and were quite substantial. Agents who were outstanding performers could double their starting salary of INR 12,000 (approx. USD 175/month) in a year and be promoted to team leader in two years. Agents' grades were based on their Customer Satisfaction (CSAT) Scores. Skillful agents made the customer feel good even when they were unable to resolve the customer's problem. The ability to bring about a certain disposition in the customer was essential to being a good agent. If customers left the call feeling that they had been heard, that the agent was helpful, and that the company could be trusted, then it was more likely that they would have positive feelings about the brand. That is why the CSAT surveys often emailed to customers right after an interaction asked how likely they were to recommend that company to others and how likely they were to reuse the products and services of that company.

Being able to achieve a high level of connectedness and empathy on a call was usually correlated with high CSAT scores. Agents were trained to accomplish this goal. While most affective labor is based on bodily copresence, BPOs were predicated on separating spatial proximity from affective intimacy (chapter 3). Using only the sense of hearing, the contact between agents and customers was in some senses a stripped-down version of face-to-face interaction; however, it was not for that reason less corporeal, nor diminished in its affectivity and no less material (chapter 4). Despite the fact that agents' entire interaction with customers was via a headset, their entire bodies were galvanized into action: they had to learn to inhabit their bodies in new ways. For example, they were trained to smile while speaking, to wear deodorant that their customers would never smell, and to adhere to a dress code at work that none of their customers could see.

How is the affective labor performed by BPO agents different from that of other segments of the (trans)national service economy—for instance, the labor performed by flight attendants, nurses, and workers in the hospitality industry? For one, it differs from the emotional labor of these workers in that it is not based on face-to-face interactions (cf. Hochschild 2012). What makes call center agents' jobs particularly challenging is that they have to manage emotions at a distance based on their verbal interactions with their clients or customers, many of whom live in cultural contexts vastly different from theirs. Affective labor in call centers also involves intense transformations in processes of embodiment: to cite just a few examples, the training of call center agents entails relearning speech patterns and the necessity of night work alters their circadian rhythms (chapter 4).

Finally, and importantly, while their labor by no means subsumes their lives or imaginations, it is affective in that it entails a profound reconfiguration of the ways in which BPO agents inhabit their worlds, indeed, in their processes of "worlding" and "world-making" (Das 2006; Stewart 2007). At the very least, it involves processes of virtual and imaginative travel (Aneesh 2015; Mankekar 2015): almost none of the workers we interviewed had traveled or, indeed, could travel to the United States, the United Kingdom, or Australia. Their affective labor involves the ability to empathize and translate the lives of others in order to better serve them. To a large extent, their affective labor profoundly shapes their *capacities* to affect and be affected in the worlds in which they now move: in this sense, then, their labor manifests what Baruch Spinoza describes as the essence of affect.

Theorists of semiocapitalism tend to focus primarily on the circulation of information; the implication is that technology and the reflexivity of capital enable the flow of information across borders. However, neither semiocapital, thus conceptualized, nor affective capitalism entails placeless production: its modes of value production and extraction are *engendered* by the particularities of history and place. The growth of BPOs in Bengaluru is intimately related to the longer genealogies, multiple histories, and divergent futurities that have made this global city the place that it is. The articulation of place with forms of BPO labor creates a particular assemblage of affective capitalism and, hence, implicates how we may theorize futurities.

In academic literature as much as in popular culture, BPOs have set off enormous debates about the offshoring and outsourcing of service sector jobs in a global economy. Observers like Thomas L. Friedman (2005) have represented BPOs and the IT industry as evidence of the capacity of countries like India to leapfrog into the twenty-first century; other commentators have depicted BPO agents as new (neoliberal) incarnations of older forms of indenture and slavery (for instance, Ramesh 2004; we interrogate the racial underpinnings of such representations later in this book). Our research on the BPO industry in Bengaluru suggests that these assumptions are as totalizing as they are reductive. We began our research intending to investigate, over the long term, the cultural implications of BPOs: how working in BPOs had reconfigured the knotty relationships between work and family, and labor and leisure, for BPO agents. As we proceeded to untangle these relationships we realized that, of all the transformations that BPOs had brought about in the lives and subjectivities of agents, what had changed most radically was not just their imagination of the future, but the future of futurity.

Futures and futurity are close kin (Campt 2017). The *futures* imbricated in development projects may bring into articulation discourses of past lack, present striving, and aspirations for a better tomorrow; narratives of past injury and current projects of ethnic cleansing and genocide may undergird an Islamophobic project of a Hindu nation that is yet to be achieved; upper-caste discourses of a purportedly golden age of the past inflame violence against Dalits, Bahujans, and other oppressed castes who allegedly no longer know their place; and rapidly rising inequality across and within geographies may lead democracies into populist and authoritarian futures.[12] *Futurity*, on the other hand, enables the capacity to imagine or strive for a future. As an affective-temporal formation, futurity is generative of action, aspiration, a drive to change things, and of emotions like passion, dread, longing, fear, or anxiety. Futurity as *immanence* implies movement and works on a temporal register by exceeding the articulation of what-has-been, what-is-now, and the yet-to-come and frequently dislodging linear temporalities by scrambling past, present, and future. Futurity as immanence is unlike futures, which may be defined by a fixed point or perhaps a horizon. Futurity gestures to the potentiality of conjunctures—the present as a conjuncture of the past, present, and future. Above all, futurity is ontological.

Most BPO agents that we interviewed were under the age of twenty-five and were experiencing upward class mobility for perhaps the first time in their lives: it is not surprising that they were concerned about the future. We had initially planned to use a semistructured interview protocol whose last three questions were to be about where agents saw themselves in the next two years, the next five years, and the next ten years. But we almost never explicitly needed to ask those questions because, in a typical interview, they would describe their hopes and fears about the future without prompting, and often nearer the beginning rather than toward the end of our conversations. Agents were eager to talk about the promises and perils that the future held for them, the trajectories that they had planned for their lives, and what they saw themselves doing after they had finished working in a BPO. Executives at senior and middle management in BPOs were also preoccupied with the future. Instability was a constant in the industry, and executives at all levels had to prepare for rapid shifts in technology, the labor market, demand, and competition. At a conclave of senior executives organized by NASSCOM in 2009, Gupta observed that most talks dealt with the question of the future of the industry. What sources would result in new business?

How could the industry and individual companies expand? It seemed that everyone was preoccupied with the future. However, the stories we heard suggested something more than simply what kinds of futures different people in the industry imagined for themselves, for their companies, and for the industry as a whole. It seemed to us that there was something crucial that was not necessarily stated explicitly but that underlaid the articulation of discrepant futures.

What our interlocutors were gesturing toward was potentiality, emergent phenomena that did not yet have a name, and about becoming as a *mode of being*. What lay beyond words and feelings was futurity, an affective-temporal formation that was impressed on bodies and geographies, and on itineraries that were existential and material at the same time. A second-order phenomenon, futurity was not observable, but it was generative of those futures that could be articulated and for which feelings could be registered. If futurity is a quality of *becoming*, that which is immanent, it is analytically distinct from futures, which we conceptualize as individual and collective states or ends imagined, aspired to, or feared. Futures that may be linked with or expressed in terms of, for example, aspiration, optimism, or pessimism.

Futurity enables the production and imagination of futures. As affective-temporal potentiality, futurity propels agency and is productive of subjectivities. Futurity is embedded in duration (durée) and is characterized by qualitative multiplicity; unlike time, duration is immeasurable, ineffable yet inexpressible, incomplete, and continuously unfolding (Bergson [1910] 2015, 122). Futurity is implicated in processes of emergence that are fundamentally open-ended, nonnormative, and presubjective. Sociality is braided into futurity rather than anterior to it; yet, futurity is irreducible to institutions, political economies, state policy, or, in the case of BPOs, regimes of affective labor. At a historic moment marked by climate change, economic volatility, and the disintegration of polities that aspired to coexistence and tolerance, theorizing the future of futurity is an urgent political project. Our research on affective labor, transnational capitalism, and the lives and worlds of BPO agents enables us to draw on the futures imagined by our interlocutors as an ethnographic site to theorize the articulations (and disarticulations) of discrepant futurities.

Visions of the future are often produced by temporalities marked by struggles for dominance. Thus, modernization theory, which became dominant during the Cold War, produced a linear and teleological temporality that took nation-states from the first stage, "traditional society," to the most advanced state, "high mass consumption." Modernization theory provided a vision for the future—advanced capitalist consumer society—buttressed by a confidence that this future was possible for the entire world. In an earlier era, futurists provided a model for a new industrial age, where speed and technology would intersect to change people's lives for the better (Berardi 2011, 17–25). Futurists saw themselves as heralding an emergent phenomenon that they were convinced would become dominant: the future of their vision of industrial life reshaped by speed, power, and technology was never in doubt.[13] Utopian visions of the future have always been accompanied by dystopian ones: the future age of modernity based on capitalist industrialization was questioned by many, from Luddites to Romanticists; the future imagined by nationalism was resisted not only by the ancien régime but by many who feared the loss of their regional, linguistic, or ethnic identity. Today, an emergent vision of the future, shaped by climate crises, the failures of global capitalism, and the exhaustion of optimistic versions of nationalism has cast doubt on whether the future has a directionality, let alone a teleology, either progressive or dystopian (Appadurai 2013; Berardi 2011). The future of futurity has itself been cast into doubt.

Our goal is not to evaluate whether these ideas of the future will turn out as envisioned. Each of these visions is the result of a struggle among discourses of futures that may align or collide with each other, or by the conviction that an emergent temporality will become dominant in the not-too-distant future. Visions of the future are encoded in mundane activities of governments, corporations, and citizens rather than solely in well-articulated ideas in the public sphere (Appadurai 2013). Public policies constitute investments in particular futures that the state tries to bring about. Or there may be moments when utopian and dystopian narratives are equally prominent and there may be a tussle as to which one will prevail.

Futurity, and its agentive potentiality, lie at the heart of our theoretical and political interventions in this book. When we first began fieldwork in December 2008, the United States was confronting a recession: people were losing their homes; storefronts were boarded up; the election of a new president brought some hope, but it was evident that the way out of the crisis was going to be difficult. In contrast, when we arrived in Bengaluru we were taken aback by an ambient sense of optimism, the crowded and busy markets and malls, and, even though it was often tinged by anxiety and nervousness, by the excitement expressed by most of the young people we met in BPOs: the future seemed bright for all those who worked in this "sunrise industry." *And yet*, it was clear that there was much to be concerned about. Youth in other sectors of the economy were in despair: unemployment and underemployment fueled the frustrations of those who had been left behind by the nation's march to the future. Farmers were committing suicide. Violence against minority communities, especially Muslims, and oppressed Dalit and Bahujan communities was surging.

Women in the BPO industry were venturing into uncharted territory with confidence and optimism, often in defiance of the restrictions and surveillance imposed on them by their families, neighbors, and community members. These women not only worked through the night but, when they could, created new pathways for themselves professionally and personally. Their lives, while marked by relentless labor, were not without joy or enchantment. They were able to imagine new kinds of futures for themselves and their loved ones. When they had the time and the means, they socialized with each other; they would window shop and dream; they partook of the pleasures offered by the enticing new world that they were now inhabiting. *And yet*, violence against women in public spaces was increasing. At the very beginning of our fieldwork, thugs from the Hindu nationalist organization, Sri Ram Sene, physically assaulted women in a pub in nearby Mangalore. This incident initially made our interlocutors fearful but, eventually, they refused to be intimidated: they persisted in seeking relief from their exhausting schedules in each other's company and, when they had the time and the money, in malls, food courts, multiplexes, and pubs. In 2012, while we were still engaged in long-term fieldwork on this project, a young woman was brutally gang-raped in Delhi; feminists and other activists took to the streets demanding that the streets be made safer for women. This incident shook the confidence of many women who had already been deeply unsettled by the murder of call center employee Pratibha Murthy in 2005.

Agents entered into dense social relationships with coworkers from cultural backgrounds completely unfamiliar to them. They forged solidarities and intimacies, webs of relationality founded on mutual aid and care for each other, despite the fact that they were often required to compete against each other. Some of them entered into intercaste and interreligious relationships in a manner that had previously been unthinkable. *And yet*, all through our fieldwork, Hindu nationalist vigilante groups were brutally attacking Muslim men for allegedly seducing Hindu women as part of a larger campaign against "love jihad," which these groups asserted would bring about a demographic shift in favor of Muslims. And Dalit and Bahujan men, and the dominant-caste women who entered into romantic relationships or marriages with them, were violently attacked and often murdered (Chowdhury 2004, 2009; Mankekar 2021a, 2021b, 2022; Rege 1998).

The capacity to aspire generates ethical horizons (Appadurai 2013, 193). Our insistence on futurity is imbricated with ethics in more than one sense of the word: the ethical formation of our interlocutors, as well as our ethical commitment to them. Redefining, theorizing, and *holding on* to futurity is, for us, an urgent political project. We cannot abandon the project of futurity: the very vulnerability of our interlocutors makes it incumbent on us to pay closer attention to the nuances of their imaginations, aspirations, and fears about the future. Anxiety, anticipation, excitement, yearning, worry, desire, and despair: the copresence of these apparently disparate emotions was precisely what made their imaginations of the future tense. The emotions expressed by our interlocutors about their futures were indexical of futurity as an affective-temporal formation. What do heterogeneous and discrepant futures, imagined both individually and collectively by BPO agents, suggest about futurity? Ineffable, unnameable, and potent, futurity marked our interlocutors as particular kinds of desiring subjects. As is the case with other affective regimes, subjects are not the locus of futurity. Instead, futurity leaves traces on their subjectivities, shaping their desires, undergirding their fears, and making them excited and tense about what lies ahead.

INTERJECTION

Cynthia's life changed dramatically after she got a job as a BPO agent about nine years ago. The only child in a poor family, she had the opportunity to attend a church-run school and learn excellent English.[14] She did not go to college and indeed could not even dream of studying further after she graduated from school. She applied for a job in a BPO and, after working as an agent for about five years, was promoted to a trainer. Because she worked in a small BPO, the security of her job depended entirely on the ability of her company to get contracts from overseas clients. Moreover, the kind of training she needed to provide constantly changed according to the clients' shifting needs. Then she fell in love with someone in an IT company. The pace of her work and the uncertainties surrounding her job made her feel that she needed to "take things a little slower" instead of "always being on the move." Sometimes she felt "dizzy," she added. She wanted to get married and have children.

By the time we concluded our fieldwork, she had had a son and quit the industry altogether. "This industry has given me a lot," she said. "But I felt the industry is always changing and I always have to move too fast to keep up.

It just didn't work for me anymore. I had to take a break and it worries me to do so. But . . . we cannot keep moving all the time: it makes your head spin."

Cynthia is certainly not the first woman to quit a stressful job to take care of her family—in the chapters that follow, we will meet others like her. Nor was her decision to take a break unique to BPO agents. Nevertheless, her words foreground some of the ways in which disjunctive futures come into conflict. There were many instances when exhaustion, disillusionment, or shifting priorities of family meant that our interlocutors would pull out of the vertiginous lifestyle enjoined by the rhythms of their labor. The collision of the temporalities of affective labor with those of the body, social relations, and religious obligation could lead to burnout. Our interlocutors, after all, were never just laborers: even as work was central to their lives, shaped their imagination of the future, and left its mark on their bodies, it rarely, if ever, subsumed their lives. Sometimes the futurities surrounding affective labor would be out of sync with the futures our interlocutors imagined for themselves. When this happened, some of them (those who could afford to do so) would quit—even when it entailed downward class mobility. Ian Klinke (2012) asserts that the "times of others" are being erased under the continuing expansion of western modernity (677). We push back against the assumption that the rhythms of affective labor erase other temporalities because it reinforces the narrative of the teleological march of "global" capitalism. For this reason, while Cynthia's narrative might appear commonplace, we place it on record precisely because it gives us pause.

We cannot keep moving all the time: it makes your head spin. We are interested in what an *in*ability to "move all the time" suggests about the relationship between futures, as imagined by individuals and collectives, and futurity as a mode of orienting oneself in the world. Furthermore, movement as a modality of navigating a rapidly changing world can be experienced as disorienting and unsettling; some futures may not be desired or coveted. Futurity as immanence implies movement. At the same time, the movement in futurity is not about a particular future. Futurity is indifferent to whether the future involves rapid movement or relative stasis.

TEMPORALITY, DURATION, AND MOVING TARGETS

Over the course of seven years of fieldwork, we were frequently struck by how rapidly the BPO industry kept changing. Some of these changes were mirrored in the different names by which the industry represented itself. In

1999, these businesses primarily did back-office work. Subsequently, voice processes became dominant, and they came to be known as call centers. By the time we began our research in 2008, this name was replaced by the term *business process outsourcing.* BPOs encompassed both call center labor and back-office work. Around the same time, Knowledge Process Outsourcing became ascendant: this entailed, for instance, reading pathology reports and MRI scans for hospitals, preparing briefs for attorneys, and assisting certified public accountants. Shortly thereafter, the abbreviation BPM (for business process management) became commonly used and, in some instances, customer-facing businesses began to be referred to as contact centers.

At the time of writing this book, technological transformations are being driven by the intersection and articulation of three changes. First, internal changes to BPO processes are being driven by artificial intelligence, Big Data, and analytics; second, changes in consumer behavior are being led by the increasing use of apps, tablets, and mobile phones; and third, the firms that contract to BPOs are demanding that they minimize costs, decrease consumer migration, and increase brand loyalty and customer satisfaction. The four major actors in this industry—the contracting corporation (for example, British Airways or Verizon); the BPO hired to perform customer contact, with operations in India, the Philippines, or another location; consumers mostly located in the United States, the United Kingdom, and Australia; and the city of Bengaluru—each have their own future trajectories in technological, organizational, and social space. Transformations in the industry respond to the articulation of these futures because they respond in the present to where they think they are headed in the future. The anticipation and production of sociotechnical futures recast the present actions of all the actors in this relationship.

What has been striking to us in studying this industry over several years is the speed of its transformation from year to year. For example, one of the companies where we did our fieldwork now operates in a manner that bears almost no resemblance to what it was doing in 2009, and similar rapid technological change is sweeping the entire industry. After our first year of intensive fieldwork in 2008–2009, when we returned to Bengaluru every subsequent summer, we would confront a transformed landscape. We chose to conclude our study in July 2016 because we realized that the industry as it existed at that moment was on the verge of momentous transformation. The city was changing at breakneck speed and the BPO industry was reconstituting itself ceaselessly. The changing names of the industry were not simply changes in nomenclature. They were symptomatic of the constantly

mutating and transformative nature of capitalism and its divergent temporalities of duration, pause, movement, and stasis.

Rather than getting frustrated and overwhelmed by the task of studying a moving target, we decided to train our ethnographic eye precisely on
these apparently contradictory forces of movement and stasis, duration and
change, acceleration and pause inherent in the industry—and in the lives
and worlds of our interlocutors. BPOs enable us to track the global expansion of affective capitalism for the extraction of surplus value; as we have
noted, the initial objective of setting them up in India was to profit from
labor arbitrage—the difference between the cost of labor in metropolitan
and peripheral regions (for instance, the United States and India, respectively). For BPO employees, the future, simultaneously full of possibility
and anxiety, beckoned.

The temporality of change also extends to the socioeconomic composition of BPO agents. The middle-class graduates initially hired by the industry
left it for more lucrative pursuits, and by the time we began our fieldwork
in Bengaluru in December 2008, the industry was hiring primarily from
what has been termed the aspirational classes. Most of these young people
had only a PUC diploma and came from either lower-income backgrounds
or from the precariously lower-middle class. Their parents were bus drivers,
auto-rickshaw drivers, welders, domestic workers, and clerks in government
offices. For most of these young people, unlike those who came from wealthier backgrounds, working in a call center was not "time-pass," something
they did to have fun or earn pocket money while they awaited admission to
college or repeatedly sat for entrance exams to the Indian Institutes of Technology (IITs), medical schools, and other elite colleges. As will be clear from
the rest of this book, the incomes our interlocutors earned were crucial to the
financial stability of not only themselves but their entire families and, often,
their broader kin network. Contrary to (middle- and upper-middle-class)
media portrayals of BPO agents as irresponsible individuals and profligate
spenders, their salaries helped to provide for the tuition of younger siblings,
pay off loans incurred by the family, contribute to the marriages of siblings
and cousins, and, most importantly, support their parents and grandparents
in their old age. BPO agents from middle-class backgrounds, whose parents
were school teachers, college professors, army officers, middle-level bureau-
crats, or bankers, would also join BPOs to supplement the family income
while going to college, but for the duration of our fieldwork, most of our
interlocutors were from socioeconomic backgrounds that were considerably
less privileged.[15] In some cases, the entry of middle-class youth into BPOs

was precipitated by the unexpected death or incapacity of their fathers. At an interview, when asked why he wanted to join a BPO, James explained that his father had died unexpectedly and because of that he had suffered a "mental setback." He worked with his uncle in a family business, but his brother urged him to leave Nagaland in northeast India and come to Bengaluru to make a career. He had tried unsuccessfully to pass the entrance exam for an engineering college, and this is why he sought a job in a BPO. Another applicant, Venkat, had worked with his father in a real estate business in Bengaluru, but when his father met with an accident, he was forced to look for work in a place where he could earn a steady income.

We also interviewed several young women who worked in a BPO at night and attended college classes during the day and, for most of these women as well, their BPO salaries were crucial to the financial stability of their families. A considerable proportion of our interlocutors came from oppressed castes but only a few self-identified as Dalit (Guru 1998).[16] Our respective caste positions played a crucial role in how we came to understand caste in the worlds of BPO agents. As mixed and dominant caste subjects who have been raised in India, our lives and family dynamics have been powerfully shaped by caste, even as we have benefited from our respective caste privileges in numerous material and intangible ways: over the course of our lives as Hindu South Asian/American subjects, we have learned to be *attuned* to how caste, as a particular kind of subject position, is inhabited. Additionally, our previous fieldwork in rural and urban India respectively sensitized us to the politics of hierarchy, disclosure, exclusion, and naming as well as the physical, psychological, symbolic, and material violence producing and surrounding caste. As a result, even when caste was not explicitly discussed, we were often able to glean the caste positions of our interlocutors from their biographies, family histories, last names, eating habits, and, at times, their bodily habitus.[17] On some occasions, our interlocutors' caste was revealed by where they lived: as we describe in chapter 1, Bengaluru has historically been segregated by caste, and new patterns of urban development have only partially changed the geography of caste in the city. At other times, the occupations of their parents and other family members would indicate their caste position.

The self-representation of BPOs stresses meritocracy, a flattening of hierarchies, and a relatively egalitarian ethos. This self-representation is in keeping both with neoliberal disavowals of structural disadvantages and systemic violence, as well as with liberal notions of modernity. All the senior managers, CEOs, COOs, and owners of BPOs that we came across were Savarna or of dominant castes: their own caste positions were invisible to them, and *herein* lay their caste privilege. Aditya Nigam (2019) has pointed out that the invisibilization of caste has historically been central to the (Savarna) modern Indian self: "The erasure of caste involved not merely its proscription or 'repression' from public discourse, in any obvious sense, rather, it was built into the formation of the self, seen as something that this 'modern Indian' had already left behind in some remote past" (122).

Many of the BPO agents with whom we worked closely did not want to talk about caste: this occlusion of caste is the result of many factors. For one, as we have just noted, the ostensible invisibility of caste is a product of the enduring structuring power of caste rather than its disappearance. Analogous with (but distinct from) the nonmarked normativity and hegemonic supremacy of whiteness in the United States, the very silence around caste produces and consolidates its power (Deshpande 2013; Soundararajan 2012).[18] Caste thus emerges as the "problem" of oppressed castes and not of those of the dominant caste: caste, as the Other of the modern, always belongs to the "lower" castes (Pandian 2002, from Mosse 2020, 1232). As Sucharita Kanjilal (2023, 10) argues, "claims to caste-blindness is common among liberal, upper-caste elites in India [Deshpande 2013, Shepherd 2019b] and especially its diasporas [Kanjilal and Mankekar 2022], serving to elide caste, while simultaneously re-signifying upper-caste practices as universally 'Indian,' and caste privilege as cosmopolitanism, secularism, or simply unmarked 'culture.'" Our interlocutors from oppressed castes were, for the most part, loath to disclose their caste identity. Perhaps the fear of being humiliated, of being subjected to overt discrimination, or an unwillingness to relive past humiliations, combined with aspirations to middle-class status, may have been why these interlocutors felt this way.[19] On our part, we felt no compulsion to push our interlocutors to disclose or speak about their caste positions. Nevertheless, as we will elaborate later in this book, the presence of caste hierarchies in the BPOs where we worked, as well in the lives of our interlocutors, was persistent, complex, and replete with contradictions (Appadurai 1986; Dumont 1981).

The place of caste in the BPO sector is a lot more complex than it is in the IT industry, which continues to be dominated by men from upper castes and workers from the middle and upper classes (Fuller and Narasmihan 2007, 2008). Indeed, BPOs drew in young people from socioeconomic backgrounds, castes, and religious communities that were considerably more diverse than the software industry (Upadhya 2016, 23). Women accounted for 40 percent of the workforce in BPOs, including at the managerial level, unlike the software industry where they continue to be underrepresented

(Upadhya 2016).[20] Last but not least, in a national context scarred by the consolidation of Hindu nationalism and economic and physical violence against Muslims, a substantial number of the agents we came across were Muslim.[21] To this (limited) extent, BPOs appear to have destabilized older hierarchies of class, caste, gender, and religion.

But let us be clear: BPOs have, by no means, done away with these hierarchies. In India as a whole, over the past few years, caste conflicts have accelerated, and violence against Dalits, Bahujan, Adivasis, and other oppressed communities has intensified; religious polarizations have sharpened as Christians, Sikhs, and, particularly, Muslims have been increasingly subjected to state-endorsed violence; disparities between rich and poor have deepened. Rather than conceive of BPOs as anachronistic or exceptional, we are interested in how the *fraught* coexistence of these disjunctive spaces—increasing caste and religious violence and deepening inequality on the one hand and, on the other, the apparently egalitarian spaces of BPOs—compels us to reconceptualize futurity.

The shifting demographics of agents have additional implications for the generation of futurities associated with the industry. Because the entry-level workforce at most of these companies was straight out of PUC, the majority of employees tended to be very young, between eighteen and twenty-five years of age. Since the industry was itself very young, people who had worked in it for more than ten years were deemed veterans. Most upper-level managers, as well as middle managers, had come up the ranks and were in their late twenties or early thirties. They were in charge of thousands of employees spread across different locations around the world. These companies were characterized by a youthful culture and were filled with ambitious people who often did not do well in India's rigid educational system. The exception to this rule was that CEOs were almost all recruited from other industries or were themselves founders of call centers or BPOs.

Why did shifting demographics make for different futurities? Unlike the first generation of middle-class, upper-class, and primarily urban agents who were working for "pocket money," during the years when we conducted our fieldwork people in the industry sought to forge careers for themselves in BPOs or, if they were unable to do so, move laterally to other branches of the service industry such as event management, hospitality, or sales. Rather than regarding their jobs contemptuously, as did so many of the earlier generation of agents, they perceived their work in BPOs as a key to future success. At the same time, they were keenly aware of the volatility of the global economy and knew that, although they earned good incomes by local standards, there was little security for them individually and for the industry as a whole.

When we started our research in 2008, the greatest challenge facing the managers and HR departments of BPOs was the retention of agents: at that time, the industry was booming and agents seemed to move continuously from one job to another. According to Maria, who worked in HR in a mid-size BPO, the main aim of the recruitment team was to curb attrition, and to continuously hire new workers, as many as two hundred every week. Her company conducted two induction ceremonies every week, one on Monday and another on Thursday, and each of them had at least ninety new recruits. They had developed what she called a "nice welcome process" that consisted of arranging a breakfast for them, giving each of them a CD about the company, and taking their photo when they first came in, developing it, and giving them a print at the end of the day.

This period was followed by a pause in the expansion of the industry during the global recession in which lateral mobility for agents became a little harder. In 2008 and 2009, organizations were devoting most of their time to recruiting and retaining agents and had few resources left for process improvements or other kinds of innovation and streamlining. The industry was then growing at breakneck rates of 20 percent year over year. Turn-over rates were extremely high: the common figure cited to us by different companies was around 40 percent annually. By 2011, the global recession finally hit the BPO industry in Bengaluru. Turnover slowed down consider-ably, and organizations reported that they could finally shift their attention to cost reduction and process efficiencies. Although elaborating on this is beyond the scope of this book, the industry again underwent momentous changes during the COVID-19 pandemic: unlike other industries, the BPO sector emerged resilient owing to its reliance on technological innovation and cloud computing. Furthermore, because of the Indian state's "Work from Anywhere" policy, BPOs were able to pivot to having agents work remotely: this was not without considerable challenges especially regarding the pri-vacy of customers and the importance of supervision, but BPOs met these challenges, with increased cybersecurity measures and virtual supervision (Mankekar and Gupta 2023.).[22]

Acceleration, stagnation, movement, emplacement, duration, pause. Our interlocutors conceived of the future in divergent ways, and these futures were refracted by the disjunctive temporalities generated by intertwined processes of rapid transformation and stagnation, aspiration and anxiety, upward social mobility and precarity. *The Future of Futurity* is intended to evoke the twinning of aspiration and insecurity for our interlocutors, the hope for a better future in a world in which the future is unpredictable and uncertain. Futurity, as an affective-temporal formation, and futures, as subjectively and collectively imagined, longed for or feared, dreaded or aspired to, and institutionalized through public policy, are frequently heterogeneous, messy, and contradictory, particularly for subjects and communities at the margins of class, caste, gender, and sexuality.

So what, then, is different about the futures and futurities surrounding BPOs, and what do these disjunctive futures teach us about the reconstitution of futurity, and its viability, in our current moment? We track how the temporalities of labor, family, intimacy, sociality, and embodiment collude and collide in the performance of affective labor in BPOs, and how they refract the production and extraction of value in affective capitalism. Conversely, the temporalities of affective capitalism, in various alignments and misalignments with the temporalities of the body, family, mobility and immobility, and translation and mis(sed)translation, have spawned distinctive futurities. How do these disjunctive temporalities compel us to reconceptualize the interweaving of work and life in the futurities generated by affective capitalism?

INTERJECTION

Delta Tech Park was built on the outskirts of Bengaluru in a peri-urban neighborhood called Green Meadows. We heard from several long-term residents that Green Meadows used to be a quiet outpost of the city: there were a few churches that served the Anglo-Indian community, a large mosque, a couple of small temples, and a warren of streets filled with small stores selling goods ranging from produce to furniture. Green Meadows used to have a bucolic air. Paddy fields lined the large lake that was the lifeline of the villages that surrounded it; cobras roamed the coconut groves that dotted the landscape while monkeys and parakeets screeched insults at each other. At the center of town was a mid-sized kalyana mandapa, a wedding hall where well-heeled Hindus celebrated the weddings of their children.

It is tempting to claim that once the IT industry arrived in Green Meadows "everything" changed. It is true that the cost of land shot through the roof, with politicians and developers "persuading" villagers to sell their lands in order to build large tech parks, malls, and gated housing communities. Two-lane streets intended for suburban drivers became perpetually, permanently, ensnarled in traffic. The city of Bengaluru, octopus-like, started to encircle Green Meadows. But it would be a mistake to assume that the IT industry "took over" life in Green Meadows. The spatiotemporalities of high-tech capital have had to coexist, and often collide, with those of religion, ritual, and community.

Other forms of life have reemerged.

These past few years, several temples have been built along the main street of Green Meadows, indicating both the irrepressibility of faith and the success of Hindu nationalist grassroots organizing. The big mosque on the edge of town has been repainted; it has acquired a larger, more powerful public address system, and groups of the faithful congregate regularly. And there are now no less than three kalyana mandapas in Green Meadows: wedding ceremonies, sometimes last several days, accompanied by music pouring out into the streets from loudspeakers hung on walls that attempt, entirely in vain, to contain the sounds of celebration, the aroma of feasts, and the flow of guests. These kalyana mandapas are a source of tremendous frustration to those who work in Delta Tech, especially those who have to commute in cabs that drive recklessly across town to get them to work, only to be stalled by traffic and the swell of wedding guests outside their gates.

The lake, so long the pride of Green Meadows, foams and froths at the mouth, much like a rabid dog: mysterious, enormous clouds of foam rise periodically from its surface to float onto the streets surrounding the tech parks, creating ever larger traffic jams and making it still harder to get to work on time (Rao 2017). And, as if to reclaim their home, cobras have found their way into the manicured lawns of Delta Tech Park and the gated communities in Green Meadows that are home to the CEOs and expatriate managers of companies.

AFFECTIVE CAPITALISM IN PLACE

Nigel Thrift characterizes cities as "roiling maelstroms of affect" (2004, 57). These maelstroms of affect swirl around the sedimented pasts, presents, and futures of Bengaluru's chronotopes. Bengaluru is not the "product" of capital: it is, fundamentally, a place that has engendered as well as been produced by multiple histories and identities which are a source of both its richness and its conflicts (Massey 1991, 27; 1994).[23] Rather than assume that "capitalism" *arrived* in this city, we turn to the sedimentation of past, present, and futures of Bengaluru to foreground how modes of value production have been shaped by history and by place (Upadhya 2016, 34). As much as the city is shaped by its IT and ITES industries, Bengaluru's political-economic and cultural pasts have mediated the growth of the BPO industry and its heterogeneous futurities. At the same time, and importantly, this is a place formed through historical patterns of in-migration and the synergy—and violence—

I.1. Small Shiva temple.

generated when different, usually hierarchically positioned, cosmologies, temporalities, and spatialities cohabit in tense adjacency (T. Srinivas 2018).

While doing justice to its rich history is beyond the scope of this book, we highlight some features that continue to shape its multiplex identities and the heterogeneous futurities that are frequently in conflict with each other. Believed to have been founded in 1537, the city that we now know as Bengaluru thrived during the rule of Kempegowda during the Vijayanagara Empire. Its topography was shaped by a network of temples and tanks that attracted merchants and artisans from surrounding regions. Bengaluru was a major center of the textile industry, which was revitalized in the twentieth century: it continues to be a center of silk production. The 1930s saw the arrival of millhands, consisting of a steady stream of migrants from surrounding areas, to work in factories (Nair 2005, 55). After Indian independence in 1947, Bengaluru became the site of public sector units set up by the postcolonial government including, in the 1970s, companies such as Bharat Heavy Electrical Limited (BHEL) and Hindustan Machine Tools (HMT) that employed over eighty thousand people.[24] As relevant as its history as a place drawing migrants from different parts of the nation is, Bengaluru's self-representation is evident in the moniker Science City, buttressed by the establishment of the Indian Institute of Science in 1909, followed after Indian independence by the National Aeronautical Laboratory (NAL) and the Indian Space Research Organization (ISRO). Its identity as a city of the future has thus preceded its current neoliberal avatar.

At the same time, despite its self-representation as a center of public sector industries and a city of science and research, Bengaluru has remained a city of multiple temporalities and spatialities (S. Srinivas 2016; T. Srinivas 2018) and, therefore, of futurities that sometimes collide with one another. The first Sufi shrines were built in the seventeenth century: many of these still exist, even if in conditions of precarious disrepair. Missionaries brought Christianity to the state of Karnataka in 1648, and in 1674 St. Mary's Basilica was built as a shrine in Bengaluru: it continues to serve as a major landmark in the city's cultural geography. After taking over Mysore in 1799, the British built a military cantonment in the city: today, some of the layout and architecture of central Bengaluru retain vestiges of colonial rule, and defense and military production remain important to the city. Bengaluru's cityscape remains a palimpsest of these histories, and it is to this "multiple city" (De 2008) that migrants come from all over the nation to find work in the IT and ITES industry.

Bengaluru's streets show evidence of the city's rich ritual and religious life (Mankekar and Gupta 2023). The Karaga Festival is an eleven-day festival during which a male priest journeys through the streets of the old city paying homage to temples and a dargah in order to receive and, eventually, embody the goddess Draupadi: the festival entails the participation of over 200,000 (two lakh) people who come from all over the region and is perhaps Bengaluru's most important civic ritual (Nair 2005, 36; see, especially, S. Srinivas 2008).[25] During the holy month of Ramadan, iftar is observed in homes but also in public celebrations in different parts of the city: on Russell Street and other streets in Shivajinagar, MM Road and Mosque Road in Frazer Town, Tilak Nagar, Rahmat Nagar, and Johnson Market. During the annual festival at St. Mary's Basilica, crowds spill onto streets in and around Shivajinagar.

But it would be a mistake to assume that Bengaluru is a site of the happy commingling of different religious communities: these sedimented pasts have cast long shadows over how its residents currently live and how it imagines its future. In 1928, the city experienced horrific Hindu-Muslim violence known as the Bangalore Disturbances, followed by a second round in 1931. As we revise this book, Bengaluru, much like the rest of the state of Karnataka, has become a laboratory for the initiation of Islamophobic projects in contemporary India, ranging from the ban on hijabs in educational institutions to the coerced removal of loudspeakers that issue calls to prayer in mosques. Given that Bengaluru represents itself as a city of the future, these developments should give us pause. In addition to the future of this city and this nation, it is the future of futurity that hangs in the balance as devastating violence simmers under the thin surface of civility.

Other inequities and hierarchies have been reconfigured or recharged as disparate visions of the future come into conflict, with concrete implications for the agentive potentiality of futurity. Bengaluru's intense linguistic politics have tended to pivot around the intersection of class, migratory status, and religion: these volatile relations continue to shape the inequalities of language in the city and its BPOs (chapter 1). Nor can we assume that migrants to Bengaluru are always welcomed with open arms. The city's topography is shaped by state-endorsed and extralegal acquisitions of land for tech parks and malls as the poor, particularly from Dalit, Bahujan, Muslim, and other marginalized communities, are pushed farther into the peripheries of the city. The pulsating energies of its streets are marked by the ebb and flow of religious fervor as well as conflict, with violence against Muslims and Dalits by majoritarian Hindus erupting in December 2015 (Mondal 2015) and again in August 2020 (Deutsche Welle 2020; *Times of India* 2022). These are the cultural and discursive factors that powerfully *refract* the multicultural and multireligious socialities, intimacies, and worlds of BPO agents, with powerful implications for how we may theorize futurities in all their multiplicity.

The spatiotemporal dimensions of these multiple futurities are manifest in the topography of the city. Bengaluru's landscape has, historically, been shaped by settlements segregated along religious and caste lines. Today, many of these neighborhoods persist and contrast sharply with tech parks, malls, and gated communities built by real estate developers for the new cognitariat—the engineers, senior managers, and venture capitalists of IT and ITES companies (Berardi 2013) (chapter 2). These gated communities were, of course, out of reach for the BPO agents with whom we worked, many of whom had to live in congested neighborhoods often at a considerable distance from the tech parks where they worked (chapter 1). Bengaluru attracts poverty-stricken people from surrounding rural areas, as well as ambitious young men and women who come to seek their fortunes from far-flung cities like Ranchi, Guwahati, Kanpur, Srinagar, and other, smaller towns and cities across India. As BPO agents commute to work and back to their homes, the chronotopes of this city refract the worlds and lives that they craft for themselves. Even as they generate disparate futurities, these chronotopes *impinge on* the futures they imagine, aspire to, or dread.

In Bengaluru, futurity is inescapably imbricated with the symbolic significance of the IT and ITES industries. Exemplifying how affective-temporal formations of futurity are institutionalized in public policy and political economy, the Indian state has directly participated and invested in the growth of these industries. For instance, state investment in telecommunications infrastructure, tax breaks to multinational companies that establish BPOs in India, the establishment of industrial parks and SEZs to house these companies, and other such policies have been essential to the rise of the BPO industry (Gupta and Sharma 2008).[26] Discourses of national sovereignty have played a crucial role in the formulation of these policies, thus foregrounding the discursive and ideological production of capital and value (Bear et al. 2015; Upadhya 2016). These policies have been predicated on the belief that national sovereignty depends on the growth of the economy in the future: the assumption is that a strong economy will result in a modern, developed, and, therefore, sovereign nation. In this way, the future of the industry is tied to the emergence of India as a modern and developed nation-state—a form of futurity that effortlessly brings together global interconnectedness with emergent national power.

Thus there are multiple ways in which futurity has become institutionalized in public policy oriented to specific visions of the future of the city, the state, and the nation. The growth of the IT and ITES industries is a direct result of close collaborations between corporate and political elites in the state of Karnataka. This became particularly evident during the "IT-friendly" government of chief minister S. M. Krishna from 1999 to 2004, who provided substantial financial and policy support to the IT, ITES, and biotech industries. This was also a period that witnessed the formation of the Bangalore Agenda Task Force (BATF), which aimed to boost urban infrastructural development; significantly, the BATF's leadership consisted primarily of prominent IT and biotech leaders who aspired to make Bengaluru the city of the future (chapter 2). Urged by IT and biotech elites to improve the telecommunications infrastructure, the state government of Karnataka and neighboring Andhra Pradesh forged direct links with multinational capital bypassing the central (federal) government (Upadhya 2016, 47). Last but not least, state policies have been hand-in-glove with the hegemony of neoliberal discourses of entrepreneurship, risk, and individual growth which have provided the ideological and discursive scaffolding for the consolidation of affective labor in the BPO industry (chapters 2 and 4; see also Mankekar 2015; Harvey 2007).

Foreign multinationals first set up offshore development centers (ODCs) in Bengaluru in 1985, starting with Hewlett Packard and Texas Instruments. Subsequently, other multinationals set up shop initially to outsource low-skilled but labor-intensive coding. First built in 1991, software technology parks offered high-speed data links as well as a range of other services and benefits to these companies. By the late 1990s, ITES industries and IT had created sixty thousand jobs (Nair 2005, 86). Nonetheless, even though Bengaluru claims to be the Silicon Valley of India, this aspiration has hit many roadblocks, ranging from infrastructural problems to so-called cultural factors. For instance, many CEOs and managers we interviewed insisted that the laid-back attitude of "locals," exemplified in the Kannada phrase *salpa adjust madi* ("just adjust a little") attributed to them, prevented workers from meeting deadlines or led to them producing shoddy work: these interlocutors disingenuously caricatured Bengalurians as too "easy going" to be productive or efficient.

Finally, the futures imbricated with BPOs in Bengaluru also need to be understood in terms of the articulation of the heady combination of excitement and anxiety about the future(s) of this city. Some of these anxieties erupted after the 1980 census, which highlighted the city's exponential growth: worried citizens groups expressed the urgent need to develop infrastructure to handle this growth. These anxieties are also expressed in terms of a desire to preserve Bengaluru's "older" way of life: this is a nostalgia that flies in the face of its history as a city that has always witnessed considerable in-migration and change (Frazier 2019). This nostalgia is sometimes countered by the dream to make Bengaluru into a technopole and, at other times, paradoxically accompanied by it (Nair 2005, 18–19). Such discourses of Bengaluru's future are inspired by the example of Singapore's purported success in merging capitalist modernity and "Asian" culture (chapter 2). Bengaluru is also home to vibrant civil society organizations and NGOs, ranging from women's organizations like Vimochana to neoliberal public-private partnerships like Janagraha that aim to address the anxieties about the city's future. The city's crumbling infrastructure and the persistence and growth of its informal economy and poor communities living in conditions of abject poverty contrast with the glitz of its tech parks, malls, and gated communities, raising troubling questions about its discrepant futurities (Benjamin 2000,

2006, 2010; Benjamin and Bhuvaneshwari 2001). For many residents, the future of Bengaluru as a world-class metropolis in the mold of Singapore is riddled with ironies. The sustainability of Bengaluru as a conurbation is very much in doubt because it lacks a dependable source of water, and climate change has made its already meager water resources unreliable. Thus, what is in play is the future of futurity in Bengaluru and not just its discrepant futures that may range from the utopian to the dystopian. And let us not forget: *other forms of life have reemerged*, undermining any assumptions we may have about the linear temporality of futurity.

STEPPING INTO THE FUTURE

Although the BPO industry generated multiple and discrepant futures, it was united in being singularly future-oriented. Future orientation was salient in BPOs for two reasons: the workforce was very young, and the industry was inherently unstable because its services and platforms changed rapidly and depended on the changing habits of consumers in different nodes of global capitalism. One important way of producing futures is through infrastructure. The material spaces of BPOs, as well as their organizational structure, generated a particular atmosphere of futurity. Agents saw their futures in terms of possibility, of crafting for themselves and their families a more comfortable life: their lives were immeasurably more hopeful than that of their parents and, indeed, that of unemployed or underemployed Indian youth, or those working in the informal economy where conditions were considerably more abject, desperate, and precarious.[27] The trope of growth was ubiquitous in how our interlocutors imagined and narrated both their futures and that of the Indian nation: theirs was a narrative that was hitched to the immanent possibilities of the present. This sense of hope for the future was materialized in the built environment in which they worked.

An Atmosphere of Futurity

The architecture of BPOs is iconic of the futurities associated with the IT and ITES industries. All the BPOs in which we did our fieldwork were located in large technology parks constructed and maintained by some of the largest real estate developers in Bengaluru. Typically, a tech park consists of a number of buildings located on a large parcel of land, from forty to one hundred acres large, in which hundreds of companies, large and small, operate. The "shiny skin" of buildings (Nair 2005, 92) consists almost entirely of glass and steel, with landscaping featuring green lawns, fountains, and other water

I.2. Embassy Golf Links Business Park (one of many technology parks in Bengaluru).

bodies, and meticulously maintained pedestrian walkways. One of the BPOs we studied was located in a tech park that had been declared an export processing zone (EPZ). This firm had two separate buildings in adjacent tech parks, one of which was part of the EPZ, and the other in the domestic tech park. The firm had to ensure that all the processes in the EPZ tech park dealt with foreign companies and that no domestic work was conducted there.

For many Bangaloreans, the chronotope of tech parks iconized the temporality of the future in contrast to the rest of the city, which, with its power cuts, water shortages, dust, and crumbling infrastructure, represents the temporality of lag (we elaborate in chapter 2). Entering a tech park felt like entering the world of the future. It was stepping into a sensorium that manifested the lure of the global and the cosmopolitan. For many agents, particularly those who came from lower-income families or communities marginalized by hierarchies of caste or religious affiliation, the allure of these tech parks lay in their promise of a future based on meritocracy and equality and, equally, in their aesthetics and sensoria. These sensoria, with their uninterrupted supply of power and water, dust-free interiors, and the diversity of languages, foods, and aromas on offer in food courts where, regardless of the time of night, it felt like the middle of the day, were also a far cry from the congested neighborhoods in which most agents lived.

I.3. List of offices near entrance of technology park.

I.4. Typical office building construction of glass and steel.

Most tech parks featured a food court with a dozen or more food outlets in a central building, small cafés dotting the park, and other services such as banks, dry cleaners, a post office, and sometimes even a grocery store on site. The twenty-four-hour food courts offered cuisines from different regions of India and Western food like burgers, pizza, and pasta: this was where many agents tasted these foods for the first time. Some tech parks also featured gyms and retail outlets. Not unlike the malls adjacent to many of them, tech parks marketed a certain lifestyle: this is what made them *invoke* a particular kind of futurity. Many agents wanted to work in tech parks because they felt that doing so would enable them to enter into the future rather than be mired in the pasts they wished to leave behind. Being in a tech park and working in a BPO was thus about inhabiting the future and not just anticipating it (Adams, Murphy, and Clark 2009). Many agents reported that when they entered a tech park for the first time, they experienced an expansion of place and time: it was no longer about being in Bengaluru or even in India but about being part of a larger world. It was the contrast between this world and that inhabited by their families and extended kin—the world in which most agents had grown up—that was most seductive in how it promised a *sense* of globality as a distinct structure of feeling and aspiration.

So strong was the seduction of these tech parks that a few agents were motivated to give up much more stable jobs to join BPOs: the built environment, the architecture, and the buzz of globality that they offered proved compelling. Maria's story typifies the allure of tech parks as workspaces. After finishing a BA in commerce, she was driving around with a friend who had just graduated from dental school. They were passing a technology park with "beautiful green lawns and fountains," and on a lark, they decided to go interview at a BPO located inside. The first stage of the interview took the form of a group discussion. They both did well and moved to the next stage; that is when they thought, "We could actually get this job." At that time, Maria knew very little about the industry, but she was curious. She made it through all the rounds of the interview process and four hours later she had a job offer in her hands. It was only then that she realized it was serious: she would have to decide whether she was going to take the job. Her friend said, "Won't it be fun to work in a place with such wonderful, big buildings?" They both accepted the offer and went into training. They were not serious about the job even during training, which they and the companies hiring them treated like an extension of college life.

When we started doing intensive fieldwork in 2009, such interlocutors were atypical. With the exception of some who had finished a bachelor's in engineering, most applicants did not have college degrees. Prashanth and Amit were applying to a BPO because they could not find a job in a software company despite having an engineering degree: their grades were below the 65 percent cutoff employed by the large software companies. They hoped that working for a BPO would give them the soft skills necessary to eventually land a job in a multinational software company, but for the time being, their best option was to work in a BPO.

Nevertheless, the story of Maria and her friend draws attention to what working in BPOs represented to even these relatively privileged young people. They chose to work in a BPO because of what they sensed when they entered these tech parks. The built environment and architecture of BPOs carried tremendous affective valence. Many people that we interviewed were captivated by what some of them described as a "modern" work environment—the ergonomic chairs, open offices, climate control, and clean bathrooms. The air-conditioned, high-tech interiors of their offices were unlike most other workplaces in Indian cities and were about as distant from the home environments of low-income agents as one could imagine. Rather than employing a vernacular aesthetic that emphasized local history and materials, these offices gestured toward a high-tech future that was technologically sophisticated and modern.

Constructions of futurity were also generated by the unique organizational structure and culture of BPOs. All the organizations where we did research were characterized by a relatively flat organizational structure in which there were only four or five levels between the CEO and the new agent on the floor. This flatness was also emphasized in the design of buildings and office spaces. In the smallest BPO where we did research, all company employees, including the CEO, sat on the same floor in open cubicles.[28] In larger companies, CEOs may have had their own cubicles, but almost everyone else sat in an open office. Agents pointed out with pride that the CEO and other managers sat in a cubicle just like them and that they could walk over and talk to senior management whenever they pleased. When we asked them how often they had done so, it turned out that nobody had ever ventured to go and speak to the senior management. However, the symbolism of the CEO and other senior managers sitting in an open office was very important to the agents. Given that many of the agents we worked with were marginalized by hierarchies of class, caste, religion, or gender (and, sometimes, all of the above), forms of deference were deeply ingrained in their habitus. The open office symbolized a relatively democratic space that appealed especially to the ambitious young people whose aspirations were to transcend their marginalized locations. We cannot stress more the affective potency of this ostensibly egalitarian work culture: their work environment contrasted sharply with that experienced by their parents and other family members. This was of tremendous significance for agents who experienced working in BPOs as a step into a more egalitarian future.

Each "shop floor" was a space that was devoted to one process and consisted of open cubicles. It could be a very large space with four hundred workers, or it could be a much smaller room accommodating as few as fifty agents. All agents in the same project or process worked for the same external company, doing almost identical tasks. For instance, if AT&T outsourced certain functions to an Indian company, all agents handling that function were part of the same process and were partitioned into a workspace that was not accessible to agents handling a different process—say, for British Telecom. The large companies we studied operated as many as forty different processes at one site, and that subdivision could be duplicated at other sites in other cities or countries. Thus, the management of these companies was an enormous logistical challenge because agents had to be trained separately for each process, kept in separate spaces within the same facility, and the different quality demands of each contracting company had to be managed and monitored. Typically, a large US corporation that was outsourcing would give the contract for a process to several Indian companies. The assumption was that this would lead to competition between companies. On the Indian side, this practice meant that a large BPO often had small contracts from a number of US, UK, Canadian, and Australian companies rather than just two or three large contracts. This had organizational as well as administrative implications in terms of where the management team spent its time and energy.

In India, some (middle-class) analysts and commentators have disparaged call center workers as "cyber coolies" who allow themselves to be placed in a subservient position to white people in the Global North by virtue of working in a BPO (for instance, Ramesh 2004; Trivedi 2003). While such criticism correctly points to the servitude engendered by national location and race in a system of global stratification, it fails to appreciate why many BPO agents desire their jobs as agents; it also problematically equates the predicament of BPO agents with indentured laborers. In fact, BPOs represented a space where some of these young people could escape from other systems of servitude ubiquitous in the world outside, where they were not forced to reenact the daily indignities of living and working as an oppressed caste or lower-income person in India. To some of them, the form of servitude that BPO work represented was far more preferable to what their parents had experienced. Historically, servitude and so-called menial labor in India have been fundamentally imbricated with caste hierarchies because labor and occupation were, at least in theory, strictly regulated by the politics of caste. From the perspective of our Dalit interlocutors and others from oppressed and marginalized communities, the servitude of BPO work was a step up from the humiliating servitude of "menial" work performed by their parents and other kin.

As we have noted, while BPOs may destabilize established class hierarchies they by no means eliminate them. Class hierarchies existed in subtle but insidious ways within BPOs and deeply shaped perspectives on labor and, therefore, the generation of discrepant futurities. The differences in the attitudes of agents to BPO work were illustrated when Gupta interviewed Suresh. He had just quit his job at a prestigious BPO and thus felt free to speak about his experiences. Suresh was a college graduate and described himself as a person from a "well-educated family." He had applied to MBA programs and was waiting to hear from schools. Since he had a few months with nothing to do, he did not want to waste time at home and that is why he applied to work at a BPO. He complained that his starting salary was the same as those with an "ordinary junior college" (pre-university) degree. He thought that was unfair and that he should have been offered a higher salary by virtue of his superior education. When he joined the BPO, Suresh experienced complete culture shock. He said that the BPO did not attract "a very good crowd." For example, most people at work, including his supervisors, "used slang and colloquial language." Some of them were college dropouts, while others only had a 10 + 2 education and were there just to make money. When he saw how happy they were with what they were doing, he thought that they were just "a bunch of losers." After working for a month on a 9 a.m.–6 p.m. shift, he was moved to a night shift, 6:30 p.m.–3:30 a.m. That is when Suresh quit. He did not see a future there and, unlike the others, he did not need to support a family.

Some recruiters and HR managers hesitated to recruit college-educated agents like Suresh because, in their experience, higher education did not correlate with better performance. One COO, in fact, told us that if he was to choose between a college-educated candidate and someone with a PUC who came from a poor family, there was "no question" that he would choose the latter. From his perspective, a candidate's ability to be a successful agent depended on factors other than their class background and even their level of English fluency: often, a person's desire to succeed, their "hunger," was far more important than having a college degree. Employees from poorer families, he insisted, made better employees because they were more likely to stick with the job and, if they had native intelligence and were trainable, they learned what was necessary to do their job well. This perspective was corroborated by HR staff in other companies who told us that they sought candidates with a "fire in the belly" and a "go-getter" attitude. Middle-class college graduates often lacked the appetite for the tough parts of the job and were easily discouraged by initial difficulties. In myriad ways, then, fractures of class deeply shaped the production of discrepant futurities. But the fractures of class operated in BPOs on a transnational scale and not just within the nation-state.

In addition to class background, there were other markers that differentiated a candidate who had potential. Maria, who had worked in the hiring team at both large and midsize BPOs, said that she knew if a person would drop out from their body language—if their body language was very casual, it did not bode well. In addition, if the job candidate "asked tricky questions," or "gave stupid reasons" for wanting to work there, or simply had not bothered to learn anything about the company or the industry, they were unlikely to survive the cut. Those who were hired received two weeks of foundation-level training and two weeks of process training. Foundation-level training was geared toward improving basic communication skills and working on issues of grammar, intonation, speed, clarity, and others. Process training consisted of learning details about the specific process for which the agents were being recruited, such as making reservations on a travel portal or a credit card security process. From the offer letter to the end of training, Maria estimated that only 60 percent of candidates survived. For example, during the month of training, if a trainee took leave for two days, they were let go.

Irfan's case illustrates some of the complex dynamics that shaped the selection of agents. He came from an upper middle-class Muslim family that owned a very large plot of land in the center of Bengaluru. He lived on one floor of a house with his wife and two children, and his mother, who had retired from a job as the head of a prestigious private school, lived on the other floor. Unlike most recruits, Irfan spoke fluent English and had no trouble constructing grammatically correct sentences. However, his educational background had been adversely impacted because he had to switch schools in his penultimate year of high school when his mother moved from a different state back to Bengaluru. In Karnataka, he was required to take Kannada as one of his subjects, and he got a failing grade in that subject because he just did not have enough time to learn it before the exams. As a result, his high-school grades were too low to gain admission to college. He drifted from one job to another without securing steady employment. When Gupta first met him, he was in his early thirties, competing to be an agent with people who were at least a decade younger than him. Irfan did very well in the foundation level course because his English skills were superior to other trainees. However, he failed to make it through the next round of training because he spoke slowly, clearly, and deliberately and that was not good enough. He could not muster enough enthusiasm and energy in his voice to engage the customer. Irfan went through several rejections at different call centers. When Gupta last spoke to him a few years later, he had separated from his wife, who now lived with their children and her natal family, and he was contemplating moving to the United States, where a close relative wanted him as a worker in their gas station business. He was ambivalent about migrating to the United States but felt he had no other choice—all other paths to upward mobility appeared blocked.

For some workers, BPO jobs not only offered them opportunities for upward mobility but also enabled their entire families to move from the precarious lower and lower-middle classes to the relatively secure middle classes (chapter 1). Many companies provided health insurance to several members of workers' families, including parents and siblings. For example, one of the larger BPOs offered 100 percent coverage for medical costs after three months of employment, and 80 percent coverage for up to four additional family members who were dependent on the employee. For most of our fieldwork from 2009 to 2016, BPO workers with some experience found themselves in a market where they could move to a better job in a competing firm. At the same time, like many corporate jobs, there was constant pressure to achieve a high level of productivity, and companies could lay off even productive workers.

What might the purported demographic expansion of the Indian middle classes have to do with the generation of futurities? NASSCOM, the trade association for the information technology industry, estimates that workers in the ITES sectors together totaled about 1.2 million employees (IANS 2018). That constitutes a fraction of the middle classes in India, which is minimally estimated at 5–6 percent of the population (approximately 70 million people) (*Economist* 2018; Kochhar 2021; Meyer and Birdsall 2012).[29] Employment growth rates have remained relatively flat because the high growth rates of the Indian economy have not been accompanied by a rapid increase in jobs, leading to what has been termed "jobless growth." One of the reasons for this may be the highly capital-intensive nature of new growth with a high organic composition of capital that fails to employ much labor. This is why, despite high GDP growth rates, the vast majority of the population cannot dream of a better future.

FUTURITIES AND THE TIME(S) OF AFFECTIVE CAPITALISM

Growth was a predominant trope for the leaders and managers of the companies in which we worked and, more significantly, for BPO agents. Growth of the self, growth of the company, growth of the industry, and growth of the nation-state were brought together in the discursive registers of BPO employees, not always without friction. Visions of the future affect what is done today and may bring about their own fulfillment: the present is constituted by the future as much as by the past.[30]

Because the industry transformed so quickly, leaders had to constantly guess which way to steer their companies. The stakes were high because predicting the future incorrectly could result in the failure of the company. It was not surprising that upper-level executives of BPOs were constantly trying to "stay ahead of the curve" and discern trends in the business, demonstrating how planned and imagined futures act recursively on the present. Futures are important to social life because the future shapes the present and represents the horizon of possibility of present action.

The centrality of the terms *growth* and *learnings* in the discourses of our interlocutors lay not only in the number of times these terms were repeated but also in the affective charge with how they were deployed in their autobiographical accounts. The term *growth* could encapsulate promotion within the organization but also personal growth and the acquisition of soft skills. *Growth* could include increases in salary, moving up the corporate hierarchy, learning new skills and technologies, or the development of the agent's own human potential. It was seemingly goal-oriented on the one hand and completely open-ended on the other. In other words, precisely because the term was so amorphous, an agent satisfied with her job and happy to be working in a particular company could claim to be experiencing growth despite no outward markers such as a pay raise or advancement in rank. Similarly, agents talked a great deal about learnings (always in the plural), especially when recounting events or incidents in which they had been successful in overcoming challenges or even when they were speaking of occasions when they had experienced failure. *Learnings* constituted a nebulous term indexing personal growth and professional development. Both *growth* and *learnings* were future-oriented—the purpose of each was not about being strongly anchored in the present; rather, the use of these terms signified the ability of agents to reach somewhere else (better, further, higher) in the future (chapter 1). Of course, the expectation of growth and learnings could work negatively on the present as well. When we asked agents who had quit their jobs why they had done so, they often told us that they felt their experiences of growth were limited in that company; similarly, agents often voiced disappointment about the slow pace of learnings. In general, since the workflow in BPOs had been heavily Taylorized, work life was experienced as repetitive and monotonous unless it was accompanied by rapid promotions or the acquisition of new skills and education. Therefore, future orientation could sometimes discourage agents from working harder (cf. Berlant 2011).

The fractures of time and space that result in discrepant futures are not unique to the BPO industry nor are they the result of postmodernity (Harvey 1991). However, their particular configuration is profoundly influenced by the industry, its location, and the (im)mobilities of class, location, and social space. There are features of the world that lie beyond the company, industry, city, or nation-state in which our interlocutors live and dream (such as climate change, nuclear war, global capitalist crises, and pandemics), and these pose an existential threat to their ability to imagine a future. Does it mean, then, that the futurity constituted by these discrepant futures is itself in doubt? It is this question mark that hangs over all possibilities, all imaginings of the future that can be thought, sensed, or experienced (Mendieta 2020). The contexts in which discrepant futures are imagined, whether utopian or dystopian, throws the future of futurity into uncertainty.

Each of the following chapters examines futurity by focusing on one important theme. We intersperse interjections throughout the book to *enact* some of the disjunctions that we witnessed and experienced during our fieldwork. These interjections break up our arguments with recollections or reflections that cannot be smoothed out or papered over by the "flow" of our analyses: our intention is to take a pause, and to interrupt our narrative.

Chapter 1 considers the fraught relationships between mobility and growth, and immobility and stagnation, in contexts shaped by mutations of racial capitalism. Mobility was central to the lives of agents and to the BPO industry as a whole. The future of agents depended on movement toward the future across geographies, social locations, and cultures. Agents often moved to cities far from their homes where BPOs were located, they moved up the class ladder and became tenuously middle-class, and they moved across cultural boundaries to be able to help clients in the Global North. The itineraries of BPO agents were physical, virtual, temporal, social, linguistic, and experiential. What threatened their future was immobility; what they feared the most was stasis, feeling stuck, not learning new things constantly. Movement, they believed, could enable them to achieve a brighter future. Movement, here, serves an existential function since it is about the ability to become, about potentiality that is fulfilling, about futurity, and about a *sense* of being on a journey. At the same time, being placed within dense social networks gave agents a grounding and rootedness that enabled them to negotiate the uncertainties and challenges that they faced at work.

Chapter 2 diagrams the relationship between the workplace and life outside work by theorizing malls as infrastructures of aspiration. The futures that BPO agents dream about are shaped by spaces such as malls. Malls function as pedagogical sites to gain knowledges that mark the agent as cosmopolitan; this is where they can acquire the cultural capital that is seen as an essential part of the "soft skills" needed for their futures. Malls enable virtual travel that is temporal as much as spatial, enabling agents to comport themselves in spaces of modernity but also providing the resources necessary for future growth, professional stability, and success. As infrastructures of aspiration, malls generate futurities through forms of becoming.

Chapter 3 focuses on BPOs as exemplars of affective capitalism built on intimate labor across geographical distance and new, previously unmonetized domains. How does affective capitalism bring together new configurations of intimacy, alienated labor, profit, and racialized value? How is the relationship between service work and servitude mediated by racial capitalism? The virtual and imaginative travel in which BPO agents are engaged, as well as the intimate relations they forge with customers and other agents at their workplaces, can interrupt the purported "flow" of affective capitalism by unleashing eruptive and disruptive potentialities. Instead of reprising the story of the ravenous expansion of capitalism into new, intimate domains of social life, about the colonization of life by capital, we highlight the uncertain directionality of the immanent, about the potential in the lines of flight created by intimacies.

Chapter 4 emphasizes how affective capitalism is imbricated in the granular embodiment of BPO agents as racialized and gendered subjects. Agents were racialized at work through aurality and not through visual markers; they experienced racial subordination, aspiration, and anxiety, viscerally, even when they were unable to articulate their feelings. Even though the regimes of labor were relentless, our interlocutors were more than just laboring subjects: the rhythms of labor collide and collude with other temporalities, including those of family, ritual, and religion. Moreover, the lines between the laboring body and the desiring body blur so as to foreground the coproduction of bodies and affective capitalism. Futurity is predicated on the entanglement of bodies with technology, of the organic with the inorganic, and of the human with the more-than-human, to produce discrepant temporalities. The body of the worker is shaped not just by regimes of labor but by the articulation, as well as disarticulation, of temporalities that result from these relationalities.

The conclusion draws out the implications for futurity in our arguments and braids together the themes of the different chapters on mobility and translation, malls, intimate labor, and corporeality and embodiment. Taken together, these themes enable us to theorize futurity in terms of potentiality and becoming. Rather than forecasting prescriptive futures for agents and the BPO industry, our focus on futurity is shaped by our interlocutors' own gesturing toward potentiality, by their own sense of becoming as a *mode of being*; futurity is, simultaneously, existential and material.

1.

MOBILITY, EMPLACEMENT, TRANSLATION

Business process outsourcing is contingent on the mobility of value, surplus, and information: BPOs hence allow us to interrogate several characteristics of mobility in semiocapitalism. Mobility, immobility, and emplacement are foundational to semiocapital and coexist in a nonoppositional, mutually constitutive relationship. The mobility of semiocapital depends on the myth of seamless communication—the circulation of information and affect— that, presumably, is enabled by information technology across locations around the world.[1] Our research problematizes the myth of seamless communication predicated on disembodiment and placelessness and, in this chapter, we turn to some of the blockages, interruptions, and disruptions that refract affective capitalism.[2]

If affective capitalism depends on mobility, so did the futures of BPO agents: their mobility, immobility, emplacement, and sense of feeling stuck deeply shaped their pathways to professional growth and personal fulfillment and their ability to carve a more secure future for their families and loved ones. For our interlocutors, mobility was about *moving toward* the future—about movement across geographies, social locations, and cultures over time—and blockages and hurdles to mobility were experienced as putting a certain kind of future in doubt. Mobility and immobility were coimbricated with futurity: they shaped not simply our interlocutors' capacity to aspire but also mediated futurity as an ontological formation that profoundly shaped their mode of being in the world. Futurity encompasses and, more significantly, exceeds and is irreducible to the aspirations of individuals and collectivities, their anticipation of the future, and their ability to speculate and take risks about the future (Adams et al 2009; Cross 2015; G. Patel 2000). Futurity entails potentiality and becoming.

The success of the BPO industry is contingent on the speed with which products of affective labor move across national borders and on the virtual mobility of BPO agents (Aneesh 2015). The networked office puts communication to work because it is predicated on "info labor" (Berardi 2009, 88; Berardi 2013; cf. Fuchs and Sevignani 2013). In the transnational networked office, the very possibility of the outsourcing of back-office work to a site thousands of miles away is enabled by the emplacement of the worker in the back office who must physically stay in place. In BPOs, the networked office has resulted in the systematic informatization and digitization of productive processes. Furthermore, the production process in BPOs is subjected to not just the elaboration and exchange of information but, more fundamentally, the circulation of affect. BPOs demonstrate some of the shifts in regimes of labor and the production of value generated by affective capitalism. The myriad ways in which the ability to communicate was cultivated by our interlocutors as an important part of the neoliberal "skill set" that would enable them to move up the corporate ladder and "grow."[3] The postindustrial workplace exemplified by BPOs is founded on affective economies shaped by the generation, circulation, and management of emotions, empathy, and socialities: communication, after all, is foundational to affective labor (Lazzarato 2007).

The worlds and lives of BPO agents foreground the potentials and limitations of information technology in semiocapitalism. According to Franco "Bifo" Berardi (2009), semiocapitalism is characterized by the manner in which digital telecommunications networks link workers, managers, and consumers through the circulation of symbols. Berardi's theorization of semiocapitalism, however, sidesteps the role of race, histories of colonialism and empire, national location, and other structures of social inequality. BPOs both exemplify Berardi's conceptualization of semiocapitalism and problematize it. In BPOs, as in other sectors within semiocapitalism (for instance, software engineering), information technology and digital networks enable the reorganization of spatial and temporal regimes of affective labor. At the same time, the circulation, dispersal, and concentration of global labor in these contexts are also imbricated with the emplacement of workers.

We seek to untangle the myriad itineraries of the mobility of BPO agents: physical, as they make their way to and from work through a city that is winding down or asleep; virtual, as they engage clients in overseas locations; temporal, as they travel across different time zones to provide service to these clients; and social, as they struggle to inch their way up a slippery slope of class mobility. We, therefore, propose a capacious conception of mobility to account for the disparate forms of border crossing engaged by BPO agents—physical, social, cultural, linguistic, and experiential—who are constantly in motion within and across these different spaces (Cresswell 2010; Sheller and Urry 2006).

BPOs demonstrate the contingency of mobility: while capital and the products of labor (affective regimes, the circulation of signs, information) move across national, cultural, and experiential borders, the bodies of BPO agents must stay in place on account of their class, race, and national location.[4] In BPOs, mobility and processes of communication were mutually imbricated. Agents' skills lay in their ability to communicate feelings of care and intimacy through and beyond linguistic forms of connectivity; put another way, their affective labor depended on their ability to connect with clients and customers whom they would never meet face-to-face. The work and worlds of BPO agents were also replete with moments of mistranslation, missed translations, partial translations, and opacity as they interacted with customers at a geographical, cultural, and experiential remove from them. When this happened, BPO agents had to confront their subjection to regimes of emplacement, and their futures as mobile subjects became precarious.

Regimes of mobility and emplacement configured our interlocutors' constructions of futurity. Situated as they were in a political-economic context marked by rampant unemployment and underemployment for a majority of youth in contemporary India, their mobility and emplacement marked their positions vis-à-vis discourses of futurity. When mobility stalled, emplacement generated a feeling of entrapment: it represented a threat to their financial and emotional well-being because it endangered their hopes for the future. When agents were unable to rise up the corporate hierarchy, or if they found themselves in a job with little scope for growth, they were placed on the brink of precarity: feeling stuck then entailed a sense of stagnancy and of fading hopes for the future (see also Allison 2013). But, at other times, emplacement produced a sense of being located: it helped our interlocutors find their bearings in a city that had become unfamiliar even to those who had grown up there. In these instances, emplacement was about trying to find one's place in these daunting surroundings. Conversely, emplacement entailed how the city, as a particular kind of place, actively mediated futures and futurities. In varying ways, mobility and emplacement were central to our interlocutors' anxious and tense anticipations of their futures.

In foregrounding affect, our analysis draws attention to the relation between mobility and emplacement on the one hand and futurity and potentiality on the other. Affect signals a capacity—or lack of capacity—for moving through and being emplaced in worlds that are frequently not of our making. It also signals the predicament of being stuck as, for example, when our interlocutors were put in their place by abusive customers because of their race or national location, or when they felt stuck in place in terms of moving up the corporate ladder because of their gender or caste. Raghavi, who had worked in two different BPOs, contrasted the sexism she faced as a mid-level manager in her current job with her previous company. Whereas the previous company had close to a fifty-fifty gender ratio, the current one had very few women, especially in management positions. Commenting on her male colleagues, she said, "They want to put you down." At management meetings where she was frequently the only woman present, she had to be careful because she was alone: "If I say something, everyone is ready to pounce. . . . Being a woman manager of guys is especially difficult," she added. Women managers had an especially difficult time in this environment because "if you get friendly with anybody [any man], they start calling you all kinds of things." She got the feeling that her male colleagues did not like having women employees because they, alleged, women "take leaves with no reason." If she promoted women, her male colleagues "say you are favoring women, you are being biased to girls." She professed to "going crazy trying to manage these things." While Raghavi blamed it, in part, on the "Indian mindset" where people "formed opinions without meeting you and it was very hard to get rid of those perceptions," her previous company was not like that because it had a "healthier atmosphere." She concluded that it all depended "on the culture of the company" and, in her current place of employment, she found it much harder to move up the corporate ladder because she was a woman. She felt stuck where she was.

In addition to the challenges that they had to negotiate with other people within their company, BPO agents engaged in experiential and cultural border crossings. These crossings were transformative in how they stretched their imaginations and sense of the possible in unprecedented ways, thus underscoring the powerful, yet fragile, web that connects mobility and futurity.

In a prescient observation, Caren Kaplan (2003) pointed to the freighted salience of the trope of mobility in contexts shaped by information technology and the digitalization of labor: as she put it, "the rhetoric of cyberspace and information technologies relies heavily on the hyperbole of unlimited power through disembodied travel" (210). She argued that, in contexts of high-tech capitalism, the self is not "released" from national (and other) locations but is very much emplaced within them. Yet, hegemonic narratives of digitalized economies emphasize speed, disembodiment, and a casting aside of constraints. Consider, for instance, the title of a book by Bill Gates, *Business @ the Speed of Thought* (2000), which foregrounds the circulation of information and capital in terms of velocity and uninterruptibility. Similarly, Berardi (2011) defines semiocapital in terms of the movement of "goods that are circulating in the economic world . . . signs, figures, images, projections, [and] expectations" (100). However, the production and circulation of these goods, whether of signs, affect, or tangible commodities, is the result of the labor of bodies that are located in particular places (Rothenberg 2015). In affective capitalism, mobility is locational, situated, and, as we will argue later in this book, embodied. The mobility and emplacement of the BPO agents with whom we worked in Bengaluru were structured by the human and more-than-human relations constituting the material environment of the city as well as by labor, race, caste, gender, and class.[5]

Movement across an Unequal City

Our analysis of the physical and social mobility of BPO agents is in dialogue with Ghassan Hage's (2009) conceptualization of existential mobility and "stuckedness" in the lives of migrants. In contrast to tourists, Hage argues, "People engage in the physical form of mobility that we call migration because they are after existential mobility" (2). A considerable proportion of the BPO agents that we met in Bengaluru were indeed migrants because they had moved from other cities, towns, and semirural areas, and their physical movement to Bengaluru was foundational to their subject formation. Extending Hage's argument about existential mobility, we theorize movement as social, imaginative, and virtual in addition to being physical. BPO agents' anxieties about being stuck were generated and precipitated by neoliberal discourses of growth and progress that equated staying in place with stagnation. Members of this precariously first-generation middle-class were preoccupied with the uncertainties associated with acquiring the cultural capital to mark their upward mobility (see also chapter 2). In this world, staying in place could very well result in downward mobility.

How is the mobility of BPO agents and, to this extent, that of semio-capital itself, itself generated by distinct socialities and spatialities? In her pioneering work on spatiality, Doreen Massey (1991) foregrounds how the differentiated mobility of social groups is entangled with "the accumulated history of a place, with that history itself imagined as the product of layer upon layer of different sets of linkages, both local and to the wider world" (29). Neither semiocapitalism nor the mobilities and immobilities that constitute it are placeless or ungrounded; the mobile selves of BPO agents are never "unhoused"; they are situated somewhere even as they move across particular kinds of spaces (Kaplan 2002, 34). The mobilities (and immobilities) of our interlocutors foreground their emplacement in the city of Bengaluru, which, as an actant, impinges on and refracts their capacity for mobility, whether physical, social, or experiential. It is the spaces of this city that BPO agents traverse as they commute to work and back home and craft worlds and lives for themselves. BPO agents navigate a city that is constantly changing and moving, anticipating the future without shedding its past. Living in Bengaluru *requires* that one becomes habituated to the heterogeneous collisions, disjunctures, and disarticulations that constitute it as a particular kind of place.

Mimi Sheller and John Urry (2006, 214) compare places to ships, themselves traveling "within networks of human and nonhuman agents." Like the streets of metropolitan centers in many parts of the world, Bengaluru's streets demonstrate the heterogeneity of the ways in which humans and more-than-humans move through it or are placed within it. Some forms of mobility have vanished, although others have survived: animal-drawn carts are becoming rare, while feral cats, cows, buffaloes, and stray dogs wind their way around the buses, cars, scooters, motorcycles, and three-wheelers that snarl through its streets. The sonic landscape of the city can sometimes feel overwhelming with the honking of vehicles, music blaring out of public address systems (and cars), and the screeching of cabs and vans transporting BPO employees that speed through choked streets. This is a sensorium that is embedded in the entanglement of the city's political and affective economies. As Hemangini Gupta and Kaveri Medappa (2020) point out, this is an unequal city: "Industrial jobs have been lost, slums are being systematically razed, and spiraling rents cause a swift turnover of residents" (1704). Although it represents itself as the city of the future, the Silicon Valley of India has also witnessed infrastructural collapse because of its uncontrollable traffic, the pollution of its water and air, and acute water shortage. Housing has become so expensive that it has pushed working families to the city's peripheries and informal workers into slums. The cost of living makes it increasingly difficult for a majority of residents to make ends meet. And nothing hinders the movement of workers across the city more than rising transportation costs, traffic jams, and the inadequacy of public transit.

Jisha Menon (2021, 4) poignantly describes Bengaluru as a "profoundly haunted place, teeming with memories of demolished buildings, of vanished neighborhoods, of the disappearing tree cover that once gave Bengaluru its moniker, 'the garden city.' The trace of these ghosted memories continues to linger in the new city, evoking nostalgic yearnings for times past." Many BPO agents are migrants from other parts of India, and the nostalgia of Bengaluru's long-time residents frequently morphs into hostility and resentment against them, shaping their pathways through the city in powerful ways (see also Frazier 2019; Menon 2021, 55). Although Bengaluru has historically been a city on the move, it is neither a "maximum city" like Mumbai (Mehta 2004) nor, like New Delhi, the center of the federal government: it is a "multiple city" that, historically, has changed constantly (De 2008). In addition to being the hub of IT and ITES industries in India, and despite its self-representation as a "Science City," Bengaluru is a city with rich and sedimented pasts (S. Srinivas 2016; T. Srinivas 2018).

Its diverse temporalities bump up against each other. In no way has the postindustrial world of BPOs done away with Bengaluru's informal economies: indeed, it has accelerated their growth. The city's shanty towns and slums remain in plain sight adjacent to the proliferation of the postmodern spaces of tech parks and malls. Race and caste have long shaped the city's landscapes and patterns of settlements. Its colonial past once transformed it into a divided city, with the cantonment area where colonial administrators and military personnel lived sharply demarcated from the bustling petes where "natives" worked, shopped, and made their worlds (Nair 2005). In postcolonial India, settlements continue to be segregated by caste and religion so that some areas such as Malleshwaram and Basavanagudi are largely inhabited by Brahmins and other dominant castes, while other parts of the city, such as Shivajinagar and Rehmat Nagar, are regarded as "Muslim areas." In some parts of the city, statues of Babasaheb Ambedkar indicate the prominence of Dalits and other oppressed castes, and in other areas the neighborhood mosque constitutes the center of sociality and community building.

Far from disappearing, caste divisions have been sharpened in this supposedly high tech city. Naveen Bharathi, Deepak Malghan, Sumit Mishra, and Andaleeb Rahman (2022) at the Indian Institute of Management Bangalore posit that Dalit, Muslim, and other oppressed communities live in "involuntary ghettos" produced by the intersection of residential segregation and spatial inequality" (2914).[6] For instance, caste segregation is stronger in areas like Whitefield and Electronics City where there is a concentration of IT and ITES companies, as compared with parts of the city like Magadi Road or Kengeri where the tech boom has been less prominent. In fact, the marginalization of Dalits and other oppressed communities is materialized in their settlement patterns: because of the high cost of housing and overt discrimination, they have been pushed either to peripheral areas of the city or into slums. A majority of the residents of slums are Dalits, Bahujans, and other marginalized communities (Sidhnath 2020). Many of these slums have been "relocated" to peripheral areas—for instance, slums in Ejipura have been moved to Sarjapur, Baiyappanahalli to Sadamangala, and from Sanjaynagar or Gandhinagar to Kudlu. According to Bharathi et al, "Eventually, this will leave a central area, much like the *agraharas*, where only upper castes stay, while the SC, ST community [*sic*] will be in the fringes" (M. Rao 2019). Even when these communities are able to afford housing outside slums and peripheral areas of the city, they are often not permitted to purchase or rent homes in upcoming areas of the city by real estate developers, brokers, and landlords.

Given its enduring power in shaping modes of stratification, exclusion, and inequality in contemporary India, it is tempting to posit that caste mobility is an oxymoron. Yet, as several scholars have pointed out, caste is dynamic, and indeed this is what makes it resilient: while caste hegemony and violence have persisted, the inequalities of caste assume variable forms in different contexts. In some contexts, caste interlocks with class and all the privileges that upward mobility brings with it; yet, and importantly, caste cannot be subsumed within class. The spatial layout of most villages and small towns are segregated by caste: to ask where someone lives is, often, to be able to locate them along hierarchies of caste. Moving from a village to a city may, in some limited contexts, allow for a certain loosening of caste hierarchies but never does away with them: physical mobility does not necessarily result in mobility across caste lines in all areas of social life. Our Dalit and other oppressed-caste interlocutors experienced the exclusions of caste most powerfully when they moved to Bengaluru from other parts of India and sought housing: as we note above, most landlords would be unwilling to rent to them, rendering fragile the myth of egalitarianism engendered by the convergence of neoliberalism and semiocapitalism.

Power Geometries: BPOs, Mobility, and Emplacement

Mobility across caste hierarchies *within* the world of BPOs was complex and replete with contradictions, entailing movement in some aspects and emplacement in others. On the one hand, most if not all government schools in Bengaluru teach English and, since Dalit and other oppressed caste (and low-income) students tend to attend these schools, they are able to acquire sufficient proficiency in English to apply for jobs in BPOs (Jayadeva 2015, 15–18). Furthermore, we frequently observed how caste rules of commensality were loosened when agents sat together and ate in the BPO's cafeteria or at restaurants in malls: these groups were seldom, if ever, segregated by caste. We also observed that agents tended to form friendship groups with individuals from different castes and religions. And, as we note in chapter 3, in light of the moral policing and Hindu nationalist violence surrounding intercaste (and, especially, interreligious) sexual relationships, and given the relative low frequency of intercaste marriages in Bengaluru, we were surprised at the number of intercaste liaisons we came across among BPO agents. However, couples entering such relationships faced considerable resistance when their families found out about them, and those attempting to marry across caste (and religious) lines had to fight very hard to do so. In some cases, these couples would be disowned by their families, thus foregrounding the enduring power of caste in shaping relations of intimacy.

The disjuncture between the apparently egalitarian world of BPOs and the harsh realities of segregation and discrimination in the city thus underscores the role of caste in mediating mobility and emplacement and, therefore, futures and futurity. While the invisibilization of caste within the world of IT in India (and indeed in Silicon Valley) has only obfuscated its force in overdetermining exclusion and access, in the ITES industry caste assumes different forms. As Chandan Gowda points out, throughout the nineteenth and twentieth centuries, Christian missionaries enabled the formal education of hundreds of Dalit children; additionally, many of the "mission schools" taught English (Ananthamurthy and Gowda 2019). This history of the access of Dalit children to education—in particular, English education—is a significant factor in the employment of Dalit and other oppressed caste youth in BPOs.

When we started fieldwork, the lateral mobility of agents was very high and the demand for agents far exceeded supply. The general rule of thumb was that it was more important to hire people who had drive and, in the words of one of the COOs we interviewed, were "hungry": they were less likely to complain about their long hours at work, were more willing to work hard, and were more likely to stay on the job, compared to those who came from more privileged backgrounds. He said that none of the interviewees who showed up at his company knew that they would have to make as many as 350 calls a day in order to get one or two sales. Most potential customers hang up, and agents need to have the strength to face repeated rejection. For those agents who stayed on, the challenge as a small company was how to retain them. Larger companies with more lucrative contracts lured their best agents. In a resigned tone, he said, "We become the training ground for larger call centers."

At the same time, we frequently heard agents complain about how supervisors and managers tended to "favor" people of their own "community" while considering them for promotion. Community sometimes referred to regional, religious, or linguistic communities, but it was also a euphemism for caste. Equally significantly, most of the COOs, CEOs, owners, and senior managers whom we met over several years of fieldwork in BPOs had last names that revealed their dominant caste or Savarna status. At the upper reaches of these organizations, caste was indisputably a gatekeeping factor: professional and social networks, educational and financial capital, and assumptions of privilege and bodily habitus enabled people from the Savarna castes to assume leadership positions and rise to the top of their companies (see also Mosse 2020). Despite this, these senior employees and an overwhelming majority of agents insisted that they worked in environments that were relatively egalitarian. Agents believed that, unlike their parents and other relatives who had faced overt discrimination, bias, and, frequently, humiliation at work, they worked in places where hard work and diligence paid off.

Our interlocutors' sense of their class positions as particular kinds of *laborers* was even more tenuous. Even when they had not been raised middle class, our interlocutors believed that they acquired middle-class status after joining BPOs. The strength of their self-representations as middle class was rooted in the indisputable fact that many of them had indeed moved across class lines: they had pulled themselves, as well as their families, into the middle classes. And while their class mobility might, at times, seem precarious, they had achieved a kind of mobility that had been unimaginable for their parents and other relatives. This had a powerful effect on their sense of their own futures as well as on the discourses of futurity that molded them into particular kinds of subjects.

Some of these self-representations were also shaped by the self-representation and history of Bengaluru as a particular kind of city. Shortly after independence, Bengaluru became famous for its public sector enterprises. Today, even as neoliberal enterprise culture and governance have reconfigured the city's politics and socialities, these industries continue to shape its social geographies and the imagination of many of its inhabitants. Historically, public sector workers were represented, and constituted themselves, as quintessentially middle class: this had consequences for the development of workers' struggles and the development of working-class identities despite the city being home to diverse social movements (Nair 2005, 87). Certainly, in all our years of doing fieldwork in Bengaluru's BPOs, not once did we hear BPO agents describe themselves as laborers: in their workplaces, in public representations, and in their own discourses, they were called (and they represented themselves as) "agents." Since most of their parents and extended families came from lower-income backgrounds, their middle-class identity was contingent on their individual struggles to achieve upward social mobility.

Many agents had migrated to Bengaluru from different parts of India, spanning Kashmir, Punjab, and Haryana in the north to Mizoram, Nagaland, and Manipur in the northeast, and Tamil Nadu, Andhra Pradesh, and Kerala in the south. They were mostly first-generation migrants and came from families that had not ventured too far from their home states or, indeed, their hometowns or ancestral villages. Most of these young people were living on their own for the first time and, for them, the experience of finding and making a home in a new city and working alongside people from diverse cultural, linguistic, and religious backgrounds was transformative.

Although Maria came from a middle-class family, her migration story is representative of the experience of many agents. She joined a BPO when she went to an interview on a lark with a friend (see introduction). She came to Bengaluru from a small town in the western part of the state. Her mother did not approve of her working in a call center because she had heard that people there drank and smoked. Maria lived alone and worked the night shift but was afraid to disclose that to her mother because she knew she would not approve of it. One day, when she reached her apartment at 4 a.m. after working her shift, she found her mother waiting for her. She said, "Pack your bags, we are going back home." Eventually, Maria prevailed and quickly rose up the ranks of the company in which she was working.

BPO agents who had migrated from tier-two cities, small towns, and rural areas were more likely to experience life in Bengaluru as fast-paced:

speed was the trope they used most frequently to describe the lifestyle engendered by this city. Its speed was also invoked by long-term residents to describe how it had changed after the advent of the IT and ITES industries: they claimed that it had been an ideal city for retirees because of its slow pace and excellent weather, but since "techies" and other migrants had moved in, the city had become more built-up, congested, full of crime, warmer, and fast-paced (Frazier 2019). On their part, our interlocutors frequently spoke to us about how, for all the challenges that these experiences threw their way, their imaginations of what the future held for them had been irrevocably altered by their migration to Bengaluru. For instance, when we first met Jayashree in 2009, she had already been living in Bengaluru for twelve years, having migrated from Kochi, a city in the neighboring state of Kerala, where she had grown up. She told Mankekar that she had never "stepped out" in her "earlier life," underscoring that her move from Kochi had enabled a transition from an earlier mode of living. She related how dazzled she was by the "speed" of Bengaluru: "This city is so fast. It is not as if nothing happens in Kochi. But here there is so much happening that I used to feel dizzy. It is exhausting but [Bengaluru] just has this buzz and it is hard to leave it. It is like I got hooked." The vertiginous energy of the city, she was suggesting, was addictive.

Jayashree met and fell in love with an agent who worked at another BPO; he was also from Kerala and, like her, never wanted to leave Bengaluru. When Mankekar asked why that was the case, she was very clear in her response. First of all, she said, career opportunities for her and her husband were "fantastic" in Bengaluru; second, even though Kochi is "not in the boonies," it could not offer the plurality of cultures and experiences of Bengaluru. She offered the following examples: "I had never met, let alone worked with, people from Mizoram or Tripura. At most I would meet some people from Mumbai or the North. But here I feel I am part of something larger. There are so many learnings I can have. I have grown so much. I have learned to communicate, get along, talk to so many different kinds of people. It helps me in my work as an agent, but it also makes me realize that the world is full of different experiences." She added: "The malls in Kochi are also quite impressive. But it isn't just about shopping. Look at the different kinds of foods we can get here. If I take a BMTC or Vajra bus or I walk down a street in Koramangala or even walk across my tech park, I can hear so many languages, see different kinds of people who look different, wearing different kinds of clothes."

Koramangala is an upscale neighborhood not far from where Jayashree's BPO was located: the diversity of its residents equals the variety of its restaurants, and it was where her manager would take the team to lunch on Fridays. But if neighborhoods like Koramangala provided a plethora of sensations, the tech park where she worked also offered the buzz of excitement and new experiences. For most of our interlocutors, Bengaluru was a city of opportunity: it allowed one to advance in one's career but also to grow in other ways. It was a place that was simultaneously dizzying, exciting, exhausting, and addictive, offering sensoria and experiences that expanded one's horizons; it promised young people who had moved from other parts of the country an opportunity to conceptualize their place in a "larger world" in unprecedented ways: moving to this city enabled them to imagine their futures anew.

In powerful ways, then, physical and social mobility were deeply intertwined and had a direct bearing on their discourses of futurity (compare with Hage 2009). Many, if not most, agents aligned their own social mobility with the purportedly upward mobility of the nation and, hence, participated in discourses of India Rising that were ubiquitous at the time when we were doing our fieldwork (see introduction). In 2009, when we first started our extended fieldwork in Bengaluru, the government then in power was loudly proclaiming that India had "arrived" and was now poised "to take its place in the sun." Apart from opportunities for personal growth and social mobility, it was the *feeling* that they were participating in the larger story of India Rising that was frequently articulated by the BPO agents. As Rajath, a young man who had just started working in a BPO, insisted: "BPOs have made India take its rightful place in the world. Now nobody can push us around."

We have already noted that information technology is popularly associated with social mobility and progress, "fuelling new hopes and disappointments" (Upadhya 2016, 36–37). Most BPO agents we met felt that they were part of the new workforce engendered by IT. And since they considered IT the harbinger of progress and (post)modernity, they saw themselves as contributing to India's economic ascendance on the global stage. BPO agents possessed neither the qualifications nor the symbolic capital of software engineers or those engaged in coding: in fact, most of them had not attended college and, instead, only had intermediate (PUC) degrees. Although they were workers in a global service economy and catered to customers in the Global North, most of them believed that working in the ITES sector provided them with a crucial, intermediate position between under-/unemployment and the high-status jobs of software engineers.

Many BPO agents experienced upward class mobility very quickly because they received relatively high starting salaries and their earnings increased sharply after just a couple of years on the job. By 2009, when we first began fieldwork, an overwhelming majority of our interlocutors were from lower-middle-class or lower-income families; several were from Dalit and other communities located on the margins of caste hierarchies. Opportunities for upward class mobility were accompanied by new ways of imagining their futures and of their roles in carving out these futures, signifying new aspirational horizons. As the CEO of one BPO explained to us, call center jobs in India were the opposite of those in the United States because these jobs were aspirational and not a dead end. What had changed from previous years was that the *expectation* of class mobility in this population had now become normal. There was thus a shift in what Arjun Appadurai (2013, 179–95) has termed "the capacity to aspire." Sazana Jayadeva (2018) quotes one lower-income woman who articulates an extreme version of this expectation of class and, especially, caste mobility: "Today, becoming an engineer is not a big thing. A sweeper's daughter [can become] an engineer. Whether her mother scrubbed the floors, washed the bathrooms, or cooked, it does not matter" (12).

At the same time, the class positions of some of our interlocutors were complex despite their relatively high salaries, excellent health benefits, attractive bonuses, and other emoluments.[7] Although some BPO agents worked in factory-like conditions, they could not be categorized as blue-collar workers, nor did they see themselves as belonging to that category. And while our interlocutors did not engage in exorbitant shopping sprees, they were deemed major players in the expansion of India's consumer economy because their discretionary incomes were relatively high. However, they worked in repetitive jobs and were subject to close supervision; certainly, at the entry level, they could not be said to occupy white-collar jobs. Furthermore, because they depended on contracts given by multinational companies to Indian BPOs, their jobs were inherently vulnerable to the volatility of global capital.

Jayashree and her husband had worked in the BPO industry for a few years and their combined salaries enabled them to rent a tiny studio apartment. But most BPO agents were not so lucky. They lived in a city that offered them the opportunity to expand their horizons, their conceptualization of the possible, and their sense of how to emplace themselves in a world that was much larger than the one in which they had grown up. But while the very experience of getting to know, sometimes intimately, people from vastly different religious, caste, and cultural backgrounds irrevocably stretched their senses of self and their ability to place themselves in a vastly expanding cultural landscape, this sense of an enlarged world contrasted sharply with the claustrophobia of their living quarters, foregrounding other modes of emplacement. Unlike Fordist manufacturing companies, which attempted to enfold all aspects of workers' lives, providing them with housing and schooling, IT companies and BPOs largely left employees to fend for themselves.

Bengaluru suffered from a paucity of rental accommodation that could fit the budgets of lower-middle-class and middle-class agents in BPOs, IT companies, and other industries. All that was available to them was often low-quality housing in informal settlements with exploitative rent. Higher-priced villas and apartments provided a greater margin to builders, so Bengaluru had a glut of high-priced homes and flats for sale at the upper end of the market, but these were out of reach for most BPO agents. Despite the fact that a three-bedroom flat in one of the upscale high-rise apartment complexes that dot Bengaluru would cost just as much to rent as what three men or women were paying for their single rooms, no landlord in a posh gated community wanted to rent their flat to three unrelated single men, much less to three women. So BPO workers were forced to find a place to stay in the informal housing market, often in unauthorized developments and without rental agreements or receipts. The situation was markedly worse for people from Dalit, Bahujan, and Muslim communities who were openly discriminated against and excluded by landlords from many areas of the city.

A majority of the BPO agents we got to know lived in informal hostels; some resided in paying guest (PG) accommodations where they would rent out rooms in larger houses; a small minority shared an apartment with flatmates.[8] Informal hostels were usually one or more floors of a house where the landlord placed as many beds as could be fitted into one room. Some young women who had migrated from other parts of the country preferred to live in "Ladies' Hostels" because they felt safer and it was considerably cheaper and less stigmatizing than renting apartments on their own. We visited one such Ladies' Hostel in a small, free-standing house in HSR Layout. The ground floor of the house was occupied by the landlord, and we had to climb a flight of ill-lit stairs to get to the upper floor, which constituted the hostel. When we went up the stairs we found a large room with a balcony. Inside the room were narrow single beds lying adjacent to each other with barely enough room to walk between them. Although it hardly seemed possible, there were about twenty beds in that room. Adjoining the room were a toilet and a separate bathroom. There were a couple of sinks outside the bathroom. We were told that breakfast and dinner were included in the rent and served downstairs where the landlord lived. The landlord

1.1. Pillar on street plastered with PG posters.

had hired a local woman to cook the meals, and the food served was very basic with a repetitive menu. We were told that unauthorized visitors were strictly prohibited from entering the house. Each hosteller paid INR 2,500 a month for this shared space.[9] Since a BPO worker's starting salary could be about INR 10,000, it meant that a worker was paying at least a fourth or more of her income as rent to live in conditions that provided no privacy and no personal space. Not all the young women who lived there were employed in BPOs: some worked in retail stores which paid even less, while a few others were students at many technical colleges that had no dormitory

1.2. Dining room of a PG accommodation with instructions.

facilities. According to our women interlocutors, they felt safer in these Ladies' Hostels but also more confined; even when landlords did agree to rent to them (and, indeed, made good money on these rents), they tended to treat them with disrespect, often making sarcastic remarks about the fact that they did night work.

Compared to cities like Delhi, Bengaluru is relatively safe for women; yet, in the past few decades, sexual harassment in public places and gendered and sexual violence have been on the rise. This was something that all our women interlocutors, including those who were relatively long-term residents, said to us. Women BPO agents were often regarded as "loose" in part because of their ability to move across distances. The city presented many challenges because they had to work at night: traversing its spaces after dark was not without its risks and presented considerable restrictions on their mobility. Massey (1991) points out that rather than "capital," conceptualized in the abstract, the power geometry of gender, class, and race powerfully shapes mobility:

> The degree to which we can move between countries, or walk about the streets at night, or venture out of hotels in foreign cities, is not just influenced by "capital." Survey after survey has shown how women's mobility, for instance, is restricted—in a thousand different ways, from physical violence to being ogled at or made to feel quite simply "out of place"—not by "capital," but by men. (21)

These power geometries of gender, class, and race were accentuated by the regimes of labor in BPOs. Although physical mobility—the ability to traverse the city to do night work—was a prerequisite for working in BPOs, gender deeply impacted mobility. Women agents frequently worried aloud about the dangers they faced not just from strangers but also from colleagues and cab drivers. As we observed in the introduction, these fears were accentuated after the widely publicized case in Bengaluru of Pratibha Murthy, an IT worker who was raped and killed by a man posing as a company-employed driver (HT Correspondent 2010). The dangers of gendered and sexual violence, and the stigma attached to women who did night work, were so acute that most BPOs provided cabs or vans that transported their employees to and from work.[10] Companies maintained detailed logs of when women employees were picked up and dropped off, and some firms had strict rules that women employees could only be transported to and from addresses registered with them. While these practices were ostensibly for the protection of women, like many protectionist discourses, they resulted in the intensification of their monitoring and surveillance (see also R. Patel 2010; Aneesh 2015). One company mobilized such protectionist discourses by designating a radius around their location that they designated as "the hiring zone." This reduced the amount of time that workers spent commuting and also cut transportation costs for the company. If an applicant lived outside the hiring zone, they were told that they would have to move in order to receive free transportation.

Gendered formations of spatiality and temporality thus converged with dominant discourses of sexuality to emplace women in distinct ways. Stereotypical media accounts of BPO agents frequenting pubs or spending most of their earnings in malls only exacerbated the suspicions and hostility these women faced from family members. Even though they were picked up from home and dropped back by company cabs, family members, particularly in-laws, often remained skeptical because they associated night work with sexual promiscuity. The social stigma attached to women who worked in BPOs had material consequences: sometimes, landlords refused to rent apartments to these women because they worked at night (see also Aneesh 2015; Mirchandani 2012; R. Patel 2010; Vora 2015).[11]

Discourses of race and perceived racial difference also constricted the mobility of some women agents. The BPO industry attracted many young people from Manipur, Tripura, Mizoram, and Nagaland in the northeast of India because they had superior English-speaking skills from having been educated in high-achieving schools run by Christian missionaries, and more importantly, because of the scarcity of jobs there (Karlsson and Kikon 2017). The inhabitants of these states have long been represented as racially and culturally Other in mainstream Indian discourses of national belonging. Women from these states who migrated to Bengaluru were extremely vulnerable to sexual and racial violence (see also Karlsson and Kikon 2017, 460). Many BPO agents who had moved to Bengaluru from these states were acutely conscious of being regarded as unassimilable foreigners because of how they looked—to put it more plainly, because they appeared racially Other. Women, in particular, tended to be frequently targeted because they appeared different, wore Western clothes, and were perceived to be sexually available. Christina was one of the first people we met when we began fieldwork at Serenity. She was from Mizoram and worked in a small BPO; she had risen up the ranks to first become a team leader, then a supervisor, and later joined the HR section of the company. The CEO of the BPO had nothing but praise for her managerial skills. She was also warmly regarded by others in the company. Yet, she told Mankekar that she felt "different" every time she stepped outside the BPO's premises because of her appearance: she stood out because she had "un-Indian" looks.

Christina related several instances of feeling vulnerable in Bengaluru. When she had first moved to Bengaluru, she and a group of her friends, also from Mizoram, had lived in a Ladies' Hostel. After a while, she and her friends wanted to escape the claustrophobia of their living quarters in the hostel and started looking for a flat that they could jointly rent. Christina was shocked when she found that some of the landlords they approached thought they were call girls. They eventually found a flat that they could rent from an elderly widow in Indira Nagar, an upper-middle-class part of town; they had to stretch their budgets to pay the high rent but they had resigned themselves to the high cost of feeling secure. Christina added that she hated that she had to deal with catcalls, wolf whistles, and strange men who deliberately tried to bump into her when she went out on her own, so much so that she and her friends were now saving up to buy a used car. She took the company cab to work, but she never felt safe taking public transport if she was on her own or when she met friends for dinner or a movie. She said: "I look different from other Indians and wear Western clothes, so some men think I am easy." She didn't feel she could go back to her hometown, no matter how acutely she missed it, because she had been so successful in her profession; at the same time, she was justifiably angry about how she was perceived by "other Indians," especially men.

Angelina, a woman from Nagaland who was working in HR, had a longer-term perspective on changes in local attitudes toward migrants. Her uncle was working in Bengaluru and encouraged her to come and study there so that she could build a career. She went to one of Bengaluru's best colleges with the goal of becoming a social worker. Living alone was not difficult because she had been living in a hostel since fifth grade. While studying, she started working in a call center. After graduating, she was of-fered a job in HR at a consulting firm that specialized in placing people in BPOs. From there, she had moved to her current position at a small call center as the head of recruitment. She recalled that when she had first moved to Bengaluru, she felt very safe to be on the streets as a single woman at night, and the city was much easier to navigate than Mumbai or Delhi. However, she had noticed that it had become less safe and friendly. She felt that increased migration from other parts of India had made a difference and that local people were now rude. According to her, most of the migration was due to the IT industry and BPOs. Growing local resentment toward migrants was a theme that was echoed by a range of people who had moved to Bengaluru from other parts of the country, and found its mirror in local peoples' com-plaints that workers in restaurants and shops no longer spoke or understood the local language Kannada.

For women, spatial mobility and, in particular, night work produced distinct temporal dislocations: these bring to the fore the politics of gender and family that constrained them and emplaced them in particular ways

(R. Patel 2010). Since they worked at night, they needed to rest during the day, and in-laws and family members would allege that they were neglecting their familial duties, whether this entailed attending family rituals and events or cooking and taking care of the home. The temporality of BPO labor thus threatened to disrupt the temporality of domesticity and of the gendered division of labor in the household, and the obligations of family and household also put pressure on regimes of affective labor. Managers did not (and could not) alter the work schedules of agents to align with the rhythms of household and family. The incompatibilities between work schedules and the temporalities of ritual and family life frequently resulted in tension within the family, eventually leading some women agents to leave their jobs at BPOs for alternative occupations that were more conducive to childcare, elder care, and housework: evidently, some rhythms of family and ritual life remained resistant to subsumption by the temporality of capital.

Mobility and temporality intersected in other complex ways for BPO agents.[12] Although BPOs spawned intimacies of their own (chapter 3), several agents felt disconnected from the rest of the city. Preethi, whom we met at the beginning of this book, reported that night work made her feel "out of sync" with the rest of Bengaluru. At the same time, those BPO agents who had moved to Bengaluru from other places also got new opportunities to expand their social world (see also Nair 2005, 323). Instead of being completely cut off from family and friends by geographic distance and asynchronous schedules, agents found ways to stay in touch. For example, the long commutes in company cabs provided means and opportunities for socializing and catching up, both face-to-face and virtually. Agents also used this time to reconnect with friends and family members on social media, exchange texts with romantic partners in the relative privacy of the vehicle, or set up meetings with coworkers during dinner or coffee breaks.

Occasionally, some of our women interlocutors would use their work as a means to visit pubs and bars after work despite being afraid of going out at night: working in BPOs enabled these women to venture into spaces that were simultaneously enticing and dangerous. Again, it is crucial that we avoid the trap of liberal notions of choice and freedom and not interpret these women's abilities to engage in these leisure activities as a sign of their "emancipation" or "progress," or assume that working in BPOs transformed them into sovereign or autonomous subjects; in fact, as we will argue in the next chapter, these very activities refracted their constitution as laboring subjects. Nevertheless, even though they were closely surveilled at work and in their neighborhoods, these women had relatively more control over their personal time than would have been the case had they been living with their families: they were able to spend what little leisure time they had with their friends and, in some cases, get away for weekends with friends and lovers. Since most large BPOs provided cafeteria facilities, a considerable amount of socializing occurred at work.[13] Some women reported that they would go to their workplaces on nights off in order to meet with their coworkers. Their move to Bengaluru and their work in BPOs offered them new opportunities for leisure: when they had the time, they were able to relax in malls, visit new cities, explore unfamiliar cuisines, wear the kinds of clothes they wanted to, and so on. As their social worlds expanded, so did their conceptions of their futures.

RACE, NATION, EMPLACEMENT

It is empirically inaccurate, analytically lazy, and politically irresponsible to draw analogies between the ITES industry and such manifestations of racial capitalism as slavery and indenture. Despite the sensationalized accounts of some journalists and commentators who argue otherwise, there is no comparison between them. BPO agents are "free" laborers in the strict sense of the term; they can quit their jobs and move laterally to other BPOs or to other sectors of the service economy; they have unprecedented (albeit far from unlimited) access to upward class mobility; they have not only the capacity to aspire but also, in some instances, the ability to accomplish some of the professional goals they set for themselves. Older paradigms of colonized labor and imperial extraction do not apply in the same way to them as they do to slaves and indentured workers. BPO agents are not coerced, abducted, or forced against their will to move away from their homes; indeed, despite the strain placed by their work on family dynamics, for the most part, their families benefit greatly from their work for BPOs. While they have to respond to the racist abuse with stoicism and "professionalism," they by no means face the same racist violence as did slaves and indentured laborers. And yet racial*ism* mediates the extraction of their labor in important ways. What do we mean by this? How do the mobility, immobility, and emplacement of BPO agents underscore the *alignment* between their regimes of labor and regimes of racial capitalism? And what are the implications of these alignments for futurity?

Cedric Robinson (2019) has argued that all existing forms of capitalism are racial capitalism (see also Kelley 2017). While early histories of capitalism were predicated on the coerced mobility of slaves and indentured laborers and the labor that was extracted from them constituted the foundation of capitalism, it is the emplacement of BPO agents within India and their inability to move to countries in the Global North that keeps their wages low and makes it profitable for BPOs to hire them. The speed at which capital, goods, and services travel sharply contrasts with, and frequently depends on, restrictions placed on the movement of agents owing to their emplacement along axes of race and national location. Because of their race, class, and national location, BPO agents based in the Global South have neither immigration rights nor citizenship in the countries to which the products of their labor travel.[14] Although the offshore outsourcing of labor demonstrates the inadequacy of nation-bound paradigms of labor and race, it is worth recalling that the expansion of outsourcing to countries like India was a direct result of nationalist, xenophobic, and race-based restrictions on the immigration of foreign laborers to many advanced capitalist countries.

Thus, while racial capitalism has conventionally been associated with the development of white supremacist capitalism—with slavery, genocide, and indenture—its contemporary mutations also deploy racialism to undergird liberal and neoliberal discourses of postracism—for instance, in discourses of meritocracy and the myth of the flattening of racial hierarchies. Previous discourses about phenotype and civilization are supplemented and, in some cases, superseded by other new-old matrices of inequality. Racial capitalism, as instantiated in BPOs, need not be based on phenotype; instead, race, or rather, racialism "permeates capitalism's economic and social processes, organizing the hyper-extraction of surplus value from racialized bodies and naturalizing a system of capital accumulation that grossly favor the global North over the global South" (Melamed 2011, 41).[15]

Although the (post)colonial histories of India and the Philippines are distinct, the complexities of race, colonial history, and capital that undergird the establishment of call centers in the Philippines resonate with the Indian experience (Padios 2018). In both countries, labor arbitrage was central to the initial establishment of call centers and BPOs. As we noted above, labor arbitrage depends on differences in salary scales between countries, and wages in turn are dependent on the cost of living. Jan M. Padios (2018) points out that lower living costs are not just a natural fact but are produced by the history of colonialism and neocolonialism that "reproduces the uneven material relations between nations and the devaluation of life on which different costs of living are based in the first place" (65). As is the case in the Philippines, the fact that Indian BPOs are paid less than their counterparts in the Global North is the result of uneven development and the differential value attached to life and labor. This is what makes labor arbitrage and outsourcing to these locations "cheap" and, therefore, profitable to globalized capital. As dependency theorists have long pointed out, cheap labor is not just found by accident in Global South locations but has been produced by the legacies of colonialism.

BPOs thus represent a mutation of racial capitalism precisely because of the emplacement and immobility of agents; as Jodi Melamed (2011) insists, "Racial capitalism is alive and well and more aggressive than ever, flexibly making use of both old and new racial procedures" (xxiii). BPOs instantiate a distinct form of transnational racial capitalism that shapes the adjudication of value and worth to the labor and lives of BPO agents in locations in the Global South. As we elaborate later in this chapter, racial capitalism refracts processes of translation and mistranslation undergirding the affective labor of BPO agents. Racialized constraints on their movement across not just national but also linguistic and experiential borders regulate their mobility, immobility, and emplacement. The outsourcing of service work to locations in the Global South such as India and the Philippines is hence both predicated on and reconfigures histories of colonialism, imperialism, and racial capitalism.

Racial capitalism is at the core of neoliberal modes of extraction throughout the Global South and draws on "historic repertoires and cultural and signifying systems that stigmatize and depreciate one form of humanity for the purposes of another's health, development, safety, profit or pleasure" (Singh 2004, 220, in Melamed 2011, 152). Financial capitalism moves promiscuously across national borders, commodities and images circulate transnationally and, as evident in the proliferation of ITES firms across the Global South, multinational investors and technocrats move across diverse locations acting in concert to shore up global capital. However, these forms of mobility do not follow in lockstep fashion: rather, as scholars argued several decades ago, these movements are disjunctive and beset with friction (Appadurai 1996; Gibson-Graham 1996; Tsing 2004). Furthermore, these disjunctures are undergirded by discourses of racialism that have less to do with phenotype or chromaticity and is founded on the systemic and systematic undervaluing of some populations for the benefit of others, thus creating modes of hierarchy and inequality that are insidious precisely because they are supple, labile, and resilient. Last but not least, as we have argued in the introduction to this book, these mutations of racial capitalism act in conjunction with uneven development to constitute geographies of power and inequality that exist both within and across territorial boundaries, thus problematizing binaristic and totalizing assumptions about North versus South or the West versus the Rest.

Capitalist expansion produces, draws on, indeed capitalizes on, divergent mobilities. From its inception, Asian American studies scholarship on migration has offered indispensable analytical tools to understand the intersection of transnational labor regimes, patterns of global migration and immigration, and hegemonic discourses of race (see, for instance, the early work of Chuh and Shimakawa 2001; Hune 1989; Lowe 1996; 2001, 2012; Ong, Bonacich, and Cheng 1994; Palumbo-Liu 1999). In the United States, software companies first began to outsource to India to take advantage of labor arbitrage. The offshore outsourcing of software, in turn, opened the door to the outsourcing of customer service and back-office work to countries like India and the Philippines; yet, as we have argued, these laboring bodies have had to stay put because of their race, class, and nationality. We, therefore, draw on and extend Asian American scholarship on the racialization and gendering of service labor to underscore how BPOs are a manifestation of the globalization of service work in which racialization occurs when workers do not, and cannot, immigrate to advanced capitalist countries (Choy 2003; Chun 2017; Chun and Agarwala 2016; Gottfried and Chun 2018; Glenn 1992; Parreñas 2001, 2005, 2008).

Class and rank within a BPO cushioned some of its senior employees from racist abuse so that the more senior an employee, the less likely they were going to be the target of racism or xenophobia. Indeed, the globalization of service work complicates analyses of race along East-West or North-South binaries (Shome 2006; Amrute 2016) because uneven development in the global economy no longer cleaves along those axes.

Likewise, the production of value in affective capitalism both draws on and problematizes colonial genealogies of labor extraction and (de)parochializes some of the premises undergirding dominant analyses of racial capitalism. The emergence of Asia as a new locus of financial and technological prowess compels us to pivot away from (North) Atlanticist conceptions of race. For one, and most obviously, captains of industry in the BPO sector in India are more likely to be Asian than European or European American; certainly, Indian owners of BPOs have been quick to expand operations in the Philippines, Guatemala, and other locations in the Global South. But, more fundamentally, the issue here is not the presence, absence, or intentions of individual capitalists but the (heterogeneous and, often, contradictory) logics of global capital*isms* and, in particular, the complex ways in which affective capitalism works both within and against prior formations of race, nation, and global political economy. Rather than adhering to nation-based analytical frames to engage new racial formations emerging in affective capitalism, these reconfigurations articulate forms of transnational governmentality that produce distinct entanglements of race and class which, nevertheless, emplace service workers within nation-bound spatialities (Ferguson and Gupta 2002).

It bears recalling that Asian alterity has been central to the production of (Western) capitalist modernity and to formations of racial capitalism in Asia.[16] In another context, Kandice Chuh and Karen Shimakawa (2001, 12) have advocated that we attend to the racialization of Asian bodies in terms of their positions within national, transnational and postcolonial terrains: we draw on their argument to theorize the forms of mobility, immobility, and emplacement of BPO agents. While it is beyond the scope of our research to interrogate how Asians and Asian labor are represented in each of the client nations that Bengaluru's BPOs served, Asian American perspectives on the complex relationship between labor, race, and purported "Asian-ness" have been tremendously valuable to our theorization of the racialization of our interlocutors and have been foundational to our theorization of racial capitalism in postcolonial India. Additionally, in our fieldwork in BPOs in Bengaluru, we witnessed how Orientalist discourses of alterity, in which the East and West were constructed in binaristic and hierarchical opposition such that the East was placed in an inferior position to the West, deeply shaped some of the encounters between our interlocutors and their overseas customers. This was particularly true of some of our women informants who were assumed to be docile and sexually alluring (and available) by some of their overseas male customers (chapter 3). Located within a global political economy striated by racial capitalism and in conjunction with gender and national location, agents in Bengaluru's BPOs were always already racialized by virtue of working in this industry. The backlash against the outsourcing of BPO jobs to countries like India and the Philippines partakes of a longer genealogy of racialized discourses about the relationship between labor, high technology, and Asia and Asians (Lee and Wong 2013; Mankekar and Gupta 2016).[17] Within the United States, the offshoring of jobs to Asia has long provoked anti-Asian racism (the most infamous instantiation of this backlash was the murder of Vincent Chin in Detroit in 1982).[18]

In focusing on mobility, immobility, and emplacement, our goal, therefore, is to theorize the *recasting* of the relationship between capitalist expansion, racial capitalism, and race in order to examine the kinds of futurities enabled or generated by transnational affective labor. The futurities imbricated with offshore outsourcing in affective capitalism exhibit continuities with the colonial past but also point to cartographies of capitalist exploitation that do not simply recapitulate metropole-colonial or North-South binaries. The BPOs where we worked, in fact, undermined older paradigms about colonial extraction: some of them were owned and managed by Indians; they were transnational and had operations in all parts of the globe, including parts of the Global North; and they were not involved either in extracting raw materials for production in the former colonial powers or in producing goods that were then sold to the former colonies. Thus, rather than argue that BPOs recapitulate colonial practices of labor allocation, we are interested in both the continuities and the disjunctures between colonial models of labor allocation and postcolonial ones in contemporary modes of racial capitalism in India. Race and racialism play a central role in this form of capitalism but in a manner that belies the notion that history is simply repeating itself through "neocolonial" relations.

The racialized extraction of value is both enabled and complicated in BPOs in distinct ways. What Karl Marx and Friedrich Engels ([1848] 1967) termed the cosmopolitan character of capitalism was evident in the fact that the profits of transnational corporations drew on the labor of BPO agents.[19] In BPOs, the cosmopolitanism of capital goes hand-in-hand with nationalist, race-based, and xenophobic immigration restrictions of countries in the Global North that aim to regulate and restrict the entry of racialized subjects ostensibly based on the "needs" of their respective economies. Berardi (2009, 90) notes that in manufacturing the "mobility of the product was made possible by the assembly line while workers had to remain motionless in space and time. Info-workers, instead, constantly move all along the length, breadth, and depth of cyberspace." However, as we have already noted, the labor of our interlocutors was profitable to BPOs and the companies that outsourced to them *because* of their immobility: their race, class, and nationality made it impossible for them to migrate to the countries where they might potentially have been paid a wage in keeping with workers living in those locations.

As is the case in the Philippines, the fact that Indian BPO workers are paid less than their counterparts in the Global North is the result of uneven development and the differential value attached to life and labor resulting from racial capitalism. This is what makes labor arbitrage and outsourcing to these locations "cheap" and, therefore, profitable to globalized capital. Simply put, the profitability of outsourcing is predicated on the immobility and emplacement of these laborers as much as it is on the mobility of the products of their labor. Thus, the immobility and emplacement of BPO agents are not epiphenomenal to semiocapitalist outsourcing; rather, mobility, immobility, and emplacement are coconstituted rather than oppositional in the production of value. In these contexts, the apparent hyperkinesis of value and capital is not opposed to emplacement but is founded on it.

Just as the Three Worlds paradigm was decentered in the post–Cold War moment (Pletsch 1981; Chuh and Shimakawa 2001, 5–6), the affective capitalism of BPOs compels us to rethink binaristic conceptions of the Global South versus the Global North while, simultaneously, foregrounding how the global economy is sedimented by new racial logics. The BPO agents with whom we worked did not migrate and were therefore differently positioned than Asian American workers in the United States. Our epistemological framework stages a conversation between Asian American studies scholarship on labor and comparative racialization on the one hand and postcolonial South Asian perspectives on capitalist expansion and social inequality on the other in order to diagram the futurities generated, envisioned, realized, subverted, and displaced in transnational BPO work.

ON TAKING FLIGHT AND FEELING STUCK

The itineraries of BPO agents are refracted by processes of emplacement in spaces that are at once regulatory and generative: the cabs that transport them across an ambivalent, sometimes hostile, city are simultaneously spaces of sociality and surveillance; even as they engage in virtual travel through their provision of services to clients all over the world, their movements within their workplaces are multiply monitored; and their precarious mobility up class hierarchies is regulated through affectively charged discourses of gender, caste, and community. For some of them, emplacement also entails being positioned in webs of relationality and affect that feel like entrapment (chapter 3); for others, it offers a map that enables them to navigate landscapes that feel confusing or daunting. It is this looping back of emplacement and mobility that we wish to unpack.

Hage (2009) makes a distinction between existential mobility and social mobility. They are intimately entangled yet can be differentiated such that "one can be in a job and climbing the social ladder within that job yet still feel stuck in it. This highlights the fact that social and existential mobility are not the same thing, even though they tend to coincide in a number of social situations"; existential mobility, he points out, is the "sense that one is 'going somewhere'" (1). Several of our interlocutors, especially those who had been working in the industry for a decade or more, frequently complained of feeling stuck.[20] On the one hand, working alongside other young people who had migrated to Bengaluru from all over the country and, sometimes, with managers and trainers from overseas, meant that their imaginations and their sense of their place in the world had expanded in ways that they could not have foreseen. At the same time, the relentless rhythms of their work schedules, the intense pressure of meeting quotas at work, the racial abuse meted out to them by customers who resented the fact that they were speaking to service providers in India, and the surveillance of neighbors and employers undoubtedly took a toll on their bodies and emotions (chapter 4). Even as they acquired upward class mobility, many of them felt burnt out or stuck in place.

Nowhere did such contradictory feelings feel more poignant than among BPO agents who worked for a major travel website. Their job was to steer vacation-goers from the United Kingdom and North America to European holiday resorts. Their training consisted of learning about and memorizing the particular character of each holiday resort in Europe in order to be able to match it with the interests and proclivities of their customers. Thus, younger customers were sent to areas that had a lot of nightlife, clubs, and the like, while those who were primarily interested in a beach vacation were directed to the famous beach towns. Agents had to know what was distinctive about each location and then find a hotel room for the guest that was within their budget. None of the agents we worked with had ever been to Europe; more importantly, none could even aspire to go there given their meager salaries and the restrictions on travel imposed by Schengen protocols. When they provided prospective vacationers with details about places that they themselves would never be able to experience, agents engaged in imaginative travel.

INTERJECTION

A confident twenty-three-year-old, Rajani struck Akhil Gupta as a bit quirky. She had very strong opinions about everything: her work, the BPO for which she worked, the community where she lived, and her neighbors. Rajani grew up in a small town not far from Bengaluru. Her family was dominant-caste but lower-middle-class with relatively few financial resources. Despite that, Rajani had long been enamored with the idea of becoming a pilot: she had dreamed of flying a commercial plane but the fees for flight school proved to be beyond the reach of her family. She toyed with the idea of taking a loan but that was a risky proposition because even with a diploma it was difficult to find jobs as a commercial pilot unless one had political or personal connections to bigwigs in the airline industry. So Rajani had settled for a job at a BPO.

But Rajani never lost her love of flying. She used her income from working in the BPO *to travel on new airplanes whenever she could. By interesting (and somewhat poignant) coincidence, she was assigned to a process for a travel portal. As her luck would have it, this was a time when India's aviation industry was expanding rapidly. As new budget airlines were established, intense fare wars were unleashed, and one could purchase relatively inexpensive tickets on brand new airplanes. Rajani made the most of this by flying to other cities as often as she could. For her, the thrill lay in flying on a new airplane, not in reaching any particular destination. On her days off, she would leave Bengaluru early in the morning to catch the first flight, spend a day at the destination city, and return the same evening. She did not have the money to stay overnight and, in any case, the destination was less interesting to her than the journey itself. Since the domestic airline industry was expanding rapidly, with new airlines and new airplanes being introduced regularly, she managed to fly on most of the new planes that were added to the domestic fleets.*

Rajani's love of flying was unusual and, relative to her income, obviously a very expensive pastime, much more so than going to the mall to see a film or buying a meal at the food court. Moreover, her parents could not contribute anything to her lifestyle; on the contrary, they would have been grateful to receive financial assistance from her. Yet, she flew as often as she could—in fact, so frequently that she had amassed a huge credit card debt. To pay off her credit card bills, she worked overtime. Her manager was aware of her passion for flying and he sat her down and cautioned her about buying new tickets when she had not yet paid back the debt from previous trips. But she never stopped flying.

Rajani's experiences with real and imaginative travel illustrate the complex and contradictory articulation of aspiration and emplacement among BPO agents. We resist the temptation to read her story as either a perversion of modernist ideals (the undisciplined BPO agent whose aspirations are out of sync with reality) or as a form of "resistance" to her emplacement and confinement by her job in a BPO. Rather, her love of flying illustrates the knotty relation between affect, mobility, and emplacement. Her imaginative world may have been shared by most of the middle-class and upper-middle-class people traveling on the plane with her, but their means exceeded hers. What might have been an inexpensive flight for other passengers was a very costly endeavor for her, but the fact that she persevered in the bodily pleasure of flying on different types of aircraft even when she could not afford it indicates the jagged edges of the temporality of global modernity that she embraced. Rajani's case illustrates the *tense* concurrence of aspiration and feeling stuck.

Unlike some of the customers in the Global North with whom Rajani spoke all night, she could not afford to travel abroad. Her itineraries were restricted by what she could afford. She had enough money to get inexpensive domestic flights, but she did not have the money to stay overnight in a hotel or pay for meals on such trips. So she did what she could with the means available to her, which meant that she never experienced flying on truly large jets or long-haul airplanes because they were never used on the domestic routes within India. Her aspirations were not different from many people who, like her, were joining the middle class or had already become middle class, but the means at her disposal thwarted her ambitions. She was mobile but her itineraries were constrained by her emplacement.

The young people with whom we worked were not underemployed, nor did they display the inertia characterizing Craig Jeffrey's (2010) interlocutors in small-town Uttar Pradesh. Yet there were many reasons why they felt stuck. While they had opportunities for promotions or for moving laterally from one company to another, their lives were full of anxiety and uncertainty: even though they felt they had "made it," they were also painfully aware that they could lose everything if their company lost the process on which they worked or if the BPO industry tanked. They were acutely conscious of the precarity of their fortunes. Those who felt emotionally and physically exhausted were often in a quandary, not least because they had become accustomed to the "high" of call centers. Sadia was a twenty-five-year-old single mother who had switched jobs to working in an event management company. Sadia compared working in a BPO to an addiction. She said, "You know it is bad for you in the long run, but it gives you a real high. The main problem is that the body cannot cope with the work, and that is what is frightening." Several agents that we interviewed hoped to move to the HR divisions of BPO firms because they claimed that they loved the industry for all the excitement it offered. Others hoped that when they were too old or too tired to "cope" with the pace of work, they could move to hospitality or other service industries. They trusted that the soft skills and networks they had acquired would stand them in good stead. They argued that their primary accomplishment was that they now had confidence in their abilities and, especially, in their facility to deal with people from all over the world. Sadia had changed careers from the BPO industry to event management because she felt she had acquired crucial social skills in her time at the BPO from interacting with overseas customers.

Like Rajani, many agents had aspirations that were "sticky" and endured, while other aspirations unraveled or had to be cast off. As was the case with Maria, some of them were able to rise up the ranks to get positions in the HR sections of their companies. Failing that, like Sadia, they moved laterally to other service jobs that had grown after the liberalization of the economy. Some found jobs in banks or the retail sector. These were jobs with regular working hours that, while more conducive to raising a family, struck many workers as lacking the glamor and buzz of working in BPOs. But going back to their hometowns or villages was not an option that they were willing to consider for even a second, no matter how tired they were or how hopeless they felt. As one of them said to Mankekar, "It will be like going back in time. Who wants to ever do that? It is so slow back there." The tempo and the disjunctive temporalities of life in Bengaluru were addictive indeed even when they proved exhausting.

BPO agents' feelings of being stuck contrasted sharply with those of some other young Indian men and women who have seen their aspirations dashed in recent years (cf. Chua 2014; Favero 2005). Some of them had escaped the tedium of their small towns to metropolitan centers like Bengaluru, a city that they felt was so full of energy that it seemed to be bursting at the seams, vertiginous, spiraling out of control. They were neither waiting nor in limbo (Favero 2005), and their lives were marked by the temporality of acceleration rather than time-pass (Jeffrey 2010). Almost all of our interlocutors had entered the world of BPOs in their early twenties, and as they approached their thirties, some of them felt they simply could not go on: they were too emotionally and physically drained to do so. Some of them felt they had no other prospects, and as we observed during our long-term fieldwork, many agents who had left BPO jobs because they were burnt out returned to them—either because they could not find jobs that paid them equally well or because they missed the buzz, the adrenaline rush, that came from working there. Those who had some knowledge of the relationship between BPOs and the world of multinational capital were particularly eloquent about how their jobs were contingent on the predatory irrationalities of global capital.[21] They were acutely aware that they were being paid considerably less than workers in advanced capitalist countries who did comparable work, and resented that their employers were profiting from their low wages.

For some BPO agents, this sense of emplacement and, indeed, of feeling stuck was exacerbated by the surveillance to which they were subjected at work. Here we extend Carla Freeman's (2000) analysis of workers in informatics outsourcing in Barbados to point to how multiple modes of surveillance resulted in the emplacement of our interlocutors. Freeman analyzes the panoptic regimes that shape workplaces and the formation of workers' subjectivities in terms of "the gaze of the computer, the gaze of supervisor, the manager, the fellow production worker, and finally the internal gaze of the self" (258). Our interlocutors' movements were tracked from the moment they got into the car that picked them up at their home: their entry into the office was monitored and recorded by magnetic cards or by the biometric registration of their fingerprints or irises. Once seated at their desks, they would log in and a dialer software program would regulate which call they would attend, and algorithms would provide them with customer profiles that would shape, to varying degrees, what they could say to their customers. They would need to log out to take a bathroom break, and CCTV cameras followed them everywhere on the premises. Coffee and lunch breaks were tightly regulated, and they would have to log in again when they returned to their desks. All their calls were recorded; analytics software was used to monitor the quality of their interactions with their customers and these reports would become the basis of their performance reviews.[22] As Raka Shome (2006, 107) points out, these new regimes of surveillance emerged from the "global regimes of telematics virtuality that characterize our moment of digitalized capitalism." For some agents the feeling of being stuck rankled very deeply: they felt trapped in their cubicles, in their jobs, and in their lives.

These processes of emplacement deeply shaped futurity for these agents. They frequently contrasted their lot with that of their parents or other relatives who had been stuck in dead-end jobs with no possibilities for growth or upward mobility. But this was all the more reason why the stakes were so high for them: feeling stuck was so threatening not merely to their aspirations for their individual futures but, more fundamentally, to their sense of futurity. Feeling stuck meant that they were in danger of not growing, and the lack of growth signified stagnation if not a slide down the ladder of professional mobility. Feeling stuck was, in fact, destabilizing because it foregrounded the precarity of their jobs. While their salaries were relatively high, they had little or no job security: BPOs could have their entire contract canceled by client companies, resulting in large-scale layoffs of agents and other workers.[23] Yet, unlike members of the precariat (the unemployed, the underemployed, the undocumented, and others liv-ing in conditions of abjection) in India and other parts of the world, our interlocutors, for the most part, did not feel hopeless. And even though they were anxious about what lay ahead of them, futurity for them was shaped by continual becoming, potentiality, and emergence.

THE INEQUALITY OF LANGUAGES

Given that affective capitalism depends on the circulation of affect and infor-mation, what happens when these circulations are blocked, interrupted, or disrupted? Rather than assume that semiocapital "flows" unimpeded across the world, we are interested in the sociohistorical formations and mutations of racial capitalism that generate these blockages, interruptions, and disrup-tions. How might these blockages, interruptions, and disruptions refract the heterogeneous futures of BPO agents and of futurity as a mode of potential-ity and becoming? Companies invest enormous resources in training agents and evaluating their effectiveness: training and quality control were two of the most important functions that enabled high customer satisfaction to be achieved.

BPO agents' mobility and emplacement were shaped by the inequality of languages that, literally as well as figuratively, mediated our interlocutors' performance of affective labor.[24] The BPO industry has, from its inception, been founded on the premise that a combination of "trainable" labor and technology will bridge physical and cultural distances between agents and their customers. Customer service work, of course, depends on connecting linguistically and, more importantly, affectively. BPO agents are trained to speak the language of their customers with the expectation that once they learn "correct" English, adopt the appropriate accent, and assume relevant speech patterns, they can flawlessly communicate with their customers. The affective labor of agents is hence predicated not simply on the transmission of information, as technocratic accounts of the BPO industry would have us believe, but on processes of cultural and experiential translation.[25]

The optic of translation enables us to draw attention to the dynamic inher-ent in communication across unequal relations of power. Postcolonial scholar-ship has challenged notions of translation as unmediated and transparent by conceptualizing it as a set of asymmetrical practices that produce subaltern subjects (Niranjana 1992; see also Bassnett and Lefevere 1990). Certainly, translation has had a complex history in colonial and postcolonial modes of knowledge production, governance, social stratification, and subject formation. In colonial India, translation was inherent in the very introduction of English during the British Raj (Niranjana 1992; see also Viswanathan 1998).

If translation was overdetermined in the colonial context, what are its modalities in postcolonial India? How does translation articulate with neoliberal governmentality, racial capitalism, and affective labor? In dialogue with A. Aneesh's (2015) analysis of cultural and accent neutralization and Kiran Mirchandani's (2012) examination of how race and gender undergird "authenticity work" in call centers, we attend to the relationship between mobility across cultural and experiential borders and the politics of translation. By translation, we refer not merely to linguistic processes (critical for voice processing) but also to other forms of communication that involve affect. The optic of translation allows us to glean moments of opacity and mistranslation that complicated our interlocutors' interactions with customers as they performed affective labor.

Linguistic translation is a "family of semiotic processes" that "purport to change the form, the social place, or the meaning of a text, object, person, or practice while simultaneously seeming to keep something about it the same" (Gal 2015, 226; see also Bassnett and Lefevere 1990). Translation involves inequalities of power and differences in institutional authority. Moving away from a common sense understanding of translation as a faithful reproduction of the original, we wish to foreground the linguistic, ontological, and social *productivity* of modes of translation (Gal 2015; Tymoczko 1990). Translation is a generative process that produces incommensurabilities, disjunctures, and power differentials that also extend to cultural and experiential interactions. Thus conceived, translation generates iterations that transform processes of signification to foreground the *irruptive* instability of meaning. Our interlocutors' efforts at translation—and the opacities and mistranslations that followed—were often incomplete, contingent on context, and refracted by unequal relations of power.

These translations occurred in contexts of what Asad (1986) has described as "the inequality of languages" to underscore how languages, cultures, and epistemologies are hierarchically positioned in the current global economy (Gupta and Ferguson 1992). In the world of BPOs, the inequality of languages is produced through the broader contexts of inequities among nations that, in turn, are part of older legacies of colonial histories of capitalist expansion. The racialization of language and labor, the hegemony of English as a pathway to social mobility, and its ascent as the language of global capitalism produce the inequality of languages that shape the mobility and emplacement of BPO agents. It was not always possible to hide the inequality of languages in the encounter between BPO agents and customers, and because agents' English and communication skills were so often a trigger for customer anger and complaints, BPOs adopted a technique called "accent neutralization" to paper over these difficulties (Aneesh 2015).

Accent Neutralization and the (Attempted) Elision of Place

According to BPO managers, trainers, and agents alike, the objective of accent neutralization (or, in the earlier years of the industry, teaching agents to adopt American, British, or Australian accents) was to smoothen the process of communication for customers: allegedly, accents got in the way of customer service. Accents were deemed to present serious blockages to the unimpeded communication of information and affect presumed to be at the heart of the production of value: not having the right accent—or having "too much" of an accent—could produce misunderstandings and, therefore, impediments to the performance of affective labor by agents.

The so-called breakdown in communication was, frequently, a euphemism for racial and cultural difference. Many prospective BPO agents who spoke English had to undergo remedial training—or accent neutralization, as it was euphemistically named—to eliminate regional and cultural particularities from their diction (Kachru 1965).[26] But such accent work could not eliminate customers' perceptions that BPO agents in Bengaluru were ignorant or incompetent because those perceptions were deeply shaped by national location, Orientalism, and agents' racial positions as service workers located in the Global South. Racist abuse, except in extreme cases when it caused debilitating distress to agents, was often glossed as a "communication problem." Trainers, team leaders, supervisors, and managers usually told agents that responding calmly to such abuse was a mark of their professionalism, often obscuring the centrality of race in how they were being treated. For example, one trainer told her students, "If customers say, 'I want to speak to an American,' it is not because they are racist, but because they cannot connect with you." Agents, too, were mostly unwilling to acknowledge that customer abuse could be racially motivated and, because their companies could not afford to alienate customers, agents were not permitted to confront their abusers. Neither agents nor their bosses confronted the racial bases of the abuse to which they were subjected, foregrounding how, in these contexts, discourses of professionalism reinforce and consolidate structures of racial capitalism on a transnational scale (see also Padios 2018).

The shift to neutral accents was a crucial strategic decision for many BPOs: a purportedly neutral accent was founded on the idea that customers would be unable to locate it and associate it with a specific place. Accent neutralization aimed at paring down linguistic (for instance, lexical stress, rate of speech, and intonation) and cultural particularities in the service of global communication (Aneesh 2015, 4). As one trainer who had previously taught agents foreign accents told us, the earlier strategy of accent training had been "costly" and "inefficient" because when companies had to cycle agents through processes with different countries, it was not easy for agents to transition from "Aussie" to "Yank" accents. As a result, many companies decided to prioritize teaching neutral accents to agents. This, in turn, entailed neutralizing their "regional" accents; hence, for example, agents working in an American process were instructed that the correct pronunciation of *schedule* is *skedule* rather than *shedule*, and *z* is pronounced as *zee* rather than *zed*, and so on.

A few years later, some companies started revisiting this issue of accent neutralization. One company reverted to teaching their agents an "American" accent when dealing with US processes because they found that customer satisfaction was much higher when agents mimicked the accent of their customers. The formula for success was to "match and mirror" how the customer was speaking. As a trainer explained to new recruits, "When the tempo is different between the customer and you, things go haywire: listen and match, match and mirror." And using an "American" accent was "the first thing you can do to match and mirror your customer." Customers from the United States felt more comfortable with agents who spoke English with an "American" accent. She claimed that when agents spoke in a neutral accent they "lost out on rapport." Customers needed someone who could talk to them in a language they understood, and that was "American" English. The trainer explained that, with a neutral accent, "the wow factor is missing," which is what separates a great agent from a good one. It was not just the new inductees who were expected to speak in an "American" accent, but this was true for all employees who interacted with clients, from managers down to agents.

TRANSLATION AND LINGUISTIC POLITICS
IN BENGALURU

Practices of linguistic and cultural translation occur in cultural and political contexts that are located *somewhere*: place matters. Linguistic and cultural translation are particularly fraught in a city like Bengaluru where issues of language and belonging loom large. Language politics were reflected in the renaming of the city from Bangalore to Bengaluru, and regional and linguistic pride have been central to the renaming of many of its streets.[27] Cultural and regional politics were exhibited by the complex and divergent reactions of Kannada speakers and other local residents to migrants from other parts of India. These tensions have been exacerbated by the increased inequalities accompanying the ascent of Bengaluru as an IT and ITES hub.

Yet, Bengaluru has always been a polyglot city. The writer U. R. Ananthamurthy puts it very well when he says, "We live in the midst of translating. At every moment of our life, we are translating from one [language] to the other without knowing that we are translating. That is the situation in multilingual spaces" (Ananthamurthy and Gowda 2019, 101). Janaki Nair (2005, 63) points out that "the composite culture of the old city was dominated by Kannada but accommodated other languages of the north as well as the south: Pushtu, Punjabi, Gujarati, Rajasthani, and Persian mingled with the sounds of Kannada, Telugu, and Tamil." In Bengaluru, cultural and linguistic translation have always gone hand in hand.[28] Yet, these translation practices have not always been harmonious and have occasionally become bitter and irreconcilable. When linguistic divisions have aligned with religious tensions, the situation has worsened. For instance, in hegemonic discourses of belonging, the Urdu language is associated with Muslims and Kannada with local Hindus. Going as far back as 1928, these tensions have become explosive during communal clashes between the two communities (Nair 2005, 63; Swamy 2020).

What are the sociohistorical forces that have shaped the linguistic politics of Bengaluru in which BPO agents' practices of translation were embedded? The linguistic politics that mediated pathways to physical and social mobility in the past continue to refract the inequality of languages in the contemporary era. In the colonial era, linguistic and cultural politics were overdetermined by the ascent of English as a language of administration and higher education, particularly with the emergence of Bangalore as a major educational center.[29] Well before the city became a destination for English-speaking IT and ITES professionals from all over the country, the hegemony of English was established and the city saw an influx of migrants from other parts of the country. During that time, popular movements arose to propagate the use of the Kannada language, with institutions like the Kannada Sahitya Parishad (founded in 1915) advocating for the preservation of Kannada, a precursor to the more recent movement to protect Kannada and make it visible on all public-facing signage in businesses and shops. Likewise, debates over the language of instruction in local schools became affectively charged against the dominance of English. By the 1940s, the rise of Kannada as a major literary language was exemplified in the emergence of the Kannada Modern in the literary sphere. Simultaneously, and not coincidentally, linguistic politics continued to refract the cultural politics of belonging, settlement, and mobility for both "locals" and migrants. By the mid-twentieth century, the very notion of local identities was up for contestation.

In the contemporary period, the relationship between language and a sense of belonging continues to be inextricable, exemplifying what Nair has termed "the right to the city" (2005, 237).[30] These tensions over language have persisted despite the reshaping of Bengaluru by technology companies and technically trained workers and despite what Nair calls "the triumphant march of computer languages such as Java and C++ through every neighborhood of Bangalore and some other parts of Karnataka" (237). Indeed, Kannada pride has become stronger because of the growth of the city as a center of the IT and ITES industries. Thus, the linguistic politics of the city are significant precisely because of its rise as a center of IT in India: uneven capitalist development has meant that working-class Kannadiga communities have felt left behind as middle and upwardly mobile lower-income locals and migrants with access to English education have secured jobs in IT and ITES industries. A person is defined as "local" if they *cannot* speak good English, and even those people who are from Bengaluru feel that something has shifted in their relationship with the place (Jayadeva 2018, 14).

As Sazana Jayadeva (2018) argues, people from adjacent states such as Tamil Nadu and Andhra Pradesh are also defined as "local" if they do not know English or speak it poorly, producing a sense of emplacement that contrasts with BPO agents who speak English and hence are seen as being "mobile." High in-migration has meant that even local people cannot get by speaking only Kannada because shop attendants, security guards, mall employees, and others are often from other states and do not understand Kannada (14). Thus, even those people who call Bengaluru home feel displaced in a city with high rates of geographic in-migration and class mobility (Gooptu 2013b). These are the affectively charged landscapes that have impinged on and shaped the inequality of languages undergirding the translation practices of BPO agents.

The inequality of languages in this node of transnational capitalism has its roots in a complex genealogy in which English has mutated from an imperial language to the language of global capital. English was central to the colonial administration's education policy of creating a class of "natives" who could assist in running India.[31] In colonial and postcolonial India, the hegemony of English and the expansion of capitalism have aligned. After Indian independence, inequalities between languages within India were reconfigured by the linguistic reorganization of states when political boundaries were drawn on the basis of language. The inequality between English and Kannada was accentuated by the dominance of English in the worlds of science, education, commerce, and, by the close of the twentieth century, IT. The influx of "outsiders" and the resulting mixing of cultures, while glossed by many middle and upper classes as cosmopolitanism, have been experienced as particularly threatening by lower-income Kannadigas.

Caste and religious disenfranchisement and marginalization have played a central part in the linguistic politics of the city. Some Dalit activists have had a tense relationship with the Kannada language movement because of its pro-Hindutva proclivities. These tensions erupted when Dalit activists fought back against dominant caste efforts to stop the unveiling of the statue of a prominent Dalit leader, Thiruvalluvar, in Bengaluru in 1991 (Nair 2005, 268).[32] The dominance of English in the New Economy promised by IT and ITES industries and its role in exacerbating social inequality was commented on by several Kannadiga intellectuals, and it is significant that caste (as a marker, symptom, and trope) is foregrounded in some of these conversations about the place of English. For instance, in a keynote speech to the sixty-ninth Kannada Sahitya Sammelan, Ananthamurthy observed: "If caste was the most unequal division of our society in the past, today it is the possession of English that produces inequalities" (in Nair 2005, 266). In an essay tellingly titled "The Caste of English" (1978), noted writer Raja Rao described English "not as a guest or friend, but as one of our own, of our caste, our creed, our sect and of our tradition" (in Kachru 1996, 143). A similar observation was made by writer and educator Vanamala Viswanatha, who said, "There is a new caste system that divides people—either you have English or you don't" (in Jayadeva 2018, 2). Each of these statements foregrounds the entanglement of caste hierarchies with access to the English language.

The position of English as a lingua franca of corporate culture in postcolonial India has been strengthened with the (re)entry of multinational capital after the liberalization of the economy in 1991. Yet, historically, English, or rather World Englishes, were pluricentric: the center of English shifted from England to other parts of the world during colonial rule when English was "nativized" and "acculturated" in different places (Kachru 1996, 138; cf. Hsu

2015). After Indian independence, English became recognized in the Indian Constitution as an "associate" official language of the nation. The growth of BPOs in India, and especially of call centers, was made possible by the presence of a large English-speaking workforce. In postcolonial India, English has continued to bear an "imperial burden" (Aneesh 2015, 6).

At the same time, Bengaluru has witnessed a relative democratization of English education, with a majority of students in the city now attending English-medium schools (Jayadeva 2018, 4, 15). Furthermore, Indians have made English our own through the regional and local inflections we have brought to it. For BPO agents, as for many other upwardly mobile classes, English is a language of aspiration, closely bound with visions of modernity and progress, because it promised that they would develop the capacity to participate in the global economy. Learning English, therefore, is associated with becoming global, modern, and professional (Jayadeva 2018, 20). It is a language that bestows status and enables multiple forms of mobility. Above all, the ability to speak English is inextricably implicated with the production of futurity in terms of living and working in a globalized world.

However, while the status of English as an Indian language cannot be denied, within the world of BPOs only a certain kind of English was valorized: Global English. Translation practices in BPOs depended on the following characteristics of Global English. For one, this is an English that is intentionally fashioned (not always successfully) as placeless so as to, ostensibly, facilitate unimpeded communication between agents and their customers in the Global North. Global English, therefore, is distinct from World Englishes because of its assumptions about the singularity and transparency of the English language (cf. Friginal 2007). Additionally, because it claims to transcend its imbrication with race and national location, Global English is complicit with a postracial discourse on language. In affective capitalism, and particularly in BPOs, the dominance of Global English as a language of exchange consolidates "a neoliberal narrative of the global economy as a marketplace in which capital and communication flow smoothly owing to English's putative ability to function as a linguistic currency with no particular national origin" (Padios 2018, 91).

The inequality of languages occurred on multiple registers in the BPOs where we conducted our fieldwork. First, it existed between BPO owners and managers at the upper echelons of companies who tended to be from upper- and middle-class backgrounds, and new and potential recruits, who were mostly lower and lower middle class. Additionally, as Mirchandani (2012) points out, "In Indian call centers, language serves as a stratification device through which class, as well as regional hierarchies, are enacted" (11). Given India's colonial and postcolonial histories, the use of English is inextricably related to inequities of race, class, region, and caste, such that fluency becomes a signifier of privilege and status (see also Aneesh 2015; Nadeem 2011; Jayadeva 2018). Recruits and employees from relatively privileged socioeconomic backgrounds and with previous access to English language education at the primary and secondary level were at an advantage as compared to applicants from poorer families or from rural and semirural areas where English language education was weak or unavailable. In Bengaluru, multiple hierarchically positioned Englishes coexisted (Jayadeva 2018, 6–7). Global English valorized the English spoken in the West or by Indian elites who had been to upper-class schools while denigrating Indian renditions as inaccurate and inferior (see also Mirchandani 2012, 39). A clear hierarchy was thus established between these different forms of English.

By the time we commenced extended fieldwork in 2009, Global English with a neutral accent was the new normal and it remained the dominant mode of training in the industry. As we discovered through our participation-observation in hundreds of recruitment interviews, finding workers who were fluent in English was not easy: despite the fact that many job candidates attended special classes that claimed to train them in "call center English," an overwhelming majority of the applicants could barely converse in English (Lockwood 2012). Second, even those who spoke English did so with such strong regional accents as to be incomprehensible to not just overseas customers but also to those living in other parts of India. Prospective employees found "Indianisms" (Indian expressions in English) hard to shed, but the biggest challenge faced by recruiters and trainers was the persistence of regional accents, or what in the industry is termed Mother Tongue Influence or MTI. The most difficult task for trainers was to teach new recruits to shed their MTI and speak with a neutral accent, by which they largely meant an English that was shorn of any influence of regional languages, dialects, or lexical stresses, and was hence deemed placeless because it was not identifiable with a particular location (see also Aneesh 2015; Jayadeva 2018; Kachru 1965; Mirchandani 2012).

In the world of BPOs, then, a hegemonic version of Global English became the language of futurity. It was considered indispensable to participating in the global economy while versions of English shaped, for instance, by regional accents or MTI were disqualified. Learning Global English, therefore, signified the acquisition of cultural capital and a means to upward mobility.[33] In these contexts, communication involved processes of interpretation and translation that were fundamentally contingent as they occurred across contexts of inequality and power. Clearly, just as linguistic translation is never a uniform transfer, the technological production of unimpeded connectivity in semiocapitalism is also a myth.

Failed or missed translation sometimes provided a context for critique and commentary from our interlocutors. One day, we were talking to a manager of a BPO who was telling us that his company had now largely moved from voice processes to chat. He said that this shift had made it much easier for him to hire agents because there were many people with good English writing skills who would never make it in a voice process because of MTI. He claimed that a big advantage of chat was that it was easier for his agents to communicate with customers in North America because one could read what they had typed. "Even with their bad spelling and poor punctuation," he said, "it is much better than voice processes." Shaking his head ruefully, he lamented, "Otherwise, it was impossible for us to understand them. You just cannot understand what they are saying."

It took a moment for us to grasp what he meant before we realized the degree to which we too had interpreted the problem of mistranslation only from the standpoint of the customer and not taken into consideration the perspective of the agent. We had not realized that the problems that customers had with the "poor English" of BPO agents were mirrored in the problems that agents had with the "poor English" of customers. On further investigation, the problem that he was describing became clearer. The agents were taught American English in a midwestern accent or the "California accent" standardized by news channels. But when they spoke to customers all over the United States, they encountered a variety of regional accents, from a Boston accent to accents from the Deep South, as well as the multiplicity of accents represented by America's large immigrant population. The agents struggled to understand these varied accents, and when they moved to chat, were happy to be relieved of the responsibility of attempting to understand this tremendous linguistic variation. What is important in this mirroring of misunderstanding and missed translations is how much greater importance was given to the complaint from customers than to the dissatisfaction voiced by agents. This is one instance where the structural inequalities of the paying customer in the Global North and the service provider in the Global South—the inequality of languages—were starkly evident.

Linguistic border crossings are inextricable from cultural and experiential ones. We now focus on the cultural and experiential translations required for the performance of affective labor that, in turn, had powerful consequences for the mobility and emplacement of BPO agents. Most of our interlocutors had to reconstitute their identities in ways that went beyond simply assuming new names, accents, or personas. Still, some cultural "habits" proved difficult to shed, thus contradicting assumptions about the erasure of agents' identities (Shome 2006).

In the recruitment sessions that we attended, concerns about hiring workers who were "trainable" dominated all discussions of the criteria for selecting agents. The most important questions recruiters asked themselves related to the ability of potential agents to connect affectively, as much as linguistically, with overseas customers. Apart from worrying about the effects of MTI on their speech and whether or not they would be able to adopt a neutral accent, their primary concerns were whether the recruit could be trained to be attuned to the needs of customers from a different culture and to respond appropriately in their interactions with them, and whether the young person could be taught to communicate with a customer who lived in a world at great remove from them. During a training session, a trainer explained one of the main reasons why customers were unable to "connect" with agents: The customer's "culture was completely different from mine. If he was Indian, it would be easy to service [him]." Agents' affective labor was hence predicated on their ability to traverse experiential and cultural borders.

Cultural translation is indispensable to the global service industry, and nowhere is this truer than when service has to be performed virtually and at a distance. Culture and cultural difference and, therefore, practices of cultural translation acquire a particular salience in processes of racialization in different parts of the world. Thus, for instance, in the Philippines, Filipino American "relatability" is "part of the structure of feeling surrounding the United States in the Philippine postcolonial imaginary and thus part of the material conditions of possibility of the present" (Padios 2018, 11). In the case of the Philippines, race and racialization are embedded in narratives of empire and nation that uphold "the exceptionalist narrative of mutual and reciprocal U.S.-Philippine relations" (11). Here again, linguistic and cultural translations go hand in hand: histories of empire and postcoloniality shape the ways in which Filipinos are assumed to be better at relating to customers in the United States than are Indians who are deemed to be *too* culturally and racially different. This was one of the reasons given to us by Indian BPO owners for opening branches of their company in the Philippines. The bigger cultural gap that purportedly separates Indian BPO agents from their customers is one reason why they are expected to work harder at cultural translation than their Filipino counterparts in communicating with their customers, making a sale, soliciting information, or solving their problems.

Thus, it was not simply the accents of BPO agents that had to be neutralized: processes of cultural neutralization were also central to their performance of affective labor. Trainers did their best to provide "cultural training" to new recruits. One trainer told the new recruits, "Try to watch serials like *Friends*. I adore it. It helps improve language, but also to understand [American] culture. . . . Stop watching saas-bahu serials [Indian serials]. Try and watch English movies. . . . But please do not pick up profanities." We found that this advice was repeated consistently across organizations. Trainers invariably instructed agents to watch Hollywood films and, depending on the country in which the process was located, television shows like *Neighbours* or *Keeping up Appearances* (see also Poster 2007, 272). They were encouraged to watch these shows in their "spare" time, which, trainers conceded to us, was unrealistic both because the young recruits did not have much time to spare and also because they were much more inclined to watch films and television shows in their own languages. A trainer at the smallest of the BPOs where we did our research told us that agents had a lot of trouble understanding British accents. However, she said, "It is not of much use asking them [agents] to see British films. All they are interested in is regional films—they would never see an English film even if we asked them to do so."

Another trainer instructed agents working in an Australian process to use the phrase "no worries" when customers thanked them rather than the more formal "you're welcome." This, she claimed, was because "Australians are very laid back and easy-going, they don't want the person who is thanking them to feel like they're imposing on them. So they say, 'No worries.'" She added that agents working in processes set in the United Kingdom were instructed to be much more formal in their interactions with customers: "It is appropriate to address customers as 'Sir' and 'Madam' when you're speaking to people in the UK because they are much more polite and much more formal there. If you say 'Sir' and 'Madam' to Aussies or to Americans, they will think we are overacting." Another trainer working with agents who were being groomed for an American process was encouraging them to step beyond their cultural upbringing by explaining that a "lot of things we like to do is because of our history; for example, we like to be subservient." Colonial history was thus being invoked only as an impediment to effective customer service because Americans liked to be spoken to as equals rather than as superiors.

BPO agents' performance of affective labor was contingent on the extent to which they could acquire "cultural competence." Importantly, these forms of cultural competence also consisted of acquiring embodied forms of knowledge ranging from how to comport oneself, how to move one's lips to produce certain intonations and accents, and what to do in one's leisure time. English training centers also emphasized that learning English involved acquiring "English" cultural style and therefore offered courses on soft skills, social English, and body language in addition to training in grammar and speaking (Jayadeva 2018, 23). From the awkward steps taken by new recruits to shed their MTI to the gradual and painstaking acquisition of fluency in idiomatic (Australian, Canadian, British, or American) English, over our seven years of fieldwork we witnessed the transformative nature of our interlocutors' efforts to reconstitute their speech patterns. In tandem with these efforts, they would learn how to coax recalcitrant (and sometimes hostile) customers in culturally appropriate ways and familiarize themselves with modes of making small talk about sports such as baseball or rugby that they had never played.

In order to effectively serve customers, BPO agents had to imaginatively travel to a different world to be able to relate to them, perform customer service, answer their questions, and, sometimes, serve as their informal therapists or confidantes. They had to engage in cultural border crossing and, additionally, engage in experiential border crossing. Not all agents were successful in performing these experiential journeys or migrations: in these instances, interactions between them and their customers were mediated by moments of opacity, mistranslation, or incomprehensibility. It was not simply language, accents, dialects, and turns of phrase that were rendered unequal. Given that our interlocutors' affective labor was directed to satisfying customers located in the United Kingdom, the United States, Canada, or Australia, it was experiences and modes of being in the world that were placed in hierarchical relations with one another.[34] The onus of doing the work of cultural and experiential translation was placed primarily on BPO agents. Although trainers attempted to explain unfamiliar phrases that agents might hear, or to identify what words or phrases that they commonly used that were likely to be misunderstood, such training was woefully inadequate to the range of encounters that agents experienced. For example, they were told never to use "cheap" to describe the company's products but rather to call them "cost-effective" or "inexpensive," and not to ask customers at the end of a call, "Do you have any doubts?" but rather "Do you have any questions?" Any ensuing mistranslations, missed translations, or partial translations were deemed markers of their failure, with material consequences that could include being passed up for promotion, demoted, or fired.

Our interlocutors came from diverse backgrounds. Some had spent most of their lives in villages and small towns and were living in a metropolis for the first time; even those who were from big cities had spent most of their lives in poor neighborhoods; many had grown up poor or on the cusp of poverty. Yet, they were expected to create an empathetic connection with their clients in the Global North. Mankekar once "barged calls" alongside Raghu, who had grown up in a semirural periphery of Bengaluru. During that call Raghu spoke in an Australian accent to a client about the weather in Sydney, made small talk with him about the last "footy" match, and then proceeded to try to sell him a cruise to the Caribbean. Mankekar never learned if he was successful in selling him the cruise but, sitting by him, she marveled at his ability to cross cultural and experiential boundaries in his interaction with this client.

However, some of our other interlocutors found themselves in situations where they could not connect with their clients: no amount of language or "cultural training" could help because their lifeworlds were so different. Pragmatic failure implies the inability to understand "what is meant by what is said" (Thomas 1984, in Aneesh 2015, 49). The likelihood of pragmatic failure, which involves one's social experiences and system of beliefs as much as one's knowledge of the language, became a major obstacle to our interlocutors' ability to move across cultural and experiential chasms.

One process involved agents remotely taking control of their customers' computers to fix problems. In one such instance, after requesting a customer's permission to do so, a young male agent took control of her computer. Unbeknownst to her, he also turned on her computer's camera and was thus able to see her and her home. She was happy that he managed to fix the problem and nothing more might have come of it. However, when she called back a few months later, she got the same agent. Once again, he surreptitiously turned on her computer's camera while he was helping her, and could not stop himself from observing, "Madam, you seem to have put on some weight." He did not intend that to be an offensive comment but lacked the cultural competence to anticipate how it would be interpreted. Additionally, having unwittingly revealed that he had done something that he was strictly forbidden from doing (use people's cameras to peer into their living spaces), the agent then had to face disciplinary action because the customer complained to the company about this infringement on her privacy.

Experiential and cultural mistranslation and opacity were most common in processes involving debt collection. Agents working in these processes were instructed on the legal aspects of debt collection. However, despite the growing popularity of credit cards among the Indian middle classes, the persistence of cultural taboos surrounding going into debt resulted in several obstacles to connecting with customers (see also Aneesh 2015, 43).[35] Some of our interlocutors would therefore be incredulous when they came across customers who went into debt over what they believed were frivolous expenses. Vandana was a young woman who had been working as a BPO agent for close to five years. She was never promoted to supervisor because, in her words, she had "blown it" with one of her customers when she had first started working. One night, as she chatted with Mankekar in the company café, she narrated how she had been removed from a prestigious debt-collection process with a multinational credit card company because she could not bring herself to be tactful or empathetic with a customer, a middle-aged woman who lived in the United Kingdom. This had happened at a time when BPOs had started emphasizing Customer Satisfaction Scores (CSAT) as a metric rather than the number of calls agents handled during their shifts. What was at stake, then, was the agents' ability to empathetically connect with clients and gently nudge them to pay their debts. Although agents had to ensure that they followed a protocol, going off script was not discouraged if it allowed the agent to meet her goals. Vandana had made several calls to this customer coaxing her to pay her debt but to no avail. This was a woman who, after her retirement, had made a hobby of going on cruises several times a year. The only problem was that she put her expenses for the cruises on her credit card and quickly amassed huge debts that she was unable to pay off, and it fell to Vandana to recover them.

Vandana called her several times and finally lost her patience: this was a huge faux pas for a customer service agent, but it was incomprehensible to Vandana that her customer could build up debts in order to go on cruises. Vandana had seen her father take out a loan with tremendous trepidation when her brother had needed an operation. She had also heard of relatives who, in sheer desperation, had taken loans when their crops failed. But to amass such huge debts to go on cruises was something she could never understand. This was a world that made no sense to her. Enraged by Vandana's impatience, her customer complained to the credit card company, which in turn threatened to withdraw the contract from the BPO. Vandana shook her head with mortification as she recounted to Mankekar what had happened.

Despite the resources that had been invested in training agents, what happened with Vandana and other agents who "failed" at cultural translation highlights how mistranslations, misunderstandings, partial translations, and moments of opacity may impede communication, the performance of affective labor, and the extraction of value in semiocapitalism. As the acronym ITES underscores, information technology is assumed to enable the provision of services across vast physical, social, and cultural distances and render movement across these boundaries seamless. The success of these firms is predicated on the premise that workers in the Global South can be trained to engage in these forms of boundary crossing: the presumption is that IT can help them do precisely that. Certainly, our interlocutors' worlds were marked by dense connectivity as they spent hours speaking with customers in a different place and time; their labor and very livelihoods depended on their ability to make a connection, sometimes an intimate one, with strangers whom they would never meet (see chapter 3). Yet, Vandana was not alone in experiencing these moments of missed translation and mistranslation: many other agents also faced situations where they were unable to do the work expected of them because they could not "relate" to their clients. In all of these instances, they were unable to bridge the cultural and experiential distances that separated them from their customers. The imaginative mobility so necessary for their work was curtailed, resulting in their sense of being put in their place and feeling stuck. In this manner, alongside the limits and constraints placed on their physical and social mobility, cultural and experiential boundary crossings were sometimes stymied by moments of opacity, mistranslations, and missed translations.

How might these mistranslations, missed translations, and moments of opacity enable us to retheorize affective capitalism, and what do they tell us about the generation of futurities? After all, BPOs are part of an industry where the extraction of value depends on the myth of uninterrupted communication promised by information technology. The primary "tool" for the production of value in this industry is communication, which, in affective economies that are contingent on the circulation of information but to the circulation of affect. Communication is the glue that holds together the labor process as well as the extraction of value: when communication fails, these processes can come unstuck.

When I think of my body and ask what it does to earn that name, two things stand out. It moves. It feels. In fact, it does both at the same time. It moves as it feels, and it feels itself moving. Can we think of a body without this: an intrinsic connection between movement and sensation whereby each immediately summons the other?

Brian Massumi, *Parables for the Virtual* (2002)

The opening pages of Brian Massumi's *Parables for the Virtual* (2002) foreground the intrinsic relationship between corporeality and movement in terms of its implications for social theory. Massumi pushes us to see movement as fundamental to affect: the unqualified, unnameable field of intensities suffusing our abilities to affect and be affected. He advocates that we "add movement back" into our conceptual frameworks for understanding social transformation (3). The mobility of the bodies of BPO agents—their ability to move through physical, virtual, and social space—is fundamental to the affective labor they perform: the sensations of movement are proprioceptive and synesthetic, blurring the boundaries between cognition, feeling, and corporeality. At the same time, their ability to inhabit and navigate the world and connect with other bodies is also shaped by their emplacement in these very spaces. Emplacement could enable them to feel grounded and rooted, providing them with a map that potentially prevented them from losing their way. But emplacement could also mean stasis and stagnation, which could make one lose sight of one's future or not be able to *move ahead*. Movement, therefore, is existential; it shapes the formation of complex subjects. Movement is about the ability to be, about becoming, and about futurity.

While keeping in play movement's literality, we have expanded it to recenter the socius by engaging mobility in terms of spatiality and temporality for their implications for futurity. Rather than placing the emphasis of class and social mobility solely on where people "ended up" or where they might end up, we are concerned with their sense of the journey on which they embarked. Hage (2009) argues that the "language of movement is not simply metaphoric but conveys a sense in which when a person feels well, they actually imagine and feel that they are moving well" (1–2). The pleasure and promise of the type of mobility provided by working in a BPO lie in the process of movement, not necessarily at the moment of arrival into an entirely new consciousness or status. This is why agents emphasized "learnings" rather than "achievements" in their conversations with us about where they preferred to work.

As we have argued throughout, mobility, immobility, and emplacement involve not just spatiality but equally temporality. These regimes of temporality are neither universal nor transcendental. Rather than dismissing the phenomenological dimension of time, we are concerned with how agents' experiences of temporality are themselves generated by specific regimes of affective labor. We are particularly interested in how subjects are produced when time becomes unhinged. Here, we are conjuring both Jacques Derrida's ([1993] 2006) discussion of the nonlinear and antiteleological temporality of capital, and Gilles Deleuze's ([1968] 1995) understanding of the disjunctive synthesis of time. For both Derrida and Deleuze, time becomes out of joint because it breaks regularity and order; it produces aporias; it generates the uncanny. This sense of temporality, a condition of our lives under capitalism, nevertheless opens up the subject to untimely forms of becoming and, therefore, to futurity.

For agents in Bengaluru's BPOs, time was out of joint in multiple ways. At its most obvious, they had to work when their overseas clients were awake: given the time difference between India and most of these countries, they went to work when the rest of the city was asleep. As we elaborate later in this book, many workers complained that the demands of working at night had drastic consequences for their health and their social lives; their spatial mobility entailed temporal disjunction. Moreover, phenomenological experiences of temporal disjunction were themselves shaped by the durée or duration of labor: this encapsulated but also extended beyond time as experienced by the body to encapsulate how time enfolded upon itself to produce certain kinds of subjects (Bergson [1889] 2001).[36] Our interlocutors made lives and worlds for themselves in a city that was called the IT hub of the nation. This was also a city where the daily rhythms of life were refracted by temple rituals that overflowed into streets to disrupt traffic, calls to prayer from neighborhood mosques, and the raucous and joyful abandon of street festivals. This was a world of multiple temporalities that collided loudly, sometimes destructively, at other times in unpredictable ways, to create a sense of time that was so fragmented as to seem unhinged.

Contrary to voluntaristic conceptions of mobility, the movement of peoples often occurs in contexts of coercion or violence, in conditions not of their choosing, as in indenture and slavery and in the aftermath of pogroms and massacres. Sedentary state systems were built on the regulation and prohibition of the movement of people, whether it was through trade routes or migration (Scott 1999). In the modern, nation-state-based global order, the movement of people is regulated through immigration policy, checkpoints, and border controls, among other regimes (Tilly 1975). As we have seen, the world of BPO agents entails multiple forms of border crossing, some of which are unsuccessful. For our interlocutors, staying put was a source of vulnerability and, very often, claustrophobia; for many, it led to an intense sense of being stuck. Their affective labor produced, and conversely, was generated by, new modalities of racialization: they were racialized in distinct ways when—and precisely because—they remained in India.

The mobility and emplacement of BPO agents are formed in contexts where the inequality of languages was reinforced and supplemented by cultural and experiential hierarchies. These linguistic, cultural, and experiential inequalities and hierarchies refracted processes of translation even as they created moments of opacity and mistranslation. Susan Gal points to the dangers of reifying differences between languages by overemphasizing incommensurability.[37] Certainly, as anthropologists have long pointed out, neither languages nor cultures are bounded systems but are, in fact, produced through encounters across difference. These encounters do not lead to unimpeded connectivity because they frequently occur in contexts shaped by unequal power relations. As our research with BPO agents taught us, connectivity depends not simply on linguistic translation but also on cultural translation and the translation of experiences. The mistranslations, partial translations, and opacities in the world of BPOs are generative articulations of meaning rather than examples of "failure."

Theorists of semiocapital who adhere to a linear teleology of capitalism assume that it follows earlier formations (or, in the case of locations in the Global South, leapfrog over them). For instance, Berardi (2009, 62) argues that this paradigmatic shift to semiocapital "gets tangled in the *slow time of culture*, social habits, constituted identities, power relations, and the dominant economic order" (emphasis added). In contrast, rather than assume that semiocapital and cultural habits and patterns exist in relations of exteriority to one another, or presume that semiocapital sweeps everything it encounters in its sway, we have pointed to how the spatiotemporalities of location and place both generate affective capitalism and place it under pressure. The threat of sexual and racial violence against women perceived as racially Other constrains the mobility of some workers in Bengaluru, and linguistic and cultural translation are shaped in a sociohistorical conjuncture marked by colonial and postcolonial genealogies of language and cultural politics. The expansive promise of the city is countered by the claustrophobia of living spaces, neighborhoods, and workplaces inhabited by BPO agents even as they engage in imaginative travel to places they will never get to see. Young people who yearn for "progress" for not just themselves but also their kin must brace against burnout and exhaustion as they acquire upward class mobility. Vertiginous speed and stagnation exist side by side, as BPO agents attempt to move across physical, social, and experiential distance to engage in affective labor.

In an early work, Kaplan (2002) posited that the myth of unfettered travel and mobility is one of the structuring fantasies of (Western) modernity. The outsourcing of labor to the Global South in the past few decades has compelled us to rethink labor migration by foregrounding the connectivities possible even when physical mobility is foreclosed by restrictions on immigration and racist and xenophobic labor policies. And when physical mobility is curtailed, the inability to move is itself productive of the formation of laboring subjects. Gendered and racialized formations of spatiality and temporality reconstituted agents' abilities to be mobile and navigate the worlds in which they found themselves. These are worlds that are suffused with opportunities as well as failures such that potentiality and vulnerability are inseparable.

Potentiality is also about the capacity to imagine and to exercise imaginative mobility. Potentiality inhered in the capacity of BPO agents to move across—and navigate—a world that was as enticing as it was anxiety-producing. The world of BPOs was contingent on the speed of the transmission of labor and of information; at the same time, race, gender, caste, national location and the inequalities of languages fixed agents' bodies in place. Their ability to be mobile was fundamental to BPO agents' sense of the potentiality of the future, just as feeling stuck brought a sense of foreclosure. BPO agents' anticipation of the future—at once hopeful and anxious—acted recursively on their experiences in the present. These tense futurities represented the horizon of possibility generated by the present.

2.

SHOPPING MALLS AS INFRASTRUCTURES OF ASPIRATION

Learning to Labor in Spaces of Leisure

If potentiality is about the capacity to navigate new worlds, Bengaluru's shopping malls were pedagogical spaces in which BPO agents acquired kinesthetic and imaginative modes of becoming and emergence. As part of larger infrastructures of aspiration, malls were important nodes in the production of affective capitalism that unleashed our interlocutors' imagination and also channeled it; they functioned as particular kinds of chronotopes where the spatiotemporality of bodies was reconstituted; they underscored potentiality but also regulated it.

As hypermediated spaces, malls are central to constructions of futurity: they foreground the biomediatization of BPO agents who, as they browsed through malls, aspired to global cosmopolitanism in ways that were frequently misaligned with the material conditions in which they lived. Malls are integral to the sensory ecologies that have proliferated in urban India since the early 1990s when the "opening up" of Indian markets to commodities from all over the world converged symbiotically with the proliferation of transnational media (Brosius 2010; Mankekar 2004; Rai 2009). These aspirations, and their misalignments, have powerful consequences for how we may theorize futurity.

Retail trade has traditionally been a vital sector of the Indian economy, second only to agriculture in providing employment (Gooptu 2009, 47). In big and mid-sized cities, smaller markets and independent shops are being

supplemented by shopping malls. The malls of Bengaluru are no exception, with their chain stores of national and international brands, fast food
restaurants, and, in some cases, high-end stores. We analyze our interlocutors' phenomenological experiences but also move beyond them to theorize
the affective regimes and futurities engendered by malls.

Agents' aspirations to upward mobility were fueled by the commodity
affect saturating malls and underscored the intimate relationship between
aspiration, self-fashioning, and emergent futurities: these aspirations were
refracted by their varying positions along axes of class, caste, and gender
(Mankekar 2015). Indian and international media have tended to exagger-
ate and sensationalize how BPO agents, because of their increased earning
capacity, have embraced the new consumer culture sweeping through India.[1]
However, we learned through our fieldwork that shopping malls represented
more than opportunities for our BPO agents to shop: they materialized and
concentrated regimes of affect, pleasure, and sensuous knowledges (cf.
Haug 1986; Rai 2009).[2] We are concerned therefore with the extraeconomic
consequences of the shopping mall that extend beyond agents' purchasing
habits.[3] Even when BPO agents did not purchase the tantalizing commodities displayed and sold there, malls were places where they browsed through
commodity spaces, socialized with each other, and were socialized as particular kinds of subjects (Gooptu 2009; Haug 1986; Mankekar 2003, 2015).[4]

It is tempting to see malls as an especially good site for demonstrating
that "the entire society now functions as a moment of production" (Tronti
1973, 105). The reproduction of labor has been a major problem for capitalism, epitomized by Fordist concerns about order, hygiene, temperance, and
discipline within the family in workers' colonies or industrial townships.[5]
Keynesianism and the welfare state generalized this concern over the whole
of the social order and led to the development of the "social worker" (Negri
1989, 75–88). The autonomists argue that the reproduction of the worker
in advanced capitalist societies now occurs within an unbounded sphere
of social life (Negri 1988). Working in a Global South context where such
sweeping generalizations about the welfare state are untenable, we instead
interpret the role of malls as *pedagogical* sites for the reproduction of labor
power. In so doing, we place the philosophical insight proposed by Louis
Althusser ([1970] 2006) in his essay on ideological state apparatuses (ISAs)
in the more sociologically and historically embedded theorization of autonomists like Mario Tronti and Antonio Negri, but also limit the scope
and ambition of their claims. We focus on affect rather than ideology as a
means to think about the process in which spaces like malls reproduce the

"good worker" who can perform the labor needed in a globally intercon-nected industry.

Malls reconstitute the aspirations of BPO agents in ways that foreground the complexity of their subject formation. Like the special economic zones (SEZs) analyzed by Jamie Cross (2015), which condense "diverse ways of knowing about, imagining, and living toward the future," malls as infrastruc-tures of aspiration have an affective salience that cannot be captured through economic logics alone (425).[6] Cross argues that the political, cultural, and affective significance of SEZs may be best understood in terms of an econ-omy of anticipation: he asserts that "it is in the economy of anticipation, as different orientations to the future become entangled, that relationships of power, consent, and struggle take shape" (435). In centering aspiration, futures, and futurity, we build on his analysis but also diverge from it.

Aspiration refers to an orientation to the future and incorporates both individual and collective horizons (Appadurai 2013, 179). Aspirations at once entail anticipation and action, desire and calculation: they foreground ways of imagining and *moving toward* those horizons through striving to accom-plish specific goals and endpoints. "Always formed in interaction and in the thick of social life" (187), aspirations also gesture toward the more nebu-lous yet powerful formation of futurities as modes of potentiality: futurities may not have a fixed end point but are nevertheless productive of agency and subjectivity. Aspirations are thus directly linked with but irreducible to futurities, which we have earlier defined as an ontological formation, a form of navigating and being in worlds that were daunting and unfamiliar for many BPO agents.

Malls generate the *capacity* to aspire (Appadurai 2013). They are cru-cibles that educate, inform, shape, and help produce those aspirations for BPO agents. They inculcate certain affective states and dispositions in people who frequent them but also habituate those people to inhabit these disposi-tions. In this sense, malls share with other infrastructures three interrelated properties. Infrastructures are concrete metaphors that serve as a physical presence in the landscape that channel communication, travel, and the transportation of goods; they are biopolitical projects that aim to address the health and welfare of the population while also facilitating discipline and control; they are also aspirational projects that function as the symbols and indices of a future becoming (Harvey and Knox 2015). While we stress the last aspect most strongly, we also address some other infrastructural functions performed by malls.

The relationship between malls and futurity needs to be situated in the larger political context that followed the liberalization of the Indian economy.[7] The "opening up" of markets in the 1980s and the influx of transnational television in the early 1990s resulted in the acceleration of consumption.[8] Although consumption did not increase as sharply as predicted by a 2007 study by the McKinsey Global Institute, it nearly doubled between 2007 and 2018.[9] Certainly, the proliferation of malls in large (and mid-sized) cities are playing their part in making this prediction come true. In postliberalization India, economic policies, ranging from the building of SEZs and the active encouragement of foreign direct investment to financial deregulation, have had a direct impact on the affective landscapes of Indian cities (H. Gupta and Medappa 2020; Goldman 2011a, 2011b; Menon 2021). Shopping malls are thus yet another example of the inextricability of political economy from affective regimes.[10] Furthermore, Bengaluru's malls demonstrate that these affective landscapes are not simply the context or the background against which BPO agents live their lives but are actants that directly shape their desires, subjectivities, and anxieties; they mold the kinds of futures to which they individually and collectively aspire. Malls display the mutual imbrication of aspiration, commodity affect, and spatiotemporality, with material consequences for the future of futurity for heterogeneous subjects.

In India, consumption data has sometimes been used to identify and measure the middle classes (Sridharan 2004, 410). Consumption practices are also deemed a mark of distinction that sets upwardly mobile groups apart from working classes (for example, Brosius 2010; cf. Bourdieu 1984; Rathore and Kundu 2016).[11] Against interpretations that stress the consumption habits of an emerging middle class in India (for example, Brosius 2010; Fernandes 2004, 2006; Fernandes and Heller 2006), we argue that it is not consumption per se but aspiration that is the most important marker of interpellation into global capitalist markets and commodity chains.[12] Aspiration is particularly salient for workers whose primary occupation is affective labor and, more broadly, for knowledge workers making the transition to the middle class: what marks their transition is the change in their aspirational horizons. Malls are an important pedagogical site that facilitates this change.[13]

During our fieldwork, we were confronted on the one hand by the ebullient excitement of BPO agents who felt that they were entering a future filled with opportunity, and on the other hand by the rampant unemployment and underemployment of other young people. Our interlocutors' excitement was hence often refracted with anxiety about their future. What if their bodies got too tired to continue to perform such grueling affective labor? What if they were unable to meet their quotas at work? What if they lost their jobs or if the BPO in which they were working folded up? After all, this was also an era marked by jobless growth, resulting in a rapid increase in income and wealth inequality. And yet, paradoxically, the rapid growth in income for those at the top of the pyramid had also opened new avenues for aspiration for those who were rising up the class hierarchy—for instance, BPO agents. The shops opened up by global retail chains in malls in anticipation of rapid growth in business became sites where the capacity to aspire was cultivated.

In addition to the expansion of the middle classes, this historical conjuncture was shaped by the spectacular intensification of caste violence, the widening of the gap between the rich and the poor, systemic and systematic violence against religious minorities, particularly Muslims, and the increasing incidence of (reported) sexual assaults against women. Malls functioned as infrastructures of aspiration against this context of suppression, brutalization, violence, inequality, and precarity on the one hand, and hope, longing, and struggles for upward class mobility on the other. As we will demonstrate below, malls organize and bring together, in material and controlled ways, a swirling of pleasures and desires, even as they produce anxieties, insecurities, and opportunities for the unpredictable and for that which exceeds regulation (Rai 2009).

"OUR CITY HAS A DATE WITH THE FUTURE"

"Our city has a date with the future": this statement, from the Bangalore Agenda Task Force (BATF) set up in 1999, aspired to make Bengaluru a "world-class city" by 2004 or 2005 (Nair 2005, 77).[14] The promised date with the future highlights how in the vision of a world-class city, shopping malls, together with the IT and ITES industry, index individual and collective aspirations as well as visions of futurity. Convened by then chief minister S. M. Krishna, who played a crucial role in facilitating the growth of the IT and ITES industry in Bengaluru, the BATF symbolized the convergence of corporate capital, political ambition, and the aspirations of upwardly mobile middle classes. The BATF consisted of prominent members of a new cohort of entrepreneurs and engineers and was set up as a public-private partnership. Neoliberal notions of growth, progress, and of the role of the state versus civil society were central to the visions of futurity produced by the BATF, which addressed itself to "stakeholders" rather than citizens (Harvey 2007; Nair 2005, 77). Its proclaimed agenda was similarly revealing. It identified the following problems in order of priority: the condition of the roads, garbage, mosquitoes, pollution, and public toilets, as opposed to public transport, public housing, and public health (Nair 2000, 1512).

To what extent did these visions of the future prevail in the growth of Bengaluru in subsequent years? In the futuristic vision of the BATF, leading politicians, and corporate elites, Singapore was touted as the model city to be emulated (S. Benjamin 2010; Nair 2000, 2005). Singapore, rather than "the West," was represented as the vision of the future to which Bengaluru should aspire because of its purported success in bringing together "Asian" cultural values, urban planning, and the remarkable transformation of its economy since its inception as a sovereign nation-state.[15] Of course, it is worth noting that if Singapore is worth emulating for its urban planning and infrastructure, it is also remarkable for how it has fostered a culture of consumption through the construction of malls and shopping centers that index capitalist modernity and progress (Chua 2003).[16] Unlike Singapore, Bengaluru's urban planning, public housing, and transport infrastructure are in shambles.

As a result, Bengaluru's vision of the future remains chronically in suspension (Gupta 2015). Roads and flyovers remain incomplete; streets in the entire city have been dug up and concrete columns have been constructed in the middle of the street every few yards in anticipation of *something*: the metro, elevated highways, or flyovers. Those projects remain open-ended possibilities because of financial constraints, judicial entanglements, or administrative incompetence. In this state of chronic suspension, completion is just one of the many possibilities that lie ahead (Gupta 2015). Other infrastructural projects fare no better: pedestrian walkways, garbage collection and recycling (Sreenath 2016), public transportation (Kalyanaraman 2021), water supply (Ranganathan 2014), and electricity distribution, all function in an unplanned and haphazard fashion. By contrast, malls, technology parks, and luxury apartments and homes are often completed on schedule.

While Bengaluru has always been a space inhabited by migrants from different parts of the country, its emergence as an IT and ITES hub also meant that, as is the case with other large cities in postliberalization India, the metrics of cosmopolitanism have been redefined and recalibrated in terms of consumption as a normative aspiration (J. Menon 2021; cf. Berlant 2011). This vision of a cosmopolitan city, and the drive for consumption aligned with this vision, has been the impetus for the construction of malls all over Bengaluru. As we will elaborate below, the very architectural style and location of many of these malls mirror those of the IT and ITES companies that have sprung up in enclaves throughout the city and are material manifestations of the production of futurities.

It is now commonplace for people to use malls as landmarks when they give directions to each other, to auto and taxi drivers, to delivery services, and even the postal service. Bengaluru's malls have been constructed by some of the city's most successful and powerful developers who have joined hands with private investors and on occasion collaborated with multinational corporations (Searle 2016). Furthermore, the growth of malls is as much the result of state policies that proactively facilitate and endorse consumption, creating a new middle-class lifestyle (Fernandes 2009). The state's active solicitation of foreign direct investment in the retail sector is only one example of how it has actively promoted a consumerist lifestyle among its middle-class citizenry. Equally crucial is the fact that, in many urban and suburban locations, malls are constructed on land that has either been appropriated from peripheral communities or by demolishing and eradicating informal settlements in the heart of these cities: in most of these cases, land is acquired through a variety of means, including extralegal and illegal ones, all of which necessitate the active involvement or collusion of local state authorities (S. Benjamin 2010; Gooptu 2009; Nair 1996).

Exemplifying a larger phenomenon of speculative urbanism, land acquisition for the purpose of building SEZs, tech parks, malls, and gated residential communities has displaced the poor, Dalit and Bahujan communities, religious minorities, and other disenfranchised social groups (H. Gupta and Medappa 2020; Goldman 2011b; J. Menon 2021). This has resulted in the creation of large settlements of informal housing with exceedingly poor infrastructure. As Menon (2021) points out, "The labyrinthine and burgeoning informal economy, which supports and facilitates the industrial sectors reveals a picture far removed from the sterile glass and chrome buildings; here the inexorable mark of poverty reveals the underbelly of the world city" (58). As part of larger projects of development and "beautification" driven by an insatiable hunger for capital accumulation, the construction of these chrome and glass buildings and the displacement of disenfranchised communities demonstrate what Menon poignantly refers to as "brutal beauty" (see also Cross 2015, 429).

The appearance of malls where farmlands and informal settlements once used to be and the juxtaposition of their ultramodern architecture with slums and shanty towns are frequently represented in the media as a contrast between the new and the old, and to borrow Raymond Williams's felicitous formulation, the emergent and the residual: the implication is that, over time, and with the overall "progress" of the city, the inhabitants of the slums and shanty towns will acquire upward mobility and ascend the class ladder; in short, these communities that have lagged behind will eventually move forward into the future. Or, on the other hand, they are represented as communities that time itself has overtaken—as having been *bypassed* by development and by the march of the city into the future. However, rather than view these divergent forms of habitation in terms of old versus new—in other words, as anachronistic juxtapositions—we posit that these informal settlements and the shiny new buildings that have replaced them are *coeval*. In addition to displaced farmers, lower-income and Dalit and Bahujan caste communities, these settlements, shanty towns, and makeshift dwellings are, oftentimes, inhabited by laborers who have built the very communities from which they are excluded (Kalyanaraman 2021). Thus, instead of exhibiting a temporality of linearity, they manifest, in the most stark and material of ways, a temporality of simultaneity.

Sensoria of Aspiration

Our interest in the BPO industry was sparked by a visit to New Delhi in 2003, where we were struck by the number of malls that had appeared suddenly in middle-class and upper-class neighborhoods. High-end malls were particularly visible in Gurgaon (now Gurugram), a suburb of New Delhi and an emerging center of the ITES industry in India. Gurgaon, a former village, had previously witnessed a construction boom of housing for retired government officials and returning nonresident Indians, or NRIs.[17] Curious about the new structures that had started to dot the landscape, we began to visit these malls and found them displaying commodities that symbolized a new set of aspirations: there were stores that showcased washing machines, dishwashers, and other household gadgets in large glass windows; a spanking new multiplex that stood at one end of the mall; apparel stores displayed expensive clothes, many of which were imported; and well-dressed retail clerks hovering about the entrances of stores eagerly inviting passing visitors to browse through their wares. Restaurants and food courts sold food from different parts of the world, displaying on large billboards their mouth-watering menus, their aromas intermingling and seductively beckoning passersby. And in this wondrous temperature-controlled space, a welcome relief from the blistering heat of a North Indian summer, there was not a speck of dust to be seen. This mall, and others that had mushroomed all over

Gurgaon, were for people who had *arrived*, or were aspiring to arrive, in a fast-moving world meant exclusively for those who were upwardly mobile, well-heeled, and cosmopolitan—ready to take their place with successful, cosmopolitan young people in the Global North. The very air smelled of wealth, with the perfume of cosmetics, chocolates from a large candy store, and fast food taking over the senses. Cafés bragging Italian-style espressos and cappuccinos greeted one with the fragrance of coffee and baked goods. It became immediately evident that the retail outlets that the mall housed were, by no means, aimed at retired people but rather at young, upwardly mobile professionals in their twenties and early thirties.

Upon making inquiries with shopkeepers and local residents, we learned that these malls catered largely to the young people who worked in the call centers, BPOs, and IT firms that had newly proliferated all over Gurgaon. (This was a time when a majority of BPO agents, or call center agents as they were known then, were upper-middle class, seeking pocket money or an opportunity to "time-pass" while they waited for more lucrative jobs in banks and multinationals—a sharp contrast to the agents we worked with many years later, most of whom came from lower-income or upwardly mobile lower-middle-class backgrounds.) It is fair to say that it was the sensoria of Gurgaon's malls that first introduced us to the world of BPO agents.

When we arrived to do research in Bengaluru five years later, we found that it contrasted with Gurgaon in multiple ways. According to Aneesh (2015, 24), the new Gurgaon has not built on the old town as much as it has broken the mold to create "an iteration of a new global template of a city." This is anything but true for Bengaluru. Like Tulasi Srinivas's (2018) Malleswaram, where "the adjacency of past and future signal other adjacencies as well . . . allowing nostalgia and futurity to live together in the imagination of the residents" (45), present, past, and future remix on the streets of Bengaluru, making the city a palimpsest of divergent maps of temporality and affect. Srinivas's assertion about the neighborhood of Malleswaram applies to the multiple chronotopes that make up the city: Bengaluru is constantly in formation and is part of a continuous "process of world-making" (37). She also argues that Bengaluru is a quintessentially middle-class city with middle-class aspirations: "The boomtown bourgeoisie of this thriving city show a muscular 'capacity to aspire,' a key metric by which the middle class can be defined [Appadurai 2004], allowing as it does for widening sets of possibilities of upward mobility" (14).

Despite being home to entrepreneurial digital capitalism, despite being one of the fastest growing cities in India, despite taking on the identity of

Silicon Plateau, the Indianized version of Silicon Valley, Bengaluru's rich cultural and economic history has held its own, and in some ways has regenerated itself even when neighborhood landmarks have been replaced by malls (S. Srinivas 2016). Bengaluru is a city of multiple, sometimes disjunctive, chronotopes and sensoria. In many neighborhoods, the gloss and dazzle of a new mall, the aggressive (post)modernism of an IT "campus," and the manicured landscaping of a gated community sit alongside the regnant silence of an old church, the fragrances and chanting emanating from a newly reconstructed temple, a crowded street heaving with the rambunctious energy of a wedding procession, or a decrepit bungalow defiant in its glorious ruination. Loss and aspiration mark the landscape, and affective regimes of nostalgia and futurity bleed into each other and, in the process, index the multiple futurities that the city *enacts*: the city's affective landscapes impinge on, and refract, the subject formation of its inhabitants.

Without a doubt, the city has been transformed by the growth of the IT industry, and at least some of this growth has been on lands taken from lower-income, Dalit and Bahujan, and other disenfranchised communities. Even so, these developments have by no means destroyed all of Bengaluru's "older" features. While many of the visual and cultural landscapes of the city have been irrevocably altered, leading to worsening traffic, greater crowds, and expanding informal settlements, it is also true that Bengaluru's rich cultural history has survived, if not thrived, even as it has been reconfigured. As Menon (2021) points out, Bengaluru is "a repository that holds multiple urban imaginaries that range from garment industries to flower markets, from *karaga* festivals to *Ashura juloos* processions, from multinational industries to the multiple informal economies that serve the needs of various urban constituencies in the city" (58). We may surmise from Aneesh's description of Gurgaon a distinct regime of temporality that materializes in the growth of that newly incarnated city as it hurls headlong into the future: this is a temporality of linearity where the past must be left behind in order to arrive at the future. Bengaluru, in contrast, consists of subcultures, communities, and neighborhoods that have remained vibrant, bursting with noisy, colorful energy despite the proliferation of malls, SEZs, and IT parks.[18] Here again, we see how Bengaluru's futurities are marked by the temporality of simultaneity rather than that of linearity.

Of course, malls are only part of the sensoria created by the media and other forms of public culture in postliberalization India, including films, television shows, hoardings, billboards, and restaurant cultures that converge to operate synesthetically—that is, not just through images and spectacles but by the mobilization of multiple senses, such as the alteration of tastes resulting from the vast range of new cuisines available in the food courts and restaurants of malls.[19] Similar processes of embodiment are enabled by the kinesthetic pleasures of wandering through malls. Thus, even when our interlocutors were unable to purchase the commodities sold in malls, their experience of malls irrevocably altered their imaginations of the world.

The hypermediated spaces of malls create new sensoria in which tastes are altered and new desires and imaginations of the future are nurtured. Asif Agha (2011) points out that while social life is mediated whenever people participate in communicative activity, mediatization refers to instances when communication is linked to processes of commoditization: mediatization transforms the very object that is being mediated. Mediatized objects and subjects are part of larger processes of semiotic mediation and cannot be isolated from them. Extending Agha's conceptualization of mediatization, we posit that BPO agents, as they walk through the hypermediated sensoria of shopping malls, become biomediatized subjects of aspiration. Upon entering the hypermediated spaces of malls, BPO agents are further transformed: they become biomediatized also through commodity affect.[20] *Commodity affect* refers to the ineffable intensities surrounding commodities and foregrounds how commodities become "vital nodes in the production and circulation of intensities that generate and refract desire, agency, relationalities, and potentialities": commodity affect is generated by the *relay* of intensities between subjects and objects, the human and nonhuman, and bodies and commodities (Mankekar 2015, 166). Rather than referring to what commodities symbolize, commodity affect "gestures toward the consequentiality of commodities—their affectivity—for subjects' actions, desires, and anxieties" (167).

In addition to being suffused with commodity affect, Bengaluru's malls are also hypermediated spaces because of the proliferation of screens within them—television screens, screens in multiplexes, CCTV cameras, screens that monitor the passage of customers, and screens positioned all over food courts. As hypermediated spaces in which visitors roam and browse, they also manifest a concentration of images, sounds, smells, and tastes that provide intensely synesthetic experiences (see also Rai 2009, 134–35). For instance, the Nexus Whitefield Mall (formerly the Prestige Forum Value Mall) boasts large, shiny glass windows and a futuristic design. A central

2.1. Exterior of Nexus Whitefield Mall (formerly Prestige Forum Value Mall).

atrium beckons customers and browsers to explore the stores and kiosks lining each of its four floors, with escalators and a glass-walled elevator promising the easy movement of people through its enchanted spaces: kinesthetically moving through the mall, visitors navigate sensuous and affectively charged spatiotemporalities (figure 2.1). This is a cross-class space (Wilson 2004), but only to a limited extent: in all our years of visiting this mall and others in the city, we have never seen very poor people there. A primary responsibility of the security guards at the entrance to these malls appears to be to keep out those reminders of communities and individuals who have been marginalized by the city's ostensible sprint to prosperity.[21] Like all of Bengaluru's malls, security is always very tight so that the movement and actions of people are highly regulated. In order to enter, one has to walk through a metal detector with guards frisking individuals and looking through purses and bags; personal items have to be checked in at the entrance of many stores, and receipts are meticulously scrutinized at every exit, ostensibly to minimize the threat of shoplifting.

As soon as one enters the Nexus Whitefield Mall, the first thing one experiences is a dizzying array of olfactory sensations: the smell of donuts emanating from a Krispy Kreme kiosk; a Body Shop store to the left releasing,

2.2. Interior of Nexus Whitefield Mall showing shops and open area.

as it were, the fragrance of lotions, perfumes, and other cosmetics; an odor of stale oil emanating from a large KFC outlet on the right. The perfume of South Indian filter coffee wafts out of a café. These different aromas swirl around the entrance, hitting the senses immediately. A large grocery store anchors one end of the ground floor: its prices make clear that its target market consists of upper-class customers. The steady hum of movement, of bodies walking past each other and of visitors chatting with one another, is softly punctuated by piped elevator music. Lining the atrium are several chain stores and outlet stores that, ostensibly, sell goods at a discount but are still too expensive for most BPO agents. Upstairs, among other high-end restaurants, is an Italian trattoria: our interlocutors could not afford to eat there and preferred to meet with each other and with us in the food court or at one of the mall's many cafés. On one of the higher floors is a large multiplex, and the smell of stale popcorn fills the senses as eager bodies, waiting to see the latest movie, throng its entrance.

INTERJECTION

Alongside the Nexus Whitefield Mall is a warren of streets, full of small, independent stores selling meat and fish, stationery, clothing, luggage, mattresses, car parts, and groceries. This buzzing market is full of shops, old as well as new—there is nothing about it that suggests that it has been "left behind" by the spatiotemporality of Nexus Whitefield Mall. This is a different kind of sensorium, with the fragrance of bhajjis (fritters) being fried outside a tiny restaurant sitting at the entrance of a narrow lane jostling with the aroma of baked goods from a bakery. The sonic landscape is different as well, with chickens squawking as they await slaughter in a nearby butcher's shop, cars honking, and loud music blaring out of stores all at once. A vegetable vendor shouts out the prices of his wares as he pushes his cart down the alleyway. The call of a muezzin from a nearby mosque fills the air periodically. These streets are full of crowded shops, the press of bodies, uneven roads lined by drains on either side. "Variety" or "Fancy" stores offer goods ranging from cosmetics to backpacks. Shops selling large, brightly colored plastic urns used for storing water sit alongside kiosks that offer photocopying facilities. Two blocks to the east is a kalyana mandapa or wedding hall, the hub of enormous traffic jams every time there is a wedding. A few streets away, the entrance to a tiny temple lies nestled among a line of stores selling flowers and other offerings. Stores selling puja items adjoin chemists' shops, and there is a range of inexpensive eateries offering everything from rice plate lunches to dosas and fruit juices. The plate lunches and dosas are cooked by hawkers on the sidewalks and this, if they can afford it, is where most working people eat. These contrast dramatically with the purportedly "modern," air-conditioned eateries in the Nexus Whitefield Mall but, nonetheless, seem to thrive.[22]

These ostensibly different spaces manifest a temporality of simultaneity; the purportedly "old" and the "new" sit cheek by jowl. As one of our interlocutors pointed out, for him the "real shopping" happened outside malls. Yet, malls were the places where he and his friends went to "chill," and having a mall next door to tech parks made it easy for BPO workers to stop by a food court to grab a bite to eat or meet friends when they took some time off. As in Gurgaon, most of Bengaluru's malls are built in close proximity to the technology parks that house BPOs. This is not surprising because, very often, the malls and technology parks are constructed by the same builders. For our interlocutors, malls and technology parks symbolize that India, in the words of one of them, has "arrived on the global stage."

2.3. Small shops near the mall.

2.4. Shops selling food and fish near mall.

2.5. Small local temple with food vendor in front.

2.6. Sidewalk restaurant serving prepared food from containers.

2.7. Food vendor with mobile payment options.

MALLS, BPOS, AND AFFECTIVE LABOR

For many BPO agents, the rapid growth of malls all over Bengaluru paralleled the rise of BPOs and IT companies as crucial indices of India's economic success. As part of larger discourses of futurity, these spaces were affectively charged for most of our interlocutors. Even though the effects of the global recession were beginning to be felt when we began our intensive fieldwork in 2009, almost all of them persisted in the belief that India was on the road to becoming an economic superpower and that BPOs (and their own role within BPOs) were central to this trajectory.

This conjunction of malls and BPOs as icons of India's purported progress was apparent in their architecture and not just in the discourses of

2.8. Tech park at night.

2.9. Mall located inside a tech park.

our interlocutors. For example, the Park Square Mall in Whitefield is inside an immense tech park, the International Technology Park Bangalore (ITPB), which houses many large IT and ITES companies. Modernist buildings, full of chrome and glass, these malls are imposing structures. The Phoenix Market City, the newest addition that is widely considered one of Bengaluru's best malls is not far away, and it too is surrounded by offices of IT firms and BPOs.

For our interlocutors, malls and BPOs were iconic of the progress of the nation largely because of how they reconstitute spatiality. For the most part, malls are equipped with backup generators to supply uninterrupted electricity, unlike the rest of the city where power cuts and blackouts blanket entire neighborhoods and markets in darkness. Like BPOs, malls are air-conditioned, and most of them are kept spotlessly clean with sparkling windows, shining marble or tiled floors, and winding escalators that transport customers (and employees) to spaces apparently disconnected from the rest of the city: the passage to a seductive new world of consumerist cosmopolitanism is accomplished kinesthetically and imaginatively all at once.[23] Malls enable those who browse through its orderly, well-maintained, and spotless interiors to hold at bay the chaos of the city, its crumbling infrastructure, and the poverty of slum dwellers and beggars.[24]

Several of our interlocutors spoke eloquently of feeling transported into the First World when they entered BPO offices: they described the computers, the orderly organization of cubicles, the uninterrupted air conditioning, even the ubiquitous presence of CCTV cameras that monitored their every move, and the biometric screening of all who entered these buildings as icons of India's progress as a truly global nation.[25] Malls have played a particularly significant role in the entry of multinational companies into the Indian retail space with retailers like Benetton and H&M positioned to introduce western-style clothes and lifestyles to all those who browse through them.[26] Apart from the fact that these hypermediated spaces are clean, orderly, and air-conditioned, their stores—which range from kiosks selling Australian cookies, Baskin-Robbins ice cream, and cinnamon rolls from Cinnabon to multinational retailers such as Benneton and Louis Vuitton and restaurants offering Italian and French cuisine—enabled our interlocutors to imagine being in a First World country, even if only temporarily. "You can now get everything here that you can get in the West," they would say to us.[27]

Thus, malls, like BPOs, provided agents with opportunities to engage in virtual travel quite similar to the virtual migration that they performed at work. This virtual travel entailed temporal as much as spatial crossings. Wandering through these malls, imbibing and inhabiting the spectacles of modernity and "development" that they offered, and, when possible, purchasing the commodities displayed there enabled agents to step into the future: they spoke of how being in a mall allowed them (albeit temporarily) to leave behind a chaotic present and enter a well-ordered future. As material and symbolic signs of India's economic progress, malls were chronotopes that enabled young people, many of whom came from small towns or from low-income families, to get a glimpse of the futures that they hoped would be just around the corner.

Malls and Sociality

Malls constituted spaces of dense sociality for BPO agents (cf. Dávila 2016; Padios 2018; Wilson 2004) (see figures 2.9–2.13). One of our initial objectives in this research was to examine ethnographically the relationship between work and family life for BPO agents. After making contact with our interlocutors in their workspaces, we tried as much as possible to meet them off-site, if possible, in their homes. But it became increasingly evident that most workers preferred to meet us in public spaces rather than in their homes, and almost all of them wanted to meet us in malls. There seemed to be many reasons for this preference. Despite their comparatively high incomes, many of our interlocutors had been forced by Bengaluru's astronomical rents to live in tiny and congested hostels or dormitory-like apartments with minimal kitchen facilities and with several people crowded into one or two rooms.[28] They felt that meeting in these crowded spaces would be awkward for them and counterproductive for us because of the lack of privacy. We also sensed that other BPO agents who lived with their families hesitated to invite us to their homes because they were embarrassed about the modest, often shabby, conditions in which they lived.

Our intuition was borne out when, several months later, some of them invited us to their homes and we saw how run-down their living spaces were. Most of them lived with their extended families (which could include grandparents and sometimes cousins, nieces, nephews, or other relatives) in tiny apartments in low-income and congested neighborhoods, with several siblings sharing a room or, if that wasn't possible, sleeping on the floor in an outer room. The electricity would often go out, the water supply was erratic, and in many of the homes that we visited, the paint was peeling off the walls. In contrast, all the malls in Bengaluru were new, relatively clean, with gleaming floors, and air-conditioned: these features made them particularly appealing to BPO agents. As one of our interlocutors pointed out, unlike their neighborhoods where there were frequent power cuts, malls were spaces where they could seek refuge from the humidity and dust of the city. This was where they could meet each other, surreptitiously enjoy a drink, and where they could engage in clandestine rendezvous with lovers. As we have noted above, not many of them could afford to go to the high-end restaurants in these malls; instead, they would congregate in food courts, fast-food restaurants, coffee shops, and, if they could afford them, pubs.

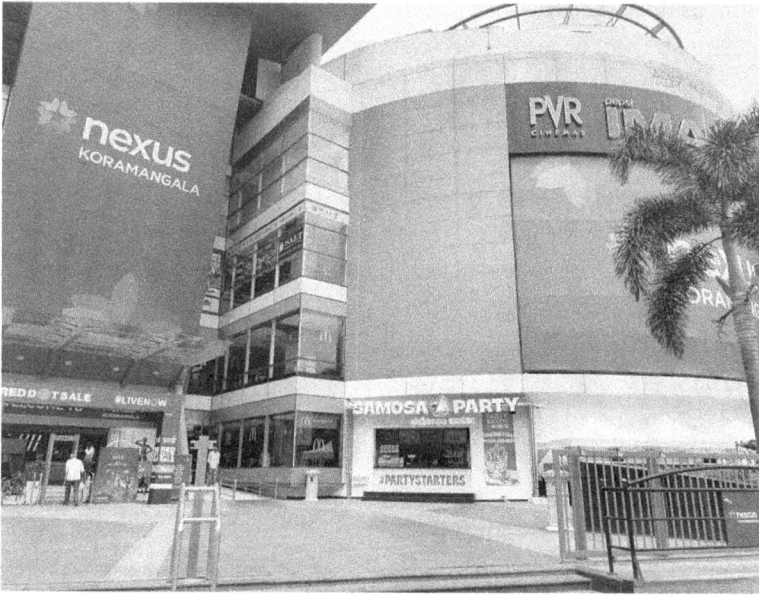

2.10. Older mall in Koramangala that was a favorite of BPO workers.

While many of them continued to shop in smaller markets in their neighborhoods, they sometimes tried to make the most of the sales and discount vouchers offered by malls to purchase gifts for their family and friends during religious festivals like Diwali, Eid, or Christmas. Even though all the companies in which we conducted our ethnographic research served dinner to their employees, some agents preferred to grab a meal, often with friends and occasionally by themselves, at food courts on their way to work. Doing so, it became clear to us, was one way in which they could engage in socialities that were relatively removed from work or keep at bay the rhythms of the workplace: the mall offered them space and time to be by themselves, away from the obligations of home and office, or be with friends so they could decompress from those pressures. The erotic possibilities of malls were especially irresistible: away from the prying eyes of family, community members, and neighbors, young couples could be spotted walking hand-in-hand or enjoying each other's company in restaurants, coffee shops, or food courts.[29]

This was particularly true of Bengaluru's multiplex cinema halls, many of which had emerged in conjunction with the construction of malls. Today, an overwhelming majority of them are within malls or are adjacent to them, offering sensory experiences that are an extension and an intensification of those offered by the mall (hence, the suitability of Rai's [2009] term "malltiplex").[30] Purnima Mankekar first experienced a multiplex when at the beginning of our fieldwork one of our interlocutors, Rukhsana Shah, suggested that they watch a movie at the mall next to her BPO. Unlike the single-screen theaters Mankekar had frequented as a teenager in New Delhi, the multiplex was air-conditioned, like the rest of the mall. As soon as she entered the lobby, she noticed other contrasts with traditional cinema theaters. The attendants who checked customers' (highly priced) tickets wore uniforms and were unfailingly polite and solicitous. Like the rest of the mall, the multiplex was spotless, its floor gleaming. The film that we watched that afternoon was only one part of the overall experience: it was almost as if our bodies were put on high alert for sensations that we were to experience even before the film began. The lobby was brightly lit; there was western music playing. The concession stand sold food and beverages that were not just very expensive but different from what Mankekar had enjoyed growing up: instead of samosas, they sold french fries, chicken nuggets, and vegetable burgers. Several different kinds of soft drinks were available along with espresso drinks. Inside the shoebox-shaped hall in which we watched the film, the seats were wide and upholstered with a soft fabric: like airline seats, these seats could recline and were fitted with tray tables. Rukhsana remarked on the cleanliness of the bathrooms, adding that these bathrooms were just as clean as the ones they had in their office. The cleanliness and order of the multiplex were equal to that of the BPO where she worked, and in sharp contrast both to the teeming, chaotic, messy city and to most people's homes or residential spaces.

In many ways, the multiplex is part of the larger pedagogical space of the mall because it enables exposure to new sensations and habits. Indeed, multiplexes have changed how urban residents who can afford tickets now watch films. Most obviously, they differ from single-screen theaters because they offer multiple screens so that viewers have a range of choices: in a polyglot city like Bengaluru, this has meant that patrons may, theoretically, choose between English, Hindi, Kannada, Telugu, Malayalam, and Tamil films.[31] However, beyond these new exhibition practices, multiplexes have led to more fundamental changes (Rai 2009, 40). The multiplex positions the biomediatized body in ways distinct from the single-screen theater: the body is reconfigured as it is opened up for new sensations and for new modes of regulation (see also Rai 2009, 36, 136–37). Older theaters organized gendered bodies differently, with young, poorer men sitting in front. "Ladies" sat in the back, with many single-screen theaters offering special "ladies seats" or enclosures for women to protect them from being seen or harassed by men. The "balcony," with its higher-priced tickets, was reserved for upper classes, and to the extent that class and caste interlock, "higher" castes. In some ways, multiplexes have reconfigured these hierarchies: their tickets are so expensive that they are generally patronized only by upper-middle-class or middle-class customers.[32] The darkness of the multiplex means that customers may interact both more freely and more clandestinely. Gender, class, and caste intersect in complex ways in the appeal of malls, as opposed to public parks, for young people in urban India. In addition to being air-conditioned and clean spaces, malls are also places where couples can spend time together, unlike parks where intercaste and interreligious couples in particular are subjected to harassment and violence by self-appointed, Hindu nationalist guardians of morality.

For women, in particular, the mall promises to be a space of safety where they may be protected from sexual harassment. For instance, Savi Murthy would always insist that we meet in malls because that was where she felt sheltered from the prying eyes of neighbors and from the harassment she faced in the streets. Savi was a single mother who had lived in Dubai until her divorce. We first met her at a training session in a BPO and quickly became friends. She told us that, when she and her women friends went to watch films at multiplexes, she was never concerned about street harassment or about "getting into trouble" with men. But, most importantly, Savi could watch films at the multiplex with her new boyfriend, who worked at the same BPO: this was, she said, a perfect place for the two of them to get to know each other. For her and other agents, multiplexes (along with the pubs that were often strategically placed across from them in malls) were highly eroticized spaces. The anonymity of the multiplex meant that this was where couples could hold hands and exchange furtive kisses; they enabled exchanges that could potentially lead to a longer, more intimate rendezvous.

Diverging from Foucauldian perspectives on disciplinary technologies or, indeed, Althusser's focus on the ISAs, our analysis of malls foregrounds how, in contemporary forms of capitalism, subject formation occurs through the *dispersal* of affect and desire across the socius. Drawing on Gilles Deleuze, Patricia T. Clough (2007) has argued:

> The production of normalization is no longer simply entrusted to the family, kin groups, or other institutions of civil society; it also involves the investment in and regulation of a market-driven circulation of

affect and attention. No longer captured in the disciplined body, the subject's desire passes beyond the enclosed spaces of the home, the school, and the labor union, beyond the opposition of normal and deviant. (19)

Malls were nodes in our interlocutors' constitution as cosmopolitan, worldly, desiring subjects. In particular, malls enabled formerly low-income, upwardly mobile young people to be exposed to a larger cultural and sensorial landscape: they expanded their *sense* of the world and these sensuous knowledges offered them opportunities to learn how to become aspirational subjects.

This sense of becoming worldly was central not just to the imagination of their own future trajectories but, perhaps more significantly, to their aspirations for their family members (see also Cross 2015). Thus, for instance, the mall represented a space where Savi and her family members learned to enjoy the fruits of her labor. She especially enjoyed bringing her eight-year-old daughter to cafés and food courts in these malls to try different kinds of cuisines. "I want my daughter to know what the outside world is like," she said to me. "I want her to see that there is a world out there, a world outside Poorva Nagar [the low-income, congested neighborhood where they lived]." Malls, therefore, were not just pedagogical sites where agents like Savi learned the skills she needed at work. They were also spaces that generated her aspirations for herself and her daughter, underscoring the complexity of the affective regimes shaping the subjectivities of our interlocutors who were not simply, or solely, laboring subjects: they were also parents, children, and siblings who struggled to improve the life chances of those for whom they felt responsible.

Malls offered BPO agents opportunities for a range of leisure activities apart from gaming arcades, food courts, pubs, and high-end restaurants. All malls have hair salons and beauty parlors (many malls have more than one hair salon, suggesting their high demand), and these became the spaces where our interlocutors learned to groom themselves. The cafés, arcades, and food courts of malls were sites of sociality for BPO agents as well as spaces where they could be socialized as cosmopolitan subjects. Malls generate and bring together new affective regimes and sensations; ideologies of gender, class, and sexuality; the biopolitical regulation and segmentation of populations; desire, anxieties, fears; aspirations and struggles; and clandestine erotics and surveillance (cf. Rai 2009).

In addition to becoming a home away from home for some of the BPO agents with whom we worked, malls were an extension of their workplaces in critical ways. Nandini Gooptu's (2009) characterization of the engineered sociality of neoliberal workplaces in terms of "fun-at-work" is particularly relevant to BPOs (see also Gregg 2010, 2011; Sonti 2006).[33] Many BPOs tried to engineer a fun-at-work atmosphere that coexisted uneasily with the workplace's hypercompetitive, target-driven spaces of surveillance. Nevertheless, the reputation of BPOs as workplaces with "fun atmospheres" was alluring to many young people. We heard this phrase repeated multiple times in the recruitment interviews in which we participated, at the inductions that we observed, and at training sessions. Agents contrasted BPOs to other workplaces because they believed them to be nonhierarchical, informal, and fun. Many new recruits were to discover eventually that this image belied a high-pressure, target-driven work environment.

Managers and human resources teams worked hard to maintain this image of BPOs as "fun" workplaces (cf. Padios 2018). Even though agents worked cooperatively within a team, theoretically, teams were supposed to compete aggressively with each other. In such a competitive environment, companies went out of their way to cultivate social relationships among agents and would organize parties, trips to pubs and restaurants, and retreats at fancy spas and resorts—all of which were designed to get agents to "bond." Furthermore, almost all managers attempted to supplement or extend this fun-at-work atmosphere by organizing fun-at-the-mall events. On Fridays, many companies took employees to lunch at restaurants in nearby malls to boost morale. These restaurants were also sites where managers would host parties for teams that had exceeded the targets set by client companies and to celebrate promotions. In conjunction with weekends and retreats at expensive resorts, these fun-at-the-mall events were central to what managers and supervisors described to us as "team building" exercises deemed indispensable to their success.

As several scholars have observed (see, especially, Dávila 2016), malls mark upward class mobility; they also represent spaces that set classes apart and play a central role in class differentiation and, to this extent, in class formation. Malls in Bengaluru vary and sometimes contrast sharply with each other in their architecture, interior layout, and the sensoria they offer according to the class identities of the customers they target, hence marking and cultivating differentiations between classes. Some malls, such as the Nexus Whitefield Mall or the Total Mall on Old Airport Road are outlet malls that seem to cater primarily (although not exclusively) to middle- and lower-middle-class customers.[34] In sharp contrast is the UB City Mall in the heart of the city with its high-end stores like Burberry, Jimmy Choo, Rolex, and Louis Vuitton. The UB City Mall is designed as a European plaza with escalators leading up to a central courtyard where expensive restaurants are placed strategically around a fountain. Barring one exception, the BPO agents with whom we worked rarely asked to meet with us in the UB City Mall. Even though they never needed to say this to us explicitly, it was clear to us that they felt too out of place and intimidated to go there. Most of them would prefer to meet with us at the Nexus Whitefield Mall because that was where they hung out with their friends and that was where they felt most comfortable.

But more pertinently for our argument, for these young people, going to the mall was a pedagogical exercise because it enabled them to learn about what an upwardly mobile and cosmopolitan lifestyle entailed. According to Nita Mathur (2010), people who visit malls can be broken down into the regulars, whom she describes as "serious buyers," as opposed to "casual buyers." The latter are interested in the latest fashions, spending time having fun without being surveilled by family members, and trying different cuisines in food courts without having to spend substantial sums of money to purchase the products being sold in the mall (221). Since most of the young people at the BPOs we studied came from relatively low-income or lower-middle-class backgrounds, almost all of them financially supported their families and, contrary to stereotypical media representations, did not have much money left for making exorbitant purchases in malls. Rather, malls provided them with opportunities to relax, fantasize about the kinds of commodities they could purchase during sales, explore unfamiliar cuisines, and most importantly, learn to negotiate spaces of modernity and globality with poise and confidence.

Affective labor is sustained by the blurring of leisure and labor, and malls represented one arena in which this occurred for BPO agents. Drawing on Negri (1999), Clough (2007) points to the reconfiguration of labor in contexts of the subsumption of life under capitalism: "With real subsumption, labor is situated in a 'nonplace' in relationship to capital—no place and all-over-the-place, where work goes on all of the time, such that labor finds its value in affect" (25).[35] As a crucial site for the socialization of BPO workers, malls constituted them as subjects of consumption and as laboring subjects.

2.11. Mall that catered mostly to a lower-middle-class clientele.

2.12. UB City Mall near downtown Bengaluru is distinguished by its faux-Italianate interiors and high-end luxury brands.

2.13. UB City Mall, featuring high-end designer stores.

When we asked agents about their motivations for seeking jobs in BPOs and in continuing to work there, discourses of growth and "learnings" stood out. For most of them, growth brought together personal *and* professional success. Almost all of them felt that growth was their personal responsibility and that it was entirely up to them to acquire and maintain the skills that would enable them to stay employed in the present and be employable in the future.[36] To some degree, then, our interlocutors seemed to be interpellated by neoliberal values of personal responsibility, entrepreneurship, and achievement.[37] Growth was measured in different ways, chief among which were upward class mobility and the acquisition of "soft skills" or social skills that would enable them to successfully navigate the worlds in which they worked or imagined working in the future.

Aspiration, Soft Skills, and Futurities

Jisha Menon (2021) insists that aspiration entails not merely personal striving but a "calculated project of renovating one's value system"; it brings together desire, instrumental reason, and barely conscious yearnings to produce specific forms of action and agency (7). She points out that aspirations "suggest yearnings that are not merely superficial or transient; instead, these yearnings are instilled with a new set of values derived from a reasoned desire. Aspiration is not autogenetic but mimetic. The striving urban subject does not simply invent a new self; rather, aspiration is mimetically generated through attachments to images and ideals that circulate as social goods" (7). For our interlocutors, the commodity affect saturating malls, and the larger sensoria of which they were a part, generated aspirations toward specific futures. While some of these aspirations involved the ability to support their families in their struggle for upward mobility, others had to do with the acquisition of specific "soft skills" that could potentially result in professional success. Soft skills included the ability to speak English fluently, and perhaps more importantly, with confidence (Jayadeva 2018; see also chapters 1 and 4). Soft skills consisted of obtaining "people skills" that, in the workplace, consisted of being able to make small talk with customers from vastly different cultural backgrounds. Central to these soft skills was the acquisition of kinetic skills—quite literally, the ability to navigate the spaces of modernity and globality with polish and confidence—and it was these very characteristics of comportment that, they believed, would enable them to seal a deal with customers or negotiate with team leaders, supervisors, and managers with dexterity.

The opportunity to learn about "the latest trends" was hence not simply about acquiring the accoutrements of upward mobility but was, in fact, essential to professional success. Browsing through malls taught them *how* to become middle class.[38] This symbolic capital was intrinsically future-oriented: the knowledge of the latest trends in fashion, acquiring a taste for different national and international cuisines, learning about the latest Hollywood films, and so on, profoundly shaped their sense of the possible, their imaginations of the future, and their understanding of their role in crafting such a future. Our interlocutors hoped that acquiring soft skills would position them more securely in a future-oriented trajectory, leading to cultural and experiential mobility, which in turn contributed positively to their performance of affective labor. Their affective labor entailed connecting with customers far removed from them in terms of geography, culture, and experience; it relied on their ability to empathetically and imaginatively connect with them; and most of all, as we have posited in the previous chapter, it was contingent on processes of cultural and experiential translation across highly asymmetrical contexts. From what we observed over our long-term fieldwork, the acquisition of soft skills was an embodied process and extended from learning how to speak with a neutral accent and knowing what clothes to wear to work and on social occasions to learning how to eat Western food (Gooptu 2009, 46; see also chapter 4).

The opportunity provided by malls to acquire the soft skills necessary for upward mobility was particularly powerful for BPO agents who believed that they did not have the requisite cultural capital. For instance, interlocutors who came from small towns or were from Dalit, Bahujan, or other oppressed and marginalized communities believed that malls provided spaces in which they could assume the habitus—the dispositions, comportments, and kinesthetic ability—required for navigating dominant-caste and middle-class spaces. Let us remember that for many of our Dalit and Bahujan interlocutors, the ability to sit with confidence alongside colleagues who were from dominant castes, and to socialize and compete with them at work, meant that some of them had to learn modes of moving in a world that had previously been closed off to them. While malls by no means provide a way to transcend caste position, they nevertheless produced structures of feeling and the capacity to aspire that were new, unfamiliar, and daunting. Malls were pedagogical spaces where previously low-income young people could potentially acquire the patina of upward class mobility.

Having been sensitized to the structural violence, stigma, and exclusion attached to Dalit, Bahujan, and other oppressed and marginalized communities during our previous fieldwork in Western Uttar Pradesh (Gupta 1998, 2012) and New Delhi (Mankekar 1999, 2015), and acutely conscious of our own caste and class privileges, both of us were attuned to these challenges for some of our interlocutors.[39] Raghu came from a low-income Dalit family and claimed that he had acquired the ability to "conduct himself" from spending time in malls. Being able to watch the latest Hollywood film at multiplex theaters and knowing what to drink in pubs complemented Raghu's efforts to learn fluent English—and these were resources and skills that he deemed essential to his personal and professional growth. In his words, people who "come from nowhere," by which he implied those from Dalit or Bahujan low-income communities, with neither professional networks in Bengaluru nor recognizable cultural capital, had to acquire soft skills in order to survive and make a future for themselves in the BPO world.

In the purportedly meritocratic world of BPOs, where neoliberal discourses of growth and personal responsibility have ostensibly invisibilized the enduring power and structural violence of caste, Raghu and other agents who were from Dalit and Bahujan communities emphasized that it was up to them to acquire the skills necessary to advance in their careers because their families lacked the resources and cultural capital to help them in any way (cf. Gooptu 2009, 2013a, 2013b; and Upadhya 2016). The ability to conduct oneself went beyond wearing "branded clothes," they would argue, and extended to one's leisure practices: in significant ways, the soft skills learned at work and in the mall complemented and reinforced each other. In this context, self-presentation, polished comportment, and "improved" grooming were all deemed essential to soft skills (see also Gooptu 2009, 48). The acquisition of these soft skills was emphasized in all the induction sessions and training that we observed in BPOs: second only to their performance evaluations, the ability to appear "smart," "with it," and self-possessed, and to nimbly and confidently navigate spaces of modernity and globality, was central to their ability to acquire jobs, stay employable, and attain professional success.

While the pressure to appear smart, confident, and "with it" was particularly burdensome for agents who were from Dalit and Bahujan communities, all our interlocutors believed that acquiring soft skills added greatly to their employability, their professional success in the present, and more pertinently to our argument, to their future prospects. Compared to government jobs there was not a lot of job security in BPOs. Yet, relative to other sectors of the economy, BPOs offered employees greater opportunities for lateral mobility, and the young agents with whom we worked took great pride in changing jobs on a regular basis. In fact, changing jobs was one way to keep oneself marketable and employable. However, it was essential to constantly "revamp" one's skills in order to be marketable. Marketability was essential to survive in this highly competitive industry because, as is the case with many jobs in the private sector, finding and, more crucially, retaining employment in BPOs was always uncertain.

Indeed, the precariousness of the Indian middle class is predicated on the constant specter of unemployment, underemployment, and unemployability. The young people with whom we worked had to learn how to survive, if not thrive, in a work environment marked by hypercompetitiveness, and in those BPOs that offered customer service, soft skills played a crucial role in maintaining their employability. Malls provided resources for the co-constitution of personal growth and professional success: the lines between labor and leisure, personal and professional identity, work and "fun" were being perpetually reconfigured in the formation of subjects who had to be self-motivated, self-regulated, and in crucial ways, looking to the future in terms of growth, professional stability, and success.

While some characteristics such as self-motivation and self-regulation were clearly shaped by aspects of neoliberalism that have now become dominant in the private sector in contemporary India (Gooptu 2009; Upadhya 2016), few of our interlocutors displayed the characteristics of hyperindividualism associated with neoliberalism. For agents in Bengaluru, aspirations to personal and professional growth existed side-by-side and in tension with a commitment to the family and community arising from a sense of duty. The renegotiated relationship between growth and progress became increasingly clear when we found that many of our interlocutors explicitly and emphatically linked their own growth with the "progress" of their families, communities, and the Indian nation.

Most agents were quite frugal, preferring to eat in food courts rather than at expensive restaurants and constantly seeking sales and discounts at clothing stores. Their frugality resulted from the fact that the largest share of their salaries went to provide for their extended families: to take care of medical bills for parents and elderly relatives, tuitions of younger siblings, paying off debts that the family had accumulated over the years, or purchasing food, white goods, cars, and if they were truly lucky, payments toward homes or apartments in their hometowns. Hence, alongside, and often superseding, discourses of personal and professional growth was the ethical imperative to support parents, grandparents, younger siblings, cousins, uncles, and aunts. What drove them were aspirations not solely of personal growth but the "progress" of their entire families; the upward mobility of agents also indexed the upward mobility of their families. When they purchased expensive commodities such as washing machines or flat-screen television sets, they were enjoyed by the entire family. This was of course true when our interlocutors lived with their families but was also frequently the case when they had moved away: festivals like Diwali and Eid provided them with opportunities to purchase these expensive commodities at discounts for families and relatives.

In her powerful indictment of the "cruel optimism" engendered by aspirational normativity, Lauren Berlant (2011, 19) asks: "What happens to optimism when futurity splinters as a prop for getting through life?" It is important to note that Berlant is referring to the pervasive precarity that has emerged after the dissolution of the Fordist compact: as we noted elsewhere in this book, these discursive and political-economic contexts are not pertinent to the lives and worlds of BPO agents, which despite the growth of neoliberal policies by the state in postliberalization India, did not mark an "end of an era of social obligation and belonging" (19; see also Amrute 2016). Furthermore, and importantly, BPO agents, unlike the subjects at the center of Berlant's analysis, do not by any means constitute a subproletarian precariat. Undoubtedly, when it came to the futures that they aspired to, many BPO agents were subjected to pressure from all sides. On the one hand, they had to deal with the exacting demands of quotas at work and the imperative to take risks, be responsible for their personal and professional growth, and constantly "revamp" their skills to stay employable in a rapidly changing industry. On the other hand, these expectations coexisted with parental and familial pressures, which ranged from the obligation to provide for their parents in their old age to taking responsibility for the education and marriages of younger siblings.[40]

Rubina Khan's case illustrates this point particularly well. Rubina attended college by day and worked in a BPO at night. Her parents were divorced and her father, who worked in the Middle East, was either unable or unwilling to remit money home on a regular basis. We were constantly struck by how hard Rubina worked. A typical day would consist of the following schedule: she went to college in the mornings, usually from 10 a.m. to about 3 p.m. She then spent the time between 3 and 4 p.m. catching up with homework or relaxing in a mall adjacent to her college. After snatching a quick bite to eat at the food court, she would leave for her shift, but because of traffic, she did not arrive there until about 6 p.m. Her shift was from 6:30 p.m. to 3:30 a.m., and by the time the company cab dropped her home, it would be close to 5 a.m. When she reached home, she would eat a snack and try to catch some sleep before leaving for class. On her days off, which sometimes coincided with weekends, she had to supervise her younger siblings' homework and help her mother with housework.

Whenever she complained of how tired she felt, her mother would suggest that she drop out of college. But Rubina was determined to get her degree: she thought that being a BPO agent was a "dead end" and that the only way she could secure her future was by getting a bachelor's and then seeking a job in a bank or in the HR section of a BPO. She believed that getting a bachelor's degree was the only way out of the rut in which she found herself and deeply resented how her mother pressured her to keep her job in the BPO but drop out of college. She felt that her mother wanted her to sacrifice what she thought was a more secure future by continuing her BPO work.

Mankekar visited Rubina's home for a celebratory Eid lunch one afternoon and was struck by the number of appliances the family possessed. Their tiny, run-down rental flat was crammed with a mixer-grinder, a microwave, a large flat-screen television set, and a small washing machine: Rubina had obviously been successful in purchasing these appliances when they were on sale. As the sole breadwinner in the family, she frequently spoke of how much she wished to make her mother's life comfortable. "My mother has struggled her entire life," she would say, "and she continues to work hard to make our lives comfortable so I must do what I can to provide her with as much as possible." At the same time, Rubina also expressed resentment toward how her mother tried to control her life. "She expects me to hand over most of my salary and I do that," she said. "But she doesn't realize that I am getting burned out. . . . I cannot do this my entire life and she doesn't realize this. I have to be able to find a better job."

Rubina's situation was not unusual in that many parents found themselves dependent on the incomes of children who worked in BPOs, even as they complained that these young people had to do night work and that they allegedly "indulged" themselves by going to malls or taking time off to relax with friends. Many of our interlocutors felt that their family members begrudged their rare attempts to spend money on themselves. Although it was a lot more stringent for young women, men too were subjected to similar pressures: parents would get accustomed to the security and comforts provided by their children but, at the same time, resent the erosion of their authority within the family.

Predictably, the desire for personal and professional growth would sometimes conflict with BPO agents' commitment to ensuring the "progress" of their families (see also Cross 2015). The pressure and the resulting friction sometimes got so acute that a few of our women interlocutors took the radical decision to branch out on their own to either live in groups or move to the dormitory-like apartments that were all that they could afford. Yet, even when they moved away from their parents, most agents would give their parents money on a regular basis: although living apart from their parents offered a degree of autonomy, many of them still felt compelled to provide for their family's financial well-being and, to the extent that they could, secure their family's future.

Futurity, then, was neither inherently nor inevitably individual-centered, nor did it exemplify a teleological movement toward neoliberal individuation.[41] Our interlocutors frequently spoke of their hopes for the future because, despite the uncertainties surrounding their jobs, they felt a lot less financially constrained than did other members of their families. They spoke of the "choices" they had in terms of the availability of the large variety of entertainment options, consumption practices, and a range of lifestyles, most of which had not existed for their parents, and all of which were offered by the malls that had sprung up all over the city. But alongside the imperative for personal and professional growth were powerful and affectively charged discourses of duty and responsibility toward building a more secure future for their family, particularly parents, children, and younger siblings.

MALLTOPIA

What do malls in India tell us about the nature and future of affective capitalism? And what do they suggest about the future of futurity in a historical conjuncture marked by economic volatility and other crises, including the impending crises of a city where the temporalities of capitalism and community coproduce, collide, or blur into each other? Affective capitalism depends on the merging of labor and leisure, and fun and work, through the constant modulation of affect. As we have argued, shopping malls were not simply places where BPO agents shopped. With their ultramodern appearance, air conditioning, uninterrupted power supply, and regulated and ordered spaces, malls are hypermediated sites that stood in sharp disjuncture with the homes and neighborhoods in which most agents were raised and lived. Equally significantly, these spaces parallel and extend the ultramodern (if not postmodern) chronotopes of BPOs. While malls were places where BPO agents went to relax with friends and thus represented spaces of sociality, they were also spaces where they acquired the cultural competence that was an essential part of the soft skills required to perform affective labor with customers across cultural and experiential chasms. Malls articulated with, and were productive of, discourses of growth and progress that were central to the formulation of discourses of futurity.

The bodies of BPO agents, which were already being transformed in conjunction with their affective labor at work, became biomediatized as they navigated the sensoria of malls. Like SEZs, shopping malls are infrastructures of aspiration and "create unique arenas in which diverse ways of knowing about, imagining, and living toward the near and distant future converge with particular intensity" (Cross 2015, 435). Elsewhere we document how the training of BPO employees consisted not just of learning about the process or the company they were serving but, equally importantly, about how to enter and leave elevators, how to use Western-style toilets, and how to use deodorants (chapter 1, Mankekar and Gupta 2016; Mankekar 2015). At first, this emphasis on personal grooming seemed to us to be not just presumptuous but also superfluous: given that customers never saw BPO employees but only spoke to them on the phone, why was it necessary for new recruits to learn how to comport and groom themselves in this manner? We quickly learned that personal grooming and "improved" comportment were central to their performance of affective labor. While training and induction sessions at work emphasized these new forms of comportment, these "learnings" were supplemented by malls that provided a wealth of opportunities for new modalities of embodiment and of navigating space (see also chapter 4). Malls were important pedagogical sites for the acquisition of some of the soft skills deemed essential for personal growth, professional success, and a secure future. This was especially critical for those of our interlocutors who came from low-income or Dalit and Bahujan families. Even as some of them were deeply anxious about the future, most of them were cautiously hopeful about what lay ahead because they had been relatively successful in climbing up the slippery slope of class mobility (see also Cross 2015, 427). Their discourses were marked by a temporality of hopefulness; they looked to the future because, they hoped, their pasts would not bring them down.

In the training of workers in the retail trade, malls serve to "create and nurture aspirations and stoke ambitions, and thus provide motivation" (Gooptu 2009, 48). Many BPO agents—especially those who came from the semiurban periphery or small towns or were from poorer households within Dalit and Bahujan communities—had to learn how to dress and comport themselves for interviews and, after getting a job, acquire the cultural competence or soft skills that would enable them to stay ahead in a highly competitive environment where becoming cosmopolitan or "global" was an important aspect of the job. In all these cases, they had to take upon themselves the responsibility of acquiring and maintaining soft skills that would preserve or increase their chances of employment in the future. Thus, while reaching and exceeding quotas set by team leaders and managers was crucial to promotions and hence to professional success and personal mobility, the imperative to acquire soft skills reinforced values of self-management and self-production.

Clough (2007) has argued that "institutions like the school, the labor union, the hospital, and the prison function as switch points for circulating bodies, along with information and capital, through channels, not with the aim of arrival, but with the aim of keeping the flows moving at different speeds" (25). As part of infrastructures of aspiration, malls functioned as "switch points" that facilitated our interlocutors' affective labor (Berardi 2009). In theorizing malls as infrastructures of aspiration, we are underlining their futurity rather than their role in present consumption. The future is produced through practices in the present of anticipation, aspiration, and imagination (Appadurai 2013; Cross 2015). But while anticipation is about attempting to *know* what might come, futurities are affective and ontological formations. Futurities are agentive, not always able to be captured in language or symbolization yet ineffable in how they generate action and agency.

As we will argue in chapter 4, affective labor depends on a modulation of affect that is granular. The modulation of affect is also constant—it happens all the time and everywhere. For this reason, theorists like Tronti (1973) and Negri (1989) argue that regimes of labor need to be conceptualized as exceeding the workplace. While the workplace was a key site for the constitution of BPO agents' identities and subjectivities, malls played a significant role as well. Although some of the formal socialization of BPO employees occurred at work, a considerable amount of their socialization took place in malls. We are not, however, arguing that subject formation of BPO agents is entirely subsumed by regimes of labor. It is important to note that our interlocutors were not merely laboring subjects: they were also parents, children, siblings, lovers, and friends who juggled, with varying degrees of success, their aspirations for themselves and for those for whom they felt a sense of responsibility. We have theorized the aspirations of BPO agents as twinned with an acute sense of precarity. Malls were crucial pedagogical spaces in which they learned not just what to aspire for but how to aspire; more profoundly, malls taught them how to inhabit and navigate emergent spaces of modernity and embody markers of growth with confidence. Even though the acquisition of symbolic and cultural capital was necessary to be a successful professional, it also indexed efforts to build a secure future for their families and loved ones.

The sensoria and spatiotemporalities of malls often contrasted dramatically with the material conditions shaping the everyday lives of the BPO agents.[42] The sensuous knowledges they obtained in malls were meant to give them the cultural capital, soft skills, and confidence to navigate a world completely at odds with the ones in which they had grown up. As their biomediatized bodies moved through spaces that were suffused with commodity affect, they dreamed of futures that were redolent with growth and class mobility for themselves as well as for their loved ones. These were futures that were at once personal, professional, and collective. These futures gestured to visions of futurity that were about becoming.

Aspirations are social facts that can be empirically studied like any other cultural phenomenon. In our reading, the mall functions as a concrete, material, infrastructural site that shapes the horizons of aspiration and imagination. In arguing that BPO workers learn to labor by crafting subjectivities and aspirations at the mall as much as at work, we are disputing the idea of the "social factory" as an accomplished fact (Tronti 1973; Negri 1989) and underlining the contradictory and disjunctural mold of ISAs (against Althusser [1971]). Instead of emphasizing discipline and the effortless reproduction of the relations of production, we wish to focus on the lines of flight opened up by the power of affective intensities (Foucault [1975] 1977). To be sure, the mall and the BPO teach people to labor; however, they also gesture to potentiality and aspiration that leave the future open and, in this manner, malls became sites that generate futurity.[43] As Jisha Menon (2021, 7) has argued, "Aspiration draws from that tension between who one is and what one desires to become." We would add that it is this very tension, this site of friction between what is, what could be, and what should be that engenders potentiality. Thus, while malls are infrastructures that are useful in producing disciplined workers, they also create potentialities that exceed that function and may destabilize it.

We reprise our earlier argument that Bengaluru is not merely a context for the world of BPOs and those that work in it but is an actant: the affective regimes that constitute this city's multiple chronotopes play a crucial role in the formation of the subjectivities of its residents. With its dug-up roads and flyovers that hover suspended over neighborhoods and tech parks, half-finished and nowhere close to completion, the futurity of Bengaluru's inhabitants seems to also remain suspended. In a city that is careening toward the future even as it threatens to fall apart at its seams, futurity might seem to have a precarious future. Nevertheless, in our theorization of the role of malls in the generation of aspiration and futurity, we lean toward stressing the "victory" of the politics of possibility over the politics of probability (Appadurai 2013, 3). As Cross (2015) has insisted in his analysis of SEZs, "Living toward the future involves not just the structural resources bestowed upon people by history but also the energy to imagine a better life" (435). As spatiotemporalities constituted by commodity affect, malls engender modes of possibility and potentiality that are controlled as well as filled with enchantment.[44]

Like other affective regimes, commodity affect refers to "bodily capacities to affect and be affected, or the augmentation or diminution of a body's capacity to act, to engage, and to connect" (Clough 2007, 2). Generative of potentiality rather than a teleological fixing of meanings, commodity affect participates in the constitution of biomediatized bodies (Mankekar 2015, 202). The biomediatized bodies of BPO agents are historically specific: they are transformed by the sensoria of malls and the chronotopes of the city; they are loci of capital investment, disciplinary regimes of labor, commodification, and consumption; they are formed through forms of desire that may be surreptitious and potentially eruptive. These biomediatized bodies demonstrate modes of becoming: herein lies the centrality of malls to modes of futurity.

Our interlocutors' aspirations were frequently contradictory and always gestured to the complexity of their subject formation. Their dreams for the future pivoted around visions of growth, professional success, and upward mobility, but they were also hungry for fun, excitement, and the glossy sheen of cosmopolitanism. If they endeavored to acquire soft skills as part of a larger project of self-construction, their sense of duty to their loved ones sometimes generated resentment and, at other times, produced a profound sense of accomplishment. Some of our interlocutors longed to break free of their parents and their hometowns; notwithstanding their heterogeneous experiences in their childhood homes, most aspired to a harmonious family life to which they could retreat when the relentlessness of work threatened to numb their souls. Several of them struggled to develop entrepreneurial skills in the hope that doing so would expand the range of options for the lives they could lead outside the world of BPOs; some of them also sought pleasure in the enchanted spaces of malls where they could, if they wished, savor new cuisines, indulge in the air-conditioned fantasies spawned by multiplexes, or, on occasion, engage in clandestine romances. Malls played a powerful role in the reshaping of the entire being of BPO agents. At once sites of sociality and socialization, erotics and surveillance, and freedom and regulation, the hypermediated spaces of malls served as infrastructures of aspiration that indexed the formation of distinct futurities.

3.
INTIMACIES AT WORK

One night Mankekar barged calls with Rohith, a young man who was highly regarded by his peers and his supervisors for being particularly adept at dealing with difficult customers. Rohith was working on a process outsourced by a utility company in the United Kingdom that was specifically set up to cater to low-income seniors (or pensioners, as they are called in the UK). We recall that night to emphasize how, despite the arduousness and frustrations of his job, Rohith never lost his bearings; he displayed an unflinching ability to treat even his recalcitrant clients with understanding, respect, and compassion, wearing his dignity like a soft but impenetrable cloak around himself.

Rohith was part of a team tasked with selling a discounted utility package that would enable potential customers to save money while also conserving energy. This was a hard sell because many customers were skeptical that the discounts the company was offering were genuine. Mankekar sat with Rohith as he cajoled a customer that he was calling for the second time. Before he began the call, Rohith informed Mankekar that this customer was an elderly man who had asked him to call him back with more information about the discount. He added: "I've compiled this additional information for him, but I don't think I'll be able to clinch the sale even this time, no matter how hard I try."

Rohith's conversation with this customer took over thirty minutes—and, as Mankekar learned later, this was not the last long conversation between them. The customer asked him the same question over and over while Rohith repeated the same information with tremendous patience. The conversation meandered, jumping from one topic to another, with the customer sometimes asking about the utility package, at other times talking to Rohith about his children who had moved to Manchester and, at yet other times, railing against the government then in power in the United Kingdom. It became apparent that the customer may have been suffering from some sort of cognitive decline because he kept straying from one topic to another, often forgetting what had been said just minutes before. Every now and then he would raise his voice in frustration and become querulous; it did not sound like he was interested in the utility package at all. He just wanted to talk and would get angry if Rohith brought the topic back to the package. The man lived by himself, and it was evident that he was desperately lonely. Yet, Rohith never lost his patience and, at the end of the conversation, asked the customer if he needed more details. After logging out, he turned to Mankekar with a gentle smile, pointing to his forehead: "He is not all there. But there is nobody to take care of him. Nobody he can talk to. I would never leave my ajja-ajji [grandpa-grandma] alone. Ever. What is the point of working if you can't take care of your loved ones?"

Attentiveness is a hallmark of intimate labor, but BPO intimacies extend beyond attentiveness to include the relay of affect between agents and their customers and among agents themselves: intimacy constitutes the foundation of affective labor in BPOs. Intimate labor includes a spectrum of work including bill collection, elder care, domestic work, sex work, and various forms of therapy: it is work that "exposes personal information that would leave one vulnerable if others had access to such knowledge" (Boris and Parreñas 2010, 5). Not all service labor is intimate labor—for example, we would not normally think of fast-food workers as performing intimate labor. BPO agents' intimate encounters with customers also problematize conceptions of intimacy predicated on face-to-face interactions. BPOs exemplify the twin movement of capitalism across geographies and domains by bringing them together, fusing the (affectively) intimate with the (geographically) distant. The world of BPOs provides us with a lens to examine the generation and regulation of intimacy for the extraction of value resulting in the recreation and reinvention of capitalism itself. When intimate relations between agents and consumers form the basis of an industry, how does it change the labor process, the products of that labor, the futurities they generate, and the futures of workers? How does the mutual imbrication of intimacy and capital implicate futurity?

At the same time, intimacy provides a basis for relationality with the potential to disrupt the imperatives of capital accumulation. BPO intimacies are generated by labor regimes but also powerfully refract these regimes; just as intimate relations have been recast by capital, so too is the production of capital refracted by intimacy (Freeman 2020; Giddens 1992; Gregg 2011; Wilson 2004; Yanagisako 2002). The intimacies agents form with each other—of solidarity, care and mutual aid, friendship, or erotics—enables us to track the dynamic entwinement of labor and attunement, dependence and interdependence, and estrangement and community. While never innocent of relations of power, relationality provides BPO agents with an ethical map for navigating a rapidly changing, sometimes confusing, and frequently exhausting terrain shaped by conflicting demands of work, family, and desire.

We resituate intimacies within heterogeneous structures of inequality while simultaneously limning them for what they suggest about potentiality and becoming—in other words, about futurity. One influential argument about the future of capitalism emphasizes the growing risks to citizens and consumers posed by the expanding role of surveillance in capital accumulation (Zuboff 2019). This conception of surveillance depends on notions of interiority, privacy, and the sovereign subject that are increasingly being brought into question by affective industries such as BPOs.[1] The intimacies at work in BPOs, spanning the relationships agents forge with customers and each other, offer an opportunity to ponder the future of futurity in contexts of affective capitalism: relationality thus becomes a lens to examine the entanglements of capital accumulation, disjunctive visions of the future, and futurity as an ontological formation.

In positing that affective capitalism in industries such as BPOs has opened up new domains for intimate labor, we are careful to distinguish between the long history of such labor as exchange value in a marketplace and its specific incorporation in capitalist accumulation. In the *Grundrisse*, Karl Marx ([1939] 1973) makes a clear distinction between the sale of intimate labor services in exchange for money within simple circulation—"From whore to pope, there is a mass of such rabble"—and the consumption of such services with the goal of capital accumulation (272). The movement of intimate labor from simple circulation to expanded reproduction has involved two intertwined transformations. First, the labor process is altered so that forms of intimate labor that previously depended on physical proximity were reconfigured and outsourced to distant locations (Vora 2015).

For example, bill collection is now conducted primarily over the phone, sex work has changed due to the growth of internet and phone sex, and therapy is increasingly done with the analyst and the patient in different locations. Second, capitalist firms have developed new methods of monetizing forms of intimate labor that were previously part of processes of simple circulation. Examples of this are corporations that franchise maid services, massage therapy, or restaurants.

Capitalism is constantly reinvented in response to challenges (Lazzarato 2014; Dyer-Witheford 1999; Upadhya 2016): industries are reconstituted, with consequences for regimes of labor, for the subjectivities of workers, and for futures longed for and dreaded. In its ceaseless search for profits, capitalism expands by bringing previously unmonetized domains of social life, or those that were within simple circulation, into the circuit of accumulation (Wilson 2016). The growth of capitalism occurs not only through geographic expansion (for example, imperialism, colonialism, and globalization) but also by monetizing domains where markets did not exist earlier.

We draw on the work of feminist and antiracist scholars who call for a radical politicization of domains of intimacy as a modality for futurity. Their critiques challenge dominant conceptions of intimacy as the property of the individual, as confined to the realm of the domestic and the conjugal, and as related to interiority "possessed" by the bourgeois subject of Western modernity (Lowe 2015, 28).[2] Intimacies at work in BPOs represent the entanglement of power and desire in contemporary conjunctures of racial capitalism.[3] BPO intimacies are enmeshed within power and capital, whether generated in asymmetrical relationships between agents and their customers at a distance, in the close relations among agents that form in the affectively—and, sometimes, erotically—charged chronotopes of BPOs, or in the fundamentally *uneven* subsumption of intimacies by capital.[4] Thus, eschewing a notion of intimacy that is unmediated by capital, commodification, or transactional exchange, we propose that intimacy, alienated labor, profit, and value are inextricably entwined in the world of affective capitalism. BPO intimacies challenge assumptions of intimacy as inhering or located within sovereign subjects or, indeed, between them (and here we build on the work of Berlant 1998 and, especially, Gregg 2011). BPO intimacies develop between bodies that are reconstituted by racialized and gendered regimes of affective labor (chapter 4). We thus conceive of intimacy in terms of a particular calculus of attributing value and worth to racialized subjects (Lowe 2015, 18).

We begin by situating BPO intimacies in a larger context of transnational mutations of racial capitalism. We then theorize the relationship between agents and customers as intimacy across distance, followed by our analysis of relationships among agents or, what we term, intimacy up close. We next interrogate the implications of both types of intimacy in relation to Marx's concept of alienation. The last section of the chapter addresses the theoretical implications of the mutual construction of intimacy and capitalism for the generation of potentiality and futurities.

INTIMACIES OF RACIAL CAPITALISM

BPO agents' service work sometimes entailed servitude to customers in client nations in the Global North. The abuse that overseas customers meted out to agents from time to time was generally articulated in racial and national terms (for example, "bloody Indians") and could be belligerent and explicitly racist. Raghavi, whom we met in chapter 1, had worked as an agent in a UK debt collection process earlier in her career. She recollected how customers would get angry at her, saying, "You are all thieves. . . . You are taking our jobs. My son does not have a job because Indians are taking our jobs." Racial capitalism in this case was built on an active forgetting and inversion of the history of looting in the British Empire. When customers persisted in the abuse, she simply hung up on them. Raghavi told us that this was particularly hard on new agents, who sometimes started crying, but, she insisted, it was "part and parcel of the business." Many young women would cry, saying that they wanted to quit, and in those cases she counseled them by talking about her own experience and telling them, "Quitting for silly reasons does not help." By diminishing their feelings of distress and calling them "silly," Raghavi at once modeled for them what true professionalism consisted of and urged them to steel themselves against such abuse if they wanted to advance in their careers. Thus, a denial of racist abuse was taken as a precondition for getting the job done.

Agents usually downplayed racism by emphasizing that only a minority of customers became angry and that they had learned how to "handle it" so that it did not bother them as much as when they first began working (see also Padios 2018 for similar disavowals of racialism among call center workers in the Philippines). In the initial years of the BPO industry, agents were required to assume "foreign" accents, names, and personas and to disguise their locations to protect themselves (and, more importantly, the company) against the racist and xenophobic backlash against the outsourcing of service jobs to the Global South. At one call center, we were told that when British customers found out that the agent with whom they were interacting was based in India, they often asked for a British supervisor. When they found that the supervisor was Indian, they slammed the phone down or yelled virulent racist abuse. Sometimes, racialized abuse was glossed as complaints about incompetence or poor communication.

By the mid-2000s, after agents were instructed to speak in "neutral" accents (chapters 1 and 4; see also, especially, Aneesh 2015), the incidence of abuse had decreased somewhat because of this change in strategy, but the virulence of the racism they experienced from customers was unabated. They were subjected to racial abuse because of several factors, including the structural inequalities produced by uneven development: they were perceived as belonging to a poor country and, because their jobs and futures depended on contracts between their BPO and companies in rich countries, they often had no choice but to tolerate the abuse.

What do these racial(ized) dynamics between agents and their customers suggest about the relationship between affective labor and racial capitalism? Affective labor here *appears* to extend the legacies of colonial rule and of racial capitalism—the inequalities and racialized division of labor of a globally interconnected economy. But one has to parse out what has changed and what has not from colonial relations of inequality in contemporary formations of racial capitalism. How does it matter that the workers are citizens of an ostensibly sovereign nation-state rather than a colony? How does it matter that they are doing service work rather than manual labor such as that on a sugarcane plantation? What difference does it make that they can quit work for an employer (unlike enslaved or indentured laborers) and go to work for another company, and perhaps go to work in another sector that does not even cater to foreigners? And, finally, how does it matter that the companies they work for are owned and managed by Indians, and that these companies hire workers in many different locations, including the United Kingdom, the Caribbean, and Central America?

As we have argued in chapter 1, such patterns reconfigure, rather than replicate or simply extend, the long legacies of colonialism and race in South Asia (cf. Vora 2015): the companies where we did our fieldwork were managed and sometimes owned by Indians, and Indian companies themselves hired people in locations as diverse as Central America, the Philippines, and the United Kingdom. Even so, performing affective labor for customers in the Global North in the context of class inequalities could expose BPO workers to racist abuse. The agents were constrained in the kind of remedies they could offer consumers by the policies of the company on whose process they were working. For example, an agent employed by the Indian company FirstCall who was working on a process for Verizon had to follow a script provided by Verizon for what to do in different circumstances. But when consumers became frustrated with Verizon's procedures, policies, or products, they vented to the BPO agents, who were not even employees of Verizon. The negative comments directed at them by their customers were often colored by racist, colonialist, and Orientalist stereotypes.

Following Lisa Lowe (2015) in "unsettling the meaning of intimacy as the privileged sign of liberal interiority" (18), we locate BPO intimacies along terrains formed by uneven development and racial capitalism. In contemporary formations of racial capitalism undergirding ITES industries, the fault lines of race, colonialism, and gender inequality *rearticulate* with the geographies of combined and uneven development across and within nations. These rearticulations compel us to revise assumptions about the geographic basis of combined and uneven development and, in turn, about the futurities of nation-states and their citizens. BPOs foreground the emergence of recharged and reconfigured formations of race. Rather than being positioned through logics of visible Otherness, BPOs foreground new ways in which the racialized bodies have been rendered invisible but remain irrevocably Other as indexed through voice, accent, and speech rather than visual appearance (chapters 1 and 4). The irrevocable Otherness of the racialized bodies of BPO agents is also part of a longer and deeper history of the representation of "Asian" labor in some of the client nations and underscores the importance of investigating, through a transnational optic, how the relationship between labor, national location, and racialization of Asians is reconstituted and rearticulated in disparate sites. To what extent are these different histories and genealogies related, and what are the disconnections that separate them?

From Servitude to Service and Back Again?

How do histories of racialized service work in diverse sites enable us to understand the positioning of BPO workers in India as "cheap" labor?[5] While, in recent years, labor arbitrage has become a less crucial factor in contracting with BPOs in India, Indian workers continue to be paid substantially less than those doing comparable work in client nations: after all, the industry depends on the cost-effectiveness of outsourcing. The BPO industry exemplifies the intersection of informational capitalism and service labor:

affective labor in BPOs lies in an intermediate position between data entry work or food service work on the one hand, and software development on the other. As Winifred R. Poster (2007) points out, "While this job can be highly routinized (like at McDonald's), it can also involve a certain degree of improvisation (to sell a cell phone plan) and/or higher technical knowledge (explaining how to fix a computer)—both of which are more complex than merely entering health insurance claims onto a screen (data entry work)" (66). One of its distinctive features is that it is affective labor performed at a distance and mediated through information technology rather than, as with flight attendants or food service workers, provided in close physical proximity to customers.

Racial capitalism works "by displacing the uneven life chances that are inescapably part of capitalist social relations onto fictions of differing human capacities, historically race" (Melamed 2015, 77). With new information and communication technology have come new forms of servitude. Many BPO agents believed that servitude was part of their job: while they certainly did not enjoy having to always defer to customers no matter how rude or ignorant they were, agents believed it was incumbent upon them to do their best to cope, even when they felt resentful and angry. When these encounters turned abusive, they felt that they had no choice but to respond with "professionalism."[6] Servitude came with the job, they believed, because it was a result of being located in India and having to provide services to rich countries. Race, racial capitalism, and location hence converged to make our informants feel emplaced or locked into a place of servitude (chapter 1). For the most part, our informants were unable to talk back, literally or figuratively, because they (and the BPOs who employed them) could not afford to lose the contracts that enabled them to keep their jobs (see also Mirchandani 2005, 113). Frustration at their servitude fueled discourses of futurity in several ways. Our informants' acute consciousness of their servitude was paradoxically what gave affective potency to their insistence that they were participating in a larger national project, that of the upward mobility of the nation. By being associated with the ITES sector, agents believed they were contributing to the larger project of India Rising and they yoked their own upward mobility to the purportedly upward and future-oriented trajectory of the nation (see also Upadhya 2016; Kaur 2012).[7]

The racialization implicit in being a citizen of the Global South, made poor by histories of colonization and racial capitalism, is the constitutive condition of imagined and possible futures and futurities distinctive to the ITES industry. As we have argued, in contexts of racial capitalism, racialism extends beyond phenotype and entails a categorization of populations in terms of purportedly innate attributes and differential worth. Some encounters with overseas customers could become coercive, particularly when intimacy veered into sexual harassment and demonstrated the inextricability of discourses of sexuality and race. One agent, Annie, shared with us how she had to put up with the sexual innuendos of a customer. She was working on an inbound process, with customers calling in with questions about a particular software program. One customer had surmised that she was Indian and, upon confirming that, kept asking her if she was a virgin. At first, Annie avoided escalating the call to her supervisor because she was afraid that the supervisor would blame her for encouraging the customer. As a result, the customer kept calling back, ostensibly with questions about the software, and would ask for Annie by name. When she eventually asked her supervisor to forward the call to another agent, the customer claimed that she had given him bad advice and that was why he continued to have problems with his software. The supervisor then insisted that she handle all his calls, and the customer continued to harass her. This customer's behavior highlights the mutual imbrication of Orientalist and racialized discourses about Indian women's sexuality.

In this instance, and in others like it, intimate encounters across transnational space acquire the form of racialized sexual harassment, underscoring the assumed availability and desirability of previously colonized women. We noted earlier that agents rarely used the words *race* or *racism* to describe the abuse they faced from customers in the Global North; nor was race or racism a frequent topic of conversation among them. Trisha asked one of her trainers, "What do we do with a customer who is flirting?" The trainer said, "You respond by saying that we are not allowed to give personal information," and proceeded to reassure Trisha that she would not encounter people like that. However, although Trisha was a new trainee at this BPO, she spoke from previous experience as she had worked in a call center before. The trainer said that if she encounters such a situation, she can tell the customer that she is going to hang up and then do exactly that. Although it is clear that Trisha experienced racialized sexual harassment, she glossed it in the much more benign language of "flirting," which implies qualities that were notably absent, such as mutuality and play. Such strategies of coping with racialized sexual harassment were common among agents.

Thus, even in ostensibly postracial workspaces like BPOs, race played a central role in the sexual harassment faced by some women agents.[8]

Racialism, combined with uneven development, reinforces inequalities within and across geographic space. Racialism in capitalism, in fact, acquires greater, more insidious power precisely when it is obscured or denied, as in contexts shaped by neoliberalism.

Scholars within the autonomist Marxist tradition have argued that capitalism works through the production and modulation of the selves (or "souls" [Berardi 2009]) of workers, but it does so across the socius rather than just within the factory or, as in our case, the BPO. Conversely, conditions of production are shaped by workplace socialities (Lazzarato 2014) and, we would add, intimacies. We diverge from the assumption that people's authentic selves are only expressed in the supposedly private sphere of the home and the family and that, by contrast, their public face is a performance or a mask.[9] A dichotomy between "false" identities and the purportedly authentic selves of BPO agents is consistently foregrounded in televisual, cinematic, and print narratives that dwell on the use of false names by agents when speaking with international customers (Mankekar 2015; cf. Hochschild 2012). In these narratives, we see the playing out of the distinction between the true, authentic selfhood of the sovereign subject, expressed through their real, domestic, private identities, and the false, inauthentic persona that the agent deploys in forming intimate relations with customers. Film titles like *Nalini by Day, Nancy by Night* and *John and Jane Toll-Free* resurrect the fantasy of a split between purportedly private and public selfhoods, between authentic, private, sovereign subjects and the inauthentic, public identities that they have to assume for their work. Rather than indicating authentic subjecthood, intimacies, in all their complexity and multiplicity, are embedded in asymmetric power relations produced by and through regimes of labor (Mankekar 2015; Berlant 1998).

Carla Freeman (2020) attests that, in contemporary formations of capitalism, "emotions have become a critical medium through which labor is performed, valued, and exchanged today, and the role these transformations have in making a life, as well as a living, is critically important within market and nonmarket practices and relations" (3). Preserving the analytical distinction between emotion and affect, we engage the emotions that suffuse the interactions of BPO agents with customers, as well as the affective regimes engendering their subject formation (see also Mankekar 2015).[10] Emotion refers to the "sociolinguistic fixing of the quality of an experience . . . the conventional, consensual point of insertion into semantically and semiotically formed progressions," while affect is unqualified (Massumi 2002, 28).[11] In terms of Peircean semiotics, if affect is about abduction, the moment before capture by language, emotions are indexical of affect. While neither emotion nor affect are located *within* subjects, affect refers to the ineffable and unqualified, yet unnameable, intensity that circulates among subjects, between subjects and objects, and between humans and more-than-humans to transect the cognitive, the visceral, and the social (Massumi 2002, 28). Although it is irreducible to the social, affect saturates sociality; affect produces and inflects domains of intimacy so as to problematize the distinction between the subjective and the collective.

For agents to perform affective labor, encounters and interactions veered into zones of intimacy so that they could, for instance, obtain the information they needed from customers or collect debts on the basis of information to which nobody else was privy. We begin by tracing the relationship between affective labor, affect, and BPO agents' cultivation of the emotions that generate intimacies. The ability of BPO agents to meet quotas set by their supervisors was predicated on their capacity to assume culturally appropriate emotions in their interactions with clients. All the trainers, team leaders, and BPO agents we worked with emphasized the importance of cultivating attention, courtesy, friendliness, empathy, and other emotions that we *retroactively* name to index the potent intensities that loop between agents and their customers. For example, since the modalities of courtesy and friendliness in the United States, the United Kingdom, or Australia (the main markets for Indian BPOs) are different from those in India, our interlocutors had to learn culturally specific modes of effecting the right affect in their voices. We have already noted that several agents working on US processes had to unlearn ostensibly "Indian" modes of respect for authority and deference in favor of adopting "American" speech patterns of informality and assertiveness. In contrast, agents working on UK processes had to deploy speech patterns that were much more formal so as to represent "British" forms of courtesy and hierarchy. Much of the training focused on such nuances and on retraining the body and the voice to produce the right affect in agents' scripted as well as unscripted encounters with customers. In training, agents were often told to smile while speaking to customers. The idea was that, even though customers could not see them smiling, they would be able to "hear" the agents' smiles in their voices. Veronica, whom we met earlier in this book, would repeatedly say to us, "It is all in the voice. You have to distill your emotions into your voice."

We learned of the importance given to cultivating empathy when we observed training sessions of BPO agents for hundreds of hours. As the example above of Rohith demonstrates, these modes of courtesy, kindness, and care engendered BPO intimacies primarily through the production of empathy.[12] Douglas Hollan (2012) alerts us to two modalities of empathy. Basic empathy occurs when mirror neurons get activated when we observe another's behavior and is, therefore, an "automatic" corporeal response (70). What happens when BPO agents interact with people that they cannot see, whose expressions they cannot observe, and who live in cultural contexts far removed from them (Throop 2012, 411)? In these circumstances, how are agents to feel empathy?[13]

Angelina, the head of recruiting at one of the large BPOs at which we conducted our research, told us that working in BPOs made people and their families more broad-minded. When agents worked on US or UK processes, they "got to know that culture." That knowledge was enhanced when clients from companies that hired the Indian BPO to manage a process "came down to talk to the agents." Dealing with overseas customers, she felt, offered agents greater exposure to the world. She unwittingly contrasted this growing cosmopolitanism when she went on to compare working on a US process with a British one. In her view, agents on a US process experienced much more abuse because people from the United Kingdom "talk sweetly and put the phone down." In other words, British customers preferred to hang up on intrusive calls rather than shout abuse at the caller. Neither set of customers displayed any interest in understanding the world of BPO agents or displayed any empathy for agents.

In interacting with overseas customers, BPO agents have to be trained to cultivate empathy because they are not engaging in face-to-face interactions with people who share their cultural repertoires. What is needed here, in particular, is what Hollan (2012) calls "complex empathy": "If empathy is merely the capacity to detect in a visceral or perceptual way when another is in a certain emotional state or involved in a certain goal-directed behavior, that is one thing. . . . Its full realization also requires knowledge that is more sensitive to situation and context, and also more prone to misinterpretation and error" (71). Complex empathy entails a more conscious awareness of other bodies and people and engagement with them (71). BPO agents are trained to become conscious of the experiences and feelings of their customers; the assumption is that with training, and over time, agents will intuitively understand their customers and hence be better able to serve them, a process that requires both emotional resonance and imagination (72). How do BPO agents acquire empathy while engaging in virtual migration and imaginative travel to the places where their customers are located, when they and their customers cannot see each other? How do they find a way to establish rapport across physical and cultural distances?

Empathy has a temporality of its own. As C. Jason Throop and Dan Zahavi (2020, 287) argue, "Empathy constitutes an orientation to another as an immediately experienced disclosure of another's lived experience through time." BPO agents become enmeshed in the feelings of their customers; they also become nodes in the transmission of affect—its relay—between themselves and their customers. Empathy is aligned with affect rather than with the repertoire of skills or emotions that BPO agents must actively, if over time nonconsciously, deploy: empathy is productive of agents' capacities to make customers comfortable, solve their problems, or solicit information from them. Thus understood, if empathy indexes a particular sense of the other that we may retroactively name as empathy, it is also productive of action.

We turn, again, to the role of the auditory—in particular, to how, in their intimate encounters with overseas customers, agents must train their ears to pick up emotional nuances in the speech, hesitations, and silences at the other end of the line just as their voices must be trained to establish rapport, express empathy, offer care and, in so doing, foster a relationship of intimacy.[14] BPO agents need to undergo intensive cultural training in order to cultivate complex empathy because they do not share the linguistic or cultural backgrounds of their customers. They cannot see firsthand the emotions, facial expressions, postures, and body language of their customers but, nevertheless, must try to sense how they are feeling and what they are thinking.

It is this ability to sense what is going on, even when they cannot name it, that enables them to establish rapport with customers and, eventually, to form intimate relationships with them: this relay, or feedback loop, of affect is critical to the formation of intimacies between agents and their customers. As Veronica asserted repeatedly in her training sessions with agents, "Try to put yourself in their shoes, look at what is happening from their point of view." She would emphasize the importance of active listening to learn how best to respond to customers so that they felt that agents "care for them." Active listening skills, as much as cultural training, were thus crucial to establishing intimacy with customers.

BPO intimacies develop in contexts shaped by stringent controls over time, space, and the bodies of workers: as we have noted in earlier chapters, surveillance is an important component of the environment in which these agents worked and set the parameters for their affective labor. If the success of agents in their jobs depended on their ability to produce appropriate emotion, they were frequently bound to the parameters set in the script they had to follow. This script was usually provided by the client company, and protocols for beginning a call and signing off had to be followed to the letter. All calls were recorded in their entirety and subjected to random checks by the quality assurance team; as we have noted earlier, a complaint from a customer to the client company could potentially cause not only the agent in question to lose his or her job but, if the complaint was serious, for the BPO to lose its contract.

Rather than being opposed to intimacy, surveillance itself generated certain kinds of intimacy. In one of the training sessions observed by Mankekar, Veronica spoke explicitly about the significance of cultivating empathy. It was past midnight but, in contrast to Mankekar, who was struggling to suppress her yawns and sit straight instead of slumping in her chair, others in the room seemed to be hanging on Veronica's every word, their bodies leaning forward with eagerness and anticipation. They were to join a debt collection process that had been outsourced to the company by a firm in the western United States. Almost everybody in the room was in their early twenties. They had just reconvened after a brief coffee break, but it seemed as if they could have done without the caffeine: their excitement about being there seemed to provide them with all the energy they needed. After a session that dwelt on supplying the new recruits with information about the client company, Veronica turned to the modes of attunement and empathy the agents needed to cultivate. What she proceeded to say made Mankekar sit up:

> If you need to get information out of them, especially if it is information that they don't usually share with anybody, for instance, about their health or about their budget or debts . . . you need to make them feel you understand [them] and that you feel close to them. If they complain, you have to respond that you understand, even when they are being abusive or ill-tempered. Stay in control of the conversation, try to change the mood of the customer if they're being hostile, especially if you're trying to sell them something they're unsure about or if you need information from them.

Understanding, rapport, and empathy here index the mobilization of affect to generate sales, solicit information, solve problems, and hence secure profits for the company: these modes of attunement lie at the core of the affective labor of customer service agents.

Of course, the empathetic relationships between agents and their customers, even when they resulted in encounters that led to intimacy, did not by any means dissolve the asymmetries between them. As Throop (2012, 410) insists, "Empathy is never simply based on shared experiences . . . it is instead an imaginative, cognitive, affective and communicative experience that *maintains* crucial asymmetries for the empathizer and empathizee alike" (emphasis added; see also Throop and Zahavi 2020). Both agents and their customers participated in the empathetic relationship but in unequal ways. The stakes were different for each of them. The expectation of empathy applied primarily to the BPO agent: customers were, by no means, expected to be empathetic to agents. The intimate encounter between agents and customers occurred between people with very different positionalities on a terrain sedimented by race, national location, and the inequalities produced by global capitalism. Agents had to try to form intimacies with customers located in the Global North even if they experienced racist and xenophobic hostility from them. If an agent had had a bad day, was ill, or was upset or frustrated about something, they were required to put their feelings aside: this, Veronica emphasized to them, was the "professional thing to do" (Padios 2018, 75). But this would place an enormous strain on agents, offering an important corrective to the unexamined assumption that intimacy connotes "familiarity and comfort" (Berlant 1998, 281). The production and mobilization of intimacy were exhausting for BPO agents, perhaps more so than for workers in other service industries. It was for this reason that the affective labor performed in BPOs led to burnout, depression, and chronic anxiety for some agents.

BPO intimacies are facilitated and shaped by technological infrastructures and suffused with the work of capital. In the ITES industry, in particular, communication technologies expand the senses in powerful ways and heighten the intimacies between gendered, sexualized, and racialized bodies. What are some of the intimacies engendered by information technology?[15] As Min Joo Lee (2020) notes in her ethnography of Korean television dramas, Hallyu fans forge transnational intimacies through online forums and fan-made music videos. Like Hallyu fans, BPO agents enter into intimacies with customers at a distance. However, this is where the similarity between Hallyu fans and BPO agents ends. Most of the Hallyu fans that Lee interviewed lived in Europe and North America and, moved by the erotic fantasies generated by Korean television dramas, had the financial resources (and passports) to travel to Korea to meet and form intimate relationships with Korean men. And, if their relationships with these men did not work out for whatever reason, they had the ability to walk away. In contrast, BPO agents located in Bengaluru had neither the means nor the opportunities to travel to the countries where their customers are located. More importantly, they did not voluntarily form intimacies with their customers: they were required to do so in order to provide customer service to them. Positioned in unequal relations of power, BPO agents cannot ordinarily hang up on their customers, no matter how exhausted, uncomfortable, or harassed they might feel. BPO intimacies hence result from the intersection of capital, labor, and the politics of race, national location, sexuality, and gender.

Carol Upadhya (2016) warns us that the reorganization of work by information technology "does not necessarily indicate a shift to a new type of society, governed by a 'post-disciplinary' logic; rather, a diversity of technologies are simultaneously in operation" (19). BPO intimacies ensue from the articulation of information technology, affective capitalism, and technologies of surveillance. On the one hand, as we will demonstrate later in this chapter, BPO intimacies are generated recursively through the moral policing to which agents, especially women agents, are subject in the media and by community members, relatives, neighbors, landlords, and indeed, by managers and colleagues in their companies. At the same time, BPO intimacies are also produced by a set of infrastructures—some technical, some organizational, all sociocultural—that enabled the industry to emerge in the first place and that shaped the type of relations that were fashioned between agents and customers.

This is not a case of intimate, local, familial life being invaded by capital (Yanagisako 2002). Rather, a new set of technological and material infrastructures enables forms of sociality and intimacy across vast distances, extending in space and time what telephones had long done in the Global North (Wilson 2016, 259–63). However, although the technology that enables high-quality voice transmission across the globe is often emphasized in the rise of BPOs in countries such as India and the Philippines, organizational innovations made by companies doing back-office work in these locations also play an important role (Aneesh 2015; Padios 2018). For example, large call centers in the United States typically consist of approximately two hundred to three hundred workers in one location; by contrast, there are many operations in India that are ten times larger. The ability to scale up allows these organizations to be more flexible in adding additional labor power when necessary, by moving people from one process to another, giving them a competitive advantage that goes beyond low labor costs. This scale, in turn, creates more possibilities for relations of intimacy to develop among the agents themselves.

The intimacies formed through BPO agents' encounters with customers were heterogeneous: they generated sentiments of compassion, sympathy, resentment, envy, and revulsion and, on occasion, involved racialized erotics.[16] Their bodies would register hostility when they had to deal with racist abuse from customers. In these instances, hostility forms "a reflux back from conscious experience to affect, it is registered as affect" (Clough 2008, 4). Hostility would become an intimate experience, one felt and registered in the body. Thus, while intimacy with customers sometimes generated empathy and solicitude (the expected outcome), at other times it produced feelings of anxiety, resentment, envy, and anger (cf. Throop and Zahavi 2020). For instance, once they had some experience in dealing with customers in the Global North, agents realized that their relatively poor economic position had little to do with their intelligence or ability but was the result of geopolitical inequality.[17] While helping customers book holidays to Mallorca or Ibiza, they wondered aloud to us why they could never dream of holidaying there, and why an accident of birth (and, we would add, racial capitalism) should privilege some people in this manner. These intimacies naturalized the inequalities of racial capitalism. Far from generating warmth or comfort for agents, they often produced "ugly sentiments" (Ngai 2005).

The quality of customer service provided by agents had material consequences for their careers and their ability to retain their jobs and was evaluated according to their abilities to make customers comfortable enough to divulge information that they were unlikely to share with others: the capacity to cultivate empathy and intimacy was thus directly connected to the kinds of futures to which they aspired. One agent eloquently described the situation thus: "We learn as much about a customer as their own family—in some cases, we know things about them that even their own family members don't know." The intimate details that they shared with agents could include information about why they had credit card charges from a foreign country, why their phone bill was so high that month, who came to get them when their car broke down, and so on. The intimacies engendered by the affective labor of BPO agents were thus not epiphenomenal but were intrinsic to the productive process. In certain kinds of processes (for example, debt collection or processes involving health care), faced with the grief, loneliness, or despair of customers, some BPO agents would respond with sympathy and compassion: the depth of these emotions was a measure of the intimacy that at times develops among ostensible strangers. Some of these encounters were fleeting; yet others stretched over weeks, if not longer; many of these encounters touched and affected our interlocutors in powerful ways.

Other agents were deeply ambivalent about the intimacy that they had to establish with customers. One young man, Andrew, felt torn about the intimate conversations that had developed between him and an elderly customer in the United Kingdom. Andrew claimed that this customer kept calling for customer service and would ask for him by name. Despite the team leader's efforts to shield Andrew from his repeated calls, he would refuse to speak with anybody else. Once on the phone, this customer would talk for hours about his deceased wife, sometimes weeping with grief, on other occasions bitterly angry that she had "left" him. At first, Andrew was deeply sympathetic and did nothing to discourage him but, as time went on, he began to dread these calls because they lasted so long and, worse, because he felt emotionally drained by them. Yet, Andrew was not in a position to disconnect the call because customer complaints could risk his job and livelihood at the BPO.

INTERJECTION

We are a month into our fieldwork with BPO agents in Bengaluru when, on January 24, 2009, forty members of the Hindu nationalist organization, Sri Ram Sene, attack young men and women at the Amnesia Pub in Mangalore, a coastal city in the state of Karnataka. They brazenly justify this attack by saying that they were protecting the honor of the young women (by publicly humiliating and beating them!) because they wore skimpy clothes, drank alcohol, and engaged in allegedly "indecent" behavior with men. Mangalore is about 350 kilometers from Bengaluru, and the BPO agents we meet are shaken by these events. Shortly thereafter, the Sri Ram Sene, along with other Hindu nationalist organizations across the country such as the Bajrang Dal and the Vishwa Hindu Parishad, launches a campaign against the celebration of Valentine's Day by young couples. The Sene's leader, Pramod Muthalik, proclaims that "Sene activists across Karnataka would not only hold protests outside colleges, hostels, and hotels where Valentine's Day celebrations are held but would also forcibly marry off couples found dating in public" (The Hindu 2009)

Distressing as these developments are, they are not surprising to us: this is not the first time that desire, especially transgressive desire, has become the target of ostracism, moral policing, and violence, and Hindu nationalist organizations have long been campaigning against Valentine's Day (Mankekar 2015). But, in recent years, desire expressed outside the confines of marriage and, in particular, sexual relationships across the boundaries of caste and religion have become the target of spectacularly violent attacks by Hindu nationalists, as evident in the brutal murders of young people who enter into intercaste liaisons and the lynching of Muslim men who are accused of waging "Love Jihad" by courting or marrying Hindu women (Mankekar 2021a, 2021b).

This is a hate-filled time for young people to fall in love. We can hear the anxiety in the voices of some of the agents that we are just getting to know, some of whom are in intercaste or interreligious relationships. They feel particularly vulnerable because of media representations of BPO agents that allege that they frequent pubs and engage in promiscuous sex (John and Tejaswi 2006). This time, our interlocutors insist, things have gone too far.

This is the mood in the state of Karnataka when we begin our fieldwork with Bengaluru's BPO agents.

INTIMACIES UP CLOSE

When we began intensive fieldwork in 2009, BPO firms were facing high rates of attrition, with agents either moving to other companies for a higher salary or what they hoped would be better working conditions or leaving the industry altogether. Trainers and managers emphasized to us that attrition was a major threat to the financial health of a BPO. Having invested many resources in training agents, HR personnel and managers believed that it was too expensive to constantly recruit and train new agents; they, therefore, had to work very hard to keep up the morale of their workers and they did this in various ways. The walls of the shop floor would be covered with inspirational messages emphasizing the personal growth of agents and their opportunities to ascend the occupational ladder; photographs and brief bios of "Agents of the Month" or "Managers of the Month" would be posted in lobbies, elevators, and other common areas. Managers hosted employee-appreciation parties at which agents would be presented with awards for meeting or exceeding quotas and took employees out to lunches on a regular basis. In addition to giving bonuses to high-achieving teams, in some cases companies hosted weekends at nearby resorts as part of "team-building exercises"; in other instances, when they had the resources, they flew high-achieving agents (and a companion) to overseas destinations like Singapore or Malaysia (we have elaborated on the "fun at work" strategies of BPOs in chapter 2).

Over coffee one night with Veronica and Raghavi, Mankekar specifically inquired about the opportunities given to agents to socialize with each other. Raghavi and Veronica both replied that the company did this to keep up the morale of workers. Raghavi added, "We want our workers to bond with each other. They do have to compete with each other, but we don't want them to hate each other; we want them to trust each other and be there for each other." Veronica added: "We take them out for lunch and to resorts because we want to show them that we care for them and don't want them to burn out. If they are able to blow off steam and relax over the weekend, [they] come back to work more energized. Burnout leads to rapid turnover and, after investing so much in training agents, BPOs cannot afford that."

The intimacies that develop among BPO agents help in the generation of profit for the company, thus underscoring the close relationship between affect and the needs of capital (Vora 2015). Yet it is also true that, more often than not, the intimacies that formed among our interlocutors, whether they were close friendships or sexual relationships, not just survived but flourished despite the competition, fatigue, burnout, lateral mobility, and other strains on their relationships: in many instances, the intimacies that developed among agents exceeded the imperative of teamwork. These relationships underscore the multiplicity of BPO intimacies: not all BPO intimacies are erotic or sexual, nor can they be subsumed or overdetermined by the imperative of productivity. In fact, management clearly saw some workplace intimacies as a threat to productivity.

Freeman (2020) critiques scholarly analyses of social formations in Barbados that tend to emphasize political economy at the expense of feelings and affect: "In this economy of value, tenderness and affection as sources of vulnerability have historically been subsumed by systems of material exchange and expressed in (mostly negative) 'socioeconomic' terms" (4). Likewise, we find analyses of BPOs and call centers in India that focus *solely* on the economic exploitation of agents unpersuasive—not because workers are not exploited but because these accounts ignore the complexity of the subject formation of agents whose lives, bodies, and futurities are, without a doubt, profoundly shaped by their labor regimes but who also have desires, aspirations, and social relationships that cannot be subsumed by the imperative for productivity. Put another way, we are wary of viewing them through a productivist lens at the expense of other aspects of their lives.

Indeed, intimate friendships, including those forged at work, were crucial to our interlocutors' senses of self, opening up new worlds of possibility both in their careers and in their personal lives (cf. Freeman 2020, 2). Many new recruits informed us that they applied for a job in a particular company either at the same time as a friend or because a friend was already working there.

Agents who became close friends would know intimate details about each other's lives, their family members, their love lives, their health crises, and their financial worries. They would spend most of their leisure time with each other, plan their futures together, and share details about their pasts. We would witness, and often join, agents as they ate together in the company cafeteria or at a nearby mall or when they went out for coffee or a drink after work. When they spent their downtime together, they commiserated about the arduousness of their work and the surveillance of their supervisors and shared and encouraged each other's dreams and aspirations. We witnessed the strength of these solidarities and intimacies as they supported each other at work, in finding new jobs, and in dealing with racist and xenophobic abuse from customers. They turned to each other during numerous personal crises stemming from the disapproval of families, the hostility of neighbors, the suspicions of community members and landlords, marital tensions, romantic breakups, health emergencies, miscarriages, and abortions. These intimate bonds were so powerful that the greatest fear of managers and HR personnel was that if one agent left the BPO to join another firm, a group of friends would follow. Raghavi wryly observed, "When one team member leaves, their friends also leave. It is like an infection [that] spreads within the team and all our hard work in training them comes to nothing."

The untimely nature of the work of our interlocutors, and the discrepant temporalities it produced, shaped a range of intimate relations implicating their bodies, each other, and their customers. In addition to the intrinsically intimate experience of having their circadian rhythms disturbed (chapter 4), BPO agents also experienced a disruption of their social life outside the workspace. Their interactions with family members, neighbors, and friends—indeed with all those who did not work the same hours—were severely curtailed. Undoubtedly, the intimacies that developed among agents were profoundly shaped by the fact that they were cut off from the family and the friends with whom they had grown up. Several agents felt that they had more in common with friends formed at the workplace than with family members or childhood friends. Rajan, who had worked in BPOs for close to seven years, pointed out to us, "My friends here can understand what we're going through. People at home have no idea what we have to deal with, so it is easy for them to criticize [us]." Like many kinds of service work, their work was intensely social, even as their labor was predicated on interactions that were highly structured by the demands of capital.

What do we make of the intimacies that formed at work or, as Melissa Gregg (2011) puts it, work's intimacy? In her nuanced ethnography of workers in Brisbane whose labor is mediated by new media technologies, Gregg points to how work has itself become a source of intimacy. Tacking back and forth between the homes and the newly configured workspaces of her informants, Gregg persuasively argues that work's intimacy occurs when it moves to the center of the everyday lives of professionals whose work has shifted online, often at the expense of other sources of intimacy and fulfillment: prior tendencies to affectively invest in work have only been exacerbated with the movement of work from offices to cafés, living rooms, and bedrooms. She argues that "the social bonds developed between co-workers in the office are a contributing factor in extending work hours" (85): work's intimacies are thus riddled with ambiguities and contradictions. This "presence bleed," she suggests, occurs when the line between work and family life is blurred and, rather than freeing her interlocutors from the demands of work, labor seems to take over their personal lives and relationships: work, domesticity, and intimacy get reconstituted as information technologies reconfigure the terrain of their labor. While technology has always constituted how we live and work, she argues, digital media enable forms of self-regulation, constant connectivity, and social networking that are intrinsic to work. Gregg points out that when work competes with family "it is work that often emerges the winner" (122).

While Gregg's theorization of work's intimacy centers on how labor is reconfigured by the literal extension of the workplace into homes and other spaces of domesticity and leisure, we are concerned with how regimes of affective labor in BPOs generate intimacies at work. Given the temporal disjunctions caused by the demands of working at night and sleeping during the day when their families and friends are awake, the rhythms of labor place an enormous strain on the family lives of BPO agents. Yet, as we have been arguing, their affective labor is also productive of other socialities and intimacies that are, undeniably, refracted by the demands of capital. Jan M. Padios (2018, 47), in her analysis of call center workers in the Philippines, argues that some of these workplace socialities and intimacies "function as the call center's own internal realm of social reproduction" (see also Aneesh 2015). Not only do work cultures foster positive social relations among workers through formal corporate culture and management practices, but the informal intimacies that emerge among them are also appropriated as "raw material of call center work" (Padios 2018, 37).

We unequivocally concur with Aneesh (2015), Padios (2018), and Gregg (2011) who caution us about the corporatization of intimacy. At the same time, some BPO intimacies also potentially push back against the demands of labor regimes. BPO intimacies frequently extended beyond the demands of affective labor.[18] While not all intimacies among our interlocutors were erotic or sexual, BPOs offered young men and women opportunities to engage in sexual liaisons.[19] Close friendships sometimes led to or coexisted with sexual relationships, including those that were socially stigmatized or tabooed—for instance, "live-in" relationships, and intercaste and interreligious sexual relationships.

Although in recent years social mores regarding sexuality in cities and among middle-class youth have shifted somewhat, these opportunities to engage in sexual liaisons contrasted with the cultural norms to which BPO agents had been previously habituated. In most Hindu communities, intercaste sexual relationships and marriages continue to be deemed transgressive because they threaten to undermine caste hierarchy. In these communities, marriage is perceived as fundamental to caste hierarchy: hence, caste continues to be crucial in "regulating sexuality, configuring ties of kinship, and representing desire" (A. Rao 2005, 715).[20] According to these hegemonic discourses of caste and sexuality, intercaste marriages represent a moral breach. For instance, when a member of a dominant caste comes into contact with someone from a former "untouchable" caste, both parties are perceived to be defiled: "Contact is a quality that is present in the 'toucher' and the 'touched'" (Sarukkai 2014, 165).[21] In addition to caste rules regarding sharing, preparation, and consumption of food (Kanjilal 2023), marriage remains a paradigmatic site for the generation and regulation of erotic desire *in terms of* caste (Mankekar and Kanjilal 2022, 2–3). The emergence of intercaste intimacies in BPOs was thus striking to us because of the persistence of taboos against them: these relationships were all the more transgressive in the context of the spectacular spike in recent years in violence against Dalit and Bahujan communities.[22]

According to the 2015 census conducted by the Karnataka state government, only 4 percent of all the married couples in Bengaluru had married outside of their respective castes, while only a little over 4 percent of the marriages were interreligious. Furthermore, as of 2015, about 92 percent of Bengaluru's residents married not only within their religion but also within their respective castes (Sidhnath 2020). Given that we conducted our fieldwork during a sociohistorical moment marked by the spectacular ascendance of Hindu nationalism, intensified caste violence, and virulent Islamophobia, we were surprised by the number of intercaste and interreligious relationships we came across in BPOs. Far be it for us to claim that these transgressive relationships undermined or subverted the structural violence and hegemony of caste or Islamophobia. Nevertheless, we continue to find remarkable how some of these relationships endured social stigma and the disapproval of family members and community hostility. For instance, Rajan, a man from an oppressed caste who identified as Hindu, had a Muslim wife, Aaliya, with whom he fell in love while working in the same office. They married after dating for three years. Rajan confided that one of the reasons why he had married Aaliya was because as a BPO agent, she understood the pressures he was under at work: in his words, they were "in the same boat." His parents, who had moved in with him, at first "threw a fit." But his parents were financially dependent first on him and, after he and Aaliya married, on both their salaries and hence realized that "they had to stop hassling [the married couple]." When asked about how things were going after their marriage, Rajan replied, "They're learning to respect Aaliya but are still not very warm to her. They respect her because she has proved herself as a good daughter-in-law. She has left the BPO and has got work in the front office of a hotel. She still has to work at night but not as often, so she took this job even though she now has a lower salary." This, Rajan claimed, was helpful because they now had a baby girl. Rajan added that after the birth of their daughter, Aaliya was accepted more fully into the fold of the family. While their marriage had caused a scandal in his extended family and community, his parents now defended her from the criticism of other relatives.

We came across several other interreligious relationships. Veronica, who is Christian, was engaged to a Hindu man whom she met when she first entered the BPO industry as an agent. Shahzia, a Muslim woman who had grown up in Chennai, married a Maharashtrian Brahmin man from Mumbai. Shahzia and her partner were in a "live-in" relationship for a year before they married. Her in-laws had grudgingly come to terms with the fact that she is Muslim. Shahzia said: "Of course, my in-laws don't live with us, who knows how it will go if they live with us. It is hard when they come to visit." Initially, Shahzia's in-laws had disapproved of her because she was Muslim and worked in a BPO. But after they learned that she had risen up the ranks and joined the HR section of the company, she added, they became "much nicer" to her. She was senior in rank and authority to her husband but that did not seem to strain their marriage. However, when he left to join another company, his supervisor was unhappy with Shahzia because he felt that their relationship resulted in the loss of a good worker. She remained with the BPO for another year but then left to join an NGO that had been started by a woman who had retired as a CEO in one of the first BPOs set up in Bengaluru. This NGO provided schooling to children in slums and Shahzia felt that, since she had made enough money, she could afford to leave and could now "give back" through community service. Furthermore, working at the NGO was not as arduous: she now had the flexibility to take care of their little son. She added that since her husband made enough money to support them all, she could finally do what she wanted. As we have previously noted in the case of Aaliya, Shahzia, and several other women to whom we became close, gendered expectations regarding biological and cultural reproduction and the division of labor in the household shape the trajectories of women agents.

Not all the intercaste and interreligious relationships that we observed survived the pressures of social and family approval. Peter, a devout Christian, was an agent in a technical process. While studying engineering, he fell madly in love with his classmate, who came from the same region but from a dominant-caste Hindu family. Peter was now working in Bengaluru while she was back in her natal home. They wanted to get married, but her parents objected, and she did not want to elope and cut off relations with her family. In the hopes of marrying her to a person who they thought was more socially appropriate, her family forced her to meet prospective suitors who belonged to the same caste group and class status as them. She refused all suitors because her heart was set on Peter. Although her parents closely monitored her so that she could not meet Peter, they talked and texted frequently via cell phone. When her parents confiscated her cell phone, she still managed to reach him by sending messages using her friends' cell phones. Finally, fed up with her intransigence, and to ensure that she could not communicate with Peter, her family shut her in a room and refused to let her leave. Her parents objected to their marriage not only because Peter was Christian but because they thought that his family was likely to be Dalit converts to Christianity. They framed their objection, however, in terms of class: they told her that they did not approve of the marriage because his family did not own land or other assets, and he himself was not working as a software engineer or in a similar high-status job with a substantial income that would guarantee a stable financial future. After many years of pining for each other, the two lovers accepted their fate and agreed that there was no future for them together. When Peter shared this news with Gupta, he was devastated; what pulled him through was his strong commitment to his faith. He accepted that they had no choice but to be reconciled to the cruelties of class and caste inequality and the prejudices and pieties that people pedaled in the name of religion.

Unlike Shahzia, most agents, men as well as women, did not have the luxury of quitting their jobs to do community service; at most, they could move laterally to jobs that paid better or had less strenuous work schedules. Some of our interlocutors spoke of the high price they paid for their high salaries. Even when they were married to people who worked in the same industry, agents worried about the strain placed on their marriages when they were unable to see their spouses for nights on end. Francis's case is illustrative. He came from a middle-class family—his father worked at a large public-sector company in northern India. After high school, he moved to Mumbai and worked in sales and marketing, dealing largely with telecommunications equipment. He moved to Bengaluru in 2001 on the urging of his sister, who had moved there after her marriage. He started a business with a friend setting up video conferencing for the growing IT industry. When his friend emigrated to Australia in 2006, the business shut down and Francis joined a BPO because several of his friends were working there. He did very well and rose up the ranks rapidly. Unlike some other agents that we interviewed, he planned to stay in the BPO business and saw himself as an operations manager or general manager for some reputable company in a few years. His wife worked from home for a medical transcription company doing quality control and had regular work hours that began in the morning and ended at 5:30 p.m., whereas Francis worked the night shift. He got up to have lunch with his wife and then went back to sleep, getting up again when her shift ended. They then spent a couple of hours together and ate dinner. After dinner, it was time for him to leave for work. Francis credited his work with helping him to develop listening skills that he was able to employ in other aspects of his life, from his relationship with his wife to that with his driver. He said his "patience level" had gone up, and he had learned to say things clearly and to finish his thoughts so that the other person understood what he intended to say. But his parents were worried about the impact that the couple's differing schedules would have on their marriage, warning him, "Koi teesra aa jaayega" (A third person might come between you). In this manner, intimacies at home could be threatened by those developed at work.

As part of team-building exercises, companies often sponsored weekend trips to resorts and those trips provided opportunities and alibis for extramarital liaisons. Veronica, who had worked in the industry for close to a decade, first as an agent and later as a trainer, spoke of the temptations that night work offered when these marriages were already under strain. Every now and then she would learn that a married agent had entered into an extramarital relationship with a coworker and that, she asserted, "creates all kinds of trouble for them and for us."

These sexual liaisons occurred in a social context in which arranged marriages continue to be the norm, sexual relations are expected to occur within marital relationships, and gender segregation is still relatively stringent. But we forcefully reject an interpretation of these relationships in terms of liberal narratives of choice, personal agency, or, worse, a sign of "progress" indexed by the supposed casting off of the shackles of "tradition" as young people enter into "modernity" beyond the disciplining gaze of parents and community members. Rather, the regimes of affective labor, the temporal disjunctions that they created, and the company's efforts to provide opportunities for young men and women to socialize and bond led to the unintended consequences of heterogeneous BPO intimacies. That many of these intimacies developed between agents of different castes, regional backgrounds, and religions made them all the more transgressive; it is perhaps no surprise, then, that BPO agents were stereotypically represented in popular media as immature or irresponsible people who engaged in allegedly licentious behavior. Let us also recall that, unless one works in a BPO, it is practically impossible to enter its premises: security guards, biometric screening, identity cards, the confiscation of cell phones, the tinted glass windows of buildings so that inhabitants of the building can look out but people outside cannot look in—all contribute to the appearance of secrecy surrounding BPOs and add to their image as spaces of potential scandal.

The Production and Regulation of Erotic Desire

The BPO industry has generated a proliferation of portrayals in feature films, novels, documentaries, and plays. In fact, we would argue that, like the software industry in contemporary India, BPOs are embedded in a representational field that is both highly mediated and mediatized (Upadhya 2016, 28). Unlike the software industry, however, BPOs have tended to attract mainly negative publicity.[23] News media have caricatured BPOs as places where young men and women, their hormones raging, do night work in close proximity and decompress by frequenting pubs and bars. By the time we began our fieldwork in 2009, Indian news media had been successful in stereotyping BPOs as spaces where sexual promiscuity flourished, and by the time we concluded in 2016, these representations had ossified into an accepted "truth," making many middle-class parents all the more suspicious when their sons and daughters started to work in this industry.[24]

We examine one such news report that exemplifies the gross exaggerations and egregious caricatures shaping some media portrayals of BPO agents. This news story appeared in the *Telegraph* on April 14, 2006, and was salaciously titled "More Sex Please, We Are BPO" (Verma 2006). It displayed a photograph of a couple locked in an overtly sexual embrace. While there did not appear to be any evidence that this couple worked in a BPO, the photograph had the following caption: "Call centers are turning into hubs where inter-personal bonding takes place. And, often, this bonding takes a sexual turn." The article claimed that a survey conducted by Durex, a manufacturer of condoms based in the United Kingdom, found that 16 percent of the employees in a call center named iEnergizer had had a one-night stand and 12.6 percent an extramarital affair, leading Durex to roll out an AIDS awareness campaign called the "Call Center Initiative." The authors alleged that "a few months ago, hidden cameras placed in a leading Mumbai-based BPO caught a couple having sex in an office cubicle." They claimed: "A Telegraph-MODE survey conducted in Calcutta, Mumbai, Delhi and Bangalore demonstrates that call centre employees let off steam by holding wild parties and seek physical comfort with the opposite sex. In Mumbai, 89 percent people polled said they regularly attend wild parties and 74 percent (55 per cent in Bangalore) said they seek the company of the opposite sex." The authors claimed that hospitals in Bengaluru had seen a surge in women seeking abortions, a phenomenon that they glibly attributed to the growth of call centers in the city. They quoted Abhijit Pakrashi, who worked as a call center executive for Accenture's BPO in the city, as saying that the sexual promiscuity of BPOs was caused by agents' work schedule: "Weird working hours means that most friendships happen in office and some of them turn intimate." The article attributed the allegedly promiscuous behavior of BPO agents variously to the "emotional loneliness" of agents who migrate from small towns; women who allegedly use the "cover" of anonymity in the big city to become "sexually adventurous"; the "identity changes" required by some BPOs that encourage young people to engage in casual sex ("BPO employees get used to playing different personalities. This helps them shrug off casual relationships more easily"); and "easy money and the opportunity to be out of the house all night." The report quoted Ashok Rau, head of a counseling center in Bengaluru, who made the following dubious allegation: "A call centre office that was visited as part of the survey reported that its drains had been found choked with condoms." While the report also quoted BPO executives who defended the industry, arguing that BPOs were similar to other workplaces that employed young people, the overall tone of the article was provocative and scandalous.

These salacious caricatures exacerbated the stigma and moral policing of all genders and (particularly) women working in the BPO industry. Sensationalistic news reports, which were ubiquitous throughout our fieldwork, and the fact that these young people engaged in night work and were newly visible in malls, restaurants, and pubs only added fuel to the fire of scandal and resulted in increased surveillance by supervisors, management, family members, neighbors, landlords, and community members. Ironically, these representations recursively *constituted* BPOs as erotically charged spaces: the workplace was itself constituted by affective intensities that swirled around agents even as it reconfigured their desires.

On their part, managers were deeply ambivalent about sexual liaisons among agents. Closed-circuit TVs were everywhere in the companies where we did our ethnographic research—in work areas, meeting rooms, photocopy rooms, hallways, entryways and lobbies, stairwells, and company cafeterias—ostensibly to discourage the abuse of drugs. However, many agents told us that the primary motivation for the surveillance was to discourage sexual liaisons in the workplace. An HR manager told us that if a couple "got intimate" during a break and were caught on surveillance video on one of the "cameras all over the place," they were given a warning letter. There were two people in the video supervision room at all times to check on agents' activities.

Thus, although managers and supervisors claimed to adopt a "don't ask, don't tell" policy toward sexual liaisons at work, they were nervous about workplace romances. As one COO said, "I don't *want* to care what my agents do outside this building, but I have to because it affects how they work. For instance, if there is a breakup [or] a pregnancy we have to face the music—or if they start a relationship they want to work in the same process." Some managers felt that they had to keep an eye on what happened even after agents left the premises. They would keep tabs on the logs kept by the cab drivers assigned to transport workers, and drivers were instructed to inform supervisors if agents asked to be dropped off at (or picked up from) addresses different from those in their personnel files. In large part, this surveillance was a response to the bad press and controversies sparked by the specter of young people of different genders doing night work and spending money in restaurants and pubs, but COOs and managers were also worried that romance would unsettle relationships in the workplace.

In many ways, the sexual intimacies that sprung up at work were instances of what Amrute (2016) has termed "affective unwork": while such intimacies, by no means, undermined the stringency of their labor regimes, they "helped loosen the investment in work" (25). They thus complicate what Kathi Weeks (2011) describes as the productive intimacy characterizing the social relationships and attachments that become productive for capital. While BPOs depended on collaborative relationships ("bonding") among workers, sexual liaisons could challenge rather than consolidate the extraction of value. As we will note in the next chapter, sexual desire, when the needs and desires of the body could not be denied, threatened to "trip up" deadlines, team morale, work schedules, and labor regimes as much as they were produced through them, underscoring that when intimacy is instantiated as desire it has the potential to "destabilize the very things that institutions of intimacy are created to stabilize" (Berlant 1998, 286). One team leader complained to us about how much he hated it when agents formed sexual relationships. He insisted that it disrupted the dynamics of the entire team and, therefore, hampered its productivity: in these instances, intimacy was, without a doubt, counterproductive. He proceeded to describe to us the many managerial challenges that ensued when a romantic triangle developed between three of his agents. Yet another supervisor informed us that she was being harassed by the parents of a young woman who had formed a romantic attachment with a man of a different religion. She felt caught between a rock and a hard place: on the one hand, she did not want to antagonize the couple because they were highly productive workers; at the same time, she was getting exhausted from having to field calls from the angry parents and was becoming increasingly worried that they would stir trouble for the company by either showing up at the office and making a scene or reporting what was happening to the local media.

As became evident from the sexual liaisons we came across during our fieldwork, the surveillance exercised by the company had its limits: the erotic energies of these young people undermined the efforts of managers and team leaders to regulate the relationships that developed among them and underscored the lines of flight—the eruptive potential—of erotics (Deleuze 1997; see also Barriteau 2014; and Lorde 1984, 1993). Of course, erotic desire between BPO agents counters neither patriarchal norms nor the conditions in which they labor, but it cannot be denied that the erotic intimacies that develop at work enable agents to make their lives meaningful and allow them to seek (and find) comfort and pleasure in the face of relentless labor. At the very least, from the perspective of agents who enter into sexual relationships with each other, the erotic highlights potentialities that gesture toward futures that are hard-won, fragile, and without sureties or guarantees (Lorde 1984; Berlant 2011).

Last but not least, if sexual harassment inflected some intimacies across geographic distance, it also occurred among workers in BPOs: in this regard, BPOs were no different from other working spaces marked by an imbalance in relations of power. Sunitha, an agent whom we met early in our research, told us that she had left the BPO where she worked because she refused to exchange sexual favors in order to get a much-deserved promotion. Sunitha believed that one of the many reasons why women who worked in BPOs were stigmatized as "loose" women was precisely because they were assumed to be so ambitious that they would "do anything" to achieve their goals. She claimed that her self-respect and dignity were more important to her than staying on at that BPO. Sunitha was able to move laterally to another BPO because at that time the industry was booming, HR sections were running hundreds of recruitment interviews a day, and well-trained and experienced agents were hard to find. There were others who, because they feared the loss of their jobs or when the economic climate changed to make BPO jobs harder to find, were less able to walk away from environments where they had to put up with sexual harassment from colleagues or supervisors.

To reiterate: it goes without saying that BPOs are, by no means, unusual with regard to sexual harassment among employees: sexual harassment is endemic in workplaces across the world where hierarchical relations of labor and patriarchal discourses of gender and sexuality shape the extraction of value. The unequal relationships between BPO agents and their supervisors as well as among agents were, predictably, fostered by dominant discourses of gender and sexuality to which BPOs were not immune. Nevertheless, extending beyond the "mixed up instrumental and affective relations of collegiality" when "desire's optimism and its ruthlessness converge" (Berlant 1998, 82), these instances of sexual harassment throw into sharp relief the close relationship between intimacy, inequality, and power in workplaces where labor regimes are predicated on hierarchy and on the biopolitical regulation of laboring bodies.

INTIMACIES, ALIENATION, RELATIONALITY

Desire is not the manifestation of a structure but has the creative power to build a thousand structures. Desire can stiffen structures, transforming them into obsessive refrains. Desire sets traps for itself.

Franco "Bifo" Berardi, *The Soul at Work* (2009)

Critics (accurately and legitimately) emphasize the relentlessness of BPO work by noting the high volume of calls that agents handle and the intense surveillance to which they are subjected. The fact that the labor of agents is affective in no way takes away from the fact that many facets of the work are repetitive and highly Taylorized: these aspects of BPO work do resemble an assembly line. The relationship between labor performed in these conditions and the development of BPO intimacies raises some interesting conundrums about alienation. Among the ways that Marx ([1844] 1978, 74) describes alienation in the "Economic and Philosophical Manuscripts of 1844" is as the alienation of the worker in the act of production itself. The routinization of work in BPOs, along with the intense surveillance of agents, represents one facet of the alienated labor of BPO agents. In Marxian terms, the self-estrangement of BPO agents is symptomatized by the fact that their labor does not comprise spontaneous activity (see also Weeks 2007, 243). At the same time, in contrast to Marx's description of estranged labor as leading to the alienation of the worker from species-being, BPO agents produce and engage a distinct form of sociality that problematizes assumptions about "pre-alienated" subjects who, through their affective labor, engage in intimate encounters with their clients. The work of BPO agents foregrounds how affective labor itself produces intimate encounters and, in the process, is generative of particular kinds of laboring subjects, thus blurring the boundaries between "pre-alienated" and alienated selfhood (Weeks 2007).

Nevertheless, these are socialities and intimacies that are produced under conditions that, as Marx points out, engender the reproduction of relations of capital and beget the dominion of the one (the capitalist) who does not produce. As we have seen, the socialities formed by a four-cornered relationship between the international capitalist firm (the client), the domestic capitalist (the BPO owner), the domestic agent, and the (usually) international customer in many instances lead to intimacies with customers and among agents. The affective labor of the BPO agents with whom we worked did result in the production of surplus: hotel bookings were made, tickets sold for flights, computers repaired, and so on. However, the fact that their labor depended on empathetic engagement and intimacy made for forms of alienation that were different from conventional production. The alienation registered by loss of control over time and the pace of one's work, shift work, and constant surveillance is familiar from product assembly lines, but the affective labor that produces and, indeed, aims for customer satisfaction has no equivalent in those forms of production: customer satisfaction, as the primary "product" of these forms of labor, is predicated on agents' ability to foster intimacies with their customers.

Unlike intimacies that are predicated on proximity that may be physical or geographic, the affective labor of our interlocutors underscores the ways in which intimacy reconstituted their very experience of time and space, proximity and distance (cf. Wilson 2016, 249). On the one hand, their success at work was contingent on their construction of a relationship of affective proximity with their clients that generated intimate encounters (cf. Holmes 2004). Although these workers did not engage in physical travel, their virtual and imaginative travel engendered new modalities of propinquity. The global care chain comprising workers who migrate from the Global South to wealthier nations to provide care and services has been rigorously analyzed by scholars in Asian American studies like Choy (2003) and Parreñas (2001): we draw on their work to highlight the coproduction of racial and affective capitalism in contexts of service work performed by Asian bodies.[25]

How do the intimacies occurring across time and space enable us to retheorize the relationship between intimacy and capitalism, and between relationality and futurity? The virtual and imaginative travel of BPO workers provokes us to rethink the place of movement in formations of intimacy, as well as our assumptions about spatiality, proximity, and distance (see also chapter 1). BPOs exemplify the global expansion of capitalism for the extraction of surplus value (Vora 2010, 2015). BPO agents work with scripts under conditions of time management and surveillance that resemble those of an assembly line, yet they are engaged in a form of labor that requires cross-cultural resources of empathy and understanding. Agents have to marshal these resources for instrumental ends, such as making a sale, but their engagement with customers goes well beyond the instrumental. Many agents repeatedly told us that what they liked most about their jobs was that they got to know people in the West intimately—how they lived, what they thought, and so on. In short, these jobs condensed an extraordinarily rich and contradictory set of determinations and meanings.

Relationality played a powerful role in the construction of their subjectivities and their visions of the future. Unlike the middle-class laboring subjects analyzed by Gregg (2011), and despite the fact that their subjectivities and conceptions of futurity were powerfully shaped by their labor, BPO agents were not so much attached to their work as they were dependent on it. Most agents joined BPOs with great excitement and, as long as they rose up the organizational ladder, remained enthusiastic about their work. However, in contrast to those in upper management whose professional identities were central to their senses of self, BPO agents, who were positioned much lower in the occupational hierarchy of their companies, were seldom so attached to their work as to feel that it was the sole or even primary source of fulfillment in their lives. Even more rarely did their work as BPO agents form the basis of their identities as social beings (cf. Weeks 2011; Gregg 2011). Their senses of self were shaped by the articulation and disarticulation of their social relationships and roles as sons, daughters, parents, partners, and siblings—in other words, by intimacies and socialities that were refracted by labor regimes but also extended outside the workplace (Amrute 2016; Upadhya 2016). At the same time, many of our interlocutors spoke of how their work in BPOs reconfigured their relations with their family members, close friends, and partners in profound ways; it also shaped their experiences of spatiality and how they navigated the multiple chronotopes that they were expected to simultaneously inhabit.

We have theorized intimacy as a form of knowing, feeling, and caring formed through affective labor, mediated and facilitated by information technology and mutually imbricated with global capitalism. But if global capitalism engenders these forms of intimacy, the intimacies that develop in BPOs also generate, impinge on, and refract the work of capital and the production and extraction of value. Commenting on the place of "positive affects" like compassion or love, Freeman (2020, 5) argues that in some studies of capitalism, "there is a tacit assumption that, like any other form of value, this emotional resource is being tapped and, in essence, depleted from its rightful and authentic, nonmarket sphere: that of the domestic, the private, and the personal" (cf. Faier 2007). In contrast, Padios (2018) identifies the deployment of empathy and relational labor in call centers in the Philippines as an example of how social relations and emotions are mobilized toward the generation of value according to the demands of capital: "By converting these subjective resources into labor power for exchange, call center work depletes and diminishes their supply" (47), resulting in emotional exhaustion (see also Ruppel, Sims, and Zeidler 2013).

There is no question that several of our interlocutors were emotionally drained by the end of their shifts. However, as Padios (2018, 47) also argues, emotions and affect are rarely completely subsumed by capital. Indeed, the worlds of BPOs generated friendships, solidarities, and intimacies that sustained workers in powerful ways. Like Filipino call center workers who are "bonded by stress" (46), solidarities and intimate friendships enabled the BPO agents with whom we became close to turn to each other both for everyday pleasures, such as visiting the mall together, and during moments of crisis. And *our* intimate relationships with some of our interlocutors enabled us to see the complex formation of their subjectivities and, in particular, the power of relationality in their lives and in how they inhabited and navigated the world: in many ways, relationality was central to their processes of world making. We are unwilling, therefore, to dismiss these structures of feeling, and the affective regimes they index, as instances of false consciousness or as the "clever ruses or manipulations" of capitalism (Freeman 2020, 5).[26]

If their ties with family, friends, and community members became more tenuous because of their relentless schedules, they were also intensified in other ways. These intimacies, even when they felt exhausting and oppressive, were deeply intertwined with the futures they envisioned for themselves *and* for their families and communities. Intimacy, friendship, compassion, and dignity were crucial to our interlocutors' senses of themselves and provided them with an ethical map to navigate a terrain that was, in equal parts, enticing and terrifying: these intimacies provided a blueprint for how to live in the everyday and how to think about the future (Mankekar and Gupta 2023).

INTIMATE FUTURITIES

Constituting more than 65 percent of India's GDP, the growth of the service sector of the Indian economy has been at the expense of agriculture; in contrast, manufacturing has remained steady at about 20 percent of GDP. A small minority of workers in the formal sector, including those who work in BPOs and IT firms, have indeed experienced Taylorization, the colonization of life by work, and the definition of work as the manipulation of symbols and codes (Berardi 2009; Weeks 2007). Nevertheless, because the rise of the service sector has not followed manufacturing, we need to think about affective labor outside conventional distinctions between Fordism/post-Fordism and material/immaterial labor. This has implications for how we envision the heterogeneous temporalities of capitalism(s) and how we conceptualize the future of futurity.

In this section, we posit that retheorizing intimacy in conjunction with relationality offers discursive and imaginative resources for thinking about futurity. BPO intimacies highlight a few of the ways in which supposedly "non-economic" forms of value generate financial capital (Upadhya 2016, 35); they demonstrate how capitalism is produced not solely by instrumental action but, equally, by sentiment and affective action (Wilson 2004; Yanagisako 2002). The intimate encounters produced by the affective labors of BPO agents are central, and not secondary, to capitalist production: these encounters constitute a vital component of the intimate industries proliferating in the current historical conjuncture. BPO agents in India face considerable uncertainty because the ITES industry keeps changing. When, for example, we concluded our fieldwork, one of the large BPOs where we worked was moving from voice-based services to chat: agents were experiencing the increasing displacement of their labor by artificial intelligence and other labor-substituting intellectual production. And in their search for ever-greater profits, companies were beginning to outsource back-office work to other countries where labor was cheaper. The futures of our interlocutors were becoming increasingly precarious.

As part of the ITES industry in India, BPOs offer a unique opportunity to rethink the relationship between intimacy, technology, and affective capitalism on the one hand and, on the other, the future of futurity. Some scholars have stressed how capitalism subsumes other aspects of life, including realms such as desire, emotions, bodily capacities, and social relations, which are then marshaled to its needs. BPO agents' emotional resources, such as empathy, care, and kindness, are put to work for the generation of profits, value, and capital. Padios, drawing on Weeks (2011), refers to this as productivism because, she argues, it represents an "orientation toward work in particular and life in general" (Padios 2018, 52). She adds that work is "increasingly linked to the very substance of our identities and our subjectivities" and has become the source of personal pleasure (53). She posits: "Productive intimacy is the form that close relationships take when they are made productive for capital. When used as a form of corporate biopower, productive intimacy allows capital to govern workers from within their relationships, putting their affective attachments to use in the creation of exchange value and surplus value" (52).

Work is undeniably powerful in the formation of BPO agents as laboring subjects. However, labor neither subsumed nor overdetermined their identities or lives. There were times when our interlocutors said they felt "pressured" by their obligations toward their families as by their labor regimes. At the same time, a deep emotional commitment to their family members was what drove many of our interlocutors to work in BPOs in the first place. The fact that their salaries could support elderly relatives, especially parents and grandparents, and improve the life chances of their younger siblings and children was one of the most important reasons why they stayed in their jobs even when, ironically, they were not able to spend much time with these family members.

Indeed, the persistence of their senses of obligation, duty, and commitment to family and community members tended to challenge the imperative of efficiency and productivity. BPO work depends on the extraction of value through regimes of affective labor that unquestionably overwhelmed our interlocutors. Even so, BPO agents are not merely or simply laborers. Even as the pace of their labor and its temporal disjunctures reconstitutes their bodily capacities and reshapes their aspirations and imaginations, their subjectivities are also formed through relationality—in particular, their relationships with friends, parents, siblings, lovers, neighbors, community members, and coworkers—by desires and aspirations that exceed their labor even as they are generated by it, and by their imaginations of worlds and lives that extend beyond the workplace. It would be a mistake to conceive of the dilemmas of BPO agents who are torn between their own aspirations to upward mobility and obligations toward family as a tussle between individualism versus collectivism/relationality (Mankekar and Gupta 2023).[27] Likewise, we remain wary of portraying women agents, who were subjected to much stronger pressure to fulfill family obligations than men, as caught between the binaristic compulsions of "tradition" and "modernity" (see also Upadhya 2016, 261; cf. Radhakrishnan 2011).

What is the point of working if you can't take care of your loved ones? Relationships and obligations to family and community, even when they felt oppressive and exploitative to our interlocutors, provided them with an ethical map that gave a purpose to their lives amid relentless labor. The complex relationalities in which they were embedded problematize voluntaristic assumptions regarding their ethical formation and their ability to imagine the future. Thus, for instance, a strong sense of duty to elderly parents compelled some of them to work in BPOs for as long as they could regardless of how frustrated and exhausted they felt.

Furthermore, and importantly, the ethical blueprint provided by relationality helped them (albeit not always successfully) juggle conflicting demands of work, family, and community. Over the years that we conducted our fieldwork and longitudinally tracked the careers and lives of agents, we learned that family obligations, which could necessitate agents' having to leave Bengaluru for their "native" (the word that many of them used to refer to their hometown or village) to attend a religious ritual or wedding or care for an elderly relative, composed some of the most common reasons for agents to leave the BPO where they were working. Particularly during the heyday of the BPO industry when jobs were plentiful, several agents would tell us that it was "not worth it" to stay on the job at the cost of neglecting significant family rituals and events and urgent family responsibilities.

While managers and HR officers were usually unable to "adjust" work schedules according to the demands placed on agents by family responsibilities, they tried to reassure family members in other ways. Two of the large BPOs where we conducted fieldwork offered health insurance for family members, which, given India's poor medical infrastructure and skyrocketing healthcare costs, helped to ensure that family members supported (or, at least, did not actively resist) the desires of young people to join BPOs. Some members of the HR team had to repeatedly call parents of recently hired workers to placate their fears. They even organized a Parents' Day at the end of product level training so that parents and other family members could see the environment in which their son or daughter was working. According to Maria, this seemed to assure many anxious parents, who said things like, "We were very worried until we came here," or "We thought it was a closed [tight] place where boys and girls work [closely] together." Seeing the glass walls and open offices that allowed anybody walking past to observe what was happening inside a security-controlled process proved reassuring to parents.

BPOs also organized events like "Family Days," a "Kiddies Carnival," "Fanfare Day," and "Hat Toss Day" when relatives were invited to visit the office to observe where agents worked: given that most of them came from low-income and lower-middle-class homes, the allure of the (post)modern architecture and plush built environment of BPOs played a crucial role in enlisting support from family members and, in the case of women agents, assuring their families of the safety and professionalism of the work environment. Managers and HR officers were acutely sensitive to the fact that family members were ambivalent, if not hostile, toward the fact that their sons and daughters had to engage in night work. While company transport was essential to maintaining a strict schedule by ensuring that agents would arrive at work on time, it was also intended to reassure family members that BPOs were concerned about the safety of their employees.

In the worlds and lives of our interlocutors, labor and leisure, work and family life, intimacy and productivity were inextricably entangled so as to mutually implicate each other in ways that were not always predictable. While BPO intimacies are produced by labor regimes, these intimacies, whether with each other or with customers, also impinge on these very regimes of labor. For instance, intimate friendships formed among agents endured, if not thrived, even when they were called on to compete with each other. Similarly, intimate relationships with overseas customers enabled agents to feel sympathy and compassion for them in ways that could jeopardize their productivity and efficiency. The intimacies that develop at work produce forms of solidarity, friendship, and dignity that inflect the conditions in which capital is produced. These intimacies underscore how regimes of affect and affective labor create (nonteleological) potentialities that offer agents opportunities for friendship, solidarity, compassion, dignity, and lines of flight when faced with exploitation, racist abuse, or sexual harassment. Apparently paradoxically, BPO intimacies consolidate forms of relationality that have the potential to interrupt the smooth functioning of capitalist efficiency and productivity.

At the same time, we steer clear of the trap of romanticizing BPO intimacies. In BPOs, the rhythms of work are coproduced with intimate relationalities. Some of the most foundational work on the relationship between capitalism and (modern) forms of intimacy conceptualizes intimacy in terms of individual choice: these frameworks are founded on universalist and unexamined preconceptions about the agency and voluntarism of a sovereign subject who becomes "individualized" and "chooses" to enter into certain kinds of relationships (for instance, Giddens 1992). But, as we have demonstrated above, intimacies may emerge in contexts that militate against these assumptions of voluntarism and sovereign agency. BPO agents do not "choose" to enter into relationships of intimacy with their customers; similarly, when they form intimate relationships with each other, the chronotopes of BPOs and their labor regimes articulate to produce these intimacies, disrupting yet again any assumptions we might have of agents as sovereign subjects.

If intimacies are produced through regimes of labor, they also refract and reconstitute how affective labor is performed, whether through disrupting the routines and rhythms of a team when two agents end a romantic relationship or when agents resist customers who try to extend, deepen, or eroticize their relationship. Intimacies between agents and their customers are short-term, flashing briefly with sharpness and vividity as they leave ineffable traces on the minds, bodies, and worlds of those that they enwrap in their force. And close and enduring intimacies develop between agents as a result of propinquity: working side by side, night after night, cut off from their daytime friends and family, these intimacies are the product of spatial as well as temporal contiguity.

Studying intimacies in terms of affect and affective labor eschews conceptions of consciousness founded on assumptions of interiority. We have retheorized intimacies through the lens of affect which we conceptualize as an intensity that is neither located in a sovereign subject nor reducible to an emotion that may be retroactively named empathy, kindness, or care. The affective intensity generated by intimacy is experienced as a force that relays between subjects and leaves traces on them and reconstitutes them; affect is never static but accumulates potency as it circulates within BPO spaces and beyond, across time zones, to refract and reconstitute the relationships agents form with each other and with their customers. These are intensities that might well remain nameless.

BPO intimacies are facilitated by labor processes that are predicated on information technology; yet, even between subjects who can neither see nor touch each other, these intimacies are not disembodied. Rather, as we will argue in the next chapter, these intimacies occur between subjects who are embodied in distinct ways through the intersection of gender, race, class, and national location; these are biomediatized subjects who are re-formed through intimate engagements with each other, with technology, and at the intersection of organic and inorganic matter (chapter 4). BPOs are contact zones for the development of intimacies.[28] These contact zones are produced through the imbrication of alienated labor with the intimacies that form when gendered and racialized bodies encounter each other within force-fields of affect and in contexts where capitalism extracts value from affect. We, therefore, align with scholars such as Ariel Ducey (2007) and Boris and Parreñas (2010) who resist the search for authenticity in their work on intimate labor. For, while the affective regimes generated by BPO work produce forms of alienation for agents, the forms of intimacy enabled by these labor practices are much more complex than familiar dichotomies of commodified versus authentic relationships (cf. Hochschild 2012). By situating the intimate labor of BPO agents within larger regimes of affective capitalism, one of our objectives is to highlight how the extractive logics of capital operate on a granular level (we elaborate on the granularity of affective capitalism in the next chapter).

Weeks (2007, 245) asks, "What are the ways by which one can advance a theory of agency without deploying a model of the subject as it supposedly once was or is now beyond the reach of capital?" Drawing on Spinoza's insistence on the ethical dimensions of affect, we conceive of the affective labor of our interlocutors and their agency in terms of potentiality and becoming, as opposed to the binary of compliance versus resistance.[29] Encapsulating but also transecting emotional, cognitive, and corporeal labor, BPO intimacies remind us of the centrality of affect to processes of worlding: the generative capacity to navigate the world. When viewed through the perspective of affect, it is agency and actions that produce the agentive subject (rather than the other way around); in this sense, affect is presubjective. Affect, and the regimes of labor with which it is coimplicated, are productive of the capacity of BPO agents to affect and be affected.

What might such a conception of agents and the intimacies that arise between them suggest about futurity? BPO intimacies enable us to rethink the relationship between technology, sociality, and affect, and between humans and the tools (machines) used in labor. BPO agents were taught to make the customer feel comfortable. They were trained to follow the cadences of the customer's speech, to make small talk to fill up dead time over the phone, and to open up the possibility of confidences being conveyed by soliciting information from customers. Whether it was an overdue payment on a credit card charge, a hospitalization, or a death in the family, customers provided details of their lives to which strangers would not ordinarily be privy. Agents had to respond to such information in a manner that was empathetic and engaged but "professional" in ways that perhaps parallel the engaged reactions of a healthcare professional or a therapist. Such interactions were mediated by technology, both the hardware that enabled high-quality, "live" conversation with someone halfway across the world as well as the software that connected callers and agents.

What, then, do we make of the intricate relationship between labor, intimacy, and futurity? Gregg (2011) makes an impassioned and eloquent plea for a "labor politics of love" that can fight the corporatization of intimacy and, hence, forge a different vision of futurity (172). In dialogue with her work, we foreground the force of intimacies formed through solidarity, loyalty, mutual aid, and care among agents in forms of relationality that enable us to theorize futurity at a time when the rapacity of capitalism(s) appears to be insatiable (see also Gottfried and Chun 2018, 1009; P. Sharma 2020). Futurity spans the individual and the collective even as it is splintered along lines of class, caste, race, and gender. Viewed through the lens of affect, futurity is imbued with potentiality and becoming; it refers to process and movement rather than arrival—the *not-yet* or the temporal lag between capacity and action. Our theorization of the intimacies of affective labor has epistemological and political implications for how we conceptualize the future of futurity.

Rejecting both a hermeneutics of suspicion, according to which relationality is viewed as a ruse of capitalism, and a hermeneutics of recuperation, whereby relationality is innocent of politics, inequality, or alienation, we advocate a theory of relationality that remains accountable to forms of interdependence among humans and between humans and more-than-humans, while *simultaneously* confronting, and accounting for, inequality, hierarchy, exploitation, and violence (Mani 2022). By foregrounding relationalities as sites of connection and oppression, desire and coercion, and solidarity and estrangement, we theorize, and hence envision, forms of futurity that are sustainable—that is, futurities that have a future.

4.

THE MISSED PERIOD

Disjunctive Temporalities, Embodiment, and the Work of Capital

Farhana Sheikh had planned to meet Purnima Mankekar at 2:30 in the afternoon at Café Coffee Day in a central Bengaluru mall. But, as always, Farhana was late, not showing up until almost 3:30 p.m. She rushed in, her hair disheveled, her dupatta awry, her face without makeup. Now, *this* was most unlike her, for Farhana was nothing if not impeccably turned out, with perfect hair and immaculate makeup. That day, however, she looked as if she had just tumbled out of bed. Most days she would go home, sleep for about five hours, and then rush to college. But that day, Mankekar concluded, she had probably decided to skip class. Farhana gave her a quick hug and collapsed in a chair, slamming her backpack to the floor. Before Mankekar could ask, Farhana told her in a hushed voice that she had missed her period the past two months. Her mother had found out and had taken her for a pregnancy test at an OB-GYN clinic in South Bengaluru, a two-hour bus ride from their home, because she did not want anybody in the neighborhood to see them. Farhana was outraged that her mother assumed that she was pregnant. "Do I have the time to have sex? To meet anybody? How could she think that of me?" she exclaimed.

Her mother's assumption that she was pregnant was in keeping with media representations of women, many of whom, like Farhana, worked night shifts in BPOs. Women employees who did night work alongside young men, away from the oversight of family members, were subject to a range of stigmatizing stereotypes: they allegedly made more money than they knew what to do with, frequented pubs and clubs with their male colleagues, had premarital sex, got pregnant, and then had abortions. In short, they transgressed all rules of middle-class female respectability. A few days later, Farhana called Mankekar to say that, as she had expected, the pregnancy test was negative. Her doctor could not explain why she had missed her periods for the past two months. All he could say was that she had lost a lot of weight, was not sleeping enough, and was working too hard. "I could have told my mother that!" she exclaimed.

Farhana worked in a BPO that contracted with a US-based company that sold dolls. With Christmas approaching, she and other agents were under tremendous pressure to increase the number of sales to customers, most of whom lived in the American South. Farhana had been working the first shift, from 6:30 p.m. to 3:30 a.m. In theory, her company's customer service agents were supposed to get regular breaks from this grueling schedule. But her process or sales campaign was on a tight deadline because they had failed to meet their quotas. In Farhana's life, there was never an opportunity to take a real break; never an interruption of the ceaseless rhythm of work, college, and work; never a lifting of the pall of surveillance that followed her from home to work and back. She said to Mankekar:

> There are times when I am so tired that I have nothing to say to my mother when I come home. She is usually up waiting for me, suspicious that I may have gone to a pub or somewhere else with a boy. I've stopped explaining to her that I get delayed because my cab is late dropping me home. I've nothing to say to her anymore.

But Farhana had a lot to say to Mankekar about her missed period. She told her that several of her women coworkers also complained that their menstrual cycles had been, in her words, "messed up": some women skipped a month or two, while others suffered debilitating bleeding. A couple of her friends had developed ovarian cysts. They were all convinced that these symptoms were a result of their long hours at work, their disrupted sleep cycles, and the fact that many women went home to another "shift" of either childcare or, as in Farhana's case, college.

The crisis engendered by Farhana's missed period indexes disjunctive temporalities at the heart of the BPO industry. As Aneesh (2015) argues in his pathbreaking book on call centers in Gurgaon, the laboring body becomes global because the integration of different time zones "requires the diurnal body to perform nocturnal labor, disconnecting and placing it into conflict with its own surroundings" (9–10). The temporalities generated by the affective labor performed by Farhana and her coworkers were embedded in specific regimes of work discipline and temporality for BPO workers (Aneesh 2015; Mankekar and Gupta 2016, 2017; Mirchandani 2012; R. Patel 2010; Poster 2007; Vora 2015). How do these temporalities intersect with the discursive practices of gender, caste, class, and race to reconstitute laboring (and desiring) bodies?[1] We trace some of the ways in which these discrepant temporalities, and the *granular* forms of embodiment with which they are entangled, implicate the futures imagined, dreaded, and yearned for by our interlocutors. What might these futures suggest about the future of futurity?[2]

Imbricated in the circulation of affect, bodies are in a state of constant becoming, thus foregrounding their inherent dynamism (Clough 2008, 1). Affect, and affective capitalism, entail processes of modulation that shape, augment, or diminish a body's capacity to act through its encounters with other bodies and objects and between organic and inorganic matter.[3] Against conceptions of disembodied labor in narratives about semiocapital, we argue that affective capitalism is contingent on the (re)embodiment of subjects. As nodes in the circulation of service labor, these bodies demonstrate the prominence of Asian bodies in transnational circuits of service labor: racialized in specific ways, these are bodies that are formed at the intersection of racial and affective capitalism. Finally, and significantly for our interest in parsing out the relationship between embodiment and futurity, these bodies demonstrate how the rhythms of affective capitalism, in conjunction or collision with the temporalities of other socialities, work at a granular level to create multiplex subjects.

CHRONOPOLITICS AND EMBODIMENT

Every time we went to a BPO at night, we were confronted by an inescapable sense of the temporal disjunctions between the company's work rhythms and those of the surrounding city. We always felt a sensory shock when we left the city's inky streets and entered the brightly lit, immaculately maintained premises of the tech parks housing BPOs. Uniformed security guards would scrutinize and record our entry, and we would be surrounded by lush green lawns, fountains, bodies of water, and postmodern buildings resplendent in chrome and glass. In contrast to the sleeping city, this was a space that pulsated with life: vehicles drove in and out, the night air was filled with aromas wafting out of restaurants and kiosks selling coffee and snacks, and everywhere groups of young people could be seen going to and from their offices. When we walked into the chilly, air-conditioned spaces of the BPO, we would feel the energy shift again, palpably, unmistakably: we would step into yet another sensorium. The air would be full of adrenaline, excitement, and anxiety. On the walls of several of the rooms would be a phalanx of clocks displaying time in different cities—San Francisco, New York, London, and Sydney—a constant reminder of the disjunctive chronotopes inhabited by BPO workers. Conference rooms would thrum with the voices of managers and administrators consulting intently with one another.

The technology that was foundational to the disjunctive temporalities of affective labor reconstituted how our interlocutors sensed and experienced time. In its reversal of work time so that agents labor at night and sleep during the day, the labor regimes of BPOs demonstrate some of the ways that globalized capital has reshaped workplace temporalities. These disjunctive temporalities are predicated on global hierarchies of time because the schedules and needs of clients in the Global North determine the timetables of workers in Bengaluru. Furthermore, the Indian state has played a central role in facilitating this time reversal by relaxing labor laws for the IT and ITES industries to, for instance, enable them to hire women to work at night (Gupta and Sharma 2006; Poster 2007).

The problematic of temporal dislocation has threaded through different sections of this book: we reprise it here to engage its implications for the embodiment of BPO agents. Because agents in India must work at night, they experience "a re-territorialization of temporalities" (Poster 2007, 56). The need to keep track of multiple time zones and the different social meanings attached to varying times is central to their performance of affective labor. For instance, in India, it is not uncommon to call someone early in the morning before they leave for work, and dinner may be eaten around 8 p.m. or later. Agents have to learn that many of their overseas customers do not like to be disturbed before 8 a.m. in the morning, that they "sleep in" during weekends, and that dinner might be eaten at (what is for them) the ridiculously early time of 6 p.m. Since adjusting their own routines of work, sleep, and leisure to their customers' timetables is a precondition of BPO work, these new hierarchies of time have generated regimes of temporality that often come at a substantial cost to the health and social relations of workers in the Global South. The chronopolitics of racial capitalism entail the subservience of regimes of temporality in the Global South to those of the Global North even when they are neither invariably nor inevitably erased by these hierarchies of time (Klinke 2012; Robinson [1983] 2020).

Agents providing customer service either worked in inbound processes, where customers can call in for information about or assistance with a product or service (such as calling a travel portal like Travelocity to make or change an airline reservation), or in outbound processes, where agents call customers to perform a service for a client company (for example, to collect payment on a bill or sell a product). These engagements occur in real time, and time discipline and punctuality are central to their performance of affective labor. So, for instance, if a customer needed help with their Travelocity reservation, they would contact an agent at a time that worked for them, even if it was 3 a.m. in Bengaluru. Similarly, if a payment had to be collected on a credit card, it would have to happen while it was daytime in the customer's country, regardless of the time in Bengaluru. Temporal dislocations are thus fundamental to agents' affective labor: irrespective of the rhythms of daily life where they were located, they had to literally and figuratively be "on call" the moment they logged in.

The work that our interlocutors performed was highly regimented and was subjected to Taylorist regimes of efficiency. Work shifts were organized by scheduling software, underscoring the algorithmic management of their time (see also Poster 2007, 78; Aneesh 2015). Tasks were broken down into simple steps, and agents were expected to follow a script on their computer screen in their interactions with customers (Woydack and Lockwood 2017). All shifts began in the afternoon or night, from 2:30 in the afternoon for a UK shift to 12:30 in the morning for the graveyard shift. BPO work was extremely taxing and sometimes entailed fielding up to two hundred calls in a work shift. Shifts were nine hours long and included a total time of one hour for lunch and two short breaks.

The embodiment of BPO agents as laboring subjects was reconfigured by the convergence of information technology with regimes of affective labor. As a result of information technology, every aspect of the labor process was monitored, archived, and mined to ensure customer service. This occurred both within the premises of the BPO and at the client company located overseas. Real-time monitoring thus occurred transnationally: managers located in the head office of the client company in the Global North could observe the computer screens of agents or listen in on their conversations with customers as they occurred. The time of each call, its length, and its outcome was logged by software programs, and online surveys recorded customer satisfaction, the results of which were also archived electronically and made available for the evaluation of the BPO, the team working on the process, and each agent. Information technology was indispensable to time management, which, in turn, was central to the production process.

The circulation of sensations and affective regimes generated by neoliberal formations of labor and consumption reconfigured the technoperceptual habits and habitations of BPO agents, entailing newly configured processes of embodiment. The laboring body of a BPO agent illustrates the "unhinging of persons from biological clocks" as a result of night work (Aneesh 2015, 3). However, the "colonization of the night" happened over a century ago: economic well-being came into conflict with social and emotional well-being because of the disconnection it produced between workers and their families and communities (Melbin 1987, 3–21). Furthermore, BPOs' labor practices, such as time discipline, drew on those of other industries even as they diverged from them. Bengaluru's long history of capitalist and public-sector enterprises has included industrial units of different sizes in a diverse array of industries, including aerospace, watch production, textiles, and machine tools (Nair 2005; Upadhya and Vasavi 2013). All these enterprises have depended on Taylorist practices of task segmentation and time efficiency. It was not entirely surprising that the first call centers followed well-established Taylorist principles of deskilling, task segmentation, and time discipline.

Even in industrial production, the unrelenting demands of industrial time discipline have produced conflicts with the lived time of working people. Analyzing how technologies of production shaped workers' experiences of time, Edward P. Thompson (1967) asked, "How far, and in what ways, did this shift in time-sense affect labour discipline and, how far did it influence the inward apprehension of time of working people?" (57). Large-scale machine-powered industry transformed working-class "time sense" and "time measurement" (Thompson 1967). Pioneering ethnographies of call centers and the informatics industry have emphasized precisely this dimension of time discipline and its effects on workers (Aneesh 2015; Freeman 2000; Mirchandani 2012; Patel 2010; Vora 2015). The examples of Farhana and many other women agents demonstrate that time discipline does not act uniformly on bodies; rather, its effects are shaped by dominant discourses of gender, race, and sexuality. The temporal disjunctions created by women's night work in BPOs share some characteristics with other capitalist enterprises.

As Emily Martin (2001) wrote of bodies that became flexible in response to the demands of capital: "The female body approximates [the] emerging new ideal of flexible adjustment to changing conditions. The female body, altering its states many times each month and undergoing dramatic adjustments to pregnancy, ovulation, or the cessation of ovulation, may become the perfect exemplar for a new modal concept of the flexibly adjusting, constantly changing body" (xxv). We extend Thompson's concern with the relationship between technologies of time sense, time measurement, and capitalist production and Martin's analysis of the relationship between capitalism and embodiment, to posit that the proliferation of affective labor in contemporary formations of affective capitalism implicates processes of embodiment for BPO agents. In BPOs, technology has informatized labor, labor practices, and the agent's body, enabling the continual transmission and modulation of knowledge and affect in dynamic and asynchronous feedback loops. Affective labor is not only central to the world of BPOs but also foregrounds the blurring of labor and leisure to generate forms of sociality and intimacy (Mankekar and Gupta 2016; see also chapters 2 and 3).

In this sense, affective labor is generative, capacious, and ontological. Indeed, by focusing on affect and affective labor we recenter the ontological in our theorization of the embodiment of BPO agents while, at the same time, avoiding the trap of conceiving of bodies as either overdetermined (scripted) by capitalism or outside of it. The affective labor of BPO agents is predicated on the continuous modulation of affect through fields of intensity that span emotion, information, corporeality, and technology to form feedback loops transecting heterogeneous social fields. These intensities were generated through encounters between the bodies of agents as they trained together and sat on the shop floor and with information technology in the course of their interactions with clients. The generation and circulation of affect also blurred the boundaries between the personal and the collective: these were intensities that spilled back and forth between the digitized workspace and other spaces of sociality to animate agents' lifeworlds in powerful ways.

The affective labor of BPO agents hence entails their entire beings and, even as it enables them to reimagine their place in an ever-expanding world, can be emotionally and physically draining for them. In these cases, affective labor is a modality for "absorbing" and "metabolizing" the negative emotions, especially the anger and frustrations, of customers: as Harris Solomon (2016) argues, the word *absorb* may be conceptualized in both its literal and figurative sense: to absorb is to preoccupy; to absorb is also to soak in, so that agents dealing with the anger of a customer might find themselves soaking in the negative feelings of their customer. Absorption is a dynamic process that renders porous the boundaries between the skin and microecologies; bodily processes and the environment; and objects, substances, technologies, and subjects.

Additionally, as a generative analytic to theorize the relationship between embodiment and affective labor, absorption also enables us to engage how bodies are nodes in the *relay* of affect across bodies and between bodies and objects. For instance, we witnessed an agent working on a debt collection process for a credit card company connect with a customer thousands of miles away thanks to fiber-optic cables and dialer software. As the agent "warmed up" his recalcitrant and increasingly resentful customer with small talk, his monitor displayed an algorithmic compilation of the customer's financial profile consisting of her purchasing records and debt history— personal information to which very few people were privy. The tension in his body was visible to us as, hunched over his desk with his fingers curled by the sides of his keyboard, the agent had to put aside his unease with the rising anger of her customer: his job was to make the customer comfortable and then persuade her to pay her debts without offending her because the "product" of his labor was a feeling of comfort that would facilitate the collection. On another night, we sat with an agent who was trying to placate an enraged customer in rural West Virginia. The agent was working on a process for a US-based HMO and his customer was furious about the bill she had received after a recent hospitalization. The agent scrolled through intimate details of the customer's medical history on his monitor as he tried to explain the HMO's policies to her. Once again, the agent had to absorb and metabolize the customer's fury to produce a feeling of comfort so that his customer did not feel that the HMO was letting her down. We suspect that he was able to collect on the bill because, when he concluded the call, the relief that coursed through his body as he stretched out in his chair was palpable. The labor process in both instances involved connecting with and engaging customers regardless of the customers' states of mind and behavior toward them: that these interactions were virtual rather than face-to-face only reinforced both the difficulty of their affective engagement and the toll it took on agents.

As we witnessed with many BPO agents, the dispositions produced by affective labor were fueled by the affective potency of aspiration as well as anxiety. Even though this twinning of aspiration and anxiety was intensely unsettling for them, they could not always articulate what was making them feel unsettled. Ironically, for people who made a living from their voice, the disjunctive temporalities of work and life were felt, sensed, and experienced more than they were voiced. The feeling of unsettlement and the unease that was created by the conflicting temporal pressures of work, family, and community were not "written" on the body but were, as we will argue shortly, refracted by other temporalities; these were highly contagious sensations that were reconstituted as they undulated with and across bodies.

The chronopolitics of these disjunctions bring into sharp relief some of the modalities of racial capitalism and their imbrication with processes of embodiment. For our interlocutors, the reversal of work time resulted in acute sleep deprivation. Nightwork produces sharp conflicts with the body's natural circadian rhythms. Drawing a distinction between long hours of work and wrong hours of work, Aneesh (2015, 118–19) argues that because our circadian rhythms are closely attuned to the earth's movement and spin, any disruption affects circulatory, respiratory, and other functions. Although circadian (sleep-wake cycle) and homeostatic processes (sleep debt compensation) are different processes, they are closely integrated at the molecular level (Franken and Dijk 2009, 1–8; Aneesh 2015). Thus, BPO agents' bodies were affected not only because they got insufficient sleep but because of when they were able to sleep. Their circadian rhythms could not adapt to the reversal of work time, which entailed working at night and sleeping during the daytime. The chronopolitics of racial capitalism, global hierarchies of temporality, the unpredictable schedule of nightwork, the toll that affective labor took on them, and the fact that agents had little or no control over their shifts reconfigured their bodies and their relations of sociality—but were also, as we will elaborate shortly, shaped by these relations of sociality. Agents experienced the rhythms of labor, predicated as they were on distinctive forms of time discipline, as relentless, as work without punctuation, without a period. Krishnan, a BPO agent in his late twenties, said to us, "Work continues while the rest of Bangalore is asleep. Customers need immediate responses. The customer cannot wait."

In turn, the rhythms of the body refracted the management and rhythms of work, foregrounding the *mutual* imbrication of processes of embodiment and the extraction of labor. To accomplish a high level of productivity, labor had to be managed carefully, stringently, and efficiently by ensuring punctuality and, hence, time discipline and spatiotemporal control. The management of time was imposed through an overriding emphasis on punctuality and the surveillance of workers' bodies. This emphasis might seem puzzling given the high priority given to customer satisfaction. Nevertheless, punctuality had to be ensured at all times by company cabs that aimed to transport agents to the office on time, the meticulous monitoring of all breaks, and the ubiquitous presence of cameras in hallways and other common areas. Punctuality was also monitored through the careful archiving of log-in and log-out times. The rhythms of labor were, therefore, predicated on the surveillance, regulation, and disciplining of the bodies of workers. So constraining was this monitoring and disciplining that it led some agents to quit the industry altogether. These processes of (re)embodiment materialize how racial capitalism and affective capitalism operate on a granular level to, once again, blur the boundaries between bodies, labor, technology, and the generation and extraction of value.

Affecting Time and Labor

The imperative to produce certain kinds of affect and the time discipline that undergirded the labor process were sometimes in a contradictory relationship. For the most part, there was a tension between the imperative of time discipline and customer satisfaction. As we noted earlier, the criteria for evaluating the performance of agents changed from the number of calls made over the course of a night to customer satisfaction. When we first started long-term fieldwork in 2009, agents' activities were closely monitored, and the chief metric used by managers to evaluate agents' work was the number of calls completed in a given shift. At that time, the corporate clients of many BPOs were paying them by the call, giving them an incentive to maximize the number of calls answered each day. This metric was soon abandoned because customers complained that agents rushed through calls.

Over time, the emphasis shifted to producing a "good outcome" (that is, the customer's comfort, well-being, sense of being cared for, or brand loyalty), which contracting companies and BPO managers glossed as "customer satisfaction." During training, agents at one BPO were told, "Although you have a target AHD [Average Handle Time], you are not driven by AHDs. Think only of the customer. Provide extra customer experience even if it takes an extra 2 minutes. [If you rush through a call], VOC [Voice of Customer] goes down. You need to keep the VOC score high because assessments are based on VOC scores." As the CEO of one BPO explained to us, the goal became to resolve the consumer's issues in one phone call because their data showed that when people called back for the same problem, they tended to be angrier and more dissatisfied with the company—the brand lost value with each repeated call. Seema, a trainer at one of the BPOs where we did our research, emphasized to trainees that their job was to "educate the customer to build brand loyalty." Earlier, they used to begin conversations by asking the customer, "How are you doing today?" but the client (the overseas company that had contracted with the BPO) felt that was a waste of time. So they now tried to get to the heart of the problem as soon as possible, leaving the question for later to prevent dead air. The trainees were told that "Americans are easy-going but very short of time—for them, time is money, so you never want to waste the customer's time." For this reason, they were told never to ask customers questions that might work as icebreakers in an Indian context and would be considered extremely intrusive by overseas customers, such as "Are you married?" "How many children do you have?" "Is your mother-in-law nice to you?"

The relationship between customer satisfaction and the imperative to be efficient was complex indeed. Even though customer satisfaction was nebulous and hard to measure, managers came to realize that it had to be given the highest priority. A good agent was one who made customers feel that the company had worked hard to look after them even when their problems had not been resolved. This gave agents some leeway while making them responsible for a more complex task—to produce the desired affect, to convince customers that the company had done its best to help them, and to emphasize that it valued them. Thus, although BPO agents made hotel and air reservations, helped people who had lost their credit cards, and restored forgotten passwords, the most important outcome of BPO work was neither a product in the sense of an object (as with factory workers) nor a string of computer code (as in the case of software engineers) but, rather, a feeling of well-being, of being looked after, and of confidence in the company.

Nevertheless, BPO managers persisted in enforcing time discipline because they believed that those skills were necessary to prepare agents for higher-order responsibilities built on task orientation. Managers maintained strict controls over workers' time because they wanted to ensure that they became accustomed to working hard and meeting deadlines. For example, if an employee wanted a bathroom break, they had to seek a supervisor's approval and, if the call volume was high, their request could be denied. At the same time, making customer satisfaction an overarching goal introduced uncertainty to the labor process that could, potentially, disrupt the temporality of affective capitalism. In some instances, managers granted high-performing agents considerable latitude as long as they received good customer satisfaction ratings. For example, Gupta was surprised when an agent named Vijay suggested that they meet in the tech park where he worked after his shift had started. Not wanting to get Vijay into trouble, Gupta asked again whether Vijay would be available at that time. Vijay responded that his manager allowed him to choose his own hours because he accomplished more in a few hours than most agents managed to do in a full shift. In fact, Vijay resisted getting a promotion because a higher position would require him to be in the office for his entire shift and be responsible for imposing time discipline on his subordinates.

Since one of the defining features of BPO labor is that it consists of "live" interaction between agents and customers, their work entails bringing together the temporal rhythms of life in vastly different geographies. In this regard, BPOs differ fundamentally from other kinds of outsourced, offshore production; for example, in a manufacturing factory in China, the rhythms of workers' labor are not connected live to customers' needs and demands. Even with just-in-time production methods and seasonal fluctuations in demand, the small temporal cushions in manufacturing disappear in BPO work because of the need for live interaction.

Live interaction had several consequences for the temporality and rhythms of BPO labor. As Alex, a British trainer who had flown into Bengaluru, impressed upon his charges, "How you say the opening lines is very important—you only have a few seconds to make an impression. You have to be enthusiastic, and speak grammatically correct sentences at high energy levels." He went on to urge them to listen carefully and emphasized that good communication skills were essential for this job. Live interaction did not give agents a second chance to get things right if they failed to make a good impression in the first few seconds. It thus placed tremendous performative pressure on the agent that was hard to sustain over a nine-hour shift.

The need to respond in real time has implications that extend beyond the fact that live connection necessitates night work and a reversal of work time. The temporalities of agents' labor were shaped by the urgency and call volumes from the geographies they were serving and by the affective nature of the encounter. A low call volume did not necessarily mean an easy shift if the calls were stressful and emotionally draining. For example, if agents had to deal with angry, abusive, or impatient clients, they experienced their shift as stressful even if there were few calls. Similarly, sudden snowstorms on the Eastern Seaboard of the United States led to stressful periods for agents on travel processes as thousands of frantic passengers called in to reschedule their arrangements.

Being "live" meant that what was happening in their clients' world had an immediate impact on their own. They had little control over those events, and their work shift could suddenly transform from being relatively easy and peaceful to a high-stress one that took an emotional toll on them. Their affective labor was thus charged, one might even say surcharged, with intensities that were fundamentally unpredictable: agents' experience of time was thus neither even nor precise. As a result and despite all their efforts, managers were unable to completely control the labor process through Taylorist techniques. Time itself did not unfold in a linear and predictable manner.

Although the experience of both the agent and the customer was shaped by their live encounter, they occupied asymmetrical positions. If a customer's day could be ruined by an unhelpful or unsympathetic BPO agent, the agent was likely to be traumatized by a customer's racist or xenophobic rant, and a complaint from a customer could lead management to discipline or fire the agent. The affective connections that were forged in these live encounters added to the stress of doing night work and spending eight hours on call intently listening to customers. Thus, although BPO work shared some features with the night work done by factory workers or janitors, it was also fundamentally different in its dependence on affective labor.

GENDERED AND RACIALIZED EMBODIMENT

How do race and gender intersect in BPO work and what are its implications for the embodiment of BPO agents? Contrary to the common presumption that BPO work is done primarily by women or is inherently feminizing, the participants in our study did not categorize their affective labor as intrinsically feminine or masculine, nor were labor processes in BPOs gender-segregated. More importantly, male BPO workers did not seem to experience or perceive their work as feminine or feminized, and they did not seem to feel that their masculinity was being undermined or threatened because they engaged in care work or affective labor. Kiran Mirchandani (2005) seeks to understand the simultaneous location of BPO work within gendered and transnational racial regimes by asking how gendered norms are shaped by race relations between workers in India and clients in the United States (107). Our diachronic research with BPO agents raises the question of how these relations need to be reconceptualized and retheorized in transnational and globalized contexts, given how the long shadow of colonialism and racial capitalism have reconfigured formations of race, caste, and class in India.

Rather than theorize our informants' labor in terms of cisgender binaries—men's versus women's work—we are concerned with whether and to what extent their performance of affective labor served to reinforce, undermine, or reconfigure hegemonic discourses of gender and sexuality. In contrast to the heteronormative gendered division of labor in transnational subcontracted work in manufacturing or data entry where, for instance, purportedly nimble-fingered Asian women are deemed to be ideal workers, BPO agents, as well as personnel up the corporate hierarchy extending to the owners and CEOs of companies, did not perceive their work in gender-stereotypical terms. In addition, contrary to Mirchandani's informants, our interlocutors generally did not perceive their work as being similar to "mothering": they framed their performance of affective labor, which depended on the cultivation of empathy and good listening skills, in terms of professional and soft skills (chapter 1; cf. Mirchandani 2005, 111–12.).[4] Yet, as we have demonstrated in the rest of this book, the consequences of affective labor were shaped by gendered expectations. For instance, while family members and neighbors were suspicious of both men and women doing night work, women workers were subjected to considerably more surveillance and stigma than were men, and women were much more vulnerable to sexual harassment within and beyond the workplace than men. Similarly, although the punishing tempo of shift work negatively impacted the health of all workers, women suffered the disruption of menstrual and ovulation cycles. Thus, the corporeal consequences of affective labor also varied sharply by gender.

By situating discourses of gender in context-specific formations of race and racialization, we underline the mutual imbrication of race and gender, rethinking prevailing paradigms of race in contexts of the transnational subcontracting of service work. Next, we examine how mutations of racial capitalism in transnational and postcolonial contexts implicate the embodiment of agents by positing that older paradigms of colonial extraction are inadequate for understanding the extraction of value from BPOs located in India. We also draw on Asian American studies scholarship that decenters nation-bound assumptions to theorize race and racialized labor from the perspective of the transnational service industry (for instance, Choy 2003; Padios 2018; and Parreñas 2001).[5]

Race, Asian Alterity, and the World of Bengaluru's BPOs

Let us revisit Cedric Robinson's ([1983] 2020) elaboration of racial capitalism: "The development, organization, and expansion of capitalist society pursued essentially racial directions, so too did social ideology. As a material force, it could be expected that racialism would inevitably permeate the social structures emergent from capitalism. I have used the term 'racial capitalism' to refer . . . to the subsequent structure as a historical agency" (2). Robinson argues that the historical development of capitalism across the world has been constituted in fundamental ways by race and nationalism (9). BPOs boast of flattened hierarchies and an egalitarian atmosphere but, as we have already seen, they are, in essence, products of networked forms of capitalist structures and logics. To the extent that these structures and logics are embedded in world-historical and transnational formations of racial inequality, they amplify the inextricability of capital flows with racialized labor and have far-reaching implications for how subjects are embodied as laborers.

Our interlocutors' interpellation as racialized subjects underscores the complex articulations of national location and race that have occurred with the proliferation of transnational subcontracting in the service economy. Tressie McMillan Cottom's (2020, 442) theorization that "global patterns of racialized labor that determine what is 'skill' and what is 'labor' mediate the value of labor and the rents the platform can extract for mediating the laborer-customer relationship" seems particularly salient to the affective labor performed by BPO agents and foregrounds, once again, the centrality of processes of embodiment for affective capitalism and semiocapitalism. The "products" of the affective labor of BPO agents (attention, empathy, and the resolution of problems) were consumed, as it were, in wealthier client nations in the Global North. At the same time, as we argued in chapter 1, while the products of the labor of BPO agents "traveled" to these client nations, they themselves were emplaced by racist and xenophobic immigration policies that, literally, kept them in place.

Racial capitalism is imbricated in embodiment because it operates through processes of hierarchical differentiation between the purported capacities and value of bodies. In her remarkable ethnography of Indian software engineers in Berlin, Sareeta Amrute asks: "Do work skills inhere in bodies?" If this question is pertinent to engineers, it is surely even more salient to how certain bodies are deployed as service providers in industries shaped by racial capitalism. Asian American scholars have demonstrated how bodies of color have historically been deployed to provide service to employers in the Global North (Chun 2022; Chun and Cranford 2018; Choy 2003; Glenn 1985, 1992, 1999, 2012; Parreñas 2005, 2008. The transnational *reconstitution* of these genealogies of race and racialized gender undergird the affective labor provided by ITES firms in countries like India and the Philippines (Padios 2018; Vora 2015).

Consider, for instance, the cover of an issue of the popular Indian news magazine *India Today* that featured a lead story in 2002 on how India has become the "electronic housekeeper to the world" (Goyal and Chengappa 2002). Published during the early years of the ITES sector in India, the article begins with a (presumably fictional) account of Meghna, a twenty-three-year-old Indian woman who becomes Michelle, providing service to a customer of a JC Penney store in Philadelphia who is requesting a credit extension:

4.1. "Electronic Housekeeper to the World" article from *India Today*, 2002.

While Meghna feeds in the request to a computer data bank, the caller is unaware that her query is being processed by someone sitting in a Third World country thousands of miles away who has never been inside such a large department store. Meghna is unruffled. Months of training, which included watching Hollywood blockbusters to pick up a wide variety of American accents and reading John Grisham thrillers to clear any linguistic obstacles, have paid off. Her computer screen even flashes the weather at Philadelphia as she tells a caller what a perfect day it is. Meghna signs off saying, "Have a good day." Outside her window it is pitch dark.

Pointing to the rapid growth of BPOs "taking care of a host of routine activities for multinational giants," the article breathlessly proceeds to describe Meghna's impersonation as Michelle as "a sophisticated subterfuge" that has resulted in bringing in millions of dollars in foreign exchange and claims that, having expanded by 70 percent in the last year, the BPO industry has ushered a "gold rush" for India. Although it makes no mention of the racialized and gendered forces enabling extractions of labor in *this* gold rush, the cover image and other images featured in the article raise several important questions about race, gender, and embodiment in regimes of affective labor.[6]

Amrute argues that the question about certain skills inhering in racialized bodies has frequently been linked to nonhuman things such as machines. Drawing on the work of Donna Haraway and Bruno Latour, she insists that "racializations occur when programmers and programming technologies meet" (Amrute 2016, 60). We extend this theorization of race to the kinds of racializations that occur in the ITES industry and argue that if "various couplings of Indian bodies and computers happen at boundaries and thresholds, where the possible relationship between coding technologies and worker subjectivity is constituted" in software companies (60), these couplings are even more ubiquitous when technology enables certain bodies to provide service to customers in the Global North. Racial capitalism in postcolonial contexts has meant that certain kinds of bodies are put to the service of those in former metropoles. The value that our informants, as well as their clients and customers, ascribed to their affective labor was powerfully refracted by discourses of uneven development, hierarchies, and inequalities between client nations like the United States, Australia, the United Kingdom, and Canada and service-providing nations like India, and the global circulation and reconstitution of discourses of race. Although the modalities of racial capitalism are far from uniform, singular, or homogeneous, the *worth* ascribed to these bodies is such that their well-being in the present and in the future is called into question. The coimplication of the labor process with the bodies of workers results from the articulation of technology, geography, the inequality of job opportunities globally, the dynamics of firms, and the policies of different governments. This is not a straightforward case of the "impact" of new technology on workers' bodies, but a highly mediated outcome contingent on many different factors and, more fundamentally, a reconfiguration of bodies through feedback loops between technology and bodies, and organic and inorganic matter.

SPEAKING DIFFERENT/CE, EMBODYING RACE

In chapter 1, we elaborated on the relationship between race and what, borrowing from Talal Asad (1986), we termed the inequality of languages. Here, we wish to trace some of the ways in which language training, accent neutralization, and Global English underscore the embodiment of BPO agents as subjects who are racialized in distinct ways. In the contemporary conjuncture of racial capitalism, processes of racialization are "unevenly detached from color lines" (Melamed 2011, 12). These processes acquire a particular force in workplaces where modes of speaking, accents, and aurality serve to emplace (re)racialized subjects on new-old terrains of inequality. As we argued in our theorization of mobility and language, national location and racialized conceptions of culture and cultural difference refract the embodied subject formation of BPO agents in concrete ways. We turn here to the convergence of colonial history, geography, and the political economy of race in the embodied racialization of BPO agents through their cultivation of "Global English."

Teaching Indian subjects English was an important strategy of colonial rule. Lord Macaulay's (in)famous *Minute on Indian Education* delivered in 1835 is a succinct elaboration of the colonial imperative to form "a class of persons, Indian in blood and colour, but English in taste, in opinions, in morals, and in intellect" (quoted in Cutts 1953, 825). In postcolonial India, even as it has been owned and reappropriated by Indians in myriad forms of "Indian English,"[7] English is not simply a language of status and class mobility but remains, to some extent, an imperial language (Aneesh 2015; Bhatt 2005). At the same time, India's competitive advantage in global services and, in particular, in the establishment of customer service BPOs stems from its large pool of young people who have learned English in school and college.[8] The lead trainer at one BPO asked new employees, "Where did we learn our English? From the British. We have to thank them."

If the imperative to learn English is implicated in racialization, it is particularly pertinent to processes of racial embodiment. At its most basic, becoming a BPO agent entails not just learning to speak English but to speak it in a particular way (Bhatt 2015). The modulation of voice is affective: it involves emotion, cognition, and the body at the same time that it is shaped by culturally specific discourses such as those of nationality, gender, class, deference, and authority. Consequently, BPOs invested considerable resources in teaching agents "proper" English and, in the early years of the industry, subjecting them to "accent training."[9] To learn to speak English in a particular way is thus to inhabit a subject position that is powerfully shaped by colonial, postcolonial, and transnational formations of race and racialism (Alim, Rickford, and Ball 2016; Hsu 2015).

In *Black Skin, White Masks*, Frantz Fanon ([1952] 2008) emphasizes the centrality of language to the formation of colonial subjects. He comments ironically that a Black person in the Antilles is seen to be whiter, "that is . . .

closer to being a real human being—in direct ratio to his mastery of the French language" (8–9). But it is not simply the ability to speak French that matters: it is *how* racialized subjects speak the language, their diction, their accent, and their modes of enunciation. Fanon points out that Black people in the French Caribbean are compelled to try to change the cadence of their speech and erase all traces of "dialect," "Creole," or allegedly inappropriate accents in an effort to learn the "proper" diction; he adds that when the acquisition of French colonial diction brings Black speakers closer to whiteness, to that extent, it also brings them closer to being human. He argues that while he is using the specific example of Black people in the French Caribbean, his description pertains to every colonized person (9). While the racial positionalities of Black men in the French Caribbean in colonial contexts can hardly be transposed onto BPO agents in Bengaluru, Fanon's theorization of language, accent, and race is instructive: accents exemplify the embodiment of race intertwined with national location.

Agents are also racialized by virtue of being located in a particular place in the world, thus highlighting the complexity of contemporary racial capitalism. How they *sound* emerges as a crucial modality by which customers locate agents in that particular place and (re)racialize them (Shome 2006; see also Aneesh 2015, 37). Fanon's argument that the ability to speak a colonial language (rather than phenotypical attributes alone) determines one's proximity to whiteness underscores how, in addition to being visual, processes of racialization are distinctly aural. For, as with racial and ethnic minorities, immigrants, and migrant workers in many parts of the world, racial difference is (re)cognized through aural cues: how we sound marks us as racialized subjects (Alim 2016).

H. Samy Alim (2016, 1) points out that language varieties are not a fixed or singular inventory of traits that map on to a given "race"; rather, speakers draw on diverse linguistic resources as they shape and engage in projects of identification (see also Alim 2009). In the United States, there has been a powerful remapping of race from biology to language so that race is increasingly constructed through perceptions of language use (Rosa 2019, 2).[10] Furthermore, as argued by Jennifer Roth-Gordon (2016), in the cultural and linguistic practices that shape everyday assessments of race in Brazil, "race is not something that you 'see' through visual cues alone—but it is, in no small part, constructed through how people 'sound.'" (51).[11]

An accent is an aural way to connote both racial difference and privilege; it goes without saying that accents are always relational.[12] Analyses of "Indian" and "South Asian American" accents in US popular culture by Asian

American scholars highlight the intersection of Orientalism with discourses of Otherness in the complex and ambiguous racialization of Indians and Indian Americans: these analyses suggest how the "Indian" accents of BPO agents may be perceived by customers in the United States and in other locations through the circulation of these representations in transnational media. In these mediatized representations, accents play a significant role in how South Asian Americans are marked as racially and culturally Other, extending significantly beyond visual identification (Davé 2013, 2; see also Mankekar 2021b).

Trainers and agents alike believed that the ability to perform affective labor was hindered if their accents identified them as racially and culturally Other. In the early years of BPOs, agents were trained to adopt the accents of the places inhabited by their customers: thus, for instance, agents working with customers in the southern United States would be trained to speak in a southern drawl, while those servicing customers in Australia would be taught Aussie accents. By the time we began our fieldwork in 2009, most companies had begun to train their employees in what they termed accent neutralization and Global English (Aneesh 2015). Rather than mimicking their customers, agents were trained to speak in an "accentless" manner that was not attempting to impersonate people in the Global North (Mankekar 2015). The purported rationale for training agents to neutralize their accents to speak in Global English was to smoothen communication with customers so as to better serve them. But even when ostensibly "neutralized," accents index racialized embodiment in complex ways: they constitute a crucial modality for locating Others along terrains produced by racial and cultural hierarchies and entail both difference and privilege. Accent neutralization and the introduction of Global English aim primarily to protect the client company from allegations that by outsourcing projects to India they are stealing jobs to which their own citizens are entitled. Accent neutralization, like accent training in the past, is aimed at mitigating some of the nationalist, xenophobic, and racist discourses inflamed by debates regarding the outsourcing of service work to the Global South (for instance, Aneesh 2015; Mankekar 2015; Mankekar and Gupta 2017; Mirchandani 2012; Nadeem 2011). However, once customers learned of the true locations of agents their anger and racism would often be exacerbated.

"Accent training" and learning a "neutral" accent are, fundamentally, implicated in the process of being (re)embodied as a racialized subject. Changing one's accent, even if to neutralize it, involves specific physiological practices: accents are "seamless expressions of the body, linking movements of the tongue, teeth, larynx, and neural wiring" (Aneesh 2015, 61). When we observed training sessions, we saw how trainees struggled to change how they spoke by learning to use their tongues and breath differently: pronouncing *t*'s and *p*'s in a supposedly neutral accent meant training oneself to aspirate differently, just as distinguishing between *v*'s and *w*'s involved new and unfamiliar movements of the lips and teeth. But beyond these obviously corporeal processes, learning to speak English a certain way and retraining one's accent was as much about retraining—and reconfiguring— the body as it was the mind.

Accent neutralization and Global English insidiously reinforced the racialization of agents and foregrounds the foundational role of racial capitalism in the ITES industry. It, once again, underscores that, far from being disembodied, the labor of semiocapitalism is performed by workers who are embodied through race and racialism. On their part, BPO agents attempted to make sense of and respond to the racism that they experienced in different ways. As we noted earlier, very few of our interlocutors specifically described customers who abused them as "racist" or in terms of racism (cf. Ghosh and Chakrabarty 2002). Instead, they often described their customers as ignorant and uneducated, in contrast to themselves as worldly and knowledgeable. They also talked about their experiences as examples of their skills in dealing with "difficult" people or as a testimony of their success in acquiring "soft skills" or people skills (see also Mirchandani 2012; for comparable responses from Filipino agents, see Padios 2018).

Second, all our interlocutors were fully cognizant of the fact that the wages they received were low in comparison with those doing the same work in the Global North and sometimes articulated extremely cogent and insightful critiques of the discrepancy in wages. Many of them said they had no choice but to accept the situation because, despite this disparity, they earned a great deal more working for BPOs than in other sectors of the Indian economy. The ITES industry exemplifies how, with the ascent of neoliberal notions of choice, opportunity, and resilience, structural inequalities ensuing from racial capitalism become naturalized such that racist abuse and exploitation are either tolerated (that is, dealt with "professionally") or, worse, deemed beneficial (as when the ability to endure abuse and exploitation is interpreted as the acquisition of professional skills).

Furthermore, agents' interpellation by discourses of nationalism, as instantiated in their self-representation as contributors to India's economic progress, enabled them to claim that they were performing their duty to the nation by tolerating racist abuse and exploitation. Like Filipino call center agents discussed by Padios (2018), our interlocutors contextualized and justified their acceptance of customer abuse as a demonstration of national responsibility (see also Mirchandani 2012). We saw how a particular trainer anticipated and deflected agents' apprehensions of abuse during a training session: "If the customer is angry, that is very good news for you," she told trainees. "It helps you to demonstrate your customer service skills. You should look forward to angry customers." Nevertheless, regardless of how they characterized or normalized it, one of the major reasons why agents experienced emotional exhaustion and burnout was the stress of dealing with racist and xenophobic abuse.

Agents constructed nationalist and racialized stereotypes of their customers, both to normalize abusive responses from them and, in some cases, to highlight educational disparities between them. For example, one manager told us that he was glad that his company was now doing a lot of processes on chat rather than voice. When we asked him why he preferred chat, he replied in all seriousness, "It was so hard to understand their [customers'] accents." He added that what made it additionally difficult was that most customers did not speak "good English." On chat, he felt, despite poor punctuation and terrible spelling, it was easier to guess what customers wanted and his agents could respond in "good"—that is, "standard"—English.

The racialized embodiment of BPO agents thus occurs in complex and unpredictable ways. In contrast to logics of race predicated on visuality, their racialization occurs despite or, more accurately, because of their invisibility: they are required to neutralize their accents and hence hide their racial and cultural identities and national location. The very masking of their racial and cultural identities works to racialize them (cf. Nakamura 2002). Furthermore, unlike processes of racialization that are contingent on the "*visible* and *interruptive* presence" of the racialized Other, BPO agents are marked as racial Others through logics of aurality: their racialization occurs through interruptive processes marked by how they sound rather than how they look (Shome 2006, 108; emphasis in original). Rather than assume that these logics of racialization are predicated on dis-embodiment (Shome 2006), we have argued the opposite. Even as they are rendered invisible, they are reembodied as racialized laboring subjects through these logics of aurality.

BPO agents' bodies are thus reconfigured to align with the demands of racial capitalism and, we would insist, coproduced with them (Bear et al. 2015; Melamed 2011). As we will see next, in contexts of affective capitalism, these are bodies of entanglement, raising complex questions about the relationship between the laboring body, information technology, and futurity.

CORPOREALITY AND THE GRANULAR PRODUCTION
OF BPO AGENTS

The embodiment of BPO agents was predicated on the production of dispositions that spanned cognition, emotion, and the corporeal. The generation of these dispositions entailed the granular modulation of bodily habits, sensations, desires, capacities, and potentialities. For instance, BPO agents trained themselves to inhabit a middle-class body in myriad ways, and, to this extent, discourses of class and their aspirations toward upward class mobility were fundamental to their formation as laboring subjects, to the generation of capital, and to futures imagined and futurities potentialized.

In addition to the transformations of the body in conjunction with time discipline, the production of these dispositions was based on reorienting and reconfiguring bodily comportment and personal habits at a granular level. We have already noted the insistence on personal grooming in all the BPOs that we studied that aimed to introduce agents to new modes of inhabiting and, indeed, configuring the body. At first we were puzzled by the emphasis on grooming; after all, unlike frontline workers in other service industries like hospitality or retail, BPO agents were not going to meet their customers in person; it therefore seemed to us to be irrelevant to their labor practices. The CEO of one BPO emphasized the importance of grooming during agent training and implemented a relatively formal dress code: as a result, in contrast to BPOs where agents wore T-shirts and jeans, all male employees had to shave regularly and wear shirts with collars and dress pants. He insisted to us that his BPO was "no place for five-o'clock shadows." He firmly believed that a "professional" appearance enabled efficiency at work.

During their training, BPO agents were taught how to enter and exit an elevator ("Stand on the side and wait for people to come out before you go in") and how to stand in the corridor ("Don't bend your knees and put your feet up against the wall"). Veronica, a trainer in a mid-sized BPO, instructed new recruits to keep their hands out of their pockets, to push in their chairs when they got up, to not interrupt others, and to learn how to ask questions and not just to provide answers. She also frequently impressed upon her trainees the importance of personal hygiene, including the use of deodorants, and spoke to them about how to use Western-style toilets. When we pressed her on why that was essential to the training of BPO agents, she replied that changing personal habits would instill in her trainees skills that could enable them to better engage with their customers. For their part, several agents explained to us in detail that learning how to eat Western food, for instance by using a fork and knife, was essential to knowing how to interact with customers living in the West.

Throughout this book we have theorized caste as a corporeal and affective formation that is resolutely social and is institutionalized in, and generated by, inequities across social domains. Hierarchies of caste have been reconfigured—and recharged—in conjunction with colonial policies, postindependence statist discourses of citizenship and rights; development, urbanization, and neoliberal governmentality; and, as we have noted, the new forms of labor that have emerged with the transnational service industry. Unlike the software industry where the majority of engineers are from dominant castes, workers in the ITES industry are comparatively diverse in terms of caste. In the BPOs in which we conducted our fieldwork, agents, HR personnel, and middle managers belonged to a range of castes; yet, senior managers, CEOs, and owners tended to be from dominant castes. Thus, while one might be tempted to surmise that the alchemy of global capitalism and information technology has leveled the field for all castes, what we observed was considerably more complex.

Contemporary mutations of caste at once articulate *and* misarticulate with the granular modes of embodiment emerging in Bengaluru's BPOs. Caste has persisted as a form of social stratification in metropolitan centers in contemporary India, even as its hold may have loosened on some aspects of social life. In some dominant discourses, caste is conceptualized in ontological terms and as inhering in one's body. In Savarna (upper-caste) discourses, specific moral characteristics are stereotypically associated with different castes: thus, for instance, Brahmins are presumed to have a predilection for learning that, in turn, is presumed to be a superior moral virtue. Sucharita Kanjilal (2023) points out that, according to Ambedkar, "the embodied, sensory response that produces caste is consistent: an 'inward feeling of defilement, odium, aversion and contempt'" (10). The notion of defilement, therefore, is not simply metaphysical (although it is that as well) but is also corporeal and moral, so much so that particular moral characteristics are deemed to inhere in the body and be hereditary. In BPOs, agents from dominant castes are trained to provide service, while those from oppressed castes which have historically been associated with menial (and purportedly defiling) labor learn to provide service in ways unknown to their parents and other kin. This is not to suggest that caste has been obliterated by any means; indeed, as Gopal Guru (2019, 203) argues in his "archaeology" of caste, it assumes deeper, more subtle forms (see also chapters 1 and 3 for how caste shapes BPO mobilities and intimacies respectively).

The laboring body of the BPO agent is shaped by its position along caste hierarchies: after all, embodiment occurs as a result of "a network of cultural material practices" (N. Menon 2019, 138). The entitlements of caste and ensuing cultural capital were manifested in the bodily habitus of BPO agents from dominant castes: acquiring the "soft skills" required for becoming a successful agent entails acquiring a sheen of confidence that often comes more easily to them because of their access to caste networks and resources (Mosse 2020).[13] Senior management, the owners of BPOs, and the angel investors were almost invariably from dominant castes. Thus, while there was certainly upward class mobility, there were several ways in which hierarchies of caste were mirrored in the corporate hierarchies of BPOs.

At the same time, as several anthropologists of Hindu South Asia have noted, discourses of personhood posit an intimate relationship between (ingested) substance and guna (moral characteristics) and, hence, between ingestion, embodiment, and personhood (Daniel 1987; see also Solomon 2016). Put another way, the ingestion of certain substances shapes the kind of person one is: therefore, the substances that enter (and constitute) one's body produce and index one's moral traits and position along hierarchies of caste.[14] As we noted in chapter 2, young men and women were exposed to diverse cuisines and their acquisition of "soft skills" often entailed learning to eat unfamiliar foods that they would never have had the opportunity to eat before joining BPOs. For instance, Brahmin agents underscored to us how, even when they remained vegetarian, they learned to eat foods that they would never before have dared to try and this, they insisted, was part of the "learnings" they needed to become successful in their careers. In this manner, some caste orthodoxies were placed under pressure and functioned to (re)embody BPO agents at a granular level. Furthermore, caste orthodoxies pertaining to commensality—that is, caste-based rules regarding whom one can eat with—were transgressed when agents from different castes and religions had food or coffee together in the BPO's cafeteria or when they went to restaurants for a meal. We cannot stress more forcefully the significance of this seemingly banal occurrence in chipping away, at least in these specific spaces, dominant rules of commensality that shaped social relations among castes and, to this extent, their granular embodiment.

In sum, in addition to teaching the skills of good listening, empathy, and assertiveness, the affective labor of BPO agents entailed transforming agents' bodily habitus: as much as the brain and the heart, agents' bodies were reconstituted in order for them to better perform affective labor. Learning to become effective BPO agents extended beyond the workplace and demonstrates the granularity of the coproduction of affective capitalism and processes of embodiment.

Bodies of Entanglement

In BPOs, technology has informatized regimes of labor as well as the body of the worker, enabling the continual transmission and modulation of knowledge and affect. These biomediatized bodies are "in-formational" and demonstrate the "dynamism inherent to bodily matter" (Clough 2008, 1), further challenging conceptions of the body as static or as an organism encased within the skin. It is important to note, however, that bodies have always been shaped, if not constituted, by modes of work in powerful ways: in other words, the coimplication of work and embodiment is not unique to modes of laboring in BPOs. Moreover, rather than being a closed "system," the body is open to the external environment, the soil on which it resides, and the social relations in which it is embedded (Daniel 1987). Indeed, the "situated, absorptive interface of bodies and surroundings" blurs the separation between the body and the environment (Solomon 2016, 15).

In the ITES industry, digital technology, and the informatization of the body suggest how the blurring of organic and nonorganic matter reconfigures, rather than merely extends, agents' bodily capacities as they perform affective labor in real time with customers at considerable geographic and cultural distances: the body is hence reconstituted as a semiomaterial assemblage (Rai 2019). Instantaneous and real-time communication occurs because of digital technology, fiber optics, and satellite technology, thus foregrounding the ubiquity of material infrastructure, software, and algorithms that enable the production of affective economies and the transmission of purportedly immaterial goods. The virtual migration of affective labor also generates particular modes of embodiment, resulting in the blurring of boundaries between technology and affective bodily capacities. For example, agents' powers of hearing and connecting were reconstituted by the hardware and software that enabled companies to transmit data across or, more accurately, under continents and oceans. This technology reconfigured agents' bodily capacities to connect with customers, extending beyond the facilitation of real-time interactions by dialer software.

But more pertinently to our argument here, the bodies of BPO agents were not simply repositories of information but were, equally, *open* to information and reconfigured by it at a level of granularity: these bodies become "resonating vessel(s) for the force of information to which it is now singularly sensitized" (Massumi 2002, 124; see also Deleuze 1992). The centrality of information technology to the performance of affective labor in the ITES industry foregrounds the "technoscientific *productions* of bodily capacities beyond the human body's organic-physiological constraints" (Clough 2007, 4; emphasis added): the entanglement of bodies with information technology blurs the line between machines, software, algorithms, and bodily capacities and, in conjunction with affective capitalism, entails the granular reconstitution of the body.

These bodies of entanglement are reconfigured and reshaped through encounters with other bodies and objects so as to constitute nodes in the circulation of affect, sensations, and intensities, which, in turn, form feedback loops that refract labor regimes. We have already theorized how the surveillance of agents' labor results in their emplacement (chapter 1); here, we analyze how these bodies are not only surveilled but are informatized through their entanglement with technology. For instance, agents' bodies were informatized in meticulous records of logins and bathroom breaks and by CCTV cameras that tracked their movements within offices. The informatization of their bodies occurred on multiple levels and in different sites: in addition to the biometric tracking of agents' entry into and exit from their offices, managers in Bengaluru and in the companies that contracted to these BPOs electronically monitored each call through agents' computer terminals. Agents' work on processes was closely tracked and quantified by quality control software tools and algorithms.[15] Put simply, the agents became data points when their bodies, as much as their labor, were subjected to digital archiving.[16]

Agents' affective labor and their affective engagements with customers became data points *but also so much more*: even as analytics made customer profiles available to agents when they worked with them, algorithmic mediations of these affective engagements engendered the virtual but often intimate interactions between agents and their customers.[17] Simply put, in the informatized workplace that is the BPO, the body is remade through its encounters with information technology because of the reorganization of its affective thresholds (Rai 2019). The affective labor of BPO agents hence demonstrates the ways in which, in affective capitalism, the relationship between the corporeal and the technological is fundamentally recast. Information technology is part of larger "assemblages of perception, sensation, habit, information, and capital" (83), underscoring the feedback loops between bodies, algorithms, capital, labor, and organic and inorganic matter.

Affective labor in BPOs demonstrates how information technology has become central to changing patterns of labor extraction under racial capitalism and, therefore, to changes in the nature of capitalism itself: it represents "even more profoundly, a mutation of capitalism" (Deleuze 1992, 6). What might the blurred boundaries between technology and bodily capacities mean for futurity? We turn to this question by engaging the intertwining of temporal disjunctions and the potentiality of the body.

BEING OUT OF SYNC AND WHAT A BODY CAN DO

The modes of embodiment enjoined by BPO agents' affective labor were imbricated with the temporal disjunctures between biorhythms and cycles of affective labor, the disruption of circadian rhythms by the durée of business cycles, and the complex articulations and disarticulations between the temporalities of BPO work and those of family and community.[18] Agents did not get fixed off days. They had two days off from work every week, but those days were rarely contiguous (e.g., they could be a Monday and a Friday) and seldom overlapped with weekends. Some processes, such as those aimed at consumer travel, could often be busier on weekends than on weekdays. Agents frequently complained that they never knew far enough in advance which days they would have off. As a result, they were unable to make advance plans for what they could do on the days that they were off work. How do these disjunctions mediate and refract the temporalities with which they seem "out of sync"?

Like Sadia, whom we met earlier in this book (chapter 1), Zareena left a BPO job to join an event management company. She claimed to be much happier with the work environment. The best part, she said, was that she did not need anyone's permission to go to the bathroom. Although there was intense work pressure in her new job, she liked the freedom to work without being monitored continuously, and she felt that the new company treated her like the adult that she was rather than infantilizing her by controlling every movement. Zareena's new job allowed her to compare different modes by which companies implemented task orientation, and much of her appreciation of her new job was due to the contrast it offered to the methods by which bodies were surveilled and disciplined in BPOs.

The inextricable entanglement of processes of embodiment with the generation of value and capital is further complicated by the fact that the laboring body is a desiring body (see chapter 3 on BPO intimacies). As semiomaterial assemblages, these bodies are not simply overwritten by the demands of labor but, also, (in)form and shape capital. These bodies get fatigued, they burn out, they get sick; they also desire and seek and find pleasure in ways that do not seamlessly or invariably synchronize with the temporalities of labor. As nodes within larger force fields of intensity that crisscross the socius with encounters between humans, technologies, objects, and organic and inorganic matter, these newly configured bodies compel us to think of affect, the ability to act and be acted on, as a form of potentiality that extends beyond individualistic (and liberal) notions of intentionality, agency, resistance, or subversion.

Proliferating Temporalities

What implications do disjunctive temporalities and their reworking of the body have for how BPO agents perceived the future and for how futurity, as an affective-temporal formation, is configured? For one, the temporalities of the body are not just reshaped in articulation with informational capitalism but also *proliferate with* it, further problematizing conceptions of the body and capital as external to each other. For instance, instead of being a sign of pregnancy, the missed period was, for Farhana and some of her friends, a manifestation of the coconstitution of embodiment and affective capitalism. That the disjunctive temporalities of affective labor had distinctive effects on women's bodies was evident from the experiences of Farhana and her women colleagues. Sleep deprivation had devastating consequences for them: nightwork, the unpredictability of their shift schedules, and the collision between the rhythms of labor and those of their bodies resulted in irregular menstrual cycles, difficulties with conception, miscarriages, premature births, and, potentially, higher rates of cancer (see also Aneesh 2015).

As we noted earlier, the temporalities of affective labor articulated as well as disarticulated with those of the family, community, and neighborhood. In particular, the demands of affective labor on women never seemed to end, leading to numbing exhaustion and emotional burnout. In addition to performing affective labor at work, for many women BPO agents, employment and financial independence generally did not alter the gendered division of labor in the family: housework, cooking, childcare, eldercare, and keeping up with social obligations and commitments continued to be perceived by family members and, for the most part, by these women themselves, as their responsibilities (see also Patel 2010). For instance, Vasanthi, who worked in one of the large BPOs where we did our research, was dismayed when she had to miss her niece's engagement ceremony and, while this did not generate the same kind of crisis as Farhana's missed period, it left her feeling very anxious: she worried that her absence from such important occasions would undermine her position in her extended family.

The rhythms of BPO work, and its relentlessness, often clashed with temporalities of ritual and religion. Vasanthi's friend and colleague, Rohini, spoke at length about how she regretted missing out on the Ganapati pujas (ritual prayers to the Hindu god Ganesha) held in her family's neighborhood of Malleswaram. Rohini was Brahmin and took her ritual obligations very seriously. These rituals were not just ceremonies that punctuated her day but were fundamental to her sense of herself as a middle-class Brahmin woman; she felt guilty also because she firmly believed that it was her duty as a daughter-in-law to participate in these rituals. The festivities extended over ten evenings but, because her office was on the other side of town, she would leave for work well before the festivities began and return after they had concluded. Ganapati pujas were scheduled in August or September according to the lunar calendar and she experienced these pujas as important markers of the passage of time: they had been a crucial component of the temporality of everyday life when she was growing up. Hence, in addition to feeling guilty about not fulfilling her duty as a daughter-in-law, she felt disoriented when she missed these pujas: her work schedule prevented her from following rituals that were deeply meaningful to her. In this instance, the temporality of ritual, which was intimately related to her embodiment as a daughter-in-law and Brahmin woman, collided with the temporality of labor at the BPO where she worked.

Similarly, Farhana complained about how difficult it was for her to fast during the holy month of Ramazan (Ramadan). The BPO where she worked set up a prayer room where Muslim employees could pray, and this was particularly helpful during Ramazan. But, while she was able to adhere to the schedule of prayers, the fact that she attended college during the day and worked at night meant that she was often dehydrated and famished when she started work. While she was sometimes able to eat the predawn sehri meal, iftar, or breaking the fast at sunset, would often be complicated because she had to rush to work for her night shifts. More important than when she could eat was the emotional valence for her of the ritual of breaking fast with family. Iftar is meant to be taken with family, she would say to Mankekar, and eating something at work just doesn't cut it. She added that Ramazan is as much about pious reflection, praying and reading the Koran regularly, and doing one's work dutifully, but it is also about taking the *time* to strengthen one's relationship to God with one's body and soul. But the rhythms of BPO work, the long commutes to college and to work, and the stringency of her schedule challenged her ability to engage in the forms of piety that mattered so much to her. It wasn't only her circadian rhythms that were interrupted and "messed up"; the temporalities of work collided painfully with those of piety and faith.

Over the course of our diachronic fieldwork, we were frequently stood up by people with whom we had made appointments. Upon making inquiries with their friends and coworkers, we would be informed that some of these interlocutors had "gone to their native"—that is, they had gone to their villages or hometowns, sometimes without giving much advance notice to their employers. While in some cases these abrupt departures were precipitated by illness or death in the family, the most common reasons had to do with their desire (and need) to participate in religious rituals, festivals, and other important events in their communities. "Going to native" was a source of tremendous annoyance to managers and supervisors. It, therefore, astonished us to learn that, in some cases, they were loath to fire these agents, even though these abrupt departures threatened to upend the schedule of a process. We have noted earlier that some agents preferred to resign from their jobs if supervisors made too much of a fuss about their going to their hometown: they did not seem to hesitate to give precedence to the temporalities of family and community over the rhythms of work. Senior managers, particularly those who had lived their entire lives in cities, would often express their frustration to us about agents "going to native," which they attributed to their lack of commitment or responsibility. We hasten to add that this was a time when it was getting increasingly difficult for BPOs to hire, train, and retain agents, and many managers would grimace in frustration to us as they described how they could not afford to fire these agents. Nevertheless, the ability of these young people to "go to native" without taking a leave in advance alerted us to the fact that they preferred to prioritize their responsibilities to their families.

Although they were not subject to the same scrutiny as women, men also felt torn between their duties to their families and their obligations at work. Another agent, Ramesh, described how his work had caused him to lose touch with his family. He lived at home with his parents and sister. When he began as a trainee, his work hours were during the day from 9 a.m. to 6 p.m. After one month of working that shift, he was transferred to the first evening shift, from 6:30 p.m. to 3:30 a.m. He now no longer saw his sister and parents because, by the time he got up, they had left for school and work. He said that this lack of contact with his family started "killing him mentally." That is when he quit.

In contrast, Zubeida, a single mother who lived with her parents, told us she preferred doing night work because it allowed her to be present when her child was awake. She could leave for work after her young daughter went to bed at 8 p.m., and when she returned home at 6:30 a.m., she could have time to make sure that her daughter was ready for school. After her daughter left, Zubeida went to bed and usually slept until her daughter returned home. Thus, she could be at home for the entire time that her daughter was awake. She felt that with a regular day job, she would have seen less of her daughter and not be able to spend quality time with her. Unlike Zubeida, however, many women were acutely unhappy about their nocturnal work schedules because they clashed with the temporalities of family and community. As if this wasn't difficult enough for them, they also tended to be subjected to close scrutiny by family members, neighbors, and landlords because they worked such unusual hours. While all agents were viewed with suspicion for doing night work, women employees had to face the brunt of surveillance and gossip about their allegedly impure behavior and loose character (chapter 1 and 3; see also R. Patel 2010). Furthermore, most women agents, including Zubeida, experienced a double workday: they had to continue to perform affective labor at home because they were primarily responsible for taking care of their families. Women who could not rely on parents or in-laws for childcare either gave up their careers or moved to less demanding jobs.

The imbrication of the temporalities of labor with those of other domains of social life were deeply entwined with modes of embodiment. Agents spent their waking hours immersed in the temporalities of their customers in another place and another time and this had tangible consequences for their processes of embodiment. As Farhana explained, "The mind has learned to adjust—I now know what to say to my clients, depending on the time of the day for them. But it is my body that gets confused." This, she insisted, was why she had missed her period. Describing the plight of some of her women coworkers, Farhana remarked, "Our bodies are so messed up that even those women who want to have children cannot—either because their bodies can't conceive or because they cannot keep [sustain] pregnancies." This was why she would get enraged by rumors—spread by media, neighbors, and extended family members—that women agents were engaging in premarital and extramarital sex and getting pregnant.

These disjunctive temporalities were devastating for women agents who had miscarriages or were unable to conceive because the disruption of circadian rhythms and the interruption of ovulation cycles sometimes resulted in infertility. Dominant discourses about women's duty to ensure social and biological reproduction intensified their sense of loss. Often under tremendous pressure from their families to have children, these women were desperate yet did not have the time or the energy to seek medical help. To the extent that futurity for these women was defined in terms of biological and social reproduction, the very future of futurity was jeopardized for them.[19]

BPO agents were only one segment of the professional class in Bengaluru who worked late into the night. Frequently attending video or audio conference calls past midnight, many software engineers in Bengaluru's IT industry also had to do night work in order to communicate with their counterparts overseas (Radhakrishnan 2011). Those who had school-age children still had to get up early to get their children ready for school and drop them off. For such workers, things like school schedules had a tangible impact on their experience of night work: school managements would not alter their schedules so parents had no choice but to adapt to them. However, as we have elaborated above, what compounded these stresses for BPO agents, unlike software engineers, was the emotional and psychic toll of their affective labor.

Furthermore, the lack of intergenerational synchrony between the schedules of different family members created temporal disjunctures that prevented the daily routines of BPO agents from mirroring those of others who worked a "normal" service sector workday. Several BPO agents would speak to us about how they felt "out of sync" with the routines of family members, many of whom they barely saw as they shuffled back and forth between work and home (see also Aneesh 2015; Patel 2010). Raghu, whom we met in chapter 1, had taken up a job in a BPO primarily to earn enough money to send his younger sister to school. He told us he rarely ever got to see her. One day, at her birthday celebration, he was shocked to see that she had grown so much that he could barely recognize her. Even worse, despite living in the same house, he and his sister did not know what to say to each other anymore. In these instances, temporal disjunctures led to a sense of emotional and social dislocation, as when our interlocutors felt out of place in their own families. This sense of estrangement was particularly distressing for Krishnan, who had been working in a large BPO for five years and remarked, "I don't even know which world is mine anymore, the world of my home or the world of my office." This sense of nonbelonging and estrangement resulted directly from being out of sync with the temporalities of family and community.

The temporalities of the body and the imperatives of capital accumulation were coimplicated in multiple ways. Many agents suffered from digestive disorders because of the impact that the BPOs' schedules and labor regimes had on their bodies. Some agents complained of a loss of appetite that led to chronic weight loss, while others felt they had become obese because of irregular mealtimes, sleep deprivation, and lack of exercise. Orthopedic and muscular ailments, such as chronic back and neck pain, were common: agents sat for long hours in front of monitors because, even though some of the larger BPOs had in-house gyms, they rarely had the time or energy to exercise. Many found it impossible to sleep after a hectic night at work, and the resulting insomnia sometimes led to clinical depression and anxiety. Chronic sleep deprivation frequently led to depressed immunity. Even though agents were under considerable pressure to not take sick days, there were times when they had no choice but to stay home. This could cause delays for the entire team and, as one of our interlocutors put it, "play havoc with the process." Ironically, the very conditions of labor made the smooth reproduction of that labor problematic. Once, when Santosh was heading to the office and complained of feeling sick, Gupta could see how conflicted he was. While Santosh felt the pressure to go to the office because his team needed him, he was clearly not feeling well enough to show up for work.

The affective labor of our interlocutors compels us, yet again, to conceive of the body as "an open system, beyond the containment of the organism" (Clough 2007, 18; see also Deleuze 1992). Focusing on the affective regimes that circulate between the body and the (working) environment enables us to track the feedback loops that give the body its dynamism and sociality. Agents who had spouses with day jobs often spoke of the strain that night work placed on their marital lives: as Krishnan remarked, "This is not a normal way to live." Francis and his wife both had full-time jobs. He worked nights at a BPO; she worked during the day at another company. They saw each other fleetingly during the day but had to wait for his days off to spend time together. In some cases, the emotional toll of being cut off from loved ones led to a sense of estrangement. Yet, laboring long hours without a break, working at night, and being away from family and loved ones while they were awake had become the "new normal." At such moments, agents acutely felt the disconnect between the present and the bright future that they envisioned for themselves.

Thus, agents' bodies were shaped by the labor regimes of BPOs—for instance, how they experienced sleep (or its absence), hunger, and a lack of exercise. The body was refracted by the demands, logics, and temporalities of affective labor; in the words of Krishnan, its "demands and needs" were shaped by that labor. Krishnan added, "My body needs sleep and rest. It gets hungry. It needs to move around. Otherwise, we get ill." If illness was registered and expressed in the body and interrupted and threatened to work to a halt, it was also brought on by the stress of affective labor.

In myriad ways, the body and capital are coimplicated rather than external to each other: the body responds to and is reconfigured by the rhythms of capital—but it also *impinges on* the rhythms of work. As we noted in the previous chapter, to some extent sexual desire was engendered by conditions at work: agents, most of whom were in their early 20s, sitting next to each other night after night, sharing experiences, confidences, frustrations, hopes, and fears for the future, relatively cut off from other social relations, sometimes had sexual liaisons. The workplace was itself constituted by affective intensities that swirled around agents even as it reconfigured their desires. Here, we wish to foreground again the place of erotics in the (re)embodiment of BPO agents to underscore how desire can disrupt the production process.

In the previous chapter, we argued that when the body's needs became difficult to ignore, sexual desire threatened to "trip up" work schedules, teams, and the management of labor: the eruptive force of desire was emphasized by several managers who complained to us that when agents entered into sexual relationships, it brought "tension" into the office. Agents involved in relationships would plead to be placed on the same shift or on the same team. Or, when agents who had previously been in a relationship broke up, it would, in the words of one manager, "destroy" the team's dynamic and derail the process. When this happened, agents would ask for a place in another process or, quite often, resign and look for another job. Thus, if exhaustion, illness, mental health challenges, or aching muscles can "play havoc with" work, so too can sexual desire (Deleuze 1997). The future of the agents and, in some cases, of the process could become uncertain, suggesting how futurity, as an agentive potentiality, is entangled with desire and the eruptions it can bring in its wake.

Bergson ([1896] 1990, 23) points to how the body engages other bodies and objects, including the more-than-human; the knowing body learns because it remembers these encounters. The gendered body must learn to anticipate, navigate, and occupy (potentially hostile) spaces of the city at night and, in the process, gets reconfigured. While faced with racist abuse the racialized body learns to sense hostility across virtual space. Bodies shaped by caste and religion are reconfigured through the rhythms of affective labor by learning (or relearning) how to provide service, their contact with other bodies, or the forms of sociality that BPO work engenders. As a contact zone, the body is traversed, and reconstituted, in articulation with myriad affective regimes and temporalities.

The knowing, desiring, or ill body reshapes capitalism and is not separate from it. The limit point for capitalism occurs when the body fails, falters, or falls apart, when it acts with a will of its own, and when its pleasures and appetites surmount the imperatives of labor: in these instances, futures may be recast in unanticipated ways and futurities are reconstituted. When imbricated in disjunctive temporalities, the body can get out of sync, and time itself gets out of joint (chapter 1). The body is not overscripted by capitalism. There is much that the body can do to reconfigure the rhythms of work through interruption and disruption.

BODIES AND FUTURITIES

We close this chapter by ruminating on the implications of embodiment and discrepant temporalities for futurity, which we have defined as an ontological condition and a quality of becoming, and for futures, as experienced and imagined by individuals and collectivities. Alondra Nelson (2002) points out that techno-utopian visions of information technology have claimed "a new era of subjectivity and insisted that in the future the body wouldn't bother us any longer" (2). We have argued that the working body of BPO agents is re-formed through discourses of gender, caste, class, sexuality, and race in distinct ways. In racial capitalism, the classification of bodies is a modality of not simply extracting labor and value but also anticipating and managing the future. These classifications offer a grid of intelligibility that, in heterogeneous modalities, has enabled exploitation, conquest, and genocide for the purpose of value extraction.

The distinctiveness of BPOs does not just lie in the fact that affective labor is central to the work process. It also lies in the (manufactured) synchronicity between the agents' time and that of the customer. Interacting with the customer "live" creates conjoined and disjunctive temporalities across spaces. Together, these properties of labor regimes in BPOs generate temporalities that differ from other types of industrial and service labor and other forms of outsourcing. These temporalities bring about a collision of business cycles, circadian rhythms, night work, and ovulation cycles on the one hand, and the rhythms of family life, community, ritual, and festivals on the other. These temporal disjunctures underscore how heterogeneous trajectories of global capitalism, rather than existing a priori, are produced through the intersection of diverse social fields and multiple power relations. What do these trajectories suggest about futurity?

Considerations of futurity are critical to our analysis both because of its implication in processes of embodiment and because, as we observed in the introduction to this book, it was a major preoccupation for our interlocutors. Agents constantly worried about maintaining the grueling pace of work, the effects of night work on their health, the emotionally draining nature of their job, and the kinds of skills that would be useful to them in the future after they had left BPO work. Furthermore, the future was central not only to the way that agents plotted their own life but to how the labor process itself was reconfigured by new technologies, movements of capital, and trade conflicts between nations, to name just a few factors.

Considerations of the future were present on at least three registers. First, call center agents' views of their own futures were heavily influenced by what they thought their bodies could endure. Most agents could not see themselves working beyond the age of thirty, either because it was too hard on their bodies or because once they had families night work would place their schedules in conflict with the rest of the family. Their worries about the future cast a long shadow on their lives and experiences in the present, foregrounding the coproduction of aspiration and anxiety.[20] Geetha worked in HR in a mid-sized BPO: she had risen up the ranks from being an agent. In her own words, she came from a "humble background": based on what she told us about her family's history, we gleaned that she was Dalit.[21] Her job had been crucial to her ability to secure the future of her younger brother who now went to college because she was able to financially support him; she was also the first in her family to have what she described as an "office job." After establishing herself in the company as a high-achieving agent, she requested a job in HR because she believed it would be less stressful. She was dating someone and dreamt of a future when she could marry him and have children, and she felt that continuing as an agent would not allow her to achieve this dream. Geetha pointed out that a job in HR would be a lot less exhausting than working as an agent because she did not have to deal with "the moods and funny behavior" of customers. When pushed to elaborate what she meant by "funny behavior," she explained that coping with abusive behavior from customers was the most difficult part of the job of an agent; compared with that, being in HR was less taxing on the emotions and the body. She also said that once she had children, she would either reduce the hours she worked in HR or leave the industry. Even in HR, she felt that the stress would leave her too physically and emotionally exhausted to take care of her children. Like Cynthia, whom we met in an earlier chapter, Geetha's aspirations and anxieties about the future highlight the impact of affective labor on the body as well as on futurity.

Thus, if futurity is an affective-temporal formation that spurs action and generates (and therefore is prior to) subject formation, it is inextricably entangled with the body and its capacities. Conceptualizing and theorizing *futurity*, therefore, entails centering bodily rhythms, frailties, desires, demands, and capacities as generative of specific kinds of *futures* for subjects who are not just workers but are, also, grandchildren, nieces and nephews, daughters and sons, lovers and friends. Futurity, after all, refers to immanence and potentiality; it inheres in duration. Futurity refers to the presence of the virtual as distinct from the actual, and this distinction is essential to our conception of multiple futures. Most importantly, futurity as agentive potentiality is, essentially, open-ended.

In this regard, futurity is distinct from anticipation. Adams, Murphy, and Clarke (2009) define anticipation as knowing (or not knowing) the future: "The future is always knowable in new ways, even as the grasping for certainty about it remains persistent" (247). In contrast, the generation of futurity/ies cannot be foreclosed; it can neither be predicted nor guaranteed. Jamie Cross (2015) defines the economy of anticipation in terms of "diverse ways of knowing about, imagining, and living toward the future" (425). Much that is unanticipated occurs in the lives of BPO agents, including getting sick or burnt out, being laid off, sinking into depression, battling anxiety, getting estranged from spouses, parents, or siblings, falling in love, getting pregnant, suffering miscarriages, dealing with the frustrations of infertility, and the devastating pain of illness or death in the family. These unanticipated events disrupt the rhythms of everyday life; moreover, they refract and, at times, interrupt the temporality of work that would otherwise continue without pause, without a period. The temporality of affective labor, in other words, is vulnerable to disruption by the temporalities of the body, underscoring how the so-called logic of capital is unstable and is more fragile than we realize: it may easily be thrown into disarray or unsettlement by that which is unanticipated. Unanticipated futures can reconfigure futurities.

Futurities, unlike futures, do not have an end point: they are about a movement forward into unknowability; they pertain to the capacity to move forward in time. Futurity pertains to a *sense*, rather than a knowledge, of what might follow; it is an orientation that potentially yields modes of imagining, anticipating, and working toward specific futures. Far from being predicated on disembodiment, the labor demanded by affective capitalism relies on the embodiment of workers. At the same time, our insistence that the agent's body is not just a laboring body gestures toward a specific way of perceiving and theorizing futurity. The embodiment of agents is also constituted by the temporalities of sociality, family obligations, ritual, faith, and piety. These discrepant temporalities push us to conceive of futurities that are predicated on relationality, on the entanglement of bodies with each other and with the more-than-human.

Futurity is central to how capitalism has been envisioned and theorized. It is tempting to read the new modes of time discipline and shifts in temporality as the colonization of extant patterns of time use by global capitalism, which, in turn, is conceptualized as inevitably "penetrating" spaces outside it (Lenin [1917] 1939; Luxemburg [1913] 2003). Alternatively, equally problematic narratives posit resistance to a hypostatized and monolithic capitalism. Both these narratives theorize capitalism as an a priori, self-organizing *system* that threatens what is outside it by colonizing human lifeworlds. In both cases, a predictable future is built into the model.

But what would happen to our analytical apparatus if, instead of thinking about what is "inside" and "outside" capitalism, we were to analyze how different forms of value extraction articulate and disarticulate with other temporalities of social life? Foregrounding the role of discrepant temporalities in processes of embodiment offers ways to track the mutual constitution of subjects, socialities, dispositions, bodies, and specific formations of contemporary capitalism. This is a much more unpredictable future, one in which the body of the worker is shaped not simply by a pregiven trajectory of capitalism. Rather, the conjunctural articulation of temporalities produces both forms of capitalism and the worker's body. BPO agents' bodies were also (re)constituted by processes of racialization that undergird how countries in the Global South (for instance, nations such as India and the Philippines) become service hubs for clients in the Global North. We have posited that the meaning and role of race in the embodiment of workers varies across locations and conjunctures. The racialization of affective labor in BPOs and, hence, the racialized embodiment of agents in India cannot be collapsed or subsumed under Euro-American and Atlanticist conceptions of race. Indeed, the racialized embodiment of BPO agents who provide service to clients and customers in the Global North ensues from the conjunctural articulation of colonial and postcolonial histories of labor, colonial and postcolonial language policies, and Orientalist and neoliberal discourses of cultural difference.

To conclude, regimes of affective labor in Bengaluru's BPOs generated modes of embodiment that were enabled, curtailed, and reconstituted by the articulation of affect, technology, labor, and the ontology of bodily matter. These were bodies that, in the words of one chief technology officer, were "trainable," by which he meant that they retained and remembered knowledge and affective regimes. However, contrary to conceptions of docile bodies that are either thoroughly disciplined by capitalism or resistant to it, the body is not a discrete organism overwritten by capital and disciplinary technologies. It is, rather, part of a force field of affective intensities that relay between and across nodes to constitute specific kinds of subjects. Rather than acting from outside them, the temporalities of business cycles and labor extraction were imbricated with the temporalities of the working body, the desiring body, and other modes of sociality. The temporal disjunctions in BPO work were produced by the combination of night work and affective labor. Agents' labor consisted of live encounters resulting in virtual migration and required them to constantly juggle different time zones. Other forms of labor (say, factory work, nursing, or coding) might share some of these properties, but not all of them simultaneously. BPO work thus produced temporal disjunctures that were specific to the industry and this, in turn, configured bodies in distinct ways. The disjunctive temporalities produced by BPO work emerged from articulations and disarticulations between the rhythms of the transnational service industry and bodily rhythms; between work schedules and the temporalities of family, the routines of schooling, obligations of ritual and religion, and the claims of important family events, such as birthdays, weddings, and funerals; and between the pressures of affective labor at work and the demands of marriages, in-laws, childcare, and eldercare.

Raghu once complained to us, "Sometimes I feel that I can never hit the Pause button." Our interlocutors' affective labor did not finish with the end of the long working night. It left traces on their minds, hearts, and bodies; for many of them, there was no closure. It was implicated in their sleep patterns, digestive systems, musculature, and the curvature of their spines; it transected their intimate relations and their engagements with family and community; in some instances, it disrupted ovulation cycles. Labor and consumption, each fully imbricated with capital, generated futures and futurities, lifeworlds and socialities, subjectivities and solidarities. The push to work ceaselessly, without a period, did not so much overwrite our interlocutors' desires or identities as produce them. And yet there were many moments when they veered off script; they entered into relations of intimacy with each other and with customers in physical and cultural landscapes far removed from their own; they engaged in forms of imaginative and virtual travel to navigate new worlds of mystery, fascination, and anxiety. They juggled other temporalities, including those of family, kinship, religion, and community. Whether it was Farhana working at night and attending college during the day, Francis and his wife not seeing each other for days on end, Ramesh struggling with the loss of contact with his family or, in contrast, Zubeida who could be at home for her daughter, or agents who had the chance to link up romantically with people whom they would not have been able to meet because of restrictions of religion, caste, or gender—the temporalities of labor, love, family, and community were seldom in synchrony. Against analyses in which the triumph of capitalism is always already foretold, our interlocutors in Bengaluru did not "internalize" the temporality of affective labor.

Let us be clear: we do not valorize the effects of disjunctive temporalities for BPO agents. Their worst effects exhausted them, sometimes bringing them to the brink of despair, at other times making them ill, and forcing some to seek alternate forms of employment. These effects brought with them high emotional and physical costs and took a toll on agents' social and intimate relationships. On the other hand, as in the example of Zubeida, it allowed for possibilities for nurturing lives that would not have been otherwise possible. The very fact that these temporalities are disjunctive rather than synchronous enables us to disavow assumptions about the teleological march of digital capitalism or the subsumption of life by neoliberalism. Against narratives that feature only the dull compulsion of endless labor that is emotionally and physically draining, our interlocutors maintained their vitality and sought and found pleasure where they could.

The disjunctive temporalities that reconfigured the bodies of BPO agents were refracted by discrepant futurities. The demands on the bodies of BPO workers were shaped by technology in the office, but technologies also changed the workers' relations to family and community. For example, chat shared with voice processes the property of being live but differed in its affective demands. Similarly, low-cost data offered by mobile networks in India made it possible for family members to record events that agents missed because of their schedules and also made it possible for agents to participate virtually in a sibling's birthday or a religious ceremony from the car transporting them to the office.

If futurity is unknowable and exists in the realm of potentiality (Agamben 2003; Mankekar and Gupta 2023), it is neither to be celebrated nor decried. The futures that agents saw for themselves, the future that CEOs and shareholders saw for their companies, the future that all of them saw for India, the future of technology, and the future of families and sociality were all evolving and developing in ways that may have been individually predictable to some degree but were unpredictable in their articulation. We could see how agents sensed this when they told us what they saw themselves doing in the future, simultaneously hopeful and keenly aware of precarity, a future that was tense because it was poised with promise but could easily turn into disappointment and despair.

The demands made on agents' bodies are unpredictable. Changing technologies, institutional cultures, national rivalries, and government policies all have implications for the future of working bodies and for futurity as agentive potentiality. Some jobs in the BPO industry may disappear, and others materialize as all these parameters shift. Agents planned their own futures in terms of the demands of the job on the body, but the future of the body is itself predicated on changes in those other realms. For example, if wages rise in India or the Philippines, or if the minimum qualification necessary for this type of labor changes due to the use of artificial intelligence, the industry might look very different in the future. If the production of the body of the BPO worker is due to specific articulations at this historical juncture, new conjunctures are likely to produce different bodies. While the focus is often on new technologies such as AI, predictive analytics, Big Data, chatbots, and process automation, the new conjunctures will emerge in articulation with changing technology, as well as new forms of global inequality, the reorganization of global capitalism in the wake of the COVID-19 pandemic, the dynamics of BPO firms, and the policies of the governments of India and other countries in which BPOs operate and those of the nation-states where consumers and corporate customers are located.

The disjunctive temporalities of BPOs throw into relief lifeworlds that do not simply endure alongside exploitation, burnout, and despair but are enabled, created, or fractured by relations of articulation and disarticulation. These disjunctive temporalities compel us to "rethink technology, time, and the ontology of bodily matter" (Clough 2007, 5). As in other forms of semiocapitalism, in the ITES industry, the transmission of information is fundamental to connectivity, but this information, we have argued throughout, is not simply cognitive but profoundly affective in how it transforms agents' bodily capacities and subjectivities. Furthermore, the disjunction between the temporalities of affective labor and other dimensions of sociality proves to be recalcitrant despite their mutual creation.

And some old habits just die hard. Mankekar last met Farhana on a humid August afternoon in 2015 after which the two of them lost touch. They met at a multiplex because they had planned to see a recently released Hindi film. Farhana badly wanted to watch this film because it starred the actor Priyanka Chopra and she was willing to miss class for it. Farhana thought she resembled Chopra in many ways: she felt that she looked like her and, like Chopra, was a strong, "self-made" woman. She reiterated that she felt stuck in a rut of "work-college–more work–my mother's taunts." But she insisted that she would find a way out. At that last meeting, she was late by an hour, and Mankekar realized that this was a woman who would never be punctual.

INTERJECTION

We revise this manuscript in Bengaluru at a moment when, it is being claimed, the worst of the COVID pandemic has ebbed. But signs of the havoc it wreaked persist, as friends, neighbors, interlocutors, and strangers recount to us harrowing accounts of loved ones lost, hospitals filled with dead and dying bodies, and desperate searches for oxygen cylinders, for medical care, for antivirals, and for hope. How do we speak of the body and futurity in the ostensible aftermath of a pandemic? We are haunted by devastating images of bodies piled up for cremation in India during the worst days of the pandemic—we will never know the accurate number of people who fell to COVID, demonstrating to us, once again, how some bodies are not just uncounted but are abandoned outside the realm of accountability. The pandemic has surely been a time of reckoning when we have learned that the fragility of the body, its vulnerability to disease and death, can bring the world to its knees.

And then there are bodies that have been lynched for desiring the Other. Bodies that have been burned alive for consuming beef. Bodies that have been marred by pellet guns, gaping holes where eyes once used to be. How do we speak of the body, and of the future of futurity, at such a moment? What must endure for there to be a sense of the future? What can the fragility of the body in these troubled times teach us about other fragilities—of the planet and of hope and of futurity itself?

What can we learn from these tense futures, futures that are not just discrepant but are in conflict with each other? Centering the body, with all its fragility and knowledges, might enable us to reckon with the "time of the gods" (Chakrabarty 2000) as well as other disjunctive temporalities that are not "outside" capitalism but are, instead, coproduced and articulate with it. What can these disjunctive temporalities teach us as we seek modes of habitation, knowing, and feeling that could, potentially, enable more sustainable futurities?

CONCLUSION

Potentiality and Future Tense

Our interest in futures and futurity emerged organically from our ethnographic research. Within a few days of beginning fieldwork, we realized that the one theme that cut across all our conversations with our interlocutors, from CEOs, COOs, and other senior executives, through middle management, to agents, was the future. What did the future hold in store for the industry? How was the future of the industry related to the future of the nation and, beyond that, to the fate of global capital? What lay ahead for BPO agents whose sense of the future had suddenly expanded? In this conclusion, we bring together the themes threading through this book to diagram the relationship between potentiality and futurity and to ruminate on the future of futurity.

What struck us the most was the manner in which joining BPOs completely altered how BPO agents had started to imagine their futures. Since a considerable number of the agents with whom we became close came from lower-income backgrounds, castes that had been historically oppressed, or religious communities that were being marginalized and demonized, these shifts in the imagination of the future acquired tremendous affective potency. Equally significant was the fact that, when they thought of the future, agents were not concerned exclusively, or even primarily, about their individual destinies. Without exception, every one of the agents we got to know believed that their futures were irrevocably linked to the futures of their families, communities, and the nation. Although many of them had been interpellated by neoliberal discourses of growth and personal responsibility, they were deeply committed to taking care of their families, even when they felt exploited by them or resented the stresses generated by these obligations. These maps of relationality, of commitment to family and loved ones, enabled them to navigate a terrain marked by precarity and anxiety. And, although they were reimagining their future in considerably more expansive terms than they had earlier, these imaginations of the future also provoked uncertainty and insecurity.

Futures and futurities are embedded in the BPO industry for a variety of reasons, only some of which we can parse here. For one, they are tied to technological transformations that, in turn, are driven by the articulation of three changes. First, while automation has not taken over the BPO industry at the current moment, internal changes to processes are increasingly being driven by artificial intelligence, Big Data, and analytics that, ostensibly, aim to improve customer service; second, changes in customer behavior are being led by the increasing use of apps, tablets, and mobile phones; and third, the firms that contract to BPOs are demanding that they minimize costs, decrease consumer migration, and increase brand loyalty and customer satisfaction. The four major actors in this industry—the contracting corporation (for example, British Airways or Verizon); the BPO hired to perform customer contact, which has operations in India, the Philippines, and other locations; consumers mostly located in the United States, the United Kingdom, and Australia; and the city of Bengaluru—each have their own future trajectories in technological, organizational, and social space. Transformations in the industry respond to the articulation of these futures because they respond in the present to where they think they are headed in the future. The anticipation and production of sociotechnical futures recast the present actions of all the actors in this relationship.

Technological and organizational transformations are one of the springboards for generating visions of the future and of futurity. While there is a long tradition in "Western" modernity to read technological transformation as being both independent of organizational forms and an exogenous generator of social utopias (and sometimes dystopias), technological change is obviously both more socially embedded and more closely related to the changing nature of firms, labor, and government policy. When we started our fieldwork in December 2008, the futures that leaders of the BPO industry were concerned about had to do with new markets and new sources of revenue for the industry. Suggestions ranged from outsourcing more work from the Indian government, taking over back-office functions of local, state, and federal government offices in the United States and other wealthy countries in the Global North, ascending the value chain through domain specialization, and building a new customer base in middle-income countries. While some of these envisioned futures came to pass, there were other unanticipated changes that were to transform the industry in subsequent years. For example, there was no hint then of how Big Data and analytics would impact the industry and, certainly, no discussion of AI; the incredibly quick shift in consumer behavior that saw a big uptick in the use of chat, apps, and websites, mostly by younger consumers, could not have been imagined; the wholesale shift of voice processes from India to the Philippines was only just beginning; and nobody anticipated changes in contracts to get a share of sales instead of being paid on a per unit basis (per call or per customer). Although many BPOs were owned and run by IT companies, they were seen as two fundamentally distinct businesses whose subsequent merger has been surprising even to some industry insiders.

After 2016, these technological and organizational changes accelerated. New contracts in the BPO industry focused on process automation, design thinking, cognitive computing platforms, innovation centers, and analytics and data science skills (Fersht and Snowdon 2016, 37). In other words, the industry has been transformed into one where human labor is increasingly displaced by programs and machines, and where new contracts emphasize the hiring of people whose skill sets are in the computing, project design, or management fields rather than low-cost workers with a high-school education to answer phone calls. Thus, technological and organizational changes have implications for the future of the industry, the future of work, and the future of employment.[1] The COVID-19 pandemic led to other technological and organizational changes, none of which were anticipated (Bhattacharya 2020; *Business Today* 2020; CRN Team 2020; Dave 2020; Frayer and Pathak 2020; Kannan 2020; Malik 2020; R. Rao 2020; Roy and Emont 2020; Saxena 2020). Hence, technological futures are not only multiple but often unanticipated, and they do not always have a tendency to move in the same direction.

CHRONOTOPES OF FUTURITY

The articulation of place with forms of BPO labor creates a particular assemblage of affective capitalism and, hence, implicates the generation of futurities. The growth of BPOs in Bengaluru is intimately related to the longer genealogies, multiple histories, and divergent futurities that have made the city the place that it is. The chronotopes of Bengaluru powerfully refracted our interlocutors' sense of the future. At once exciting and daunting, the city, considered by many to have a "Date with the Future," is an important node in the generation and circulation of futurity as an affective-temporal regime. The human and more-than-human jostle for survival in gated communities, in older, middle-class neighborhoods, and in the city's slums; incomplete flyovers are iconic of a future that is, materially and quite literally, in suspension (H. Gupta 2015; see also S. Srinivas 2016).

Furthermore, Bengaluru's chronotopes shape the desires of its residents as much as it is shaped by them. As an actant, the city actively participates in the formation of not simply heterogeneous futures for its inhabitants but also discrepant forms of futurity. Construction never seems to stop, with each new building or bridge gesturing toward a future, while the pile of rubble on the streets appears to point toward the temporality of the past, the detritus of that which has seemingly been left behind. New flyovers fly over, and thereby bypass and exclude, poor neighborhoods and slums as they enable the traffic of those trying to get from gated communities and newly built skyscrapers to gleaming tech parks. These new constructions spawn discrepant futurities by materially excluding those who are deemed to inhabit the temporality of lag.

Bengaluru has always been notorious for its traffic, and, in some ways, its flows and gridlocks evoke the fraught relationship between physical mobility, social mobility, and futurity. Vans and cabs carrying BPO workers to and from work career through the city, sometimes resulting in fatal accidents for pedestrians and for others who are not, and cannot, be associated with the temporality of speed. At the same time, traffic jams and gridlocks defy the efforts of companies to impose strict time management schedules on their employees: the mobility of workers is hampered by human and more-than-human socialities outside tech parks and BPOs. A boisterous wedding procession, a stray dog hit by a speeding van, feral cats slinking obstinately across a street, or crowds spilling out of a roadside temple can hold things up for agents who need to get to work on time. The city's multiple temporalities frequently collide to produce discrepant futurities.

Contrary to conceptions of semiocapitalism as placeless, according to which information and capital "flow" across the world at the speed of light, this is a world in which the city, with its slums, gated communities, glitzy malls, street bazaars, and the congested dormitories and PG hostels that house many BPO agents, is not just a silent backdrop or a mute ethnographic "context." The city's spaces are reconfigured by the desires of its new migrants and older residents who are simultaneously emplaced by the chronotopes that they must learn to inhabit and navigate. In Bengaluru, one form of futurity is inescapably imbricated with the symbolic significance of the IT and ITES industries. Exemplifying how affective-temporal formations of futurity are institutionalized in public policy and political economy, the Indian state has directly participated and invested in the growth of these industries. Even as the city is imploding upon itself, it continues to attract new workers, migrants, and dreamers of expansive futures. The ostensibly dichotomous landscapes of expansion and implosion of the "City of the Future" are allegorical of the fate of futurity(ies) in how they gesture, at once, to promise and catastrophe.

But what does it mean to ruminate on futurity when the futures of BPO agents are at odds with those of other lower-income youth in India, and in other parts of the world, who face unemployment, poverty, marginalization, or the snuffing out of a chance to have a future at all? The tense optimism of our interlocutors was not simply in opposition to the youth who engaged in "time pass" or who committed suicide in despair (Chua 2014; Jeffrey 2010; see also *Indian Panorama* 2022). Rather, these apparently discrepant modalities of futurity were intimately, inextricably entwined and, to a large extent, coproduced.

INTERJECTION

We are in the office of Sanjay Gopinath, the CEO of a BPO that caters to a multinational department store headquartered in the United Kingdom. Sanjay is describing to us his career trajectory: he received an MBA from a university in London and began working for Harrods. He next moved laterally to other jobs, proving his mettle in marketing and customer service. By the time he was in his early forties, he was being wooed by several companies for CEO positions. Customer service was then being redefined by being outsourced to countries like India and the Philippines. He was excited by the new possibilities presented by this shift to offshore outsourcing. When he was offered the opportunity to head a BPO in Bengaluru that would service a multinational store, he couldn't pass it up. His children were growing up; his parents were getting older and more frail with every passing year. So he had strong personal reasons as well for moving to Bengaluru.

When we meet him, he is very optimistic about the future of the ITES industry and believes that with AI and robotics the industry will only become more profitable. "Voice processes are now becoming a thing of the past," he insists. *Made uneasy by what he is saying, Mankekar asks what would happen to BPO agents who were part of voice processes. Will they be laid off once AI becomes dominant in the ITES industry? Will they become redundant? What will these young people do? He dismisses her concerns by responding, enthusiastically, that they can be trained to do other kinds of tasks. For instance, they can perform customer service through chat. "But the main thing is," he asserts, "we are finding new ways to provide customer service with efficiency."*

When we inquire about how he feels the BPO industry is impacting the Indian economy, he is candid and unequivocal. He says: "I live in a gated community in Green Meadows. I am surrounded by expatriates and other NRIs. When I enter Malibu Heights [the housing development where he owns a villa] I feel I am leaving the craziness of the city. But one day that craziness will enter Malibu Heights. They won't wait until they're invited. People are losing patience. Angry people from Nammahalli [the village right outside the gates of Malibu Heights] will storm in."

People are losing patience. Bengaluru's topography is shaped by state-endorsed, often extralegal acquisitions of land for gated communities such as Malibu Heights, tech parks, and malls like the Nexus Whitefield Mall, while the poor, particularly from Dalit, Bahujan, Muslim, and other marginalized communities are literally pushed farther out to the peripheries of the city. When Sanjay spoke of the "craziness of the city," he was referring not simply to the bustle and congestion of the city outside his manicured gated community but to the rising frustrations and anger of people who felt sidelined by where their city was headed. The coproduction of gated communities, with their uninterrupted power supply, large mansions, swimming pools, and clubs, and the villages and slums whose inhabitants barely eke a living and have only the most tenuous access to running water or electricity, where clogged drains line their ramshackle homes, where the best (or only) jobs available are for drivers and domestic help in the homes of the wealthy, and where the frothing, foaming lake seems to bubble over in rage felt to him (and to us) like a highly combustible situation. What might futurity look like in such a context?

In a situation marked by the emergence of discrepant futures, what can we say about futurity, about that which is immanent? Our intervention is not to gaze into a crystal ball and produce speculative accounts of the future of futurity. If our conception of futurity is antiteleological, it is also invested in a way of theorizing, imagining, and working toward a different future. Narratives emerging from India's ruling classes—governments in power and India Inc.—are of an economy that has grown faster in the last two decades than any other country except China (Press Trust of India [PTI] 2017a, 2017b). Such good tidings, however, fail to account for the growing number of farmers' suicides, a forceful Maoist uprising, and the increasingly remote chances of improvement in the lot of large numbers of poor people, rural and urban. BPO workers are themselves participants in uneven development within India because they, like IT workers and others who are connected to the global economy, earn a lot more than those workers whose labor caters entirely to the domestic market. A worker in the retail or hospitality business serving domestic clients in India with exactly the same credentials (a PUC diploma) as a BPO worker, but without fluency in English, earns a third or fourth of the salary of BPO workers. The gap between the richest and poorest within a city like Bengaluru has widened, as has the gap between Bengaluru and other parts of the state of Karnataka, especially between urban and rural parts of the state. These heterogeneous and conflicting futures are immanent in neoliberal capitalism.

The creative destruction resulting from capitalist expansion leads to new possibilities as well as to ruination, often at the same time, within nation-states as much as across them. Studying a sunrise industry such as BPOs and working with people who were painstakingly climbing the class ladder offer us clues to a more complex and dynamic understanding of the contradictory nature of contemporary capitalisms. While some citizens of India are ascending the class ladder to a middle-class lifestyle, others remain poor or slip down. The temporalities of life and work for BPO workers may diverge from those of their neighbors or other family members, the trajectories of their lives may be drastically different from their classmates or siblings, and their possible and realized futures may be deeply heterogeneous. The futures of BPO workers and those in the IT industry are, obviously, very different from their uneducated or "less-skilled" compatriots. These disjunctive temporalities and their discrepant futures provide us with critical insights into the place of global capital, labor, and technology in our rapidly changing world. The futures that are likely to emerge are shaped by combined and uneven development operating not (just) across territorial space but across social space. A radically rethought version of combined and uneven development, based on new geographies of accumulation, helps us conceptualize this mix of different stages of the neoliberal moment of capitalist development. BPOs demonstrate the articulation of the spatial movement of capital with its tendency to create social inequality within places. BPO workers are taking the first tentative steps into a middle-class lifestyle and some entrepreneurs in India are becoming wealthy by global standards, while most of the rest of the Indian population lacks employment and is caught in a low-level "equilibrium." The future of India is unlikely to be one where the entire population gets richer and "catches up" with living standards in the Global North. Different segments of India's population are likely to experience different futures: combined and uneven development drives these discrepant futures and is thus a form of futurity and of potentiality.

But theorizing futurity is predicated on remapping it. Geographies of capitalist firms from the Global North spreading in a colonial or imperial manner in the Global South are less persuasive now than a few decades ago. In many traditional manufacturing sectors, the expansion of firms from the Global South to the Global North is just as conspicuous as the movement in the other direction. Capitalist expansion in services has become even more multinational and horizontally distributed and ranges from banking and financial services to consulting, IT services, and, of course, BPOs. Having learned their lesson from the backlash in the Global North to the outsourcing of lower-end services such as call centers, higher-value services in IT, business consulting, banking, accounting, and other industries have quietly and unobtrusively globalized, moving many higher-end functions to the Global South (Alsop 2020; Statista Research Department 2020). The meaning of the "headquarters" for many companies has changed completely, and, even before the COVID pandemic, it had become commonplace for someone working in an office in Los Angeles to be reporting not to someone in his or her own building but to a person in Singapore or Bengaluru. The futures encoded in Global South–centric globalization move us very far away from conventional narratives of "recolonization" or "empire" and help us think of global economic power in a manner that has multiple poles and centers and that is networked and densely interconnected. Of course, such a movement is never linear. The reassertions of autocracy during COVID and the rise of populist authoritarian nationalisms all over the world pose a serious challenge that may alter the directions in which existing formations are headed.

As capitalist firms, BPOs are located in what, inspired by Raymond Williams, we might term a structure of futurity. Within those structures of futurity, BPOs are distinctive as nodes of affective capitalism. In capitalism, there is a particular directionality and structure given to the future by the process of expanded reproduction: the search for surplus value through expanded reproduction makes the capitalist system inherently dynamic and unremittingly future-oriented. Technological change and infrastructural development drive this process. The conflict with labor that is central to capitalism results in a rising organic composition of capital (fixed capital increases relative to variable capital).

In other words, capital intensity increases but, because of that, the payback period is often longer. If the future does not turn out as planned, the initial investment will not be paid back and may result in bankrupting the company. Even in the best of circumstances, "demand" is elusive despite the massive investment made in advertising and persuasion. There is thus always instability associated with the closure of the circle of expanded reproduction. Furthermore, competing fractions of capital in different sectors of the economy invest in different futures as do competing companies within the same sector. Betting on the future puts individual companies at great risk because the wrong bet could bankrupt any individual corporation, but it also puts entire sectors at risk depending on how the future actually unfolds (G. Patel 2000). Hence, capitalist expansion is predicated on and produces multiple and disjunctive temporalities. The larger point about futurity here is that technological optimism, geographic expansion, infrastructural development, *and* labor suppression are the distinctive features undergirding capitalist potentiality.

After Donald Trump's election in 2016, we witnessed the stabilization and consolidation into common sense of a particular narrative of the decline of the US middle class. According to this narrative, the declining fortunes in the United States of (mostly white) formerly middle-class professionals and blue-collar workers are the result of their jobs being "stolen" by immigrants and workers overseas in countries such as China and India. Software engineers and BPO workers seem to fit well in this narrative, which remains centered on the nation-state and perceives the broader context of capitalist globalization in terms of a zero-sum logic whereby offshoring has resulted in the loss of manufacturing jobs at home (cf. A. Ong 1999, 2006; P. Ong, Bonacich, and Cheng 1994). However, an explanatory framework centering on the post-Fordist rise of precarity, downward mobility, and future uncertainty for understanding capitalist modernity in the present fails to understand the dynamic, heterogeneous, and contradictory logics of capitalism(s) across the world (Brenner and Glick 1991). Most workers in China and India are unlikely to close the gap in living standards with people in the Global North, and the future imagined by a geography of zero-sum economic nationalism is improbable. We are already witnessing upward mobility on the part of some formerly lower-income communities in China, India, Brazil, and Southeast Asia. BPO workers are part of this small sliver of India's population, constituting the lower end of the emerging middle classes in India.

However, the trend is for inequality to grow within geographic regions and within nation-states. Rather than the majority of the population of countries like China and India becoming richer, what we are seeing is the growth of highly differential wealth.[2] The future is open and we will end up with highly unequal societies across the world if present trends persist. But the crucial point here is that such a trajectory for the future is not inevitable—how futurity as potentiality unfolds will depend on political organizing and political activity.

Eschewing the temptation to naturalize a particular temporality of capitalist development in which nation-states move from industrialization based on manufacturing to the service economy, from Fordism to post-Fordism, and from manual labor to immaterial labor, we retheorize the teleologies of development thinking when nation-states such as India move from agriculture to services without going through a manufacturing phase. Such unscripted developmental trajectories not only suggest heterogeneous and discrepant futures but also call into question the futures that were imagined by the planning practices of the nation-state (Koselleck 2004). Futurity as potentiality, and as immanence, opens up to futures that veer from the traditional developmental script. As climate change, pandemics, and other world-changing events unfold, it becomes ever more untenable that poorer countries will follow the script of development that simply repeats and replicates the history of "the West."

Neoliberal globalizers led by the International Monetary Fund anticipated a future in which more open markets and democratic governments would result in the convergence of living standards across spatial boundaries. The hope that poor nation-states would get richer faster than the rest was predicated on the idea that faster growth rates would make the lives of everyone better in the Global South. The paradox has been that inequality has risen in all nation-states, rich and poor, and, as a result, large segments of the population in fast-growing nation-states have been left out of the new wealth. At the same time, formerly comfortable people in the Global North have slipped from a middle-class existence down the class ladder. While this has created the conditions for a zero-sum narrative, such a spatial story about development anchored in nation-states misses the truth of contemporary capitalism. Capitalist expansion in the contemporary moment is not creating "areas" of wealth and poverty (colonial or neocolonial) that are moving in different directions. Instead, the discrepant futures of capitalism in the present are creating wealth and poverty across social space as much as across territorial space. To the extent that futurity continues to be imagined in terms of the potentiality of the nation-state form, we will misconstrue the fractures created by contemporary capitalism and fail to see the discrepant futures associated with "the same" population.

The rise of BPOs and the offshore service economy hence cannot be enfolded into a narrative of dichotomous contrasts between the Global North and the Global South. The growing numbers joining the middle classes in an overall context of increasing inequality constitute an analytical challenge for social theorists. Some analysts of capitalism in India have emphasized processes of "primitive accumulation," precarity, and growing immiseration, but this leaves unexplained the growth, reproduction, and expansion of new middle classes (Sanyal 2013). Instead, a dystopian future and a hopeful one are both immanent, but for different parts of the population. Rejecting the teleology of modernization theory or theories that posit the totalizing march of neoliberalism, what kind of movement are we able to conceptualize when we think of futurity? Futurity involves movement in multiple directions rather than toward a predetermined or singular direction (cf. Hardt and Negri 2005; Harvey 2000). Futurity consists of movements that are zigzag and discontinuous, rather than linear or teleological, across multiple spatiotemporal domains.

It is impossible to talk about futurity, whether at the individual level of the aspirations and anxieties of our interlocutors or at a collective level of national(ist) fantasies, without engaging the interrelationship between different aspects of the future. BPO employees did not share a singular future that we could project or predict. Similarly, our job is not to predict a particular future for the BPO industry. Even if we focused on one agent, they articulated at different times futures that were discrepant. For example, an agent might be hopeful that their financial support of their younger siblings would propel those siblings into a bright future yet despair at their own ability to move on from a job at a BPO or worry that staying in their job would make it difficult for them to be able to marry and raise a family. Futures were multiple, discrepant, and conflicted, whether one saw them at the levels of the individual, the family, the firm, or the industry.

RELATIONALITY, FUTURITY, POTENTIALITY

Our conception of futurity is restricted neither to the futures spawned by affective capitalism nor to technofuturities, whether utopian or dystopian. We have insisted on perceiving BPO agents as laboring subjects who are more than just workers: we thereby foreground futurities untethered to productivist conceptions of their subjectivities. Put another way, we have resisted abstracting labor from other dimensions of the lives of our interlocutors, such as the rhythms of family, the temporalities of religious life, the irruptions of erotic desire, the flows and gridlocks of traffic in the city, the landscapes of enchantment in shopping malls, and, last but not least, the recalcitrance of laboring bodies even as they are put to the service of affective capitalism. Relationality lay at the core of how most of our interlocuters positioned themselves and navigated the world, even when they chafed against the constraints that seemed to undermine their aspirations.

As we have argued throughout this book, racial capitalism works within systems of value extraction that attribute differential worth to human life, labor, and well-being (Appel 2019; Kelley 2020; Robinson [1983] 2020). Racial capitalism inflects the labor of BPO workers through several interwoven formations: the political-economic, affective, and institutional factors that converge to facilitate the shift in the outsourcing of service work from the Global North to locations in the Global South; the differential value attributed to service workers in the Global South, exemplified in the disparity between their incomes and those of workers in the Global North; the politics of language and cultural translation that undergird the affective labor of BPO workers; and the policies and ideological structures that shape the immobility and emplacement of these workers in the Global South. Focusing on specific aspects of the lives and worlds of BPO agents— their embodiment, the intimacies and social relationships that they formed, the disjunctive temporalities of affective labor, their forays into spaces of enchantment, and the excitement of mobility as well as the dread of the em- placements it could entail—provide us with optics to theorize futurity. At a time when the future of futurity seems precarious because of predatory capitalism, climate change, surging inequality, structural violence against communities placed at the margins of nation-states, and the proliferation of authoritarian regimes in different parts of the world, what does our em- phasis on relationality suggest?

Foregrounding relationality in the lives of BPO agents is itself a theo- retical and political intervention.[3] In this context, we turn to the work— and exhortations—of postcolonial and antiracist scholars who insist on the imperative to underscore that relationality is "the precondition of our very existence" (Mani 2022, 6). This emphasis on relationality seems, to us, to be particularly salient to BPOs and other formations of affective labor and ra- cial capitalism. Drawing on Ruth Gilmore, Jodi Melamed (2015) points out that racial capitalism depends on "invalidating processes of relationality by separating forms of humanity so that they may be connected in terms that feed capital" (78). If racism is a technology of *antirelationality*, our effort to reclaim relationality as a means of finding spaces of rupture within racial capitalism is integral to imagining, theorizing, and working toward particular futurities. We hence align ourselves with antiracist and queer scholars of color who urge us to go "beyond anti-relationality" (Muñoz 2006, 825–26; see also Muñoz 2009; cf. Puar 2009). Rather than assume a priori that the affective labor of BPO agents has resulted in social death or the death of intimacy, we have analyzed how they build relationships founded on mutual aid and care, their defiance of powerful social sanctions against intercaste and interreligious relationships and marriages, and even their apparently banal acts of visiting the mall together to indulge in window shopping or try out new cuisines.[4] Our interlocutors built community and forged intimacies in the face of burnout. Their strong sense of responsibility toward the people they loved provided them with an ethical map that enabled them to navigate a daunting present as they reached toward the future. By taking these everyday acts of care, desire, and commitment seriously we conceptualize them as practices that are indexical of futurity. These intimacies were not simply a mechanism by which they coped with or escaped from burnout. Indeed, these intimacies, and the dense socialities in which they were embedded, *materialized* particular kinds of futurities.

Put another way, futurities for BPO agents are founded on their ability (their potentiality) to create ethical maps of relationality that enabled them, at least some of the time, to not lose their way in unfamiliar terrains—and this was true even when these relationalities felt oppressive or exploitative. We theorize futurity in terms of what made life meaningful for our interlocutors, even as they faced precarity and exhaustion, the soaring of aspirations, and the crashing of dreams, sometimes all at once. Rather than attempt to track moments of resistance, our conception of futurity entails moving away from a master-slave dialectic that oscillates between domination or compliance versus resistance.[5] Moreover, we have refused to see our interlocutors as victims: as one of our interlocutors said to us, sinking into despair is a luxury we cannot afford.

We theorize futurity in recognition of the fact that there are multiple, interlinked futurities: of supposedly inert matter and the more-than-human, the economic and the planetary, the rhythms of affective capitalism and the body—all of which are coconstituted but also, often, positioned at odds with each other. The embodiment of BPO agents reminds us that the rhythms of the body, even when out of sync, cannot be overscripted: even as the body falters and fails, it also surprises us. Futurity inheres in what a body can do, in duration as constant unfolding, in movement itself rather than an endpoint (Bergson [1896] 1990).

THE TIME(S) OF FUTURITY

Futurity is about constant motion and movements that impinge on each other. In BPO work, time was simultaneously conjoint and out of joint. Agents had to work at night when the rest of the people in Bengaluru were asleep because that was when people in North America and the United Kingdom were awake. Similarly, the cadence of their work was determined by what was happening in the geographies that they served, not where they lived. They had to reach their office in time and be ready to work even if a tropical rainstorm flooded the streets of Bengaluru and their clothes were all wet, but a hurricane on the Gulf Coast in the southern United States could lead to an intensely stressful night at work. There is another reason why time is out of joint for workers in the BPO industry. The rapid growth of the service industry in India is not simply reprising the story of European modernity or repeating the history of capitalist development in the West. As a nation-state, India is not following a normative trajectory of development in which countries move from agriculture to manufacturing and finally end up in services. Development has not mimicked the trajectory of European nation-states while merely lagging behind; what we witness instead is an economy that has largely bypassed manufacturing while maintaining high rates of growth, but where growth has not been accompanied by an expansion of jobs. The BPO workers are not part of a nation-state where "all boats are rising": they are unlike most of their fellow citizens in becoming middle class. Without a history of Fordism, they do not suffer from Fordist nostalgia. Nor are they similar to citizens of the industrialized world who suffer because of deindustrialization. The conditions in which they encounter global neoliberalism are thus quite different from those of their counterparts in the Global North (Brenner and Glick 1991). In underlining the disjunctive temporalities that make time out of joint, we wish to critically witness the aspirations and potentiality of workers, neither dismissing them for their naivete nor treating them with disdain as people who insufficiently understand their own historical condition.

As we learned from the disjunctive temporalities of the missed period, of agents whose bodily rhythms both collude and collide with the demands of affective labor, and of the clash of ritual time with the time of capitalism, theorizing futurity necessitates that we retain multiple senses of time rather than a sense of time predicated on progress or predictability.[6] While attending to the sense of time in phenomenological terms and its material effects on the agency of agents, futurity entails conceptualizing temporality as a sociopolitical force that shapes lives and worlds. The allegedly "different" sense of time humorously and, at times, condescendingly associated with Bangaloreans—what some decry as the SAM principle of "salpa adjust madi" (just adjust a little)—suggests how the inflexibility of productivism and time management may collide with the purportedly unpunctual and untimely worlds of our interlocutors. What managers and, in particular, expatriate managers condemn as the lack of punctuality and the alleged lack of "work ethic" of Bangaloreans may also index an inhabitation of multiple temporalities that cannot be subsumed by capital (Emont 2020). Ritual time, biorhythmic times, the time of labor and of love, circadian rhythms, the speedy passage of time and its stasis—all informed our interlocutors' experiences of the passage of time even as it implicated the generation of futurity for them. The agentive quality of futurity was always striking to us. Thus, while this book is about affective labor, outsourcing, and global capitalism, it is also about the *capacity* of young people engaging in affective labor to imagine otherwise (Chuh and Shimakawa 2001), live otherwise, and think of their future and the futures of their families and communities in ways that intermix anxiety, desperation, and exhaustion with hope, aspiration, and excitement.

At the same time, as we complete this book in the (supposed) aftermath of the COVID pandemic and the throes of an accelerating climate crisis, we cannot but ponder what the fragility of the body tells us about other fragilities—of the planet, of the economy, and of hope. What must endure for there to be a sense of the future? The limit for many BPO agents was when the body faltered, broke down, made demands of its own, or refused to be overwritten by the time of labor. As we ruminate on the future of futurity, the pandemic has forced us to reckon with what happens when the body fails at a moment when time is out of joint.

FUTURITY AS POTENTIALITY

For my own part, I have always been interested in movement—individual and social—and how to live otherwise than in the putatively inevitable repetition of the degradations and depredations that injure us.

Avery Gordon, "Some Thoughts on Haunting and Futurity" (2011)

It takes more than a discursive shift to resolve social problems. But our rhetoric and framework can either nourish our capacity to stay the course or else unintentionally serve to inhibit it.

Lata Mani, *Myriad Intimacies* (2022)

At a time when predatory capitalism, climate change, and precarity seem to have jeopardized the future of futurity, our theorization of futurity is inspired by the urgency of possibility in the work of women of color feminists (such as Campt 2017; Chuh and Shimakawa 2001; Gordon 2011; Hartman 1997; hooks 1984, 1986; Moraga and Anzaldúa 1983); the scholarship on Afrofuturism (for example, Capers 2021; Dery 1994; Nelson 2002; Wabuke 2020; Womack 2013; Yaszek 2005); Latine futurism (for example, Ramirez 2008); Indigenous futurity (for example, Hickey 2019); and Dalit studies (including but not restricted to Ciotti 2010; Datar 1999; Guru 1998, 2017; Guru and Sarukkai 2019; Gajarawala 2020; Ramberg 2016; Rege 1998; Soundararajan 2020, 2022; Teltumbde 2016; Teltumbde and Yengde 2018) to theorize *and insist on* futurity. The politics of the projects of futurity may potentially be marshaled to a denaturalization of common-sense (hegemonic) notions of the present, to social justice, and to rethinking one's place on the planet.

Tina Campt (2017), for instance, insists on futurity as a political project. Distinguishing between futurity and hope, she asserts the importance of thinking about futurity "through a 'tense.' . . . A tense of a tense of anteriority, a tense relationship to an idea of possibility that is neither innocent nor naïve. Nor is it necessarily heroic or intentional" (33). She describes Black feminist futurity as "a grammar of possibility that moves beyond a simple definition of the future tense as *what will be* in the future. It moves beyond the future perfect tense of *that which will have happened* prior to a reference point in the future. It strives for the tense of possibility that grammarians refer to as the future real conditional or *that which will have* had to *happen*" (33; italics in original).[7]

As we conceptualize it, futurity is potentiality because it refers to what *can* be and what *must* be. We draw, in particular, on Campt's (2017) insistence on the agentive potentiality of futurity as the "performance of a future that hasn't yet happened but must. . . . It is an attachment to a belief in what should be true, which impels us to realize that aspiration" (34). We have argued that theorizing futurity involves centering the will as much as the fragility of the body, and all that that teaches us about other fragilities in our worlds. As our interlocutors taught us, theorizing futurity also entails centering everyday acts of care, loyalty, and desire in the face of uncertainty and vulnerability: relationality provided them with an ethical map for navigating a daunting terrain. Relationality also offers *us* a modality for conceptualizing futurity in contexts scarred by racial capitalism, class and gender inequality, the marginalization of religious and racial Others, and the structural violence of caste.

However, holding on to, and theorizing, futurity as a political project entails an acutely reflexive reckoning of privilege and safety in the face of exclusion, minoritization, and violence. The anticasteist scholarship of Sharmila Rege is particularly instructive in shaping how we, as scholars privileged by class, caste, religion, and citizenship, must reckon with our own positionalities, even as we take care to not consolidate a "narrow identitarian politics" by reducing the complex subjectivities of our interlocutors to their caste positions or religious identities (1998, ws39).[8] Additionally, working with theories of futurity proposed by Dalit feminists is particularly important because it enables us to push back against conceptions of semiocapitalism as placeless and as purportedly transcending the structural violence of race and, particularly in the case of Indians in the world of IT and ITES, of caste.[9]

Indeed, it is the affective force of futurity that generated the ability of our interlocutors to act and be acted on, to affect and be affected. By charting the itineraries of agents as they navigated unfamiliar and daunting worlds, we have sought to foreground the relationship between futurity and potentiality. Transecting individual and collective futures, futurity is agentive: it generates particular kinds of actions. Futurity is also, in many ways, content-less: at stake is not, for instance, whether a particular person would get promoted or laid off, but their ability to act in certain ways; in short, futurity is about potentiality.

Elusive and yet palpable, futurity indexed the potentiality of the multiple and discrepant futures to which BPO agents aspired to, desired, dreamt of, or feared. Giorgio Agamben (2003) argues that potentiality exists in two modalities: the ability to act or not to act, or what he terms *impotentiality*. He adds, "To be potential means: To be one's own lack to be in relation to one's own incapacity" (182). Potentiality and impotentiality are inseparable. Potentiality is *conjoined* with the vulnerability of BPO agents. Their sense of vulnerability congeals around the fear that their bodies will no longer be able to keep up with the stresses and fast pace of night work; the fear of being stuck and unable to accumulate skills fast enough and rise up the hierarchy to be able to stay relevant for changes in this job or qualified for others; the fear of racial abuse and exploitation; the fear of losing connection with friends and family who may provide an anchor in a rapidly changing world; and the fear of not finding a person with whom to share one's life.

Affective labor in the context of global racial inequalities has meant that agents were emplaced as workers in the Global South and put in the service of consumers in the Global North. Their relations with these consumers could be intimate, and these intimacies depended on their ability to translate across geographic and cultural distance. Affective capitalism is predicated on the mutual entanglement of value extraction with other domains of human experience and emotion. In this world of affective capitalism, intimacy, alienated labor, profit, and value are inextricably intertwined. In such contexts, potentiality refers to a wide range of capacities: the ability (or not) of the body to deal with discrepant temporalities, forge relationships with family and friends, build new ones with coworkers and romantic partners, bridge physical, cultural, and emotional distances, learn new skills on the job and in the mall, and maintain hope despite the precarity of their jobs, feelings of "stuckedness," and the mercurial irrationalities of global capitalism. Futurity inheres in how agents' lives are shaped by continual becoming, potentiality, and emergence.

Potentiality is that affective intensity that enabled agents to make a life in rapidly and constantly shifting circumstances, and in their exercise of imaginative mobility; potentiality entailed their capacity to move across— and navigate—a world that was as enticing as it was anxiety-producing. Many newspaper and magazine reports focus on the vitality and hopefulness that characterizes the lives of so many BPO agents. Our immersion in their worlds through long-term fieldwork made their vitality and hopefulness even more remarkable because of how they seemed to endure in the face of the volatility of their lives. The electrifying energy of the shop floor, the creativity that agents displayed off script when dealing with a difficult customer, the dense ties of duty, care, and loyalty that they displayed toward their family and friends, and their ability to find joy and socialize and enter and sustain romantic liaisons, all while working long hours at an exhausting job, made it impossible not to think about the eruptive potentiality of becoming. There is no contradiction in, on the one hand, maintaining that BPO workers were exploited by global capitalism and, on the other, insisting on the creativity that they brought to their work. Our ethnographic sensibilities were attuned to those moments of opening, creativity, and dignity that we gleaned in the face of vulnerability and the tedium of seemingly unending labor.

Potentiality is precisely about not knowing the end point of agents' trajectories. Potentiality is itself an emergent quality of movement, whether that movement is physical, virtual, temporal, social, linguistic, or experiential. Agents' abilities to move were not driven just by bodily intentionality. Instead, their bodies were active and dynamic nodes in feedback loops in affective dispositions that congealed around regimes of labor, aspiration, and the worlds that they inhabited and navigated (Mankekar and Gupta 2017). The world of BPO agents is comprised of a contradictory mix of affective regimes, emotions, sensations, and feelings: disjunctive temporalities, aspiration, chronic anxiety, a strong sense of duty to loved ones; excitement, burnout, and enchantment.

As one of our interlocutors said to us, "Vulnerability is a good teacher. When we feel vulnerable, we learn to not despair, for to despair would be to drown in our fears." Potentiality was revealed in the journeys that agents undertook while working at BPOs rather than in a trajectory toward a predetermined end point: how they sought enchantment, however ephemeral, in the face of uncertainty and an unknowable future and in how they navigated a world in which the ground beneath their feet shifted constantly. This was a world marked by environmental degradation and pollution, traffic jams, road blockages, and speeding vehicles that crash and kill; of health hazards caused by the city's unthinking sprint into the "Future"; and of financial precarity and imminent job loss. Fear and wonder, dignity and depression, hope and frustration were part of the temporality of struggle for BPO agents.

At the same time, an agent's ability to "connect" with the person at the other end of the line, for example, extending compassion to an elderly retiree across geographic and cultural divides, drew on their imaginative travel and ability to engage in cultural translation. Providing high-quality customer service that made the customer feel good about the brand and satisfied that they had been treated well by the company was anything but a seamless process. Although the ability to talk to another person halfway across the world in real time promised a vision of global capitalism predicated on the frictionless circulation of information and affect, the reality was somewhat different: it was mediated by emplacement, interruptions, and blockages. Agents' lives were marked by movement toward the future in the form of professional growth, change of physical location, new "learnings," and the sense of striving by constant work on the self that is so much the hallmark of neoliberalism. Their itineraries were physical, virtual, temporal, social, linguistic, cultural, and experiential, shaped by continual becoming and emergence.

Agamben describes the ability to become a being—the process of becoming—as contingent on potentiality.[10] He reminds us that humans are made as such not through a moment of arrival but in the process of trying to get to an unknown and often unknowable end point. Neither arrival nor the possibility of achieving one's potential is inevitable. Potentiality is irreducible to actuality: it maintains itself as potentiality per se. BPO agents' sense of potentiality, of futurity, was always constructed in the shadow of the specter of failure, of the fear of losing their way in new, unfamiliar worlds. If affect is a form of "intelligence about the world" (Thrift 2004, 60), our interlocutors remind us that potentiality is an intelligence that inheres in the sense of *making* and *finding* one's place in the world. Massumi (2002, 9) posits, "Potentiality is unprescribed. It only feeds forward. . . . Potentiality is the immanence of things to its still indeterminate variation. . . . Immanence is process." Potentiality, therefore, is inherently open-ended; it is this open-endedness that we wish to center in the imagination of futurity among many, if not most, of our interlocutors. We, therefore, engage an anthropology of potentiality that is not naïve in its insistence on open-endedness but remains accountable to the struggles, privations, and accomplishments of our interlocutors. To refuse to ignore what they felt makes their lives worth living is not to occlude the place of exploitation and power dynamics that shape their lives; rather, it is to see what breaks through, not despite but in conditions marked by, exploitation and power dynamics (Ortner 2016).

We have learned a great deal about the future of futurity from our interlocutors. For BPO agents, futurity entails a capacity for moving through and being emplaced in worlds that are frequently not of their making: movement is an existential condition, and that is why futurity, and potentiality, are so important in understanding their lives. Their potentiality inhered in their persistence in acting, even when they did not always know the consequences of their actions, and in learning anew to respond to the worlds in which they found themselves. Agamben (2003, 181) argues:

> If potentiality were, for example, only the potentiality for vision and if it existed only as such in the actuality of light, we could never experience darkness (nor hear silence, in the case of the potentiality to hear). But human beings can, instead, see shadows (*to skotos*), they can experience darkness: they have the *potential* not to see, the *possibility of privation*. (italics in original)

For our interlocutors, potentiality inhered in the fact that they lived under the shadow of darkness. The ever-present specter of failure, of the vortex of depression and emotional paralysis, of the fear of losing their way in new, unfamiliar worlds—these forms of darkness engendered and shaded BPO agents' senses of their potentiality. The relationship between darkness and potentiality is, hence, crucial to our theorization of futurity.

Our theorization of potentiality also aligns closely with Berardi's conception of *futurability*, which he describes as "a layer of possibility that may or may not develop into actuality" (2019, 3; see also Berardi 2012 and, especially, Campt 2017). Futurity is indeterminate: as we have noted above, its significance lies not in its content (as, for example, in representations of the future in utopian versus dystopian terms) but in its very possibility.[11] But this possibility is "limited by the inscribed impossibilities of the present" (Berardi 2019, 1) and is, therefore, not infinite. Thus conceptualized, futurity pertains to immanence that is inscribed in the present, bearing in mind that there are many conflicting possibilities that are always present. Yet, let us recall that futurity is antiteleological; as Berardi insists, "If we assume that the future is necessarily inscribed in the present constitution of the world, we attribute a teleological meaning to the immanence, and inscription is turned into *prescription*" (13; italics in original).

Ultimately, potentiality is about the *sense* of the not-yet-here that propels action and agency in the here and now. We hence conceptualize potentiality as subjects' ability to say "I could" rather than "I will." Over the course of our fieldwork, we began to conceive of potentiality in terms of the ability to strive in the face of possible failure: potentiality is irreducible to arrival or success, much less to liberal or indeed neoliberal constructions of freedom or choice. Potentiality evokes the presence of the possible rather than its lack; but it is also the zone of a presence that, by necessity, implicates its simultaneous absence. Potentiality does not index the essence of being human but is, instead, about one's emergence into being and about the fullness of life rather than its reduction to bare life. If potentiality indexes the capacity to navigate a world that is wondrous and terrifying in equal measure, futurity is about movement in all its unpredictability; it is about the desire to live otherwise, even if there are no guarantees; it is about the striving for a more just world.

Notes

1   A PUC diploma is also known as "10 + 2" to indicate twelve years of schooling.

2   Our research was conducted with three BPOs that catered to international customers. There is a large, and growing, BPO industry that caters to the domestic market that is considered to be a less desirable source of employment. Wages and working conditions in domestic BPOs are not as high as those that provide global services, and they are considered less prestigious places to work. Many workers whose English is not good enough to work in international BPOs end up working in domestic BPOs. Some see such work as a first step toward a job in an international BPO.

3   The first call center we visited was in 2003, a small mom-and-pop operation that was being run in a large house in Gurgaon (now renamed Gurugram), a suburb of New Delhi that was fast becoming the home of call centers and IT firms (Aneesh 2015). At that time, the largest call center in Gurgaon was Daksh eServices, whose six thousand employees became part of IBM when the company was acquired in 2004.

4   Compare with Andrea Muehlebach (2011). Unlike Muehlebach's interlocutors, most of the agents we worked with were from lower-income or lower-middle-class backgrounds and belonged to socioeconomic strata that had never benefited from the promises of Fordism or harbored fantasies of it.

We propose that postcolonial affect rather than post-Fordist affect might be a more generative framework for understanding BPOs. Muehlebach and Shoshan's claim that Fordist nostalgia pervades even those places that may not have experienced Fordism does not have much empirical purchase in a country like India (2012). Fordism does not have an afterlife even as a pipe dream in India where, for most rural people, the fantasy of a life with a social safety net constructed by the state, combined with a future as industrial workers in high-wage occupations, had little purchase.

While the analytical framework of post-Fordist affect can be tremendously productive, it cannot be transposed to countries such as India, where more than 90 percent of workers have historically been employed in the informal sector. The issue is not simply of empirical or historical specificity but of the theoretical and analytical traps inherent in an assumption that capitalist formations, and workers' experiences of them, are the same everywhere. This assumption is particularly problematic because it proceeds from beliefs about the universality of historical and political-economic formations of the Global North and attributes a singularity and homogeneity to capitalism.

5   "Thus, while capital must on one side strive to tear down every spatial barrier to intercourse, i.e. to exchange, and conquer the whole earth for its market, it strives on the other side to annihilate this space with time, i.e. to reduce to a minimum the time spent in motion from one place to another. . . . There appears here the universalizing tendency of capital, which distinguishes it from all previous stages of production" (Marx, in Smith 2010, 127).

6   Our work is in dialogue with analyses of the relationship between capitalism and temporality in India's New Economy; in particular, Aneesh (2015); Amrute (2016); Poster (2007); Upadhya (2016); and Vora (2015).

7   At first, the hope was that uneven development would allow nation-states in the Third World to leapfrog stages of development (Trotsky 2010; Gerschenkron 1962), and this idea is central to the notion that development would level standards of living across the world. However, over time, it became clear that the unevenness produced by capitalist development is systematically reproduced across both regions in the world and within nation-states. As Ashman (2012, 65) succinctly puts it: "Neoliberal globalization has produced neither convergence nor catch-up."

8   Wallerstein's oeuvre is extremely important in rethinking beyond and across the nation-state (1991, 1997, 1999).

9   In the decade in which we studied the industry, BPOs changed from being heavily dependent on voice processes to becoming much more software mediated, from the use of chatbots to analytics to track customers' desires and anticipate their needs. Although we may not yet live in Berardi's dystopian

vision of a global hive in which all workers are gig workers inputting code into a giant interconnected machine whose form and overall shape is clear to none. An analysis of the impact of AI on "the future of work" is beyond the scope of this book.

10   Gottfried and Chun (2018, 998), for instance, foreground how care work has become a "robust site for theorizing about the global and the transnational."

11   Compare Castells's (2000, 21) theorization of the informational society as "a specific form of social organization in which information generation, processing, and transmission become the fundamental sources of productivity and power because of new technological conditions emerging in this historical period."

Even though the BPO sector involved the creation and exchange of intangible commodities, unlike software, it was never considered a "knowledge industry" (Amrute 2016; Upadhya 2016).

12   Pivoting away from the hypostatizing and fetishization of caste on the one hand, and its invisibilization on the other, we theorize caste as a *dynamic* mode of stratification that has taken on new forms in conjunction with the globalization of capital, neoliberal governmentality, and the ascent of Hindu nationalism. We follow David Mosse's (2020) insistence that "'caste' is not a transhistorical social category, but refers to any of a wide variety of phenomena including the identity of endogamous groups (*jatis*) or clusters of them, a division of labor, a social classification, the attribution of inherent or cultural difference, a public representation of social rank, a network, a set of values, social judgements or discriminations (of people, spaces, markets, practices), an administrative or legal category, among others" (1225–26).

The term *Dalit* refers to a sociological and political identity claimed by those who, within a dynamic system of caste hierarchies, are deemed to be "lower" caste. Its etymology may be traced to the Sanskrit where it refers to that which is crushed or broken. The political mobilization of Dalits draws substantially from the work of B. R. Ambedkar, a Dalit scholar and political leader, who was the author of the Indian constitution. From the 1960s onwards, a powerful social movement emerged in Maharashtra that aimed to seek liberation from caste hierarchies. Inspired by the Black Panthers movement, the Dalit Panthers appropriated the term *Dalit* to invert the symbolic markers of their oppression and signify their pride in their Dalit self-identity (Govinda 2022). Since the 1990s, there has been a surge in Dalit political mobilization which has "coincided with the liberalization of the Indian economy, and the struggles for dignity born of social experiences of continuing discrimination and humiliation in the age of the market" (Mosse 2020, 1233).

In our discussion of caste in the worlds of BPO agents, we have preferred the terms *Dalit*, which refers to the political self-representation of the Ambedkarite movement, and *oppressed caste* over *low* or *high caste*. We also use the term *Bahujan* to refer to the larger political identity of Dalits, other subordinated castes like the Sudras and OBCs ("Other Backward Classes," as inscribed in the Indian constitution) and, in some political contexts, tribal populations and Muslims (for a detailed elaboration of these terms, see Nigam 2021, 133). However, as Nivedita Menon (2019) points out, while the term *Dalit Bahujan* refers to the political alliance of non-Brahmin castes against the Brahminical order, it is important that we not assume a concurrence of political goals between Dalits and OBCs because "the latter are also the proximate exploiters that Dalits face in many contexts, even more than relatively distant Brahmins" (153–54).

13   Without reflecting on the limits of his narrative about the century of the future, Berardi (2011) constructs ethnocentric conceptions of the future as universal history, both the story about the faith in the future brought about by the Enlightenment, as well as the "idea that the future is over" (18).

14   In our engagement with intersections of caste, class, and gender, we are particularly indebted to activism and scholarship in Dalit feminism, including but not limited to the work of Omvedt (1979); Dietrich (1992); Manorama (1992); A. Rao (2005, 2009, 2017); Rege (1998, 2000, 2010); Sivakami (2006); Moon and Pawar (2008); Paik (2014); and Sharma and Geetha (2010). We have already noted that, as a political category, the term *Dalit* does not refer to a fixed or static identity, and this is particularly crucial to note with regards to Dalit women. In her foundational discussion of Dalit feminist epistemology, Rege (1998) insists on the heterogeneity of Dalit women's experiences. She also foregrounds that a Dalit feminist standpoint perspective is an epistemological and political project ensuing from learning and unlearning from the lived experiences of heterogeneous Dalit women: she insists that, rather than a static or essentialist "position," Dalit feminist standpoint perspectives can transform subjectivities and privilege can be unlearnt such that non-Dalit feminists can aim to "reinvent themselves as Dalit feminists" (WS-45). Rege's formulation of the transformation of non-Dalit feminists has been interrogated and critiqued by several scholars, some of whom are Dalit, who are concerned about the appropriation of Dalit women's experiences; see, for instance, Datar (1999); Kulkarni (2014); and Guru (2005).

15   The scholarship on Indian middle classes is too voluminous to cite here. On the dynamic and heterogeneous formation of the middle classes in postcolonial India, see Mankekar (1999). While Fernandes (2006) and Fernandes and Heller (2006) present a sociological perspective on the "hegemonic" formation of the Indian middle class in postliberalization India, Mazzarella (2005) interrogates and unpacks the aspirations and anxieties in discourses of middle-classness (see also Kapur, Sircar and Vaishnav 2017; Krishnan

and Hatekar 2017). Jayadeva (2018) demonstrates the importance of the English language to middle-class identity. There is also a large literature specifically on the formation of Bengaluru's middle classes. On the relationship between the IT industry and the formation of Bengaluru's middle classes, see, especially, Radhakrishnan (2008, 2011); Upadhya (2016); and Nisbett (2007, 2010).

16   For a thoughtful commentary on the politics of naming surrounding the category of Dalit, see Gopal Guru (1998). Guru posits: "The category dalit provides both an element of negation (to state constituted categories or harijan) and permits the conjunction of categories belonging to the same logical class (Buddhist, bahujan)" (6).

17   On the inextricability of caste with the gastropolitics of food, see Sucharita Kanjilal (2003).

18   Several Dalit feminist scholars have theorized the productive articulation of Dalit feminist and African American feminist theories. See, for example, the pioneering theorization of Dalit feminist standpoint theory by Sharmila Rege (1998); as well as Devika et al. (2013); Govinda (2022); Jyothirmai and Ramesh (2017); Paik (2014); and Soundararajan (2012).

        There has been a lively debate about the pertinence of analogies between caste, as experience and episteme, in India and race in other parts of the world (see, for instance, chapters in the volume *Racism after Apartheid* edited by Vishwas Satgar [2001]; see also Pandey 2013; Wilkerson 2020). Engaging this debate is beyond the scope of our analysis.

19   In an essay aptly titled "Dalit Middle Class Hangs in the Air," Gopal Guru (2017) argues that Dalits who acquire middle-class status are sometimes hesitant to publicly declare their caste status.

20   This is despite the fact that, according to Upadhya (2016), IT and software are considered a suitable occupation for women notwithstanding the long hours that they demand; this is not true of BPOs where women tended to be stigmatized, in media representations and by landlords, neighbors, family and community members, because they worked there.

21   This may, in part, have been a result of the fact that Muslims form the largest minority community in Bengaluru and in the state of Karnataka (Government of India, Ministry of Home Affairs 2011).

22   For some examples, see Phartiyal and Ravikumar (2020); GEP (2020); CXOtoday.com (2022); Akhouri (2022); and Rely Services (n.d.).

23   We align with Doreen Massey's (1991) advocacy of an "extroverted" sense of place, in particular, her argument that "what gives a place its specificity is not some long internalized history but the fact that it is constructed out of a particular constellation of social relations, meeting and weaving together at a particular locus" (27).

24　These figures did not, of course, account for the large numbers of people employed in the informal economy who, by 1991, amounted to close to 70 percent of the total workforce (Nair 2005, 83).

25　Because it involves a visit to a Muslim dargah, the Karaga Festival has also been described as a festival of communal harmony (Shilpa 2022).

26　For insightful and nuanced analyses of the symbolic importance of IT to Indian nationalism, see Amrute (2016) and Upadhya (2016).

27　Only 10 percent of India's labor force of more than 470 million people is in the formal sector (Kumar 2017).

The term "cruel optimism" (Berlant 2011) may be more applicable to the many poor young people who migrated to Bengaluru from other parts of Karnataka and neighboring states than to BPO agents. These young people expected it to be a city of opportunities, only to struggle to find jobs commensurate with their abilities or expectations because of their poor English. Given their educational qualifications or technical knowledge, they thought that such opportunities were within their grasp, yet jobs proved elusive (Jayadeva 2018, 10).

28　See, especially, Carla Freeman's (2000) powerful analysis of the politics of "open offices" in the informatics industry in Barbados.

29　The middle class is variously defined in terms of consumption patterns, employment, and political orientation (Fernandes 2006, xiv–xix). In 2005, the business consulting firm McKinsey estimated the size of the middle classes to be around 5 percent of the total population. The firm projected that approximately 41 percent of the population, or 583 million people, would be middle class by 2025. However, ten years from the time that that report was prepared, it does not appear that the numbers of middle-class people have expanded as much as was once predicted (RUPE 2015). In fact, Kochhar (2021) estimates that the middle class in India shrank by 32 million due to the pandemic in 2020 and was now approximately 66 million strong.

30　We can modify Koselleck's (2004) account of open futures by drawing on Appadurai's (1981) investigation of the history of a temple in South India that revealed how heterogeneous constructions of the past were used by different groups to legitimize their actions in the present.

CHAPTER 1. MOBILITY, EMPLACEMENT, TRANSLATION

1　Our theorization of mobility and emplacement in this chapter is indebted to Caren Kaplan's foundational work on mobility in contexts of high-tech capitalism, and that of other feminist scholars who have theorized the politics of mobility—in particular, Ahmed (2000, 2006); Ahmed, Casteda, and

Fortier (2003); Grewal (1996); Grewal and Kaplan (1994); Kaplan (1996, 2002); and Massey (1991, 1994).

2   In chapter 4, we diagram the coproduction of the (re)embodiment of BPO agents and affective labor.

3   Communication skills are also deemed central to the skill set of software engineers, thus underscoring its importance to cognitive labor: in software companies, "communication also refers to information flows that are critical to the production process" (Upadhya 2016, 219).

4   Sheller and Urry (2006) draw attention to differential mobilities: "There are new places and technologies that enhance the mobility of some peoples and places and heighten the immobility of others, especially as they try to cross borders" (207). We would add to this insight that the same person may simultaneously experience forms of mobility and immobility through these places and technologies.

5   Kaplan (2002, 36) made the important point that "the value placed on mobility in representations of subjectivity in cyberspace or new technologies is not new . . . but can be seen to be the full articulation of something old: travel."

6   Kalyanaraman (2021) demonstrates the negative effects on educational achievement and employment of this process of displacement of Dalit and Bahujan communities. On caste and spatial segregation in Bengaluru, see also M. Rao (2019).

7   For a nuanced analysis of the ambiguous class positions of women working in the informatics industry in Barbados, see Freeman (2000).

8   Confusingly, almost all the informal hostels were also called "PG" accommodations.

9   INR 2,500 was roughly equivalent to USD 40 in 2015.

10   It is important to note that women who work in BPOs are better protected than many other women who do night work—for example, sex workers or women nurses who do night shifts.

11   Compare this with Allison's (2009) pioneering analysis of how gender, sexuality, and labor undergird the performance of night work in hostess clubs in Japan.

12   We elaborate on the social and corporeal impact of night work in chapters 3 and 4.

13   On the social and intimate relations generated by affective labor in BPOs, see chapter 3.

14   This is as true of affective capitalism as it is for the outsourcing of manufacturing. See, especially, Mirchandani (2012) for an important discussion

of the continuities and discontinuities between call centers and the offshore outsourcing of manufacturing.

15   Our discussion of racial capitalism and BPOs is especially indebted to Cedric Robinson's ([1983] 2020) theorization of racialism.

16   For early discussions of the relationship between capitalist modernity and Asian alterity, see Lowe (2001) and Palumbo-Liu (1999).

17   See, especially, Amrute (2016) for a pathbreaking analysis of the racialization of Indian software engineers in Berlin.

18   For a powerful analysis of Vincent Chin's murder, see Renee Tajima-Peña (1987). Indeed, anti-Asian racism extends beyond the offshore outsourcing of jobs in the late twentieth century and can be traced back to the xenophobic backlash against the arrival of Asians as laborers in the late nineteenth century (Takaki 1989; for an account of the backlash against South Asian workers, see Leonard 1992).

19   In *The Communist Manifesto*, Marx and Engels ([1848] 1967, 83) posit, "The bourgeoisie has through its exploitation of the world market given a cosmopolitan character to production and consumption in every country."

20   For portrayals of call center work as a dead end in the Philippines, see Padios (2018). See also Hage (2009) on the predicament of "waiting it out": he argues that the "heroism of the stuck" who persist in waiting represents a form of governmentality (8).

21   Amrute (2016) makes a similar argument about the critiques formulated by her interlocutors in Berlin.

22   Zuboff (2019) points out that such surveillance is the new normal for most people in the age of informatics. While BPO agents were thus not exceptional, they experienced greater surveillance at work than many other people who are part of the industries that comprise semiocapitalism.

23   The volatility of the outsourcing industry is also commented on by Padios (2018) in her research on call centers in the Philippines.

24   We borrow the phrase "inequality of languages" from the germinal essay by Talal Asad (1986).

25   Scholars have analyzed the training of call center agents by foregrounding mimicry (Nadeem 2011) or cultural neutralization (Aneesh 2015). Nadeem (2011) proposes that mimicry entails appropriation and transformation because linguistic and cultural cues are transplanted to a different terrain (9). We find Aneesh's (2015) use of the trope of mimesis, which emphasizes *re*coding, more useful. Aneesh argues, "Instead of simply copying, mimesis recodes cultural expressions with non-cultural functions without making it apparent, triggering a transmutation that allows global business communication to appear as everyday cultural communication" (68).

26 Cultural neutralization is by no means unique to the BPO industry. See Ameeriar (2012, 2015) for an ethnography of how South Asian immigrants to Canada undergo similar training.

27 We have elected to use *Bengaluru* rather than *Bangalore*, except when we cite other sources or quote our interlocutors. We also use *Bangalore* while referencing its formation as a colonial city and in the discourses of futurity that emerged immediately after Indian independence.

28 Referring to the process of translating epics from one Indian language to another, U. R. Ananthamurthy says, "Tulsidas's Ramayana, the Tamil Ramayana and the Kannada epics, these are all-India texts which are translated not in the sense of how we use the word 'translation' but something like *anuvaada*, i.e., to come closer to a text" (Ananthamurthy and Gowda 2019, 102). Later, he distinguishes between vak (speech) and artha (meaning), arguing that the translation of epics was intent on preserving only the meaning, not the poetic structure "mantra" or the literal words (115).

29 We are intentionally using the colonial name of the city here.

30 The explosive mix of linguistic tensions and the right to the city reached a peak when Rajkumar, a leading actor and cultural icon of Kannadigas, was kidnapped in July 2000. The frustrations of Kannada associations and Rajkumar fan clubs spilled over into city streets because he had come to embody pride in the Kannada language. Since the person who had kidnapped him, Veerappan, was a Tamilian, these tensions became transposed into conflicts between Tamilians and Kannadigas. See, especially, Niranjana (2000) on the class and gendered implications of the Rajkumar kidnapping and of the assertions of Kannada linguistic nationalism leading up to and surrounding the kidnapping.

It is important to note that tensions between Tamilians and Kannadigas both encapsulate and extend beyond conflicts over language. For instance, the Cauvery water dispute between Tamil Nadu and Karnataka has also been central to tensions between these two communities.

31 We elaborate on the significance of this policy later in this book.

32 The year 1991 also saw some of the worst anti-Tamil riots in Bengaluru and some other parts of Karnataka over conflicts over the sharing of the waters of the River Cauvery between Karnataka and Tamil Nadu (Press Trust of India 2013).

33 Jayadeva (2018) gives the example of a language trainer who adopted a "posh" accent when she wanted to give the impression that she had "roamed the world" (29). English similarly provides call center agents in the Philippines with an avenue for upward mobility by signifying cultural capital that correlates with economic privilege (Padios 2018, 73).

34 One of Jayadeva's (2018, 18–23) observations about adults learning English at training centers was how they viewed English as providing access to

superior knowledge, as well as being more polite and refined than Kannada or Tamil.

35 The *Hindu Business Line* concluded that "just 21 million credit cards in a country with 1,300 million people and 900 million mobile phones and nearly 700 million bank accounts, is appalling" (Vageesh 2015).

36 We elaborate on the corporeal dimensions of these temporal disjunctions in chapter 4.

37 On debates about translation in Euro-American scholarship, see Gal (2015, 227–28).

CHAPTER 2. SHOPPING MALLS AS INFRASTRUCTURES
OF ASPIRATION

1 On similar expressions of moral outrage against the consumption behavior of call center workers in the Philippines, see Padios (2018). See also Chua (2003) on the discourses of morality surrounding young people's consumption behavior in Singapore.

2 In his theorization of the commodity aesthetics undergirding the "technocracy of sensuality" in contexts of capitalism, Wolfgang F. Haug draws on Norbert Elias's ([1939] 1978) thesis on "affect moulding."

3 Some of the most illuminating analyses of the extraeconomic dimensions of consumption have been pioneered by feminist anthropologists. For examples of some of this work, see Louisa Schein's (1996) early, trenchant interrogation of the fraught relationship between race, consumption, and desire among the Miao; Carla Freeman's (2000) important theorization of consumption among women informatics workers in Barbados, which foregrounds the place of professional dress in how women fashion middle-class identities while, simultaneously, reconfiguring enactments of femininity; and Ara Wilson's (2004) subtle analysis of how consumption reshapes social lives and desires.

For examples of early analyses of consumption from anthropological and cultural studies perspectives, see Daniel Miller (1987, 1995), Meaghan Morris (1993), and Chua Beng Huat (2000).

4 Shopping malls have long been analyzed as spaces where people browse as much (or, in many cases, more than) they shop, as Chua Beng Huat (2003, 42) observes in his study of shopping malls in Singapore. Later in this chapter, we examine how shopping malls spawn dense socialities and desires, including erotic desire.

5 See especially Edward P. Thompson's (1967) classic essay on the difficulties encountered by capitalists in imposing a sense of factory time discipline on the first generation of industrial workers.

6   See also Adams, Murphy, and Clarke (2009) for a pathbreaking analysis of the politics of anticipation.

7   Compare this with Freeman's (2014) analysis of the impact of structural adjustment and discourses of neoliberalism on the aspirations and futurities of middle-class women in Barbados.

8   On the close relationship between consumerism, the expansion of the Indian middle classes, and the proliferation of transnational media in the immediate aftermath of economic liberalization, see Mankekar (1999, 2004, 2015) and Rajagopal (1998, 2001a, 2001b, 2001c).

9   Figures for consumption data are from the World Bank: https://data .worldbank.org/indicator/NE.CON.TOTL.KD?locations=IN&most_recent _value_desc=false (accessed July 8, 2024).

10   We are particularly indebted to Cross's (2015) analysis of how SEZs are places of "imagination and aspiration" and are places of "future worlds for themselves and others, establishing the zone as a promissory infrastructure" for workers (424–25).

11   See, especially, Freeman's (2000) insights on how consumption practices enable women informatics workers in Barbados to distinguish themselves from working-class women.

12   Compare with Amrute's (2016) caution about the attribution of a singularity and homogeneity to the Indian middle classes in terms of their purported conspicuous consumption (19). See, especially, Mazzarella's (2005) discussion of the Indian middle class.

13   See Upadhya (2016) and Amrute (2016) on the relationship between aspiration and work in the lives of software engineers.

14   The hailing of Bangalore as a city of the future builds on historical precedence. In the early years of independence, Prime Minister Jawaharlal Nehru opined in a speech to the city's residents: "Most of the old cities represent the past of India. They represent history, whereas your city represents the future we are trying to mould" (Heitzman 2004, 61, in J. Menon 2021, 56).

15   For astute analyses of the unsuitability of the so-called Singapore model to a city like Bengaluru, see S. Benjamin (2010) and Nair (2000). Nair points out that the enthusiastic advocacy of the Singapore model by upper-class residents was subsequently "tempered" by S. M. Krishna who argued, instead, for the development of "strips of Singapore" (1512). Not surprisingly these "strips of Singapore" were to be created around the IT corridor and were to be particularly advantageous for the growth of the IT and ITES industry in Bengaluru.

        For more details on the politics leading up to Krishna's backpedaling on the Singapore model, see S. Benjamin (2010). Solomon Benjamin also closely analyzes the investment of the Singaporean government and companies in real estate developments in Bengaluru, chiefly, in malls and IT parks like ITPL; as he points out, "the well-publicised 'Singaporean connection' to Bangalore images as being much more than mere imagery" (102).

16   See, especially, Chua's (2003, 19) careful delineation of Singapore's long history of modernity.

17   See Aneesh (2015) for an excellent delineation of the relationship between call center and ITES industries and the growth of Gurgaon.

18   This is similar to Wilson's (2004, 9) claim about the "power of and limits on the global economy's ability to remake social worlds."

19   Whether conceptualized as media convergence (Jenkins 2006), media assemblages (Rai 2009), or sensorial ecologies (Mankekar 2015), it is impossible to think of media as operating in isolation from each other. Elsewhere, Mankekar (2012) has analyzed how lifestyle programs on Indian television underscore and reinforce for middle-class viewers new ways of navigating space and time, and indeed, inhabiting the body.

20   See also Rai (2009, 78) on the relationship between malltiplexes, biomedia, and subject formation.

21   Several scholars have pointed to how urban space is a site of contestation between classes. See, especially, Kaviraj (1997) for an astute and eloquent reflection on public space in Calcutta (Kolkata).

22   It should be evident by now that, in our description of the markets adjoining Forum Value Mall, we resist Orientalist clichés about the Indian/Eastern bazaar in terms of a temporal lag or backwardness: on the contrary, we underscore and reiterate that in existing—and thriving—literally and figuratively *alongside* the mall, these spaces demonstrate a temporality of simultaneity.

23   On the erotics of commodity affect, see Mankekar (2003 and 2015).

24   In some elite neighborhoods in Bengaluru, malls adjoin exclusive gated communities that are often built by the same developer (for instance, the Forum Mall and the Forum Value Mall have been built by Prestige Group which has also constructed expensive residential enclaves adjoining them).

25   This also seems to be the case in Bangkok, where according to Wilson (2004, 107), malls have come to symbolize the modernity of the Thai nation.

26   See, especially, Chua's (2003, 60–64) analysis of "inadvertent" and "intimidated" browsers in Singapore's shopping centers.

27   We stress the role of imagination because very few of them had actually been to or were likely to go to the "West."

28   We describe one such hostel in chapter 1.

29   As in Thailand, where public expressions of heterosexual desire are frowned upon (Wilson 2004, 125), Bengaluru's malls provide a space for expressing identities and relationships that are encouraged by the mall itself. See also Chua (2003, 48–50) for a similar discussion of the intimate spaces of malls in Singapore. For youth in many cultural contexts, malls provide spaces of relative protection from the surveillance of parents and other authority figures (see, for example, Dávila 2016.)

30   See also Aparna Sharma (2003) on multiplexes in India. The rise of multiplexes has gone hand-in-hand with audience segmentation strategies of Bollywood producers, the rising fortunes of distributors and exhibitors, and the demise of the single-screen theaters—all of which have occurred in sync with the changing economies of Indian film industries.

31   Several scholars have analyzed linguistic politics in Bengaluru: see, for instance, Nair (2000, 2005) and Niranjana (2000). We elaborate on the politics of language in the city's BPOS in the previous chapter.

32   Amrute (2016) underscores the dynamism and shifting power of the Indian middle class(es) in her discussion about how multiplexes and shopping malls reestablish middle class control over urban space. She argues that such spatial hegemony is always contested, as witnessed by the "plebianization" of parks (162).

33   Filmmaker Gautam Sonti (2006) captures this atmosphere perfectly in a segment about Sun Microsystems in India entitled "Fun@Sun."

34   Total Mall has a large grocery store that sells food and other commodities at relatively low prices and constantly advertises discounts and sales. The Nexus Whitefield Mall has a more mixed clientele: while many of its retail outlets sell discounted clothes, as we have noted above, it also has a high-end multiplex cinema theater and an expensive Italian restaurant. Compare with the expansion of transnational cosmopolitan consumption to low-income communities in Bangkok (Wilson 2004, 112.)

35   Clough takes from Negri the idea that in the welfare states of the Global North, the whole of society is subsumed by capital (the "social factory"), so that there is no autonomous sphere or even a pericapitalist space for the reproduction of the worker. In such a world, "work goes on all the time" because laborers are reproducing capitalist relations even when they are not working (for example, during leisure time, with their families, etc.). We have argued that postcolonial spaces that have never been Fordist or Keynesian cannot be assumed to be operating under a similar dynamic. This is why malls can function as "pedagogical" spaces—because the reproduction of workers is not always already subsumed by capital, they have to learn how to be capitalist subjects.

36   Upadhya (2016) makes a similar point in her discussion of the self as a "skill set" for software engineers in Bengaluru. She argues that these workers need to "absorb particular social skills and dispositions that contribute to their development of the desired class habitus as well as to their careers" (305).

37   As Freeman (2014, 1) puts it, "The self as an entrepreneurial 'project' under constant renovation is a key signpost of neoliberalism and its perpetual quest for flexibility in the changing global marketplace." On discourses of entrepreneurship in the lives of BPO workers in India, see Mankekar (2013, 2015); for a broader discussion of "enterprise culture" in postliberalization India, see Gooptu (2013a).

38   This is similar to Wilson's (2004) observations about malls in Bangkok, where the "explosion" of malls and the "retail revolution" they brought in their wake "invited spending of the growing middle-class population as well as of the populations who had previously been excluded from 'modern' transnational consumption: lower-middle-class and working-class Bangkok residents, including even migrant workers from the countryside" (112). See also Padios (2018).

39   See Mankekar (2015) on the caste marginalization and consumerist fantasies of cosmopolitanism, and Gupta (1998). Our argument about the place of malls and BPOs in the construction of visions of the future for our Dalit and Bahujan interlocutors resonates with what Jamie Cross (2015, 430) posits for SEZs: "For many young Dalit men the zone was *imagined* as a potential catalyst for social reform, a moment of rupture that would create an unparalleled opportunity to rebuild and recreate new kinds of inter-caste relationships" (emphasis added).

40   Compare with the tension between neoliberal individualism and obligations to community and family for middle-class "entrepreneurial subjects" in Barbados (Freeman 2014).

41   We are not interested in whether young people in India are less or more individualistic than their counterparts in the West: such a question presumes teleological narratives of individualization that leave unproblematized the culturally particular and historically specific concept category of the individual and the self.

42   Our insistence on foregrounding this contrast aligns with Jisha Menon's (2021) powerful theorization of the aspirations of new urban subjects in contemporary India.

43   Wilson's (2016) example of bathrooms in public parks that were repurposed as sites for sex between men shows that the uses for which infrastructure is intended do not always coincide with its future employment.

44   Much thought has already been given to the relationship between capitalism and dis/enchantment—see, especially, the work of Weber ([1905]

2002), who underscored the relationship between capitalism, instrumental rationality, and dis/enchantment. In critical theory associated with the Frankfurt School, for instance, disenchantment is associated with capitalism and secularization and is deemed a necessary component of capitalist modernity; see, in particular, Adorno (1991), Horkheimer and Adorno ([1947] 2002), and W. Benjamin ([1982] 2002, [1935] 1968). For critiques of the relationship between secularization and disenchantment, see Taylor (2016). We use the term *enchantment* in cognizance of its centrality to capitalist modernity (W. Benjamin [1982] 2002, [1935] 1968). However, engaging the relationship between secularization, instrumental rationality, and disenchantment is beyond the scope of this chapter.

CHAPTER 3. INTIMACIES AT WORK

1   The danger of surveillance lies in its surreptitiousness: subjects do not know that they are being surveilled and may not wish to share knowledge of activities that they regard as private and confidential. However, the growth of affective capitalism has been accompanied by changing ideas of what is considered private and intimate for customers, citizens, and workers.

2   Lisa Lowe's (2015) critique of liberalism as rationalizing, obfuscating, and, therefore, enabling settler colonialism, slavery, and indenture offers a particularly generative critical reading practice and methodology for critiquing the close relationship between violence and intimacy *across* different scales and spatial regimes. Lowe uses the concept of intimacy as a heuristic to examine the world-historical processes that produce modern liberal subjects (17). See also Nayan Shah (2011) on intimacy and racialization, Pratt and Rosner (2006, 2012) on the global and the intimate, and Povinelli (2007, 2011) on intimacy and biopolitics.

3   Ann Stoler (1989, 2006) and other scholars of colonial intimacy have argued that the sphere of the intimate is a crucial site of colonial governance.

4   On the shift from formal to real subsumption in informational capitalism, see Clough (2008).

5   Furthermore, as Gottfried and Chun (2018) argue, "The social aspect of paid care work implicates the self, emotions, and the body (and thereby gender and race)" (1003). We diagram coproduction of the affective labor and the gendered and racialized body in the following chapter.

6   In chapters 1 and 4 we unpack how these discourses of professionalism occlude an acknowledgment of race and racialization and are undergirded by neoliberal and postracial conceptions of autonomy and agency. See Padios's (2018) astute analysis of the coimplication of empire, race, racialization in experiences of servitude and discourses of professionalism in call centers in the Philippines.

7   The alignment of individual progress with the progress of the nation also appears to have been very strong for call center agents in the Philippines (Padios 2018).

8   See Amrute (2016) for an important discussion of the centrality of race in the purportedly postracial workplaces of Indian engineers in Berlin. Compare with the responses of Filipino call center workers who respond to the racism and xenophobia of their customers in the Global North in terms of discourses of professionalism and Filipino-American relatability (Padios 2018).

9   See, especially, Amrute (2016) and Upadhya (2016) on the formation of the selves of Indian software engineers in Berlin and Bengaluru respectively.

10   We take seriously Freeman's (2020) caution about how "in studies of capitalism, feelings have emerged most often as an expression of alienation, a by-product of oppressive extractive relations between owners and producers" (5).

11   We build on the rich anthropological literature on the cultural specificity of emotion: this scholarship is too voluminous to cite but it is interesting to note that much of this work has emerged from feminist anthropology—for instance, Abu-Lughod (1986), Lutz and Abu-Lughod (1990), Lutz (1986), and most significantly, the ground-breaking theorization of emotion in Rosaldo (1984).

12   Padios (2018) observes that call center workers in the Philippines are, likewise, urged to "think like a customer"; thus, rapport and empathy, which she describes as relational labor, are indispensable to the "emotional economy in which call center labor produces value" (42–43). As one call center employee said to her, "You have to have the highest level of EQ [emotional quotient] to be here" (44).

13   While our focus is on the role of empathy in the affective labor of BPO agents, Throop and Zahavi (2020) point out that empathy is not restricted to the affective: it can also involve cognitive and conative states (285). Throop and Zahavi address the relationship between empathy, attunement, and embodiment thus: "When oriented to another empathically, we experience the intensity, rhythm, and pitch at which another is living through a given embodied situation" (287).

14   We build on Throop's (2012) analysis of the significance of touch and the haptic in his analysis of Yap healing. Foregrounding empathy's dynamism and complexity, Throop posits it as a multimodal process that "not only involves perception, intellection, affect, and imagination, but also the bodily and sensory aspects of lived experience" (408).

15   There exists a rich and voluminous literature on the relationship between technology and intimacy, and we refer here only to some of the most early

and foundational theorizing on this subject. Within anthropology, Nicole Constable (2003, 2007) pioneered research on the role of information technology, the internet in particular, in the formation of intimate relationships at a distance and across racial, national, and cultural lines. Constable's (2013) research is also exemplary in how it foregrounds the heterogenous and, sometimes, contradictory desires that undergird these relationships which can range from the erotic to the "counter-erotic." Likewise, an early and foundational text in the scholarship on technology and the intimate is the anthology edited by Chris Berry, Fran Martin, and Audrey Yue, *Mobile Cultures: New Media in Queer Asia* (2003). See also Cupples and Thompson (2010); David and Cambre (2016); Elwood and Leszczynski (2018); Keeling (2019); Kuntsman (2004); Miles (2017); and Valentine (2006) for groundbreaking analyses of technology and intimacy.

16   On the non-equivalence of the sexual and the erotic, see Mankekar and Schein (2013).

17   On similar articulations of critique and self-reflexivity on the part of call center workers in the Philippines, see Padios (2018).

18   Compare with Amrute's (2016) persuasive analysis of how software engineers in Berlin forge relationships that enable them to find meaning and pleasure outside the workplace.

19   In this regard, the workplace socialities of BPOs seem to contrast with those of software companies analyzed by Upadhya (2016) where cross-gender interactions remain relatively formal with little socializing between men and women occurring outside the workplace (162).

20   It is equally important to note that, far from being static, caste endogamy is highly contingent: it is fundamentally shaped by temporally specific dynamics of power. Social reformers and activists like Tarabai Shinde, Jyotirao Phule, E. V. Ramaswamy Naicker, and B. R. Ambedkar challenged upper-caste practices of marriage, sexuality, and kinship. Furthermore, the contingency of caste endogamy is predicated on everyday forms of power and inequality generated, in turn, by historically specific hierarchies (Abraham 2014, 56; A. Rao 2005; Rege 2003). For instance, the bodies of lower-caste women are deemed accessible to upper-caste men both within and outside marriage, thus foregrounding the intersection of discourses of sexuality and caste (Abraham 2014, 57; Geetha 2007, 191–92; Mankekar 2021a; Mankekar and Kanjilal 2022, 3).

21   It is not simply, or only, the haptic that is at work in the maintenance or transgression of hierarchies. Caste is affective as much as it is political-economic and sociological: it is deemed to mobilize a range of emotions such as reverence and humility (toward dominant castes) or disgust and repulsion (toward members of the oppressed castes). The corporeality of caste is implicated in how it functions, at least in part, as an affective

regime: for a member of a dominant caste to touch or be touched by an "untouchable" is to act and be acted upon (Kanjilal 2023).

22   Much of this violence is also part of a broader backlash against the political mobilization and (precarious) upward class mobility of Dalits, Bahujans, and other oppressed communities (Mankekar 2021b).

23   See Upadhya (2016, 299) for an analysis of the sharp contrast between representations of women workers in software companies and BPOS respectively.

24   On the anxieties and moral panics surrounding the sexuality of young call center workers in the Philippines, see Padios (2018).

25   Indeed, the prominence of Asian bodies in contemporary formations of the transnational service industry display the "historical legacies of intertwined systems of hierarchy" (Gottfried and Chun 2018, 999).

26   See, especially, Amrute (2016) on the power of eros in the subject formation of Indian engineers in Berlin.

27   See also Ortner (1995) for an early, and incisive, critique of such binaristic assumptions.

28   We borrow the term *contact zone* from Mary Louise Pratt's *Imperial Eyes* (1992).

29   See also Saba Mahmood's (2011) critique of the liberal "resistant" subject.

CHAPTER 4. THE MISSED PERIOD

1   For an important synopsis of genealogies of bodily comportment in South Asia, see Amrute (2016). As Amrute reminds us, these genealogies (whether those of precolonial Yogic or Sufi techniques of asceticism, meditation or breath control, or anticolonial legacies such as those promoted by Swami Vivekananda and Hazrat Inayat Khan, or the "neo-Yogic" practices of bodily discipline in contemporary Hindu nationalist times) have been deeply intertwined with technologies of political control (149–50). See also Daniel (1987) on the relationship between embodiment and substance in "being a person the Tamil way," and Solomon (2016) on corporeality, metabolism, and urban living in contemporary Mumbai (2016).

2   In his critique of canonical Marxist historiography, Dipesh Chakrabarty (2000) has insisted on the disjunction between, for instance, the time of capital and what he calls "the time of the gods." Compare with Bear et al.'s (2015) critique of conceptions of capitalism as unilinear, singular, and outside other social formations.

3   Our theorization of embodiment, technology, and temporality in this chapter owes much to the work of scholars like Balsamo (1995); Clough (2007);

Grosz (2018); Haraway (1985, 1991); Mankekar (2021b); Puar (2007); and Rai (2019).

4   Our argument contrasts with perceptions of call center workers in the Philippines as performing intrinsically feminine labor, and foregrounds historically and culturally specific discursive conjunctions of gender, labor, and care work (Padios 2018).

5   We draw inspiration from Grace Hong and Roderick Ferguson's (2011) conception of the "strange affinities" as a methodological framework to rethink the historical particularities, positionalities, and alliances *across* (and within) racialized and queer of color communities in the United States. While an analysis of the strange affinities between BPO workers in Bengaluru and at other nodes of the transnational service economy is beyond the scope of our research, our approach relies on a relational rather than comparativist epistemology.

6   As Asian American scholars, it is impossible for us to not be reminded of the extraction of Asian labor during the gold rush in the western United States in the nineteenth century. The transnational circulation and (perhaps inadvertent) adoption of such racialized terms is striking to us. Recall, also, the use of the term "cyber coolie" for BPO agents (see introduction).

7   We elaborate on the politics of Indian English in chapter 1.

8   While the growth of BPOs and the subject formation of workers in India and the Philippines respectively have much in common in how they manifest the intertwined legacies of empire, postcolonialism, and the racialized politics of language (Padios 2018; Tupas and Salonga 2016), important differences also exist. For instance, according to Padios (2018, 113), "Filipinos are described as having neutral or light accents that are easy to understand, with tacit or sometimes explicit comparison to Indian accents, which U.S.-based customers not only find difficult but also recognize as Indian."

9   As we noted in chapter 1, accent training of the early years of BPOs must not be confused with the strategy of accent "neutralization" that became more widespread by the late 2000s.

10   Rosa (2019) argues that standardized English becomes "the normative language variety for official business" and in this process, Spanish-inflected language, for instance, becomes structurally stigmatized. Rosa is concerned with an intermediary, phenotypically heterogeneous ethnoracial population—Latinx communities—located unstably between Blackness and Whiteness. Arguing against a purely phenotypical understanding of race that does not tell us as much about historical, political, and economic circumstances, Rosa posits the Black-White binary as one powerful racial logic among many racial assemblages. He focuses on how "semiotic ideologies recruit linguistic practices to homogenize Latinxs as racial others"

(3) and argues that race and language are not objectively observable or embodied phenomena; instead, they are "historically and institutionally constituted subject formations that are rooted in the rearticulation of colonial distinctions between Europeanness and otherness" (150).

11 Roth-Gordon (2016) proposes the concept of racial malleability "to foreground the role of linguistic practices in the racial shifts that are made possible through daily interactions" (54). She argues that bodies are given racial meaning and also remain racially malleable so that they may be read as more or less white based on a range of daily practices that include bodily aesthetics, patterns of consumption (from clothing to music) and, critically, language use.

12 Davé (2013) posits that Indian accents are indexical of the ambiguous status of Indians vis-a-vis other racial minorities in the United States: while representing Otherness, Indian and Indian American accents also represent a privilege based on mastery of the English language. This, in turn, then marks the ability of (upper- and middle-class and, presumably, dominant caste) Indian Americans to be "not too different," and therefore more easily assimilated into European America.

13 As we have elaborated in chapters 1 and 2, the confidence (and, to a large extent, the ability) of BPO agents to navigate the new worlds in which they find themselves is that much harder for those from oppressed castes who have been deprived of the social networks and resources ensuing from, and constituting, caste and class privilege.

14 For a powerful (and elegant) elucidation of the relationship between ingestion, substance, and personhood, see Daniel (1987).

15 See Aneesh (2006) for a brilliant discussion of algocracy and the algorithmic control of labor processes.

16 In informatized societies all bodies have become data points due to the ubiquity of information technology, ranging from smartphones to internet browsers, in our everyday lives.

17 We address the intimacies of affective labor in the previous chapter.

18 In some ways, the disjunctive temporalities inhabited by BPO agents were similar to those experienced by factory laborers. The Taylorization of labor in the factory meant that workers' minute actions had to be harnessed to attain maximum productivity.

19 The hegemonic injunction to reproduce and the (assumed) metonymy between biological and social reproduction indexes heteropatriarchal normativities dominant in the United States as much as in India. In the United States, the relationship between social reproduction and futurity has elicited much debate in queer theory: for instance, Edelman's 2004 polemic against "reproductive futurism."

20   The aspirations experienced (and accomplished) by our interlocutors are not representative of those of youth in other sectors of the Indian economy or in other parts of the country. For example, they differ from the attenuated aspirations of youth in the northern Indian town of Meerut (Jeffrey 2010). Youth suicides in Kerala draw an even starker contrast with the aspirations of many of our interlocutors (Chua 2014). These suicides can be seen as the "fallout" of failed aspiration, spiraling out of control when the "disappointed, frustrated, and demoralized refuse[d] to live" (2).

21   See, especially, the work of scholars such as Govinda who have insisted that we interrogate the "processes by which the category of 'Dalit woman' comes into being, is embraced, questioned, and negotiated" (2022, 78).

CONCLUSION

1   This is decidedly not a book about the future of work. Nevertheless, emerging uses of process automation, AI, voice recognition, Big Data, and analytics are poised to change the labor process in fundamental ways, all of which have implications for the somatic and psychic health of workers. Some of those technologies will no doubt displace existing call center workers, but many will change job definitions and labor processes—the manner that BPO workers interact with technology and are reconstituted by it (Ford 2015).

   The literature on the future of work is as voluminous as it is heterogeneous. For some of the most generative analyses of the relationship between information technology, the logics of neoliberal capital, and regimes of labor, see Dyer-Witheford (1999); Dubal (2020); Forrester and Weigel (2020); Fuchs (2019); Gregg (2011); and Weeks (2011).

2   For this reason, the optimistic projections of an "Asian century" are also likely to be wrong (Frank 1998).

3   We do not presume that friendships at work necessarily translate to relationships of solidarity (cf. hooks 1986).

4   As we insist in chapter 3, the intimate relationships they formed with each other and with their customers were never separate from affective labor; in fact, these intimacies inflected and reconstituted the rhythms and imperatives of affective labor. These intimacies cannot be disentangled from affective labor produced and commodified by semiocapitalism: there is no space of purity or innocence in contexts of affective capitalism.

5   BPO workers thus blur the distinction between becoming "autological subjects" who make their own history and subjects of a genealogical society where they are defined by belonging to a collectivity (Povinelli 2017, 302).

6   Mani (2022, 74) posits, "Our lives are lived along multiple timelines: geo-logical, seasonal, political, ritual, historical, biorhythmic, cultural, cellular, cosmic, and so on."

7   This grammar of possibility is also what Appadurai (2013) calls for when he advocates for the "victory" of a politics of possibility over a politics of probability (3).

8   As a non-Dalit scholar, Rege teaches us about the importance of self-critique and self-reflexivity regarding our participation and collusion in relations of oppression and exploitation and a vigilance against uncon-sciously reproducing caste dominance. Drawing on African American feminist theorizing, Rege insists that confronting casteist practices is not the "sole responsibility" of Dalit, Bahujan, and other communities mar-ginalized by Brahminical and Hindu supremacies. We would add that for class- and caste-privileged researchers like ourselves, this would necessarily involve a project of *nonidentification* with less privileged subalterns based on a confrontation with our complicity in the consolidation of difference and inequality between our positionalities.

   Rege's theorizing of a Dalit feminist standpoint theory has been cri-tiqued for not emphasizing sufficiently the importance of the lived expe-rience of Dalit women and for privileging educated Dalit women at the expense of those at the margins of the community (Datar 1999; Guru 2005).

9   Toral Gajarawala (2020, 44, 45) posits Dalit futurism as "radical futurity" by drawing on older anticaste movements (including, for example, the self-respect movement led by Periyar E. V. Ramasamy in South India and the Ambedkarite movements) and, simultaneously, tracking the transna-tional travels of caste and anticasteist struggles—for example, through the Dalit Solidarity Network and the multigenre interventions of Thenmozhi Soundararajan (2020). Although our focus has been on the ITES indus-try, which has a considerably more caste-diverse employee pool than the Savarna-dominated IT industry (Upadhyay 2016), we are indebted to the work of Equality Labs (www.equalitylabs.org) and, in particular, Sounda-rarajan for foregrounding the reconstitution and consolidation of caste in the world of IT in the United States (Soundararajan 2012; Soundararajan and Varatharaja 2015). See Saritha Rai (2021) on caste in Silicon Valley and, more generally, in the IT industry. We place this discussion in dialogue with Ajantha Subramanian's (2019) research on how caste structures the training of engineers at the elite Indian Institutes of Technology in India, many of whom work in IT and ITES in India as well as overseas.

   We are also indebted to Ramberg, who draws our attention to the par-allels between Dalit studies and queer theory in how both "denaturalize and resignify embodied stigma to mobilize forms of political and social transformation" (2016, 224). On the temporality of lag associated with

Dalits, see Ramberg (2016, 224). On Dalit-futurist feminism as manifest in contemporary science fiction, see Naik (2021).

10   In *Homo Sacer*, the condition of bare life or mere being arises when a human being is denied potentiality (Agamben 1998).

11   On "dialectical utopianism," cf. Harvey (2000).

References Cited

Ablett, Jonathan, Aadarsh Baijal, Eric Beinhocker, Anupam Bose, Diana Farell, Ulrich Gersch, Ezra Greenberg, Shishir Gupta, and Sumit Gupta. 2007. "The 'Bird of Gold': The Rise of India's Consumer Market." McKinsey Global Institute, May 1, 2007. https://www.mckinsey.com/featured-insights/asia-pacific/the-bird-of-gold.

Abraham, Janaki. 2014. "Contingent Caste Endogamy and Patriarchy: Lessons for Our Understanding of Caste." *Economic and Political Weekly* 49 (2): 56–65.

Abu-Lughod, Lila. 1986. *Veiled Sentiments: Honor and Poetry in a Bedouin Society.* Oakland: University of California Press.

Adams, Vincanne, Michelle Murphy, and Adele E. Clarke. 2009. "Anticipation: Technoscience, Life, Affect, Temporality." *Subjectivity* 28 (1): 246–65.

Adorno, Theodor. 1991. *The Culture Industry: Selected Essays on Mass Culture.* Edited by J. M. Bernstein. London: Routledge.

Agamben, Giorgio. 1998. *Homo Sacer: Sovereign Power and Bare Life.* Translated by Daniel Heller-Roazen. Stanford, CA: Stanford University Press.

Agamben, Giorgio. 2003. *Potentialities: Collected Essays in Philosophy.* Stanford, CA: Stanford University Press.

Agha, Asif. 2011. "Meet Mediatization." *Language and Communication* 31 (3): 163–70.

Ahmed, Sara. 2000. *The Cultural Politics of Emotion.* London: Routledge.

Ahmed, Sara. 2006. *Queer Phenomenology: Orientations, Objects, Others.* Durham, NC: Duke University Press.

Ahmed, Sara, Claudia Casteda, and Anne-Marie Fortier, eds. 2003. *Uprootings/Regroundings: Questions of Home and Migration*. London: Routledge.

Akhouri, Piyush Raj. 2022. "Covid Impact: How IT Outsourcing Is Booming Worldwide. *India Today*, March 17, 2022. https://www.indiatoday.in /business/story/covid-impact-how-it-outsourcing-is-booming-worldwide -1926464-2022-03-17.

Alim, H. Samy. 2009. "Translocal Style Communities: Hip Hop Youth as Cultural Theorists of Style, Language, and Globalization." *Pragmatics* 19 (1): 103–27.

Alim, H. Samy. 2016. "Who's Afraid of the Transracial Subject? Raciolinguistics and the Political Project of Transracialization." In *Raciolinguistics: How Language Shapes Our Ideas About Race*, edited by H. Samy Alim, John R. Rickford, and Arnetha F. Ball, 33–50. Oxford: Oxford University Press.

Alim, H. Samy, John R. Rickford, and Arnetha F. Ball, eds. 2016. *Raciolinguistics: How Language Shapes Our Ideas About Race*. Oxford: Oxford University Press.

Allison, Anne. 2009. *Nightwork: Sexuality, Pleasure, and Corporate Masculinity in a Tokyo Hostess Club*. Chicago: University of Chicago Press.

Allison, Anne. 2013. *Precarious Japan*. Durham, NC: Duke University Press.

Alsop, Thomas. 2020. "Cisco Employees by Region 2010–2019." Statista, March 2, 2020. https://www.statista.com/statistics/350519/cisco-employees-by-region/.

Althusser, Louis. (1970) 2006. "Ideology and Ideological State Apparatuses (Notes Towards an Investigation)." In *The Anthropology of the State: A Reader*, edited by Akhil Gupta and Aradhana Sharma, 86–98. Malden, MA: Blackwell Publishing.

Althusser, Louis. 1971. *Lenin and Philosophy, and Other Essays*. New York: Monthly Review Press.

Ameeriar, Lalaie. 2012. "The Sanitized Sensorium." *American Anthropologist* 114 (3): 509–20.

Ameeriar, Lalaie. 2015. "Pedagogies of Affect: Docility and Deference in the Making of Immigrant Women Subjects." *Signs: Journal of Women in Culture and Society* 40 (2): 467–86.

Amrute, Sareeta. 2016. *Encoding Race, Encoding Class: Indian IT Workers in Berlin*. Durham, NC: Duke University Press.

Ananthamurthy, U. R., and Chandan Gowda. 2019. *A Life in the World: U. R. Ananthamurthy in Conversation with Chandan Gowda*. Noida: HarperCollins.

Aneesh, A. 2006. *Virtual Migration: The Programming of Globalization*. Durham, NC: Duke University Press.

Aneesh, A. 2015. *Neutral Accent: How Language, Labor, and Life Become Global*. Durham, NC: Duke University Press.

Appadurai, Arjun. 1981. "The Past as a Scarce Resource." *Man* 16 (2): 201–19.

Appadurai, Arjun. 1986. "Is Homo Hierarchicus?" *American Ethnologist* 13 (4): 745–61.

Appadurai, Arjun. 1996. *Modernity at Large: Cultural Dimensions of Globalization*. Minneapolis: University of Minnesota Press.

Appadurai, Arjun. 2004. "The Capacity to Aspire: Culture and the Terms of Recognition." In *Culture and Public Action*, edited by Vijayendra Rao and Michael Walton, 59–84. Stanford, CA: Stanford University Press.

Appadurai, Arjun. 2013. *The Future as Cultural Fact: Essays on the Global Condition*. London: Verso.

Appel, Hannah. 2012. "Offshore Work: Oil, Modularity, and the How of Capitalism in Equatorial Guinea." *American Ethnologist* 39 (4):692–709. https://doi .org/10.1111/j.1548-1425.2012.01389.x.

Appel, Hannah. 2019. *The Licit Life of Capitalism: US Oil in Equatorial Guinea*. Durham, NC: Duke University Press.

Asad, Talal. 1986. "The Concept of Cultural Translation in British Social Anthropology." In *Writing Culture: The Poetics and Politics of Ethnography*, edited by James Clifford and George E. Marcus, 141–64. Berkeley: University of California Press.

Ashman, Sam. 2012. "Combined and Uneven Development." In *The Elgar Companion to Marxist Economics*, edited by Ben Fine, Alfredo Saad-Filho, and Marco Boffo, 60–65. Cheltenham, UK: Edward Elgar.

Assadi, Muzaffar. 2002. "Hindutva Policies in Coastal Region: Towards a Social Coalition." *Economic and Political Weekly* 37 (23): 2211–13.

Bajaj, Vikas. 2011. "Philippines Overtakes India as Hub of Call Centers," *New York Times*, November 25, 2011.

Balsamo, Anne. 1995. *Technologies of the Gendered Body: Reading Cyborg Women*. Durham, NC: Duke University Press.

Barriteau, Violet Eudine. 2014. "A (Re)Turn to Love: An Epistemic Conversation between Lorde's 'Uses of the Erotic' and Jonasdottir's 'Love Power.'" In *Love: A Question for Feminism in the Twenty-First Century*, edited by Anna G. Jonasdottir and Ann Ferguson, 77–96. London: Routledge.

Bassnett, Susan, and André Lefevere, eds. 1990. *Translation, History, and Culture*. New York: Pinter Publishers.

Bear, Laura, Karen Ho, Anna Lowenhaupt Tsing, and Sylvia Yanagisako. 2015. "Gens: A Feminist Manifesto for the Study of Capitalism." *Fieldsights*, March 30, 2015. https://culanth.org/fieldsights/gens-a-feminist-manifesto-for-the-study -of-capitalism.

Benjamin, Solomon. 2000. "Governance, Economic Settings and Poverty in Bangalore." *Environment and Urbanization* 12 (1): 35–56.

Benjamin, Solomon. 2010. "Manufacturing Neoliberalism: Lifestyling Indian Urbanity." In *Accumulation of Dispossession: Transformative Cities in the New Global Order*, edited by Swapna Banerjee-Guha, 92–124. New Delhi: SAGE Publications India.

Benjamin, Solomon, and R. Bhuvaneswari. 2006. "Urban Futures of Poor Groups in Chennai and Bangalore: How These Are Shaped by the Relationship between Parastatal and Local Bodies." In *Local Governance in India: Decentralization and Beyond*, edited by Niraja Gopal Jayal, Amit Prakash, and Pradeep K. Sharma. New Delhi: Oxford University Press.

Benjamin, Solomon, and R. Bhuvaneswari. 2001. *Democracy, Inclusive Governance and Poverty in Bangalore*. Birmingham, UK: International Development Department.

Benjamin, Walter. (1935) 1968. "The Work of Art in the Age of Mechanical Reproduction." In *Illuminations*, translated by Harry Zohn, 217–52. New York: Schocken Books.

Benjamin, Walter. (1982) 2002. *The Arcades Project*. Translated by Howard Eiland and Kevin McLaughlin. Cambridge, MA: Belknap Press of Harvard University Press.

Berardi, Franco "Bifo." 2009. *The Soul at Work: From Alienation to Autonomy*. Translated by Francesca Cadel and Giuseppina Mecchia. Los Angeles: Semiotext(e).

Berardi, Franco "Bifo." 2011. *After the Future*. Edited by Gary Genosko and Nicholas Thoburn. Stirling: AK Press.

Berardi, Franco "Bifo." 2012. *The Uprising: On Poetry and Finance*. Los Angeles: Semiotext(e).

Berardi, Franco "Bifo." 2013. "What Does Cognitariat Mean? Work, Desire and Depression." *Cultural Studies Review* 11(2): 57. https://doi.org/10.5130/csr.v11i2.3656.

Berardi, Franco "Bifo." 2019. *Futurability: The Age of Impotence and the Horizon of Possibility*. London: Verso.

Bergson, Henri. (1889) 2001. *Time and Free Will: An Essay on the Immediate Data of Consciousness*. Mineola, NY: Dover Publications.

Bergson, Henri. (1896) 1990. *Matter and Memory*. Translated by N. M Paul and W. S. Palmer. New York: Zone Books.

Berlant, Lauren. 1998. "Intimacy: A Special Issue." *Critical Inquiry* 24 (2): 281–88. https://www.jstor.org/stable/1344169.

Berlant, Lauren. 2011. *Cruel Optimism*. Durham, NC: Duke University Press.

Berlant, Lauren, and Michael Warner. 1998. "Sex in Public." *Critical Inquiry* 24 (2): 547–66. https://www.jstor.org/stable/1344178.

Berry, Chris, Fran Martin, and Audrey Yue. 2003. *Mobile Cultures: New Media in Queer Asia*. Durham, NC: Duke University Press.

Bharathi, Naveen, Deepak Malghan, Sumit Mishra, and Andaleeb Rahman. 2022. "Residential Segregation and Public Services in Urban India." *Urban Studies* 59 (14): 2912–32. https://doi.org/10.1177/00420980211072855.

Bhatt, Rakesh M. 2005. "Expert Discourses, Local Practices, and Hybridity: The Case of Indian Englishes." In *Reclaiming the Local in Language Policy and Practice*, edited by A. Suresh Canagarajah, 25–54. Mahwah, NJ: Lawrence Erlbaum.

Bhatt, Rakesh M. 2015. "Landmarks English as a Second Language: Pedagogy, Paradigms, and Politics." *Language and Language Teaching* 4 (2): 54–61.

Bhattacharya, Ananya. 2020. "Genpact's Response to Coronavirus Is a Lesson in What Not to Do during a Pandemic." *Quartz India*, March 25, 2020. https://qz.com/india/1824158/genpacts-insensitive-coronavirus-response-riles-indian-employees/.

Boris, Eileen, and Rhacel Salazar Parreñas. 2010. Introduction to *Intimate Labors: Cultures, Technologies, and the Politics of Care*, edited by Eileen Boris and Rhacel Salazar Parreñas, 1–12. Stanford, CA: Stanford University Press.

Bourdieu, Pierre. 1984. *Distinction: A Social Critique of the Judgment of Taste.* Translated by Richard Nice. Cambridge, MA: Harvard University Press.

Brenner, Robert, and Mark Glick. 1991. "The Regulation Approach: Theory and History." *New Left Review*, 1st ser., no. 188, 45–119. https://newleftreview.org/I/188/robert-brenner-mark-glick-the-regulation-approach-theory-and-history.

Brosius, Christiane. 2010. *India's Middle Class: New Forms of Urban Leisure, Consumption, and Prosperity*. London: Routledge.

Business Today. 2020. "Permanent 'Work From Home' for IT Employees Now Possible! Govt Relaxes Rules." November 6, 2020. https://www.businesstoday.in/technology/news/permanent-work-from-home-for-it-employees-now-possible-govt-relaxes-rules/story/421254.html.

Camiscioli, Elisa. 2013. "Women, Gender, Intimacy, and Empire." *Journal of Women's History* 25 (4): 138–48.

Campt, Tina. 2017. "Quiet Soundings: The Grammar of Black Futurity." In *Listening to Images*, 13–47. Durham, NC: Duke University Press.

Capers, Bennett. 2021. "Afrofuturism and the Law." *Critical Analysis of Law* 9 (1): 1–7.

Castells, Manuel. 2000. *The Rise of the Network Society: The Information Age— Economy, Society, and Culture, Vol. I*. 2nd ed. Oxford: Blackwell Publishing.

Chakrabarty, Dipesh. 2000. *Provincializing Europe: Postcolonial Thought and Historical Difference*. Princeton, NJ: Princeton University Press.

Chowdhury, Prem. 2004. "Caste Panchayats and the Policing of Marriage in Haryana: Kinship and Territorial Exogamy." *Contributions to Indian Sociology* 38 (1–2): 1–42.

Chowdhury, Prem. 2009. "'First Our Jobs Then Our Girls': The Dominant Caste Perceptions on the 'Rising' Dalits." *Modern Asian Studies* 43 (2): 437–79.

Choy, Catherine C. 2003. *Empire of Care: Nursing and Migration in Filipino American History*. Durham, NC: Duke University Press.

Chua, Beng Huat, ed. 2000. *Consumption in Asia: Lifestyle and Identities*. Abingdon, UK: Routledge.

Chua, Beng Huat. 2003. *Life Is Not Complete without Shopping: Consumption Culture in Singapore*. Singapore: NUS Press.

Chua, Jocelyn Lim. 2014. *In Pursuit of the Good Life: Aspiration and Suicide in Globalizing South India*. Berkeley: University of California Press.

Chuh, Kandice, and Karen Shimakawa, eds. 2001. *Orientations: Mapping Studies in Asian Diaspora*. Durham, NC: Duke University Press.

Chun, Jennifer Jihye. 2017. "Building Political Agency and Movement Leadership: The Grassroots Organizing Model of Asian Immigrant Women Advocates." In *Building Citizenship from Below: Precarity, Migration, and Agency*, edited by Marcel Paret and Shannon Gleeson, 103–19. New York: Routledge.

Chun, Jennifer Jihye. 2022. "Protesting Precarity: South Korean Workers and the Labor of Refusal." *Journal of Asian Studies* 81 (1): 107–18. https://doi.org/10 .1017/S0021911821001479.

Chun, Jennifer Jihye, and Rina Agarwala. 2016. "Global Labour Politics in Informal and Precarious Jobs." In *The SAGE Handbook of the Sociology of Work and Employment*, edited by Stephen Edgell, Heidi Gottfried, and Edward Granter, 634–50. London: SAGE.

Chun, Jennifer Jihye, and Cynthia Cranford. 2018. "Becoming Homecare Workers: Chinese Immigrant Women and the Changing Worlds of Work, Care, and Unionism." *Critical Sociology* 44 (7–8): 1013–27.

Ciotti, Manuela. 2010. "Futurity in Words: Low-Caste Women Political Activists' Self-Representation and Post-Dalit Scenarios in North India." *Contemporary South Asia* 18 (1): 43–56.

Clough, Patricia T. 2007. Introduction to *The Affective Turn: Theorizing the Social*, edited by Patricia T. Clough with Jean Halley, 1–33. Durham, NC: Duke University Press.

Clough, Patricia T. 2008. "The Affective Turn: Political Economy, Biomedia and Bodies." *Theory, Culture and Society* 25 (1): 1–22.

Constable, Nicole. 2003. *Romance on a Global Stage: Pen Pals, Virtual Ethnography, and "Mail Order" Marriages.* Berkeley: University of California Press. https:// www.jstor.org/stable/10.1525/j.ctt1pnr50.

Constable, Nicole. 2007. "Love at First Site? Visual Images and Virtual Encounters with Bodies." In *Love and Globalization: Transformations of Intimacy in the Contemporary World*, edited by Mark B. Padilla, Jennifer S. Hirsch, Miguel Muñoz-Laboy, Robert E. Sember, and Richard G. Parker, 252–70. Nashville, TN: Vanderbilt University Press.

Constable, Nicole. 2009. "The Commodification of Intimacy: Marriage, Sex, and Reproductive Labor." *Annual Review of Anthropology* 38 (1): 49–64. https://doi .org/10.1146/annurev.anthro.37.081407.085133.

Constable, Nicole. 2013. "Correspondence Marriages, Imagined Virtual Communities, and Countererotics on the Internet." In *Media, Erotics, and Transnational Asia*, edited by Purnima Mankekar and Louisa Schein, 111–38. Durham, NC: Duke University Press.

Cottom, Tressie McMillan. 2020. "Where Platform Capitalism and Racial Capitalism Meet: The Sociology of Race and Racism in the Digital Society." *Sociology of Race and Ethnicity* 6 (4): 441–49.

Credit Suisse. 2015. *Global Wealth Report.* Switzerland: Credit Suisse Research Institute.

Cresswell, Tim. 2010. "Towards a Politics of Mobility." *Environment and Planning D: Society and Space* 28 (1): 17–31.

CRN Team. 2020. "Surge of WFH Jobs in India and How It Impacts the IT Industry." *CRN India*, September 18, 2020. https://www.crn.in/news/surge-of-wfh -jobs-in-india-and-how-it-impacts-the-it-industry/.

Cross, Jamie. 2015. "The Economy of Anticipation: Hope, Infrastructure, and Economic Zones in South India." *Comparative Studies of South Asia, Africa and the Middle East* 35 (3): 424–37. https://doi.org/10.1215/1089201x-3426277.

Cupples, Julie, and Lee Thompson. 2010. "Heterotextuality and Digital Foreplay: Cell Phones and the Culture of Teenage Romance." *Feminist Media Studies* 10 (1): 1–17.

Cutts, Elmer H. 1953. "The Background of Macaulay's Minute." *American Historical Review* 58 (4): 824–53. https://doi.org/10.2307/1842459.

CXOtoday.com. 2022. "Pandemic and New Age Technologies Drive Rapid Expansion of BPOs in India." August 25, 2022. https://cxotoday.com/interviews/pandemic-new-age-technologies-drive-rapid-expansion-of-bpos-in-india/.

Daniel, E. Valentine. 1987. *Fluid Signs: Being a Person the Tamil Way.* Berkeley: University of California Press.

Das, Veena. 2006. *Life and Words: Violence and the Descent into the Ordinary.* Berkeley: University of California Press.

Datar, Chhaya. 1999. "Non-Brahmin Renderings of Feminism in Maharashtra: Is it a More Emancipatory Force?" *Economic and Political Weekly* 34 (41): 2964–68.

Dave, Sachin. 2020. "European Firms, Banks Take Outsourced Jobs Back Home Fearing Data Leaks amid Covid-19." *Economic Times*, August 11, 2020. https://economictimes.indiatimes.com/tech/ites/european-firms-banks-take-outsourced-jobs-back-home-fearing-data-leaks-amid-covid-19/articleshow/77465621.cms?from=mdr.

Davé, Shilpa S. 2013. *Indian Accents: Brown Voice and Racial Performance in American Television and Film.* Urbana: University of Illinois Press.

David, Gaby, and Carolina Cambre. 2016: *Screened Intimacies: Tinder and the Swipe Logic. Social Media + Society* 2 (2): 1–16.

Dávila, Arlene. 2016. *El Mall: The Spatial and Class Politics of Shopping Malls in Latin America.* Berkeley: University of California Press.

De, Aditi. 2008. *Multiple City.* New Delhi: Penguin India.

Deleuze, Gilles. (1968) 1995. *Difference and Repetition.* Translated by Paul Patton. New York: Columbia University Press.

Deleuze, Gilles. 1992. "Postscript on the Societies of Control." *October* 59 (Winter): 3–7. https://www.jstor.org/stable/778828.

Deleuze, Gilles. 1997. "Desire and Pleasure." In *Foucault and His Interlocutors,* edited by Arnold I. Davidson, 183–92. Chicago: University of Chicago Press.

Deleuze, Gilles and Félix Guattari. 1988. *A Thousand Plateaus.* London: Athlone.

Derrida, Jacques. (1993) 2006. *Specters of Marx: The State of the Debt, the Work of Mourning and the New International.* Translated by Peggy Kamuf. New York: Routledge.

Dery, John. 1994. "Black to the Future: Interviews with Samuel R. Delany, Greg Tate, and Tricia Rose." In *Flame Wars: The Discourse of Cyberculture,* edited by John Dery, 179–222. Durham, NC: Duke University Press.

Deshpande, Satish. 2013. "Caste and Castelessness: Towards a Biography of a General Category." *Economic and Political Weekly* 48 (15): 32–39.

Deutsche Welle (English edition). 2020. "Bangalore Riots: India's Tech City Sees Deadly Violence over Anti-Islam Facebook Post." August 13, 2020. https://www.pressreader.com/germany/deutsche-welle-english-edition/20200813/281973200010701.

Devika, J., Mary E. John, Kalpana Kannabiran, Samita Sen, and Padmini Swaminathan. "Sharmila Rege (1964–2013): Tribute to a Phule-Ambedkarite Feminist Welder." *Economic and Political Weekly* 48, no. 32 (2013): 22–25.

Dietrich, Gabrielle. 1992. *Reflections on the Women's Movement in India: Religion, Ecology, Development*. New Delhi: Horizon India.

Dubal, Veena. 2020. "Digital Piecework." *Dissent* 67 (4): 37–44.

Ducey, Ariel. 2007. "More Than a Job: Meaning, Affect and Training Health Care Workers." In *The Affective Turn: Theorizing the Social*, edited by Patricia T. Clough, Jean O. Halley, and M. Hardt, 187–208. Durham, NC: Duke University Press.

Dumont, Louis. 1981. *Homo Hierarchicus: The Caste System and Its Implications*. Chicago: University of Chicago Press.

Dyer-Witheford, Nick. 1999. *Cyber-Marx: Cycles and Circuits of Struggle in High-Technology Capitalism*. Urbana: University of Illinois Press.

Economic Times. 2021. "Indian IT-BPM Sector Saw Recovery in Revenue Growth at 7.9% in FY20: Economic Survey 2020–21." January 29, 2021. https://economictimes.indiatimes.com/tech/information-tech/indian-it-bpm-sector-saw-recovery-in-revenue-growth-at-7-9-in-fy20-economic-survey-2020–21/articleshow/80586683.cms?from=mdr.

Economist. 2018. "India's Missing Middle Class." January 11, 2018. www.economist.com/briefing/2018/01/11/indias-missing-middle-class.

Edelman, Lee. 2004. *No Future: Queer Theory and the Death Drive*. Durham, NC: Duke University Press.

Elias, Norbert. (1939) 1978. *The Civilizing Process, Vol 1: The History of Manners*. Translated by Edmund Jephcott. New York: Urizen Books.

Elwood, Sarah, and Agnieszka Leszczynski. 2018. "Feminist digital geographies." *Gender, Place and Culture* 25 (5): 629–44.

Emont, Jon. 2020. "Is That a Rooster on My Customer-Support Call? Yes, Blame Coronavirus." *Wall Street Journal*, May 14, 2020. https://www.wsj.com/articles/customer-support-call-animal-noises-rooster-coronavirus-11589465454.

Errighi, Lorenza, Charles Bodwell, and Sameer Khatiwada. 2016. "Business Process Outsourcing in the Philippines: Challenges for Decent Work." ILO Asia-Pacific Working Paper Series, December 14. https://www.ilo.org/publications/business-process-outsourcing-philippines-challenges-decent-work.

Everest Group. 2019. "Everest Group BPS Top 50." https://www.everestgrp.com/wp-content/uploads/2019/04/Everest-Group-BPS-Top-50-2019.pdf.

Faier, Lieba. 2007. "Filipina Migrants in Rural Japan and Their Professions of Love." *American Ethnologist* 34 (1): 148–62.

Fanon, Frantz. (1952) 2008. *Black Skin, White Masks*. New York: Grove.

Favero, Paolo. 2005. "India Dreams: Cultural Identity among Young Middle-Class Men in New Delhi." PhD diss., Stockholm University.

Ferguson, James, and Akhil Gupta. 2002. "Spatializing States: Toward an Ethnography of Neoliberal Governmentality." *American Ethnologist* 29 (4): 981–1002.

Fernandes, Leela. 2004. "The Politics of Forgetting: Class Politics, State Power and the Restructuring of Urban Space in India." *Urban Studies* 41 (12): 2415–30. https://doi.org/10.1080/00420980412331297609.

Fernandes, Leela. 2006. *India's New Middle Class: Democratic Politics in an Era of Economic Reform*. Minneapolis: University of Minnesota Press.

Fernandes, Leela. 2009. "The Political Economy of Lifestyle: Consumption, India's New Middle Class, and State-Led Development." In *The New Middle Classes: Globalizing Lifestyles, Consumerism, and Environmental Concern*, edited by Hellmuth Lange and Lars Meir, 219–34. New York: Springer.

Fernandes, Leela, and Patrick Heller. 2006. "Hegemonic Aspirations: New Middle Class Politics and India's Democracy in Comparative Perspective." *Critical Asian Studies* 38 (4): 495–522.

Fersht, Phil, and Jamie Snowdon. 2016. "Making the Leap from Effective to Strategic BPM." HFS Research, September 19, 2016. Accessed August 8, 2024. https://www.hfsresearch.com/research/making-leap-effective-strategic-bpm/.

Ford, Martin. 2015. *Rise of the Robots: Technology and the Threat of a Jobless Future*. New York: Basic Books.

Forrester, Katrina, and Moira Weigel. 2020. "Bodies on the Line." *Dissent*. https://www.dissentmagazine.org/article/bodies-on-the-line.

Foucault, Michel. (1975) 1977. *Discipline and Punish: The Birth of the Prison*. Translated by Alan Sheridan. New York: Pantheon.

Frank, Andre Gunder. 1998. *ReOrient: Global Economy in the Asian Age*. Berkeley: University of California Press.

Franken, Paul, and Derk-Jan Dijk. 2009. "Circadian Clock Genes and Sleep Homeostasis." *European Journal of Neuroscience* 29 (9): 1820–29. https://doi.org/10.1111/j.1460-9568.2009.06723.x.

Frayer, Lauren, and Sushmita Pathak. 2020. "India's Lockdown Puts Strain on Call Centers." NPR, April 24, 2020. https://www.npr.org/2020/04/24/841698386/indias-lockdown-puts-strain-on-call-centers.

Frazier, Camille. 2019. "Urban Heat: Rising Temperatures as Critique in India's Air-Conditioned City." *City and Society* 31 (3): 441–61.

Freeman, Carla. 2000. *High Tech and High Heels in the Global Economy: Women, Work, and Pink-Collar Identities in the Caribbean*. Durham, NC: Duke University Press.

Freeman, Carla. 2014. *Entrepreneurial Selves: Neoliberal Respectability and the Making of a Caribbean Middle Class*. Durham, NC: Duke University Press.

Freeman, Carla. 2020. "Feeling Neoliberal." *Feminist Anthropology* 1 (1): 71–88. https://doi.org/10.1002/fea2.12010.

Friedman, Thomas L. 2005. *The World Is Flat: A Brief History of the Twenty-First Century*. New York: Farrar, Straus and Giroux.

Friginal, Eric. 2007. "Outsourced Call Centers and English in the Philippines." *World Englishes* 26 (3): 331–45. https://doi.org/10.1111/j.1467–971X.2007.00512.x.

Fuchs, Christian. 2019. *Rereading Marx in the Age of Digital Capitalism*. London: Pluto.

Fuchs, Christian, and Sebastian Sevignani. 2013. "What is Digital Labour? What is Digital Work? What's their Difference? And Why Do These Questions Matter for Understanding Social Media?" *TripleC* 11 (2): 237–93.

Fuller, Chris, and Haripriya Narasimhan. 2007. "Information Technology Professionals and the New-Rich Middle Class in Chennai." *Modern Asian Studies* 41 (1): 121–50.

Fuller, Chris, and Haripriya Narasimhan. 2008. "From Landlords to Software Engineers: Migration and Urbanization among Tamil Brahmans." *Comparative Studies in Society and History* 50 (1): 170–96.

Gajarawala, Toral. 2020. "The Postman and the Tramp: Cynicism, Commitment, and the Aesthetics of Subaltern Futurity." *Cultural Critique*, no. 108, 40–68.

Gal, Susan. 2015. "Politics of Translation." *Annual Review of Anthropology* 44 (1): 225–40.

Gatade, Subhash. 2014. "Pawns In, Patrons Still Out: Understanding the Phenomenon of Hindutva Terror." *Economic and Political Weekly* 49 (13): 36–43.

Geetha, V. 2007. "History and the Caste Imagination: Some Notes on Contemporary Tamil Fiction." In *History and Imagination: Tamil Culture in Global Context*, edited by R. Cheran, Darshan Ambalavanar, and Chelva Kanayanagakam. Toronto, ON: TSAR Publications.

GEP. 2020. "The Impact of COVID-19 on the BPO Industry." May 18, 2020. https://www.gep.com/blog/mind/the-impact-of-covid-19-on-the-bpo-industry.

Gerschenkron, Alexander. 1962. *Economic Backwardness in Historical Perspective*. Cambridge, MA: Harvard University Press.

Ghosh, Amitav. 2016. *The Great Derangement: Climate Change and the Unthinkable*. Chicago: University of Chicago Press.

Ghosh, Amitav, and Dipesh Chakrabarty. 2002. "A Correspondence on Provincializing Europe." *Radical History Review* 2002 (83): 146–72.

Gibson-Graham, Julie Katherine. 1996. *The End of Capitalism (as We Knew It): A Feminist Critique of Political Economy*. Oxford: Blackwell.

Giddens, Anthony. 1992. *The Transformation of Intimacy: Sexuality, Love and Eroticism in Modern Societies*. Stanford, CA: Stanford University Press.

Glenn, Evelyn Nakano. 1985. "Racial Ethnic Women's Labor: The Intersection of Race, Gender and Class Oppression." *Signs: Journal of Women in Culture and Society* 17 (3): 86–108.

Glenn, Evelyn Nakano. 1992. "From Servitude to Service Work: Historical Continuities in the Racial Division of Paid Reproductive Labor." *Signs: Journal of Women in Culture and Society* 18 (1):1–43.

Glenn, Evelyn Nakano. 1999. "The Social Construction and Institutionalization of Gender and Race." In *Revisioning Gender*, edited by Myra Marx Ferree, Judith Lorber, and Beth B. Hess, 3–43. Walnut Creek, CA: AltaMira.

Glenn, Evelyn Nakano. 2012. *Forced to Care: Coercion and Caregiving in America.* Cambridge, MA: Harvard University Press.

Goldman, Michael. 2011a. "Speculating on the Next World City." In *Worlding Cities: Experiments and the Art of Being Global*, edited by Ananya Roy and Aihwa Ong, 229–58. Malden, MA: Wiley-Blackwell.

Goldman, Michael. 2011b. "Speculative Urbanism and the Making of the Next World City." *International Journal of Urban and Regional Research* 35 (3): 555–81.

Gooptu, Nandini. 2009. "Neoliberal Subjectivity, Enterprise Culture and New Workplaces: Organised Retail and Shopping Malls in India." *Economic and Political Weekly* 44 (22): 45–54.

Gooptu, Nandini, ed. 2013a. *Enterprise Culture in Neoliberal India: Studies in Youth, Class, Work and Media.* London: Routledge.

Gooptu, Nandini. 2013b. "Servile Sentinels of the City: Private Security Guards, Organized Informality, and Labour in Interactive Services in Globalized India." *International Review of Social History* 58 (1): 9–38.

Gordon, Avery. 2011. "Some Thoughts on Haunting and Futurity." *Borderlands* 10 (2): 1–21.

Gottfried, Heidi, and Jennifer Jihye Chun. 2018. "Care Work in Transition: Transnational Circuits of Gender, Migration, and Care." *Critical Sociology* 44 (7–8): 997–1012.

Government of India, Ministry of Home Affairs, Office of the Registrar General and Census Commissioner. 2011. "Census Tables." Accessed July 25, 2024. https://censusindia.gov.in/census.website/data/census-tables.

Govinda, Radhika. 2022. "Interrogating Intersectionality: Dalit Women, Western Classrooms, and the Politics of Feminist Knowledge Production." *Journal of International Women's Studies* 23 (2): 72–86.

Goyal, Malini, and Raj Chengappa. 2002. "India Becomes World Leader in Call Center Business; BPO Emerges as New Sunshine Sector." *India Today*, November 18, 2002. https://www.indiatoday.in/magazine/cover-story/story/20021118 -india-becomes-world-leader-in-call-centre-business-bpo-emerges-as-new -sunshine-sector-759851-2012-03-06.

Grand View Research. 2022. "Business Process Outsourcing Market Size, Share and Trends Analysis Report by Service Type (Customer Services, Finance and Accounting), by Outsourcing Type (Onshore, Offshore), by Deployment, by End-Use, by Region, and Segment Forecasts, 2024–2030." Accessed July 26, 2024. https://www.grandviewresearch.com/industry-analysis/business-process -outsourcing-bpo-market#.

Gregg, Melissa. 2010. "On Friday Night Drinks: Workplace Affects in the Age of the Cubicle." In *The Affect Theory Reader*, edited by Melissa Gregg, Gregory J. Seigworth, and Sara Ahmed, 250–68. Durham, NC: Duke University Press.

Gregg, Melissa. 2011. *Work's Intimacy*. Cambridge: Polity.

Grewal, Inderpal. 1996. *Home and Harem: Nation, Gender, Empire and the Cultures of Travel*. Durham, NC: Duke University Press.

Grewal, Inderpal. 2005. *Transnational America: Feminisms, Diasporas, Neoliberalisms*. Durham, NC: Duke University Press.

Grewal, Inderpal, and Caren Kaplan. 1994. *Scattered Hegemonies: Postmodernity and Transnational Feminist Practices*. Minneapolis: University of Minnesota Press.

Grosz, Elizabeth. 2018. *The Incorporeal: Ontology, Ethics, and the Limits of Materialism*. New York: Columbia University Press.

Gupta, Akhil. 1998. *Postcolonial Developments: Agriculture in the Making of Modern India*. Durham, NC: Duke University Press.

Gupta, Akhil. 2012. *Red Tape: Bureaucracy, Structural Violence, and Poverty in India*. Durham, NC: Duke University Press.

Gupta, Akhil, and James Ferguson. 1992. "Beyond 'Culture': Space, Identity, and the Politics of Difference." *Cultural Anthropology* 7 (1): 6–23. https://doi.org /10.1525/can.1992.7.1.02a00020.

Gupta, Akhil, and Aradhana Sharma. 2006. "Globalization and Postcolonial States." *Current Anthropology* 47 (2): 277–307. https://doi.org/10.1086/499549.

Gupta, Akhil, and Aradhana Sharma, eds. 2008. *The Anthropology of the State: A Reader*. Malden, MA: Blackwell.

Gupta, Hemangini, and Kaveri Medappa. 2020. "Nostalgia as Affective Landscape: Negotiating Displacement in the 'World City.'" *Antipode* 52 (6): 1688–1709.

Gupta, Kristina. 2015. "Compulsory Sexuality: Evaluating an Emerging Concept." *Signs: Journal of Women in Culture and Society* 41 (1): 131–54.

Guru, Gopal. 1998. "The Politics of Naming." *Seminar*, no. 471, November 1998. https://www.india-seminar.com/2018/710/710_gopal_guru.htm.

Guru, Gopal. 2005. *Atrophy in Dalit Politics*. Mumbai: Vikas Adhyayan Kendra.

Guru, Gopal. 2017. "Dalit Middle Class Hangs in the Air." In *Middle Class Values in India and Western Europe*, edited by Imtiaz Ahmad and Helmut Reifeld, 141–51. London: Routledge.

Guru, Gopal. 2019. "Archaeology of Untouchability." In *The Cracked Mirror: An Indian Debate on Experience and Theory*, edited by Gopal Guru and Sundar Sarukkai, 200–222. New Delhi: Routledge.

Hage, Ghassan. 2009. "Waiting Out the Crisis: On Stuckedness and Governmentality." In *Waiting*, edited by Ghassan Hage. Melbourne: University of Melbourne Press.

Haraway, Donna. 1985. "A Cyborg Manifesto: Science, Technology, and Socialist-Feminism in the Late 20th Century." *Socialist Review*, no. 80, 65–108.

Haraway, Donna. 1991. *Simians, Cyborgs, and Women: The Reinvention of Nature*. New York: Routledge.

Hardt, Michael. 1999. "Affective Labor." *boundary 2* 26 (2): 89–100. http://www
.jstor.org/stable/303793.

Hardt, Michael, and Antonio Negri. 2005. *Multitude: War and Democracy in the
Age of Empire*. New York: Penguin.

Hartman, Saidiya. 1997. *Scenes of Subjection: Terror, Slavery, and Self-Making in
Nineteenth-Century America*. New York: Columbia University Press.

Harvey, David. 1991. *The Condition of Postmodernity: An Enquiry into the Origins
of Cultural Change*. Cambridge: Blackwell.

Harvey, David. 2000. *Spaces of Hope*. Edinburgh: Edinburgh University Press.

Harvey, David. 2007. *A Brief History of Neoliberalism*. New York: Oxford University Press.

Harvey, Penny, and Hannah Knox. 2015. *Roads: An Anthropology of Infrastructure
and Expertise*. Ithaca, NY: Cornell University Press.

Haug, Wolfgang F. 1986. *Critique of Commodity Aesthetics: Appearance, Sexuality
and Advertising in Capitalist Society*. Translated by Robert Bock. Minneapolis:
University of Minnesota Press.

Heitzman, James. 2004. *Network City: Planning the Information Society in Bangalore*. New Delhi: Oxford University Press.

Hickey, Amber. 2019. "Rupturing Settler Time: Visual Culture and Geographies
of Indigenous Futurity. *World Art* 9 (2): 163–80.

The Hindu. 2009. "We'll Not Spare Dating Couples on Valentine's Day: Muthalik."
February 6, 2009. https://web.archive.org/web/20120308160858/http://www
.hindu.com/2009/02/06/stories/2009020657590100.htm.

Hochschild, Arlie R. 2012. *The Managed Heart: Commercialization of Human Feeling*. Berkeley: University of California Press.

Hollan, Douglas. 2012. "Emerging Issues in the Cross-Cultural Study of Empathy." *Emotion Review* 4 (1): 70–78. https://doi.org/10.1177/1754073911421376.

Holmes, Mary. 2004. "An Equal Distance? Individualisation, Gender and Intimacy
in Distance Relationships." *Sociological Review* 52 (2): 180–200.

Hong, Grace Kyungwon, and Roderick A. Ferguson, eds. 2011. *Strange Affinities:
The Gender and Sexual Politics of Comparative Racialization*. Durham, NC:
Duke University Press.

hooks, bell. 1984. *Ain't I a Woman: Black Women and Feminism*. New York: Pluto.

hooks, bell. 1986. "Sisterhood: Political Solidarity Between Women." *Feminist Review*, no. 23, 125–38.

Horkheimer, Max, and Theodor Adorno. (1947) 2002. *Dialectic of Enlightenment:
Philosophical Fragments*. Edited by Gunzelin Schmid Noerr, translated by Edmund Jephcott. Stanford, CA: Stanford University Press.

Hsu, Funie. 2015. "The Coloniality of Neoliberal English: The Enduring Structures
of American Colonial English Instruction in the Philippines and Puerto Rico."
L2 Journal 7 (3): 123–45. http://dx.doi.org/10.5070/L27323549.

HT Correspondent. 2010. "Cabbie Who Raped and Killed Pratibha Escapes
Death." *Hindustan Times*, October 8, 2010. https://www.hindustantimes

.com/india/cabbie-who-raped-and-killed-pratibha-escapes-death/story
-MDyvrMBZHhW6C1q1eHzt1H.html.

Hune, Shirley. 1989. "Expanding the International Dimension of Asian-American Studies." *Amerasia Journal* 15 (2): xix–xxiv.

IANS. 2018. "Indian BPM industry largest in the world" *Business Standard*, October 4, 2018. https://www.business-standard.com/article/news-ians/indian-bpm -industry-largest-in-the-world-nasscom-118100400881_1.html.

Indian Panorama. 2022. "Budget 2022: India's Job Crisis Leading to a 'Nowhere Generation.'" February 5, 2022. https://www.theindianpanorama.news/opinion /perspective/budget-2022-indias-job-crisis-leading-to-a-nowhere-generation/.

Jayadeva, Sazana. 2015. "Overcoming the English Handicap: Seeking English in Bangalore, India." PhD diss., University of Cambridge.

Jayadeva, Sazana. 2018. "'Below English Line': An Ethnographic Exploration of Class and the English Language in Post-Liberalization India." *Modern Asian Studies* 52 (2): 576–608. https://doi.org/10.1017/s0026749x16000639.

Jeffrey, Craig. 2010. *Timepass: Youth, Class, and the Politics of Waiting in India.* Stanford, CA: Stanford University Press.

Jenkins, Henry. 2006. *Convergence Culture: Where Old and New Media Collide.* New York: New York University Press.

John, Sujit, and Mini Joseph Tejaswi. 2006. "Sex and BPO: Crackdown On." *Times of India*, October 8, 2006. https://timesofindia.indiatimes.com/india/Sex-BPO -Crackdown-on/articleshow/2116438.cms.

Jyothirmai, D., and K. Sree Ramesh. 2017. "African American Womanism Speaks to Dalit Feminism: Special Reference to Telugu Literature." *Roopkatha Journal on Interdisciplinary Studies in Humanities* 9 (1): 140–50.

Kachru, Braj B. 1965. "The *Indianness* in Indian English." *Word* 21 (3): 391–410. https://doi.org/10.1080/00437956.1965.11435436.

Kachru, Braj B. 1996. "World Englishes: Agony and Ecstasy." *Journal of Aesthetic Education* 30 (2): 135–55. https://doi.org/10.2307/3333196.

Kalyanaraman, Jananie. 2021. "Window Seats: Making Connection through Transport and Mobility in Bengaluru, India." PhD diss., University of California, Los Angeles.

Kang, Milliann. 2010. *The Managed Hand: Race, Gender, and the Body in Beauty Service Work.* Berkeley: University of California Press.

Kanjilal, Sucharita. 2023. "The Digital Life of Caste: Affect, Synesthesia, and the Social Body Online." *Feminist Media Studies*, July 2023, 1–16. https://doi.org /10.1080/14680777.2023.2229053.

Kannan, P. V. 2020. "Customer Service Continuity and Lessons Learned during the COVID-19 Pandemic." *[24]7.ai*, April 10, 2020. https://www.247.ai /blogs/customer-service-continuity-and-lessons-learned-during-covid-19 -pandemic.

Kaplan, Caren. 1996. *Questions of Travel: Postmodern Discourses of Displacement.* Durham, NC: Duke University Press.

Kaplan, Caren. 2002. "Transporting the Subject: Technologies of Mobility and Location in an Era of Globalization." *Publications of the Modern Language Association of America* 117 (1): 32–42. https://doi.org/10.1632/003081202x63492.

Kaplan, Caren. 2003. "Transporting the Subject: Technologies of Mobility and Location in an Era of Globalization." In *Uprootings/Regroundings: Questions of Home and Migration*, edited by Sara Ahmed, Claudia Castaneda, Anne-Marie Fortier, and Mimi Sheller, 207–24. London: Berg.

Kapur, Devesh, Neelanjan Sircar, and Milan Vaishnav. 2017. "The Importance of Being Middle Class in India." In *The New Middle Class in India and Brazil*, edited by Dawid Danilo Bartelt and Axel Harneit-Sievers, 39–58. New Delhi: Academic Foundation.

Karlsson, Bengt G., and Dolly Kikon. 2017. "Wayfinding: Indigenous Migrants in the Service Sector of Metropolitan India." *South Asia: Journal of South Asian Studies* 40 (3): 447–62. https://doi.org/10.1080/00856401.2017.1319145.

Kaur, Ravinder. 2012. "Nation's Two Bodies: Rethinking the Idea of 'New' India and Its Other." In *Interrogating India's Modernity: Democracy, Identity, and Citizenship*, edited by Surinder Jodhka, 221–42. New Delhi: Oxford University Press.

Kaviraj, Sudipta. 1997. "Filth and the Public Sphere: Concepts and Practices about Space in Calcutta." *Public Culture* 10 (1): 83–113.

Keeling, Kara. 2019. *Queer Times, Black Futures*. Durham, NC: Duke University Press.

Kelley, Robin D. G. 2017. "What Did Cedric Robinson Mean by Racial Capitalism?" *Boston Review*, January 12, 2017. https://www.bostonreview.net/articles/robin-d-g-kelley-introduction-race-capitalism-justice/.

Kelley, Robin D. G. 2020. "'Western Civilization Is Neither': Black Studies' Epistemic Revolution." *Black Scholar* 50 (3): 4–10.

Klinke, Ian. 2012. "Chronopolitics: A Conceptual Matrix." *Progress in Human Geography* 37 (5): 673–90.

Kochhar, Rakesh. 2021. "In the Pandemic, India's Middle Class Shrinks and Poverty Spreads While China Sees Smaller Changes." Pew Research Center, March 18, 2021. https://www.pewresearch.org/fact-tank/2021/03/18/in-the-pandemic-indias-middle-class-shrinks-and-poverty-spreads-while-china-sees-smaller-changes/.

Koselleck, Reinhart. 2004. *Futures Past: On the Semantics of Historical Time*. New York: Columbia University Press.

Krishnan, Sandhya, and Neeraj Hatekar. 2017. "Rise of the New Middle Class in India and Its Changing Structure." *Economic and Political Weekly* 52 (22): 40–8.

Kulkarni, Pragati. 2014. "Reconstructing Dalit Feminist Standpoint Theory: Looking at Sharmila Rege's Work'" August 27, 2014. https://www.academia.edu/9914284/Reconstructing_Dalit_Feminist_Standpoint_Theory_Looking_at_Sharmila_Reges_work?auto=download.

Kumar, Gudipati Rajendera. 2017. "An Analysis on the Role of India's Informal Economy." *The Hans India*, July 14, 2017. https://www.thehansindia.com

/posts/index/Hans/2017–07–14/An-analysis-on-the-role-of-Indias-informal
-economy/312388?infinitescroll=1.

Kuntsman, Adi. 2004. "Cyberethnography as Home-Work." *Anthropology Matters* 6 (2): 1–10.

Lazzarato, Maurizio. 2007. "Machines to Crystallize Time: Bergson." *Theory, Culture and Society* 24 (6): 93–122. https://doi.org/10.1177/0263276407078714.

Lazzarato, Maurizio. 2014. *Signs and Machines: Capitalism and the Production of Subjectivity.* Translated by Joshua David Jordan. Los Angeles: Semiotext(e).

Lee, Min Joo. 2020. "Touring the Land of Romance: Transnational Korean Television Drama Consumption from Online Desires to Offline Intimacy." *Journal of Tourism and Cultural Change* 18 (1): 67–80. https://doi.org/10.1080/14766825.2020.1707467.

Lee, Rachel C., and Sau-ling Cynthia Wong, eds. 2013. *Asian America.Net: Ethnicity Nationalism and Cyberspace.* New York: Routledge.

Lenin, Vladimir Il'ich. (1917) 1939. *Imperialism: The Highest Stage of Capitalism.* New York: International Publishers.

Leonard, Karen. 1992. *Making Ethnic Choices: California's Punjabi Mexicans.* Philadelphia: Temple University Press.

Lockwood, Jane. 2012. "Are We Getting the Right People for the Job? A Study of English Language Recruitment Assessment Practices in the Business Processing Outsourcing Sector: India and the Philippines." *Journal of Business Communication* 49 (2): 107–27. https://doi.org/10.1177/0021943612436975.

Lorde, Audre. 1984. *Sister Outsider: Essays and Speeches.* Berkeley, CA: Crossing Press.

Lorde, Audre. 1993. "The Uses of the Erotic: The Erotic as Power." In *The Lesbian and Gay Studies Reader,* edited by Henry Abelove, Michèle Aina Barale, and David M. Halperin, 339–43. New York: Routledge.

Lowe, Lisa. 1996. *Immigrant Acts: On Asian American Cultural Politics.* Durham, NC: Duke University Press.

Lowe, Lisa. 2001. "Epistemological Shifts: National Ontology and the New Asian Immigrant." In *Orientations: Mapping Studies in the Asian Diaspora,* edited by Kandice Chuh and Karen Shimakawa, 267–76. Durham, NC: Duke University Press.

Lowe, Lisa. 2012. "Reckoning Nation and Empire: Asian American Critique." In *A Concise Companion to Asian American Studies,* edited by John Carlos Rowe, 229–44. Hoboken, NJ: Wiley-Blackwell.

Lowe, Lisa. 2015. *The Intimacies of Four Continents.* Durham, NC: Duke University Press.

Lutz, Catherine. 1986. "Emotion, Thought, and Estrangement: Emotion as a Cultural Category." *Cultural Anthropology* 1 (3): 287–309. https://doi.org/10.1525/can.1986.1.3.02a00020.

Lutz, Catherine, and Lila Abu-Lughod, eds. 1990. *Language and the Politics of Emotion.* Cambridge: Cambridge University Press.

Luxemburg, Rosa. (1913) 2003. *The Accumulation of Capital*. Translated by Agnes Schwarzschild. London: Routledge.

Macaulay, Thomas B. (1835) 1979. *Macaulay's Speeches: A Selection*. New York: AMS Press.

Mahmood, Saba. 2011. *Politics of Piety: The Islamic Revival and the Feminist Subject*. Princeton, NJ: Princeton University Press.

Malik, Bismah. 2020. "Malware Attacks Threaten Companies as Hybrid Workspace Model Gains Prominence." *New Indian Express*, November 15, 2020. https://www.newindianexpress.com/business/2020/nov/15/malware-attacks -threaten-companies-as-hybrid-workspace-model-gains-prominence -2223772.html.

Mani, Lata. 2022. *Myriad Intimacies*. Durham, NC: Duke University Press.

Mankekar, Purnima. 1999. *Screening Culture, Viewing Politics: An Ethnography of Television, Womanhood, and Nation in Postcolonial India*. Durham, NC: Duke University Press.

Mankekar, Purnima. 2003. "Off-Centre: Feminism and South Asian Studies in the Diaspora." In *At Home in Diaspora: South Asian Scholars and the West*, edited by Jackie Assayag, Vironique Binio, and Véronique Bénéï, 52–65. Bloomington: Indiana University Press.

Mankekar, Purnima. 2004. "Dangerous Desires: Television and Erotics in Late Twentieth-Century India." *Journal of Asian Studies* 63 (2): 403–31.

Mankekar, Purnima. 2012. "Television and Embodiment: A Speculative Essay." *South Asian History and Culture* 3 (4): 603–13.

Mankekar, Purnima. 2013. "'We Are Like This Only:' Aspiration, Jugaad, and Love in Enterprise Culture." In *Enterprise Culture in Neoliberal India: Studies in Youth, Class, Work and Media*, edited by Nandini Gooptu, 27–41. London: Routledge.

Mankekar, Purnima. 2015. *Unsettling India: Affect, Temporality, Transnationality*. Durham, NC: Duke University Press.

Mankekar, Purnima. 2021a. "'Love Jihad,' Digital Affect, and Feminist Critique." *Feminist Media Studies* 21 (4): 697–701.

Mankekar, Purnima. 2021b. "Mobile Love: Moral Panics, Erotics and Affect." In *The Routledge Companion to Romantic Love*, edited by Ann Brooks, 80–95. London: Routledge.

Mankekar, Purnima, and Akhil Gupta. 2016. "Intimate Encounters: Affective Labor in Call Centers." *Positions* 24 (1): 17–43. https://doi.org/10.1215 /10679847-3320029.

Mankekar, Purnima, and Akhil Gupta. 2017. "Future Tense: Capital, Labor, and Technology in a Service Industry." *HAU: Journal of Ethnographic Theory* 7 (3): 67–87.

Mankekar, Purnima, and Akhil Gupta. 2023. "Affective Sovereignties: Mobility, Emplacement, Potentiality." In *Sovereignty Unhinged: An Illustrated Primer for the Study of Present Intensities, Disavowals, and Temporal Derangements*, edited by Deborah A. Thomas and Joseph Masco, 113–138. Durham, NC: Duke University Press.

Mankekar, Purnima, and Sucharita Kanjilal. 2022. "Over-the-Top: Online Media and the Transnational Travels of Caste." In *The Routledge Companion to Caste and Cinema in India*, edited by Joshil K. Abraham and Judith Misrahi-Barak, 117–31. London: Routledge. https://doi.org/10.4324/9781003343578.

Mankekar, Purnima, and Louisa Schein. 2013. "Mediation and Transmediations: Erotics, Sociality, and 'Asia.'" In *Media, Erotics, and Transnational Asia*, edited by Purnima Mankekar and Louisa Schein, 1–32. Durham, NC: Duke University Press.

Manorama, Ruth. 1992. "Dalit Women: Downtrodden among the Downtrodden." In *Dalit Solidarity*, edited by Bhagwan Das and James Massey, 165–76. New Delhi: SPG Publications.

Martin, Emily. 2001. *The Woman in the Body: A Cultural Analysis of Reproduction*. New York: Beacon.

Marx, Karl. (1844) 1978. "Economic and Philosophic Manuscripts of 1844." In *The Marx-Engels Reader*, 2nd ed., edited by Robert C. Tucker. New York: W. W. Norton.

Marx, Karl. (1939) 1973. *Grundrisse: Foundations of the Critique of Political Economy*. Translated by Martin Nicolaus. New York: Vintage.

Marx, Karl, and Friedrich Engels. (1848) 1967. *The Communist Manifesto*. Translated by Samuel Moore, introduction by A. J. P. Taylor. Harmondsworth, UK: Penguin Books.

Massey, Doreen. 1991. "A Global Sense of Place." *Marxism Today* 35 (6): 24–29.

Massey, Doreen. 1994. *Space, Place, and Gender*. Minneapolis: University of Minnesota Press.

Massumi, Brian. 2002. *Parables for the Virtual: Movement, Affect, Sensation*. Durham, NC: Duke University Press.

Mathur, Nita. 2010. "Shopping Malls, Credit Cards and Global Brands: Consumer Culture and Lifestyle of India's New Middle Class." *South Asia Research* 30 (3): 211–31.

Mazzarella, William. 2005. "Indian Middle Class." In *South Asia Keywords*, edited by Rachel Dwyer. Online encyclopedia, SOAS. Accessed August 6, 2024. https://d3qioqp55mx5f5.cloudfront.net/anthrolpology/docs/mazz_middleclass.pdf.

Mehta, Suketu. 2004. *Maximum City: Bombay Lost and Found*. New Delhi: Penguin.

Melamed, Jodi. 2011. *Represent and Destroy: Rationalizing Violence in the New Racial Capitalism*. Minneapolis: University of Minnesota Press.

Melamed, Jodi. 2015. "Racial Capitalism." *Critical Ethnic Studies* 1 (1): 76–85.

Melbin, Murray. 1987. *Night As Frontier: Colonizing the World After Dark*. New York: Free Press.

Mendieta, Eduardo. 2020. "Toward a Decolonial Feminist Imaginary: Decolonizing Futurity." *Critical Philosophy of Race* 8 (1–2): 237–64.

Menon, Jisha. 2021. *Brutal Beauty: Aesthetics and Aspiration in Urban India*. Evanston, IL: Northwestern University Press.

Menon, Nivedita. 2019. "Marxism, Feminism, and Caste in Contemporary India." In *Racism after Apartheid: Challenges for Marxism and Anti-Racism*, edited by Vishwas Satgar, 137–155. Johannesburg: Wits University Press.

Meyer, Christian, and Nancy Birdsall. 2012. "New Estimates of India's Middle Class." CGD Note, Center for Global Development, Washington, DC. Accessed August 6, 2024. https://www.cgdev.org/sites/default/files/archive/doc/2013 _MiddleClassIndia_TechnicalNote_CGDNote.pdf.

Miles, Sam. 2017. "Sex in the Digital City: Location-Based Dating Apps and Queer Urban Life." *Gender, Place and Culture* 24 (11): 1595–1610.

Miller, Daniel. 1987. *Material Culture and Mass Consumption*. Hoboken, NJ: Blackwell.

Miller, Daniel. 1995. "Consumption and Commodities." *Annual Review of Anthropology* 24:141–61. https://doi.org/10.1146/annurev.an.24.100195.001041.

Mirchandani, Kiran. 2005. "Gender Eclipsed? Racial Hierarchies in Transnational Call Centres." *Social Justice* 32 (4): 105–19.

Mirchandani, Kiran. 2012. *Phone Clones: Authenticity Work in the Transnational Service Economy*. Ithaca, NY: Cornell University Press.

Mondal, Sudipto. 2015. "Spike in Communal Tension Touches Karnataka's Cosmopolitan Bengaluru." *Hindustan Times*, December 30, 2015. https://www .hindustantimes.com/india/spike-in-communal-tensions-touch-karnataka-s -cosmopolitan-bengaluru/story-VDYasR2DPi1XHVaH5b2hKI.html.

Moon, Meenakshi, and Urmila Pawar. 2008. *We Also Made History: Women in the Ambedkarite Movement*. New Delhi: Zubaan.

Moraga, Cherríe, and Gloria Anzaldúa. 1983. *This Bridge Called My Back: Writings by Radical Women of Color*. New York: Kitchen Table.

Morris, Meaghan. 1993. "Things to Do with Shopping Centres." In *The Cultural Studies Reader*, edited by Simon During, 295–319. New York: Routledge.

Mosse, David. 2020. "The Modernity of Caste and the Market Economy." *Modern Asian Studies* 54 (4): 1225–71.

Muehlebach, Andrea. 2011. "On Affective Labor in Post-Fordist Italy." *Cultural Anthropology* 26 (1): 59–82.

Muehlebach, Andrea, and Nitzan Shoshan. 2012. "Introduction." *Anthropological Quarterly* 85 (2): 317–43.

Muñoz, José Esteban. 2006. "Feeling Brown, Feeling Down: Latina Affect, the Performativity of Race, and the Depressive Position." *Signs: Journal of Women in Culture and Society* 31 (3): 675–88.

Muñoz, José Esteban. 2009. *Cruising Utopia: The Then and There of Queer Futurity*. New York: New York University Press.

Nadeem, Shehzad. 2011. *Dead Ringers: How Outsourcing is Changing the Way Indians Understand Themselves*. Princeton, NJ: Princeton University Press.

Naik, Preetigandha. 2021. "Dalit-Futurist Feminism: New Alliances through Dalit Feminism and Indian Science Fiction." *Journal of International Women's Studies* 20 (10): 106–22.

Nair, Janaki. 1996. *Women and Law in Colonial India: A Social History*. New Delhi: South Asia Books.

Nair, Janaki. 2000. "Singapore Is Not Bangalore's Destiny." *Economic and Political Weekly* 35 (18): 1512–14.

Nair, Janaki. 2005. *The Promise of the Metropolis: Bangalore's Twentieth Century*. Oxford: Oxford University Press.

Nakamura, Lisa. 2002. *Cybertypes: Race, Ethnicity, and Identity on the Internet*. New York: Routledge.

Nasscom. 2018. "Indian BPM Industry Shows Consistent Growth Capitalising on Newer Technologies and Re-skilling." Report presented at the BPM Strategy Summit, Bengaluru, Karnataka, October 4–5.

Nasscom. 2020. "BPM Council: Programs and Initiatives to Catalyse Growth of Indian BPM Industry." Nasscom website. Accessed August 28. https://www.nasscom.in/about-us/what-we-do/industry-development/bpm-council.

Negri, Antonio. 1988. *Revolution Retrieved: Writings on Marx, Keynes, Capitalist Crisis, and New Social Subjects*. London: Red Notes.

Negri, Antonio. 1989. *The Politics of Subversion: A Manifesto for the Twenty-First Century*. Cambridge: Polity.

Negri, Antonio. 1999. *Insurgencies: Constituent Power and the Modern State*. Minneapolis: University of Minnesota Press.

Nelson, Alondra. 2002. "Future Texts." *Social Text* 20 (2): 1–15.

Ngai, Sianne. 2005. *Ugly Feelings*. Cambridge, MA: Harvard University Press.

Nigam, Aditya. 2019. "Hindutva, Caste, and the 'National Unconscious.'" In *Racism after Apartheid: Challenges for Marxism and Anti-Racism*, edited by Vishwas Satgar, 118–36. Johannesburg: Wits University Press.

Niranjana, Tejaswini. 1992. *Siting Translation: History, Post-Structuralism, and the Colonial Context*. Berkeley: University of California Press.

Niranjana, Tejaswini. 2000. "Alternate Frames? Questions for Comparative Research in the Third World." *Inter-Asia Cultural Studies* 1 (1): 97–108.

Nisbett, Nicholas. 2007. "Friendship, Consumption, Morality: Practising Identity, Negotiating Hierarchy in Middle-Class Bangalore." *Journal of the Royal Anthropological Institute* 13 (4): 935–50.

Nisbett, Nicholas. 2010. *Growing Up in the Knowledge Society: Living the IT Dream in Bangalore*. New Delhi: Routledge.

Omvedt, Gail. 1979. "The Downtrodden Among the Downtrodden: An Interview with a Dalit Agricultural Laborer." *Signs: Journal of Women in Culture and Society* 4 (4): 763–74.

Ong, Aihwa. 1999. *Flexible Citizenship: The Cultural Logics of Transnationality*. Durham, NC: Duke University Press.

Ong, Aihwa. 2006. *Neoliberalism as Exception: Mutations in Citizenship and Sovereignty*. Durham, NC: Duke University Press.

Ong, Paul, Edna Bonacich, and Lucie Cheng. 1994. *The New Asian Immigration in Los Angeles and Global Restructuring*. Philadelphia: Temple University Press.

Ortner, Sherry B. 1995. "Resistance and the Problem of Ethnographic Refusal." *Comparative Studies in Society and History* 37 (1): 173–93. http://www.jstor.org/stable/179382.

Ortner, Sherry B. 2016. "Dark Anthropology and Its Others: Theory since the Eighties." *Hau: Journal of Ethnographic Theory* 6 (1): 47–73.

Padios, Jan M. 2018. *A Nation on the Line: Call Center as Postcolonial Predicaments in the Contemporary Philippines*. Durham, NC: Duke University Press.

Paik, Shailaja. 2014. "Building Bridges: Articulating Dalit and African American Women's Solidarity." *Women's Studies Quarterly* 42 (3–4): 74–96.

Palumbo-Liu, David. 1999. *Asian/American: Historical Crossings of a Racial Frontier*. Stanford, CA: Stanford University Press.

Pandey, Gyanendra. 2013. *A History of Prejudice: Race, Caste, and Difference in India and the United States*. Cambridge: Cambridge University Press.

Pandian, MSS. 2002. "One Step outside Modernity: Caste, Identity Politics and Public Sphere." *Economic and Political Weekly* 37 (18): 1735–41.

Parreñas, Rhacel Salazar. 2001. *Servants of Globalization: Migration and Domestic Work*. Stanford, CA: Stanford University Press.

Parreñas, Rhacel Salazar. 2005. *Children of Global Migration: Transnational Families and Gendered Woes*. Stanford, CA: Stanford University Press.

Parreñas, Rhacel Salazar. 2008. *The Force of Domesticity: Filipina Migrants and Globalization*. New York: New York University Press.

Parreñas, Rhacel Salazar, and Eileen Boris. 2010. *Intimate Labors: Cultures, Technologies, and the Politics of Care*. Stanford, CA: Stanford University Press.

Parreñas, Rhacel Salazar, Hung C. Thai, and Rachel Silvey. 2016. "Intimate Industries: Restructuring (Im)Material Labor in Asia." *Positions* 24 (1): 1–15. https://doi.org/10.1215/10679847-3320017.

Patel, Geeta. 2000. "Ghostly Appearances: Time Tales Tallied Up." *Social Text* 18 (3 [64]): 47–66.

Patel, Reena. 2010. *Working the Night Shift: Women in India's Call Center Industry*. Stanford, CA: Stanford University Press.

Phadnis, Shilpa. 2020. "IT/BPM Services Biz to Slow to 4–6%: Everest," *Times of India*, April 7, 2020. https://timesofindia.indiatimes.com/business/india-business/everest-sees-services-biz-slowing-to-4-6/articleshow/75018238.cms.

Phartiyal, Sankalp, and Sachin Ravikumar. 2020. "India's Huge Outsourcing Industry Struggles with Work-From-Home Scenario." *Reuters*, March 24, 2020. https://www.reuters.com/article/health-coronavirus-india-outsourcing-idCNL4N2BH3AT/.

Pletsch, Carl E. 1981. "The Three Worlds, or the Division of Social Scientific Labor, circa 1950–1975." *Comparative Studies in Society and History* 23 (4): 565–90. Accessed March 21, 2021. https://www.jstor.org/stable/178394.

Poster, Winifred R. 2007. "Who's On the Line? Indian Call Center Agents Pose as Americans for U.S. Outsourced Firms." *Industrial Relations: A Journal of Economy and Society* 46 (2): 271–304. https://doi.org/10.1111/j.1468–232X.2007.00468.x.

Povinelli, Elizabeth A. 2007. "Disturbing Sexuality." *South Atlantic Quarterly* 106 (3): 565–76. https://doi.org/10.1215/00382876–2007–015.

Povinelli, Elizabeth A. 2011. *Economies of Abandonment: Social Belonging and Endurance in Late Liberalism.* Durham, NC: Duke University Press.

Povinelli, Elizabeth A. 2017. "The Ends of Humans: Anthropocene, Autonomism, Antagonism, and the Illusions of our Epoch." *South Atlantic Quarterly* 116 (2): 293–310. https://doi.org/10.1215/00382876–3829412.

Pratt, Geraldine, and Victoria Rosner. 2006. "Introduction: The Global and the Intimate." *Women's Studies Quarterly* 34 (1/2): 13–24.

Pratt, Geraldine, and Victoria Rosner. 2012. *The Global and the Intimate: Feminism in Our Time.* New York: Columbia University Press. https://doi.org/10.7312/prat15448.

Pratt, Mary Louise. 1992. *Imperial Eyes: Travel Writing and Transculturation.* London: Routledge.

Press Trust of India (PTI). 2013. "Thiruvalluvar's Statue Unveiled in Bangalore." *Business Standard*, January 20, 2013. https://www.business-standard.com/article/economy-policy/thiruvalluvar-s-statue-unveiled-in-bangalore-109081000076_1.html.

Press Trust of India (PTI). 2020. "Nasscom Pegs IT-BPM Sector Revenue at USD 192 Billion in FY20." *Business Standard*, February 12, 2020. https://www.business-standard.com/article/pti-stories/nasscom-pegs-it-bpm-sector-revenue-at-usd-192-billion-in-fy20-120021201709_1.html.

Press Trust of India (PTI). 2021. "Indian IT-BPM Sector Saw Recovery in Revenue Growth at 7.9% in FY20: Economic Survey 2020–21." *Economic Times*, January 29, 2021. https://economictimes.indiatimes.com/tech/information-tech/indian-it-bpm-sector-saw-recovery-in-revenue-growth-at-7-9-in-fy20-economic-survey-2020-21/articleshow/80586683.cms?from=mdr.

Puar, Jasbir K. 2007. *Terrorist Assemblages: Homonationalism in Queer Times.* Durham, NC: Duke University Press.

Puar, Jasbir. 2009. "Prognosis Time: Towards a Geopolitics of Affect, Debility and Capacity." *Women and Performance: A Journal of Feminist Theory* 19 (2): 161–72. https://doi.org/10.1080/07407700903034147.

Radhakrishnan, Smitha. 2008. "Examining the 'Global' Indian Middle Class: Gender and Culture in the Silicon Valley/Bangalore Circuit." *Journal of Intercultural Studies* 29 (1): 7–20.

Radhakrishnan, Smitha. 2011. *Appropriately Indian: Gender and Culture in a New Transnational Class.* Durham, NC: Duke University Press.

Rai, Amit S. 2009. *Untimely Bollywood: Globalization and India's New Media Assemblage*. Durham, NC: Duke University Press.

Rai, Amit S. 2019. *Jugaad Times: Ecologies of Everyday Hacking*. Durham, NC: Duke University Press.

Rai, Saritha. 2021. "How Big Tech Is Importing India's Caste Legacy to Silicon Valley." *Bloomberg*, March 11, 2021. https://www.bloomberg.com/news/features /2021-03-11/how-big-tech-is-importing-india-s-caste-legacy-to-silicon-valley.

Rajagopal, Arvind. 1998. "Advertising, Politics and the Sentimental Education of the Indian Consumer." *Visual Anthropology Review* 14 (2): 14–31.

Rajagopal, Arvind. 2001a. *Politics after Television: Hindu Nationalism and the Reshaping of the Public in India*. Cambridge: Cambridge University Press.

Rajagopal, Arvind. 2001b. "Thinking about the New Middle Class: Gender, Advertising and Politics in an Age of Globalization." In *Signposts: Gender Issues in Post-Independence India*, edited by Rajeswari Sunder Rajan, 57–100. New Brunswick, NJ: Rutgers University Press.

Rajagopal, Arvind. 2001c. "The Violence of Commodity Aesthetics: Hawkers, Demolition Raids, and a New Regime of Consumption." *Social Text* 19 (3): 91–113.

Ramberg, Lucinda. 2016. "Backward Futures and Past Forwards. *GLQ* 22 (2): 223–48.

Ramesh, Babu P. 2004. "'Cyber Coolies' in BPO: Insecurities and Vulnerabilities of Non-Standard Work." *Economic and Political Weekly* 39 (5): 492–97.

Ramirez, Catherine S. 2008. "Afrofuturism/Chicanafuturism: Fictive Kin." *Aztlán: A Journal of Chicano Studies* 33 (1): 185–94.

Ranganathan, Malini. 2014. "'Mafias' in the Waterscape: Urban Informality and Everyday Public Authority in Bangalore." *Water Alternatives* 7 (1): 89–105. www.water-alternatives.org.

Rao, Anupama. 2005. "'Sexuality and the Family Form." *Economic and Political Weekly* 40 (8): 715–18.

Rao, Anupama. 2009. *The Caste Question: Dalits and the Politics of Modern India*. Berkeley: University of California Press.

Rao, Anupama. 2017. "The Word and the World: Dalit Aesthetics as a Critique of Everyday Life." *Journal of Postcolonial Writing* 53 (1–2): 147–61.

Rao, Mohit M. 2017. "What Leaves Bengaluru's Washing Machines Ends Up in Its Lakes, and Dinner Plates." *The Hindu*, June 11, 2017. https://www.thehindu.com /sci-tech/energy-and-environment/more-than-a-bit-of-froth/article18936458.ece.

Rao, Mohit M. 2019. "Study Reveals Caste-Based Segregation in Bengaluru." *The Hindu*. January 20. https://www.thehindu.com/news/cities/bangalore/study -reveals-caste-based-segregation-in-bengaluru/article26039905.ece.

Rao, Rukmini. 2020. "Big IT Sector Reform! Permanent Work From Home Will Boost Global Competitiveness." *Business Today*, November 20, 2020. https://www.businesstoday.in/current/economy-politics/big-it-sector-reform -permanent-work-from-home-will-boost-global-competitiveness/story /421289.html.

Rathore, Udayan, and Tadit Kundu. 2016. "How Can India Bridge the Gap between Its Middle and Median Class?" *Livemint*, July 27, 2016. www.livemint
.com/Opinion/uMcYLhhViH2IOX9jdzvHcM/How-can-India-bridge-the-gap
-between-its-middle-and-median-c.html.

Rege, Sharmila. 1998. "Dalit Women Talk Differently: A Critique of 'Difference'
and Towards a Dalit Feminist Standpoint Position." *Economic and Political
Weekly* 33 (44): WS39–WS46.

Rege, Sharmila. 2000. "'Real Feminism' and Dalit Women: Scripts of Denial and
Accusation." *Economic and Political Weekly* 35 (6): 492–95.

Rege, Sharmila. 2003. "More Than Just Tacking Women on to the 'Macropicture':
Feminist Contributions to Globalisation Discourses." *Economic and Political
Weekly* 38 (43): 4555–63.

Rege, Sharmila. 2010. "Education as *Trutiya Ratna*: Towards Phule-Ambedkarite
Feminist Pedagogical Practice." *Economic and Political Weekly* 45 (44–45):
88–98.

Rely Services. n.d. *The Impact of Covid-19 on the BPO Industry*. Accessed July 24,
2024. https://www.relyservices.com/impact-of-covid-19-on-the-bpo-industry.

Research Unit for Political Economy (RUPE). 2015. "India's Middle Class Is Actually the World's Poor." *Quartz India*, December 21, 2015. https://qz.com/562578
/indias-middle-class-is-actually-the-worlds-poor/.

Reuters. 2008. "India's Outsourcing Revenue to Hit $50 Bn." *Financial Express*, Jan-
uary 29, 2008. https://www.financialexpress.com/archive/indias-outsourcing
-revenue-to-hit-50-bn/266661/.

Robinson, Cedric J. (1983) 2020. *Black Marxism: The Making of the Black Radical
Tradition*. Chapel Hill: University of North Carolina Press.

Robinson, Cedric J. 2019. *On Racial Capitalism, Black Internationalism, and Cultures of Resistance*. Edited by H. L. T. Quan. London: Pluto.

Rofel, Lisa, and Sylvia J. Yanagisako. 2019. *Fabricating Transnational Capitalism:
A Collaborative Ethnography of Italian-Chinese Global Fashion*. Durham, NC:
Duke University Press.

Rosa, Jonathan. 2019. *Looking Like a Language, Sounding Like a Race: Raciolinguis-
tic Ideologies and the Learning of Latinidad*. Oxford: Oxford University Press.

Rosaldo, Michelle Z. 1984. "Toward an Anthropology of Self and Feeling." In *Culture Theory: Essays on Mind, Self, and Emotion*, edited by Richard A. Shweder
and Robert A. LeVine, 137–57. Cambridge: Cambridge University Press.

Rothenberg, Janell. 2015. "The Social Life of Logistics on the Moroccan Mediter-
ranean Coast." PhD diss., University of California, Los Angeles.

Roth-Gordon, Jennifer. 2016. "From Upstanding Citizen to North American Rap-
per and Back Again." In *Raciolinguistics: How Language Shapes Our Ideas about
Race*, edited by John R. Rickford, H. Samy Alim, and Arnetha F. Ball, 51–64.
New York: Oxford University Press.

Roy, Rajesh, and Jon Emont. 2020. "Coronavirus Sends Outsource Workers Home,
Causing a Ripple Effect." *Wall Street Journal*, April 1, 2020. https://www.wsj

.com/articles/coronavirus-sends-outsource-workers-home-causing-a-ripple
-effect-11585738803.

Ruppel, Cynthia, Randi Sims, and Peter Zeidler. 2013. "Emotional Labour and Its Outcomes: A Study of a Philippine Call Centre." *Asia-Pacific Journal of Business Administration* 5 (3): 246–61. https://doi.org/10.1108/APJBA-02-2013-0008.

Sanyal, Kalyan. 2013. *Rethinking Capitalist Development: Primitive Accumulation, Governmentality, and Postcolonial Capitalism.* New Delhi: Routledge.

Sarukkai, Sundar. 2014. 'The Phenomenology of Untouchability." In *The Cracked Mirror: An Indian Debate on Experience and Theory,* edited by Gopal Guru and Sundar Sarukkai, 157–99. New Delhi: Oxford University Press.

Saxena, Kritika. 2020. "COVID-19: IT, BPO Sectors Lose 30,000 Jobs, Likely to Let Go of More." CNBCTV18, July 10, 2020. https://www.cnbctv18.com/information -technology/covid-19-it-bpo-sector-job-losses-india-6301801.htm.

Schein, Louisa. 1996. "The Other Goes to Market: The State, the Nation, and Un-ruliness in Contemporary China." *Identities: Global Studies in Culture and Power* 2 (3): 197–222.

Scott, James. 1999. *Seeing Like a State: How Certain Schemes to Improve the Human Condition Have Failed.* New Haven, CT: Yale University Press.

Searle, Llerena G. 2016. *Landscapes of Accumulation: Real Estate and the Neolib-eral Imagination in Contemporary India.* Chicago: University of Chicago Press.

Shah, Nayan. 2011. *Stranger Intimacy: Contesting Race, Sexuality and the Law in the North American West.* Berkeley: University of California Press.

Sharma, Aparna. 2003. "India's Experience with the Multiplex." *Seminar,* no. 525, May 2003. http://www.india-seminar.com/2003/525/525%20aparna%20sharma .htm.

Sharma, Bhushan, and K. A. Geetha. 2010. "Casteing Gender: Intersectional Op-pression of Dalit Women." *Journal of International Women's Studies* 22 (10): 1–7.

Sharma, Preeti. 2020. "Irresponsible State Care and the Virality of Nail Salons: Asian American Women's Service Work, Vulnerability, and Mutuality." *Jour-nal of Asian American Studies* 23 (3): 491–509.

Sheller, Mimi, and John Urry. 2006. "The New Mobilities Paradigm." *Environment and Planning A* 38 (2): 207–26.

Shilpa. 2022. "Bengaluru Gears up for Festival of Harmony—Karaga—on April 16." *New Indian Express,* April 7, 2022. https://www.newindianexpress.com/cities /bengaluru/2022/Apr/08/bengaluru-gears-up-for-festival-of-harmony— karaga—on-april-16-2439428.html.

Shome, Raka. 2006. "Thinking Through the Diaspora: Call Centers, India, and a New Politics of Hybridity." *International Journal of Cultural Studies* 9 (1): 105–24. https://doi.org/10.1177/1367877906061167.

Sidhnath, Mimansa. 2020. "Caste Pervades Every Aspect of Life in Bengal-uru: Panel Discussion." Citizen Matters, December 2. https://bengaluru .citizenmatters.in/how-caste-works-in-bengaluru-panel-discussion-housing -governance-jobs-academics-solutions-53951.

Sivakami, P. 2006. *The Grip of Change*. Hyderabad: Orient Longman.

Smith, Neil. 2010. *Uneven Development: Nature, Capital, and the Production of Space*. Athens: University of Georgia Press.

Snowdon, Jamie, and Phil Fersht. 2016. "The HFS Market Index–IT Services and BPO Market Size and Forecast 2016–2020." HFS Research, July 12, 2016. Accessed August 6, 2024. https://www.hfsresearch.com/research/it-services-and -bpo-market-size-and-forecast-2016–2020/.

Solomon, Harris. 2016. *Metabolic Living: Food, Fat, and the Absorption of Illness in India*. Durham, NC: Duke University Press.

Solomon, Jay, and Kathryn Kranhold. 2005. "In India's Outsourcing Boom, GE Played a Starring Role." *Wall Street Journal*, March 23, 2005. https://www.wsj .com/articles/SB111151806639186539.

Sonti, Gautam, dir. 2006. *Coding Culture*. In collaboration with Carol Upadhya. Film, 85 minutes.

Soundararajan, Thenmozhi. 2012. "The Black Indians." *Outlook*. Accessed January 2019. https://www.outlookindia.com/magazine/story/the-black-indians /281938.

Soundararajan, Thenmozhi. 2020. "It's Time to Dismantle Caste in the U.S." Yes! Solution Journalism, September 1, 2020. https://www.yesmagazine.org/opinion /2020/09/01/caste-race-united-states.

Soundararajan, Thenmozhi. 2022. *The Trauma of Caste: A Dalit Feminist Meditation on Survivorship, Healing, and Abolition*. New York: North Atlantic Books.

Soundararajan, Thenmozhi, and Sinthujan Varatharajah. 2015. "Caste Privilege 101: A Primer for the Privileged." *The Aerogram*, February 10, 2015. https:// theaerogram.com/caste-privilege-101-primer-privileged/.

Sreenath, Shreyas. 2016. "On Demonetization and Its Impact on Bangalore's Waste Pickers and Recyclers." Waste Narratives, November 25, 2016. https:// wastenarratives.com/2016/11/25/on-demonetization-and-its-impact-on -bangalores-waste-pickers-and-recyclers/.

Sreenath, Shreyas. 2020. "Black Spot: An Account of Caste, Contract, and Discards in 21st Century Bangalore." PhD diss., Emory University.

Sridharan, Eswaran. 2004. "The Growth and Sectoral Composition of India's Middle Class: Its Impact on the Politics of Economic Liberalization." *India Review* 3 (4): 405–28.

Srinivas, Smriti. 2008. *In the Presence of Sai Baba: Body, City and Memory in a Global Religious Movement*. Hyderabad: Orient Blackswan.

Srinivas, Smriti. 2016. "Roadside Shrines, Storefront Saints, and Twenty-First Century Lifestyles: The Cultural and Spatial Thresholds of Indian Urbanism." In *Place/No Place: Spatial Aspects of Urban Asian Religiosity*, edited by Joanne Waghorne, 131–47. Singapore: Asia Research Institute–Springer Asia Series.

Srinivas, Tulasi. 2018. *The Cow in the Elevator: An Anthropology of Wonder*. Durham, NC: Duke University Press.

Statista Research Department. 2020. "General Electric: Number of Employees in the U.S. 2007–2019." Statista. Accessed August 29, 2020. https://www.statista.com/statistics/220723/number-of-employees-at-general-electric-in-the-us/.

Stewart, Kathleen. 2007. *Ordinary Affects*. Durham, NC: Duke University Press.

Stoler, Ann L. 1989. "Making Empire Respectable: The Politics of Race and Sexual Morality in 20th-Century Colonial Cultures." *American Ethnologist* 16 (4): 634–60. https://www.jstor.org/stable/645114.

Stoler, Ann L. 2006. *Haunted by Empire: Geographies of Intimacy in North American History*. Durham, NC: Duke University Press.

Subramanian, Ajantha. 2019. *The Caste of Merit: Engineering Education in India*. Cambridge, MA: Harvard University Press.

Swamy, Rohini. 2020. "Bengaluru Has Seen Eight Major Riots since 1986—Including Two over Prophet Muhammad." *ThePrint*, August 13. https://theprint.in/india/bengaluru-has-seen-8-major-riots-since-1986-including-two-over-prophet-muhammad/481085/.

Tajima-Peña, Renee, dir. 1987. *Who Killed Vincent Chin?* Film News Now and WTVS. Film, 87 minutes.

Takaki, Ronald T. 1989. *Strangers from a Different Shore: A History of Asian Americans*. Boston: Little, Brown.

Taylor, Charles. 2016. "Can Secularism Travel?" In *Beyond the Secular West*, edited by Akeel Bilgrami, 1–27. New York: Columbia University Press.

Teltumbde, Anand. 2016. *Dalits: Past, Present and Future*. London: Routledge.

Teltumbde, Anand, and Suraj Yengde. 2018. *The Radical in Ambedkar: Critical Reflections*. New Delhi: Penguin.

Thomas, Jenny. 1984. "Cross-Cultural Discourse as Unequal Encounter." *Applied Linguistics* 5 (3): 226–35.

Thompson, Edward P. 1967. "Time, Work-Discipline, and Industrial Capitalism." *Past and Present* 38 (1): 56–97.

Thrift, Nigel. 2004. "Intensities of Feeling: Towards a Spatial Politics of Affect." *Geografiska Annaler: Series B, Human Geography* 86 (1): 57–78. https://doi.org/10.1111/j.0435-3684.2004.00154.x.

Throop, C. Jason. 2012. "On the Varieties of Empathic Experience: Tactility, Mental Opacity, and Pain." *Medical Anthropology Quarterly* 26 (3): 408–30. https://doi.org/10.1111/j.1548-1387.2012.01225.x.

Throop, C. Jason, and Dan Zahavi. 2020. "Dark and Bright Empathy: Phenomenological and Anthropological Reflections." *Current Anthropology* 61 (3): 283–303.

Tilly, Charles. 1975. *The Formation of National States in Western Europe*. Princeton, NJ: Princeton University Press.

Times of India. 2022. "Noise Check in Bengaluru: Police Notice for 125 Mosques, 83 Temples, 22 Churches for Ban on Loudspeakers for Azaan." April 6, 2022. https://timesofindia.indiatimes.com/city/bengaluru/noise-check-in-bengaluru-police-notice-for-125-mosques-83-temples-22-churches/articleshow/90675299.cms.

Trivedi, Harish. 2003."CyberCoolies." *Little India*, October 5, 2004. https://littleindia.com/cybercoolies/.

Tronti, Mario. 1973. "Social Capital." *Telos: Critical Theory of the Contemporary*, no. 17, Fall 1973, 98–121. https://doi.org/10.3817/0973017098.

Trotsky, Leon. (1938) 1973. *The Transitional Program for Socialist Revolution: With Introductory Essays by Joseph Hansen and George Novack*. 1st ed. New York: Pathfinder Press.

Trotsky, Leon. (1918) 2008. *History of the Russian Revolution*. Translated by Max Eastman. Chicago: Haymarket.

Trotsky, Leon. (1919) 2010. *The Permanent Revolution and Results and Prospects*. Seattle: Red Letter.

Tsing, Anna Lowenhaupt. 2004. *Friction: An Ethnography of Global Connection*. Princeton, NJ: Princeton University Press.

Tsing, Anna Lowenhaupt. 2015. *The Mushroom at the End of the World: On the Possibility of Life in Capitalist Ruins*. Princeton, NJ: Princeton University Press.

Tupas, Ruanni, and Aileen Salonga. 2016. "Unequal Englishes in the Philippines." *Journal of Sociolinguistics* 20 (3): 367–81.

Tymoczko, Maria. 1990. "Translation in Oral Tradition as a Touchstone for Translation Theory and Practice." In *Translation, History, and Culture*, edited by Susan Bassnett and André Lefevere, 46–55. New York: Pinter.

Upadhya, Carol. 2016. *Reengineering India*. Oxford: Oxford University Press.

Upadhya, Carol, and Aninhalli R. Vasavi. 2013. *In an Outpost of the Global Economy: Work and Workers in India's Information Technology Industry*. New Delhi: Routledge.

Vageesh, N. S. 2015. "Credit Card Penetration Remains Dismally Low." *Hindu Business Line*, June 15, 2015. https://www.thehindubusinessline.com/money-and-banking/credit-card-penetration-remains-dismally-low/article7318930.ece.

Valentine, Gill. 2006. "Globalizing Intimacy: The Role of Information and Communication Technologies in Maintaining and Creating Relationships." *Women's Studies Quarterly* 34 (1/2): 365–93.

Van der Linden, Marcel. 2007. "The 'Law' of Uneven and Combined Development: Some Underdeveloped Thoughts." *Historical Materialism* 15 (1): 145–65.

Verma, Varuna. 2006. "More Sex Please, We Are BPO—'It's Common to Find Couples Cuddling in the Cafeteria.'" *Telegraph*, May 14, 2006. https://www.telegraphindia.com/opinion/more-sex-please-we-are-bpo-it-s-common-to-find-couples-cuddling-in-the-cafeteria/cid/1025123.

Viswanathan, Gauri. 1998. *Outside the Fold: Conversion, Modernity, and Belief*. Princeton, NJ: Princeton University Press.

Vora, Kalindi. 2010. "The Transmission of Care: Affective Economies and Indian Call Centers." In *Intimate Labors Cultures, Technologies and the Politics of Care*, edited by Eileen Boris and Rhacel Salazar Parreñas, 33–48. Stanford, CA: Stanford University Press.

Vora, Kalindi. 2015. *Life Support: Biocapital and the New History of Outsourced Labor*. Minneapolis: University of Minnesota Press.

Wabuke, Hope. 2020. "Afrofuturism, Africanfuturism, and the Language of Black Speculative Literature." *Los Angeles Review of Books*, August 27, 2020. https://lareviewofbooks.org/article/afrofuturism-africanfuturism-and-the-language-of-black-speculative-literature/.

Wallerstein, Immanuel Maurice. 1991. *Unthinking Social Science: The Limits of Nineteenth-Century Paradigms*. Philadelphia: Temple University Press.

Wallerstein, Immanuel Maurice. 1997. "Eurocentrism and its Avatars: The Dilemmas of Social Science." *Sociological Bulletin* 46 (1): 21–39.

Wallerstein, Immanuel Maurice. 1999. *The End of the World as We Know It: Social Science for the Twenty-First Century*. Minneapolis: University of Minnesota Press.

Weber, Max. (1905) 2002. *The Protestant Ethic and the "Spirit" of Capitalism*. Edited, translated, and with an introduction by Peter Baehr and Gordon C. Wells. London: Penguin.

Weeks, Kathi. 2007. "Life within and against Work: Affective Labor, Feminist Critique, and Post-Fordist Politics." *Ephemera: Theory and Politics in Organization* 7 (1): 233–49.

Weeks, Kathi. 2011. *The Problem with Work Feminism, Marxism, Antiwork Politics, and Postwork Imaginaries*. Durham, NC: Duke University Press.

Wilkerson, Isabel. 2020. *Caste: The Origins of Our Discontents*. New York: Random House.

Wilson, Ara. 2004. *The Intimate Economies of Bangkok: Tomboys, Tycoons, and Avon Ladies in the Global City*. Berkeley: University of California Press. https://www.jstor.org/stable/10.1525/j.ctt1pnd8z.

Wilson, Ara. 2016. "The Infrastructure of Intimacy." *Signs: Journal of Women in Culture and Society* 41 (2): 247–80.

Womack, Ytasha. 2013. *Afrofuturism: The World of Black Sci-Fi and Fantasy Culture*. Chicago: Lawrence Hill.

World Bank. "Final Consumption Expenditure (Constant 2015 US$)—India." Accessed July 8, 2024. https://data.worldbank.org/indicator/NE.CON.TOTL.KD?locations=IN&most_recent_value_desc=false.

Woydack, Johanna, and Jane Lockwood. 2017. "'Scripts Are Beautiful': Managers' and Agents' Views of Script Use in Call Centers." *International Journal of Business Communication* 58 (3): 333–57. https://doi.org/10.1177/2329488417738512.

Yanagisako, Sylvia. 2002. *Producing Culture and Capital: Family Firms in Italy*. Princeton, NJ: Princeton University Press. https://doi.org/10.2307/j.ctv10crfv6.

Yaszek, Lisa. 2005. "An Afrofuturist Reading of Ralph Ellison's Invisible Man." *Rethinking History* 9 (2–3): 297–313.

Zuboff, Shoshana. 2019. *The Age of Surveillance Capitalism: The Fight for Human Future at the New Frontier of Power*. New York: PublicAffairs.

Index

Page numbers followed by *f* refer to figures.

labor (continued)
    capitalism and, 216; alienated, 45,
    140, 168, 176, 239; arbitrage, 4, 22,
    69–71, 73, 143; artificial intelligence
    and, 172; Asian, 72, 143, 261n6; BPO,
    14, 67, 190, 224; of BPO agents, 12, 14,
    20, 68, 70, 73, 157, 168–69, 173, 176,
    190, 193, 205, 218; BPO intimacies
    and, 152, 177; of BPO workers, 233;
    changing nature of, 223; cheap, 4–5,
    70, 143; cognitive, 249n3; consump-
    tion and, 218; digitalization of, 51;
    division of, 161, 245n12; embodied, 7;
    emotional, 13; feminine, 261n4; gen-
    der and, 191, 249n11, 261n4; gendered
    division of, 67, 191, 207; global, 48;
    global division of, 4; histories of, 217;
    intimacy and, 158; intimate, 45–46,
    138–40, 176; invisible, 12; ITES indus-
    try and, 3; laws, 182; management
    of, 213; market, 15; media technolo-
    gies and, 158; power, 101, 152, 170;
    practices, 176, 184–85, 201; processes,
    12, 95, 138–39, 176, 183, 186, 188–91,
    195, 215, 262n15, 263n1; racialized,
    192–93; racialized division of, 142;
    racialization of, 81; relational, 170,
    258n12; reproduction of, 101; rhythms
    of, 46, 158, 187, 207; of semiocapital-
    ism, 199; service, 71, 138, 143, 181, 214;
    Taylorization of, 262n18; temporali-
    ties of, 27, 67, 207–8, 210, 219; time
    of, 236; union, 122, 134; of workers
    in Global South, 4. See also affective
    labor; intimate labor
laborers, 20, 56–57, 73, 107, 173, 193,
    255n35; Asian, 250n18; factory,
    262n18; foreign, 69; indentured, 39,
    68, 142
labor processes, 12, 186, 188–91, 195, 215,
    263n1; algorithmic control of, 262n15;
    communication and, 95; information
    technology and, 183; intimacy and,
    138, 176; intimate labor and, 139
labor regimes, 139–40, 156, 165–67, 172,
    205, 240, 263n1; affect and, 177; BPO,
    46, 48, 64, 182, 204, 211–12, 214;
    disciplinary, 136; intimacies and,

139, 146, 158–59, 170, 174–75; racial
    capitalism and, 68; technology and,
    204; time and, 182; transnational, 71;
    workplace and, 134
Ladies' Hostels, 61, 63, 65
language, 4, 80, 83–88, 91–93, 196–97,
    251n28; affect and, 147; body, 41, 92,
    149; colloquial, 40; conflicts over,
    251n30; futurities and, 134; inequality
    of, 31, 80–82, 84–85, 87, 89, 98, 195,
    250n24; of movement, 96; policies,
    217; politics of, 233, 255n31, 261n8;
    postcolonial genealogies of, 98; race
    and, 262nn10–11; racialization of, 81;
    training, 195, 251n33. See also English
    language; Kannada
learnings, 43–44, 58, 97, 126, 133, 203, 240
leisure, 68, 124, 129, 132, 158, 174, 185; ac-
    tivities, 67, 122; BPO agents and, 14,
    182; practices, 128; time, 68, 92, 157
lifeworlds, 5–6, 9–10, 93, 185, 217–18, 220
Lowe, Lisa, 143, 250n16, 257n2

malls, 17, 18, 27, 31, 33, 37, 45–46, 53,
    100–111, 115–17, 225, 233, 252n4,
    256n39; acquisition of land for, 227;
    in Bangkok, 254n25, 256n38; BPO
    agents and, 55, 58, 65, 68, 101–2, 110,
    113, 115–19, 121–24, 126–29, 131–36,
    165; gated communities and, 254n24;
    middle class and, 255n32; as pedagog-
    ical spaces, 45, 100–101, 103, 120, 122,
    124, 127, 133–34, 255n35; Singaporean
    government investment in, 254n15;
    surveillance and, 255n29. See also
    Nexus Whitefield Mall; Total Mall;
    UB City Mall
Manipur, 57, 65
Mankekar, Purnima, 58, 65, 78, 94–95,
    131, 155, 179–80, 208, 220–21, 227; call
    barging and, 93, 137–38; on commod-
    ity affect, 254n23; on cosmopolitan-
    ism, 256n39; on entrepreneurship,
    256n37; on middle classes, 253n8,
    254n19, 264n15; multiplexes and, 120;
    on the non-equivalence of the sexual
    and the erotic, 259n16; training ses-
    sions and, 150

spatiality, 52, 96–97, 117, 169–70; of capitalist expansion, 6; gendered formations of, 65, 99

spatiotemporality, 103, 113; of bodies, 100

special economic zones (SEZS), 32, 102–3, 106, 109, 133, 136, 253n10, 256n39

speech patterns, 13, 80, 92, 147

Spinoza, Baruch, 14, 176

Srinivas, Tulasi, 108

Sri Ram Sene, 18, 154

stagnation, 26, 44, 51, 79, 96, 99

stuckedness, 51, 239

subsumption, 67; of intimacies, 140; of life, 124, 219; real, 124, 257n4

success, 25, 45, 83, 123, 150, 169, 242; professional, 126–29, 133–34, 136

surplus, 8, 47; production of, 9, 168. *See also* value: surplus

surveillance, 74–75, 79, 122–23, 149, 157, 165–66, 168–69, 180, 250n22; capital accumulation and, 139; danger of, 257n1; erotics and, 122, 136; intimacy and, 150; of labor, 205; malls and, 255n29; state, 5; technologies of, 152; women and, 18, 64, 192, 210; of workers' bodies, 187

Tamil, 84, 252n34; films in, 120

Tamil Nadu, 57, 85, 251n30, 251n32

Taylorization, 171, 262n18

technology, 2, 14–15, 46, 158, 172, 182, 185, 188, 218, 220, 260n3, 263; affect and, 12; bodies and, 195, 204–6, 219; BPO intimacies and, 176–77; communication, 3–4, 6, 144, 151; companies, 85; disjunctive temporalities and, 228; high, 72; intimacy and, 258–59n15; labor and, 80; parks, 34–37, 35f, 36f, 105, 113, 116f; racism as, 234; software, 33; speed and, 17. *See also* information technology (IT); Information Technology Enabled Services (ITES)

teleology, 17; of capitalism, 98; of modernization theory, 232

Telugu, 84, 120

temporal dislocation, 66, 182–83

temporality, 7, 67, 217, 236, 260n3; of acceleration, 78; affect and, 108; of affective capitalism, 189; of affective labor, 216, 219; of BPO labor, 190, 208; capitalism and, 244n6; of capitalist development, 231; of capitalist expansion, 6; of change, 22; emergent, 17; of empathy, 149; of the future, 35; of futurity, 34; gendered formations of, 65, 99; global hierarchies of, 187; of global modernity, 77; of hopefulness, 133; of lag, 35, 225, 264n9; of linearity, 107, 109; mobility and, 96–97; racialized formations of, 99; of the past, 225; regimes of, 97, 181–82; of simultaneity, 107, 109, 113, 254n22; of struggle, 240; teleological, 16; of work, 216. *See also* disjunctive temporalities; spatiotemporality

Throop, Jason, 149, 151, 258nn13–14

Total Mall, 124, 255n34

translation, 80–81, 83–85, 89–92, 95, 98, 127, 233, 240, 251n28, 252n37; cultural, 83, 90–91, 95, 98, 233, 240; affective capitalism and, 11, 27; BPOS and, 87; mobility and, 46; racial capitalism and, 4, 70. *See also* mistranslation

Tronti, Mario, 101, 134

UB City Mall, 124, 125f

underemployment, 18, 49, 104, 129

unemployment, 18, 49, 59, 103, 129, 226

uneven development, 70–71, 85, 142–43, 195, 244n7; BPO intimacies and, 143; BPOS and, 69, 73; combined and, 6–7, 143, 228–29; racialism and, 146

United Kingdom, 3, 14, 91, 138, 142, 148, 154, 164; affective labor and, 2, 195; business process outsourcing (BPO) and, 2–4, 137, 147, 226, 235; consumers/customers in, 21, 92, 94, 223; vacationgoers from, 75

United States, 7, 14, 42, 147, 195, 264n9; affective labor and, 2; Asian American workers in, 74; Asian labor in, 261n6; BPOS and, 3–4, 22; call centers in, 5, 60, 152; customers in, 21, 83, 89, 91–92, 191, 198, 223; decline of middle class in, 230; Indians in, 262n12; outsourcing and, 71–72, 150, 224; Philip-

www.ingramcontent.com/pod-product-compliance
Lightning Source LLC
Chambersburg PA
CBHW030821290525
27270CB00016B/145